MANAGEMENT PRINCIPLES FOR HEALTH PROFESSIONALS

Second Edition

Joan Gratto Liebler, MPA, RRA
Temple University
Philadelphia, Pennsylvania

Ruth Ellen Levine, EdD, OTR
Thomas Jefferson University
Philadelphia, Pennsylvania

Jeffrey Rothman, PT, EdD
College of Staten Island,
City University of New York
Staten Island, New York

AN ASPEN PUBLICATION®
Aspen Publishers, Inc.
Gaithersburg, Maryland
1992

Library of Congress Cataloging in Publication Data

Liebler, Joan Gratto
Management principles for health professionals/
Joan Gratto Liebler, Ruth Ellen Levine, Jeffrey Rothman.—2nd. ed.
p. cm.

Includes bibliographical references and index.
ISBN 0-8342-0287-5
1. Health services administration. 2. Management. I. Levine,
Ruth Ellen. II. Rothman, Jeffrey, Ed. D.
[DNLM: 1. Health Facilities–organization and administration.
2. Health Occupations. 3. Health services–organization &
administration. 4. Organization and Administration. WX 150 L716m]
RA393.L53   1992
362.1'068—dc20
DNLM/DLC
for Library of Congress
91-31710
CIP

Editorial Services: Barbara Priest

Library of Congress Catalog Card Number: 91-31710
ISBN: 0-8342-0287-5

Printed in the United States of America

1 2 3 4 5

Table of Contents

Contributors

Maureen Freda, MS, OTR/L
Director
Occupational Therapy Department
National Rehabilitation Hospital
Washington, DC

Ellen L. Kolodner, MSS, OTR/L, FAOTA
Assistant Professor
Field Work Coordinator
Undergraduate Program Coordinator
Department of Occupational Therapy
College of Allied Health Sciences
Thomas Jefferson University
Philadelphia, Pennsylvania

Preface

This book is intended for use by health care personnel who participate in the classic functions of a manager—planning, organizing, decision making, staffing, leading or directing, communicating, and motivating—yet have not had extensive management training. Health care practitioners may exercise these functions on a continuing basis because they are department heads or unit supervisors, or they may participate in only a few of these traditional functions. In any case, a knowledge of management theory is an essential element in professional training, as no one function is carried out independently of the others. In this book, emphasis is placed on definitions of terms, clarifications of concepts, and, in some cases, highly detailed explanations. Examples are drawn from the health care setting.

Every author must decide what material to include and at what level of detail. Samuel Johnson observed that "a man will turn over half a library to make one book." We have been guided by experience gained in the classroom and in many continuing education workshops for health care practitioners. Three basic objectives determined the final selection and development of material:

1. Acquaint the health care practitioner with management concepts essential to the understanding of the organizational environment within which the functions of the manager are performed. Some material challenges assumptions about such concepts as power, authority, influence, and leadership. Some of the discussion focuses on relatively new concepts, such as the systems approach, input-output analysis, and networking. Practitioners must not be afraid of such concepts; indeed, they should guard against "being the last to know."
2. Present a base for further study of management concepts. Therefore, the classic literature in the field is cited, major theorists noted, and terms defined, especially where there is a divergence of opinion in management literature. We all stand on the shoulders of the management "giants" who paved the way in the field; a return to original sources is encouraged.

3. Provide sufficient detail in selected areas to enable the practitioner to apply the concepts in day-to-day situations. Several tools of planning and control, such as the PERT network, management by objectives, work sampling techniques, and the flow chart, are explained in detail. Detailed examples of job descriptions, policy statements, procedures, and training objectives are also included.

We have attempted to provide enough information to make it possible for the reader to use these tools with ease at their basic level. It is the authors' hope that the reader will turn to more advanced applications as a result.

Joan Gratto Liebler
Ruth Ellen Levine
Jeffrey Rothman

Acknowledgments

The authors wish to acknowledge the continuing contribution of physical therapy examples and applications developed for the first edition of this work by Professor Emeritus Hyman Dervitz, Temple University, Philadelphia, Pennsylvania.

Part I

Selected Management Functions

Chapter 1

Introduction to Management

CHAPTER OBJECTIVES

1. Define management.
2. Differentiate between management as an art and management as a science.
3. Identify the basic functions of the manager.
4. Identify the major phases in management history.

Management has been defined as the process of getting things done through and with people. It is the planning and directing of effort, the organizing and employing of resources (both human and material), to accomplish some predetermined objective. Within the overall concept of management, the function of administration can be identified. The practical execution of the plans and decisions on a day-to-day basis requires specific administrative activities that managers may assign to executive officers or administrators. Managers may find that their role includes specifically administrative activities in addition to overall management responsibilities. The workday of a typical department head in a health care institution contains a mix of broad-based managerial functions and detailed administrative actions.

MANAGEMENT: AN ART OR A SCIENCE?

Especially since the turn of the century, management's scientific aspects have been emphasized. The scientific nature of management is reflected in the fact that it is based on a more or less codified body of knowledge consisting of theories and principles that are subject to study and further experimentation. Yet, management as a science lacks the distinct characteristics of an exact discipline, such as chemistry or mathematics.

The many variables associated with the human element make management as much an art as a science. Even with complex analytical tools for decision making, such as probability studies, stochastic (random) simulation, and similar mathematical elements, the manager must rely on intuition and experience in assessing such factors as timing and tactics for persuasion.

FUNCTIONS OF THE MANAGER

A manager's functions can be considered a circle of action in which each component leads to the next. Although the functions can be identified as separate sets of actions for purposes of analysis, the manager in actual practice carries out these activities in a complex, unified manner within the total process of managing. Other individuals in the organization carry out some of these activities, either periodically or routinely, but the manager is assigned these specific activities in their entirety, as a continuing set of functions. When these processes become routine, the role of manager emerges. The traditional functions of a manager were identified by Gulick and Urwick[1] based on the earlier work of Henri Fayol.[2] Chester Barnard brought together the significant underlying premises about the role of the manager in his classic work, *The Functions of the Executive*.[3]

Classic Management Functions

Management functions typically include

- planning: the selection of objectives, the establishment of goals, and the factual determination of the existing situation and the desired future state.
- decision making: a part of the planning process in that a commitment to one of several alternatives (decision) must be made. Others may assist in planning, but decision making is the privilege and burden of managers. Decision making includes the development of alternatives, conscious choice, and commitment.
- organizing: the design of a pattern of roles and relationships that contribute to the goal. Roles are assigned, authority and responsibility are determined, and provision is made for coordination. Organizing typically involves the development of the organization chart, job descriptions, and statements of workflow.
- staffing: the determination of personnel needs and the selection, orientation, training, and continuing evaluation of the individuals who hold the required positions identified in the organizing process. (The staffing function, rather than viewed as a separate function, is classed by some theorists within the organizing function.)

- directing or actuating: the provision of guidance and leadership so that the work performed is goal-oriented. It is the exercise of the manager's influence, the process of teaching, coaching, and motivating workers.
- controlling: the determination of what is being accomplished, the assessment of performance as it relates to the accomplishment of the organizational goals, and the initiation of corrective actions.

Figure 1-1 summarizes the classic functions of the manager and their relationship to each other. In addition, managers must continually establish and maintain internal and external organizational relationships to achieve an effective working rapport. They must monitor the organization's environment to anticipate change and bring about the adaptive responses required for the institution's survival.

At different phases in the life of the organization, one or another management function may be dominant. In the early stages of organizational development, for example, planning is the manager's primary function. When the organization is mature, however, controlling functions are emphasized.

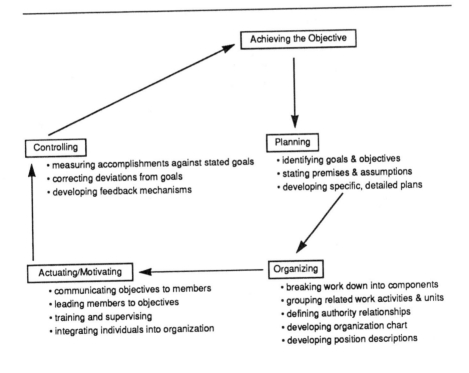

Achieving the Objective

Controlling
- measuring accomplishments against stated goals
- correcting deviations from goals
- developing feedback mechanisms

Planning
- identifying goals & objectives
- stating premises & assumptions
- developing specific, detailed plans

Actuating/Motivating
- communicating objectives to members
- leading members to objectives
- training and supervising
- integrating individuals into organization

Organizing
- breaking work down into components
- grouping related work activities & units
- defining authority relationships
- developing organization chart
- developing position descriptions

Figure 1-1　Interrelationship of Management Functions

The Health Care Practitioner as Manager

In the specialized environment of a health care institution, qualified professional practitioners may assume the role of unit supervisor, project manager, or department head or chief of service. The role may emerge gradually as the number of patients increases, as the variety of services expands, and as specialization occurs within a profession. A physical therapy staff specialist, for example, may develop a successful program for patients with spinal cord injury; as the practitioner most directly involved in the work, this individual may be given full administrative responsibility for that unit. The role of manager begins to emerge as budget projections need to be made, job descriptions need to be updated and refined, and the staffing pattern needs to be reassessed and expanded.

An occupational therapist may find that a small program in home care flourishes and is subsequently made into a specialized unit. Again, this credentialed practitioner in a health care profession assumes the managerial role. The medical technologist who participates in the development of a nuclear medicine unit and the dietitian who develops a nutrition counseling program for use in outpatient clinics may also find themselves in this position.

Practitioners who develop their own independent professional practices assume the role of manager for their business enterprises. The role of the professional health care practitioner as manager is reinforced further by the various legal, regulatory, and accrediting agencies that often require chiefs of service or department heads to be qualified practitioners in their distinct disciplines. The role of manager then becomes a predictable part of the health care practitioner's tenure in an institution. Table 1-1 shows how activities in a typical workday of a department head in a health care institution reflect the functions of a manager in their classic form.

Table 1-1 The Chief of Service as Manager: Examples of Daily Activities

Activity	Management Function Reflected
Readjust staffing pattern for the day because of employee absenteeism	Staffing
Review cases with staff, encouraging staff members to assume greater responsibility	Controlling Planning Leading/motivating/actuating
Counsel employee with habitual lateness problem	Controlling Leading/motivating/actuating
Present departmental quality assurance plan for approval of Risk Management/Quality Assurance Committee	Planning Leadership
Conduct research to improve treatment techniques	Planning Leadership
Dialogue with third-party reimbursement manager about coverage for innovative services	Planning Leadership

THE HISTORY OF MANAGEMENT

An organization is shaped by past practices. By studying the history of management, managers can become aware of the major areas that have been emphasized during the various periods of the organization's life. As health care organizations assume more and more features of business enterprises (rather than philanthropic services), health care managers may identify certain features that are adaptations of management practices in business and industry, such as the application of industrial engineering techniques, the use of incentive wages and bonuses, and an emphasis on human relations.

A knowledge of the history of management provides a framework within which contemporary managerial problems may be reviewed. Modern managers benefit from the experiences of their predecessors. They may assess current problems and plan solutions by using theories that have been developed and tested over time. Contemporary executives may take from past approaches the elements that have been proved successful and seek to integrate them into a unified system of modern management practice.

In an examination of the phases in management history, it must be remembered that history is not completely linear and that any period in history involves a dynamic interplay of components that cannot be separated into distinct elements. The analysis of selected processes of the various historical periods tends to obscure the fact that each period is part of a continuum of events. The specific features of management history phases given here are intended to exemplify the predominant emphasis of each period and are only highlights. The second caution is in regard to dating the various periods. The dates given here for the various periods of management history are intended as guides. There is no precise day and year when one school of thought or predominant approach began or ended. As with any study of history, the dates suggest approximate periods when the particular practices were developed and applied with sufficient regularity as to constitute a school of management thought or a predominant approach.

Scientific Management

The work of Frederick Taylor (1865–1915) is the commonly accepted basis of scientific management. Taylor started as a day laborer in a steel mill, advanced to foreman, and experienced the struggles of middle management as the workers resisted top executives' efforts to achieve more productivity. He faced the basic question: What is a fair day's work? With Carl G. L. Barth (1860–1939) and Henry L. Gantt (1861–1919), Taylor made a scientific study of workers, machines, and the workplace. These pioneers originated the modern industrial practices of standardization of parts, uniformity of work methods, and the assembly line.

Frank Gilbreth (1868–1924) and Lillian Gilbreth (1878–1972) developed a class of fundamental motions, starting with the *therblig* (*Gilbreth* spelled backwards but with the *t* and *h* transposed) as the most basic elemental motion. Lillian Gilbreth may be of particular interest to occupational therapists, since much of her later work concerned the efficiency of physically handicapped women in the management of their homes. Scientific management became an accepted, codified concept as a result of a famous case on railroad rate structures heard by the Interstate Commerce Commission. Louis D. Brandeis, who later became a Supreme Court justice, argued against rate increases by citing the probable effects of the application of "scientific management."[4] The concept emerged as the predominant approach to management during this era.

The Behavioralists and the Human Relations Approach

Although the major figures in the development of scientific management emphasized the work rather than the worker, concern for the latter was apparent. Lillian Gilbreth, for example, was a psychologist and tended to stress the needs of the employee. Frank Gilbreth developed a model promotion plan that emphasized regular meetings between the employee and the individual responsible for evaluating the employee's work.

Unlike adherents of the scientific management approach, who considered the worker only secondarily, behavioralists focused primarily on the worker. The application of the behavioral sciences to worker productivity and interaction was exemplified in the Hawthorne Experiments conducted by Elton Mayo and F. J. Roethlisberger at Western Electric's Hawthorne Works. Through these studies, the importance of the informal group and the social and motivational needs of workers were recognized. The behavioral science and the human relations approaches may be linked because both emphasize the worker's social and psychological needs, and stress group dynamics, psychology, and sociology. Theorists associated with these approaches include Douglas MacGregor, Rensis Likert, and Chris Argyris. The Deming approach with its emphasis on quality alert groups, quality circles, and total quality management is a contemporary example of the human relations approach.

Structuralism

Since work is done within specific organizational patterns and since the worker-superior roles imply authority relationships, the structure or framework within which these patterns and relationships occur has been studied. Structuralism is based on Max Weber's theory of bureaucracy or formal organization. Robert K. Merton, Philip Selznik, and Peter Blau, major theorists in the structuralist school of thought, gave particular attention to line and staff relationships, authority structure, the decision-making process, and the effect of organizational life on the individual worker.

The Management Process School

The special emphasis in the management process approach is on the various functions that the manager performs as a continuous process. Henri Fayol (1841–1925), a contemporary of Taylor, studied the work of the chief executive and is credited with having developed the basic principles or "laws" that are associated with management functions. His writings did not become readily available in English until 1939 when James D. Mooney and A. C. Reiley published a classification and integrated analysis of the principles of management, including Fayol's concepts.[5] Chester Barnard could be considered a member of this school of thought in that he explored the basic processes and functions of management, including the universality of these elements.

The Quantitative or Operations Research Approach

Problem solving and decision making with the aid of mathematical models and the use of probability and statistical inference characterize the quantitative or operations research approach to management. Also called the management science school, this approach includes the various quantitative approaches to executive processes and is characterized by an interdisciplinary systems approach. The urgency of the problems in World War II and in the space program speeded the development of mathematical models and computer technology for problem solving and decision making.

THE SYSTEMS APPROACH

Each school of management thought tends to emphasize one major feature of an organization:

1. Scientific management focuses on work.
2. Human relations and behavioralism stress the worker and the worker-manager relationship.
3. Structuralism emphasizes organizational design.
4. Management process theory focuses on the functions of the manager.

5. Management science theory adds computer technology to the scientific method.

The search for a management method that takes into account each of these essential features led to the systems approach. This focuses on the organization as a whole, its internal and external components, the people in the organization, the work processes, and the overall organizational environment.

Historical Development of the Systems Model

The systems model is generally accepted in the area of computer technology, but its use need not be limited to such an application; at its origin, it was not so restricted. A more flexible use of this approach provides the manager with a framework within which the internal and external organizational factors can be visualized. The systems approach to management emphasizes the total environment of the organization. The cycle consisting of input, transformation to output, and renewed input can be identified for the organization or for any of its divisions. The changes in organizational environment can be assessed continually in a structured manner to determine the impact of change.

Management theorists turned to biologists and other scientists to develop the idea of the organization as a total system. With this ecological approach, a change in any one aspect of the environment is believed to have an effect on the other components of the organization. The specifics are analyzed, but always in terms of the whole. The institution is considered an entity that "lives" in a specific environment and has essential parts that are interdependent.

General systems theory as a concept was introduced and defined by Ludwig von Bertalanffy, a biologist, in 1951.[6] His terminology is the foundation for the basic concepts of the general systems theory.[7] Kenneth E. Boulding developed a hierarchy of systems to help bridge the gap between theoretical and empirical systems knowledge. He noted that the general systems approach furnished a framework or skeleton for all science but that each discipline, including management science, must apply the model, add the flesh and blood of its own subject matter, and develop this analytical model further. Included in Boulding's hierarchy of systems is the concept of the open system and the idea of the social organization with role sets.[8]

Many contemporary studies of various aspects of organizations are based on the systems model. Areas of specific application include

- cybernetics: the science of communication and control[9]
- data-processing systems: systems used to guide the flow of information, usually by means of computer technology

- rhochrematics: the science of managing material flow, including production and marketing, transporting, processing, handling, storing, and distributing goods[10]
- network analysis: the process of planning and scheduling (e.g., PERT networks and the critical path method)
- administrative systems: the planned approach to activities necessary to attain desired objectives

Basic Systems Concepts and Definitions

A system may be defined as an assemblage or combination of things or parts forming a complex or unitary whole, a set of interacting units. The essential focus of the systems approach is the relationship and interdependence of the parts. The systems approach moves beyond structure or function (e.g., organization charts, departmentation) to emphasize the flow of information, the work, the inputs, and the outputs. Systems add horizontal relationships to the vertical relationships contained in traditional organizational theory.

The systems model is made up of four basic components: (1) inputs, (2) throughputs or processes, (3) outputs, and (4) feedback (Figure 1-2). The overall environment also must be considered.

The Nature of Inputs

Inputs are elements the system must accept because they are imposed by outside forces. The many constraints on organizational processes, such as government regulation and economic factors, are typical inputs imposed by outside groups. Certain inputs are needed in order to achieve the organizational goals; for example, the inputs often are the raw materials that are processed to produce some object or service. The concept of input may be expanded to include the demands made on the system, such as deadlines, priorities, or conflicting pressures. Good will toward the organization, general support, or the lack of these also may be included as inputs.

A systematic review of inputs for a health care organization or one of its departments could include

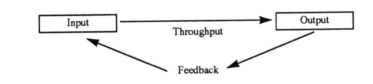

Figure 1-2 Basic Systems Model

- characteristics of clients: average length of stay, diagnostic categories, payment status
- legal and accrediting agency requirements: federal conditions of participation for Medicare programs, institutional licensure, and licensure or certification of health care practitioners
- federal and state laws concerning employers: collective bargaining legislation, the Occupational Safety and Health Act, Workers' Compensation, Civil Rights Act
- multiple goals: patient care, teaching, research

The Nature of Outputs

Outputs are the goods and services that the organization (or subdivision or unit) must produce. These outputs may be routine, frequent, predictable, and somewhat easy to identify. The stated purpose of the organization usually contains information on its basic, obvious outputs. For example, a fire department provides fire protection, a hospital offers patient care, a department store sells goods, a factory produces goods, and an airline supplies transportation. Managers control routine and predictable outputs through proper planning.

Other necessary outputs are infrequent but predictable. By careful analysis of organizational data over a relatively long time period, these infrequent outputs can usually be identified. For example, hospitals or programs are reaccredited periodically, and plans can be made for the reaccreditation process because it is predictable. An organization that is tied directly to political sponsorship could take the cycle of presidential and congressional elections into account. Again, proper planning through identification and anticipation of such special periodic demands on the system leads to greater control and, consequently, stability.

Most managers face a third category: the nonpredictable outputs for which they can and must plan. Certain demands on the system are made with sufficient regularity that, although the exact number and time cannot be calculated, estimates can be made. This is an essential aspect of proper planning and controlling. In an outpatient clinic, for example, the number of walk-in and/or emergency patients is not predictable. In order to plan for these relatively random demands on the system, the manager studies the pattern of walk-in patients, their times of arrival, and the purposes of their visits. Some patient education would probably be done to help clients take advantage of orderly scheduling. Staffing patterns would be adjusted to meet the anticipated needs. The planning is designed to shift the nonpredictable to the predictable as far as possible. Other examples of nonpredictable outputs for which plans can be developed include telephone calls, employee turnover rates, and even activities required by certain kinds of seasonal disasters (e.g., tornadoes or hurricanes) or by seasonal changes in the numbers and types of clients (e.g., in a resort area).

Some outputs are unexpected, such as those that become necessary because of natural disasters or sudden economic chaos. Even in these instances, managers can anticipate and plan for Armageddon in any of its symbolic or real forms. Disaster planning, for example, is a required part of institutional health care management.

Some outputs for health care institutions are

- maintenance of accreditation and licensure status
- compliance with special federal programs concerning quality assurance or health care planning
- provision of acute care services for medical, surgical, obstetric, and pediatric patients
- provision of comprehensive mental health services for clients in a specific area

Outputs in health care institutions may be refined even further by adding specific time factors, quality factors, or other statements of expected performance:

- processing of specified laboratory tests within ten hours of receipt of specimen
- retrieval of patient medical record from permanent file within seven minutes of receipt of request
- 100 percent follow-up on all patients who fail to keep appointments

It may be useful to group outputs with the related inputs by formulating input/output statements. It should be noted, however, that not every input generates a direct output; there is no one-to-one relationship of inputs to outputs. It may be necessary to consider a cluster of inputs in relation to a single output. For example, the goal (output) of retrieving the medical record of a patient who enters the walk-in clinic without an appointment and cannot be treated until the chart has been obtained may require the following considerations (inputs):

Inputs	Output
Hospital policy concerning chart availability for patients before receiving treatment	Retrieval of patient chart within seven minutes of request
Random arrival of patient and therefore of request for medical record	
Patient identification incomplete	
Incomplete or unavailable charts	
Misfiles within storage area	

Throughputs (Withinputs)

Throughputs are the structures or processes by which inputs are converted to outputs. Physical plant, workflow, methods and procedures, and hours of work are throughputs. Inputs originate in the environment of the organization; throughputs, as the term implies, are contained within the organization. Throughputs are analyzed by work sampling, work simplification, methods improvement, staffing patterns, and physical layout analysis.

Managers may be severely limited in their ability to control inputs, but the processes, structures, organizational patterns, and procedures that constitute the throughputs are normally areas of management prerogative. For example, a chief of service cannot control patient arrivals for walk-in service in a clinic; this input is imposed on the system. The policies and procedures for processing walk-in patients, however, constitute a cluster of throughputs that can be determined by the manager. The physical space allotment for a department may be imposed; the manager must accept this input, but the final and detailed physical layout of the department is under the manager's control.

In a specialized service, the control of throughputs is directly related to the manager's professional knowledge. For example, procedures for processing patient flow within a clinic are developed by the chief of service because of that person's knowledge of patient care procedures, priorities, and the interrelationships among components of the treatment plan. The policies and procedures for the release of information from patients' medical records are aspects of highly technical processes that are the domain of the professional medical record practitioner.

In some cases, elements that theoretically belong to the throughput category are considered inputs. These are elements that are imposed by the environment (i.e., the organization as a whole). Managers may not be able to exert direct control over some aspects of the work (e.g., in the case of physical space limitations, budget cuts, and personnel vacancies), and these elements could be listed as special inputs.

Feedback

Changes in the input mix must be anticipated. In order to respond to these changes, managers need feedback on the acceptability and adequacy of the outputs. It is through the feedback process that inputs and even throughputs are adjusted to produce new outputs. The communication network and control processes are the usual sources of organized feedback. Routine, orderly feedback is provided by such activities as market research and forecasting in business organizations, client surveys in service organizations, periodic accreditation surveys in health care institutions, periodic employee evaluations in work groups, and periodic testing and grading in an educational system. The management by objectives process, short interval scheduling, and program evaluation review technique (PERT) networks constitute specific management tools of planning and controlling that include structured, factual feedback.

If there is an absence of planned feedback, if the communication process is not sufficiently developed to permit safe and acceptable avenues for feedback, or if the feedback actually received is ignored, a certain amount of feedback will occur spontaneously. In this case, the feedback tends to take a negative form, such as a client outburst of anger, a precipitous lawsuit, a riot, a wildcat strike, a consumer boycott, or an epidemic. Spontaneous feedback could take a positive form, of course, such as the acclamation of a hero or leader after a crisis or an unsolicited letter of satisfaction from a client.

Some feedback is tacit, and the manager may assume that, since there is no overt evidence to the contrary, all outputs are fine. The danger in such an assumption is that problems and difficulties may not come to light until a crisis occurs. The planning process is undermined because there are no reliable data that can be used to assess the impact of change and to implement the necessary adjustments.

Closed Systems versus Open Systems

Systems may be classified as either closed or open. An ideal closed system is complete within itself. No new inputs are received, and there is no change in the components; there is no output of energy in any of its forms (e.g., information or material). Few, if any, response or adaptation systems are needed because such a closed system is isolated from external forces in its environment and internal change is self-adjusting. Examples of closed systems include a chemical reaction taking place in a sealed, insulated container; a sealed terrarium; and a thermostat. In certain approaches to organizational theory, organizations have been viewed as closed systems, that is, the emphasis has been placed on the study of functions and structure within the organization without consideration of its environment and the consequent effect of environmental change on its processes.

An open system is in a constant state of flux. Inputs are received and outputs produced. There is input and output of both matter and energy, continual adaptation to the environment, and, usually, an increase of order and complexity, with differentiation of parts over time.

An open system constantly seeks internal balance, or homeostasis, by means of an adjustive function of stimulus-response. A change in the organizational environment (stimulus) makes it necessary to take some action (response) to maintain this balance. Notterman and Trumbull, using a laboratory model, noted three processes necessary for a system to maintain this self-regulating cycle[n]:

1. Detection. For regulation to take place, the disparity between the disturbed and normal (or desired) state must be detectable by the organism. Obviously, if the organism cannot sense a disturbance (perceptually or physiologically), measures cannot be taken for its correction. Equally apparent is the fact that individuals vary in both the quality and quantity of information they require in order to detect a disturbance.
2. Identification. The disparity must also be identified. Corrective action cannot be specific unless a given disturbance is successfully discriminated from other possible disturbances. Here again, individual differences in the form and quantity of information necessary for identification undoubtedly exist.
3. Response Availability. Upon detection and identification of the disturbance, the organism must be permitted by environmental, physiological, or laboratory conditions to make the correction.

The management functions of decision making, leadership, and, particularly, correction of deviation from organizational goals are necessary for the detection, identification, and proper response to changes in the organization's environment. In the open system, the adjustment to the environmental change is made through the input-output cycle and the development of appropriate feedback mechanisms. Another major management function, then, becomes the systematic monitoring of change.

All living organisms have the capacity for maximum disorder, disintegration, and death. This tendency toward disintegration is termed *entropy*. The open system is characterized by the continual striving for negative entropy *(negentropy)*. It tries to overcome disintegration by taking into itself more inputs or higher level inputs (i.e., whatever it needs to produce the required outputs). Obvious examples of this include a bear storing body fat and changing its metabolism for winter hibernation or the human body building up immunity. In the management context, an organization may build a reserve of money or client good will against potential hard times.

Application of General Systems Theory

The systems approach enables managers to focus on the organization as a whole and to view each particular division or unit in the organization in relation to the whole. Through the systems approach, managers can cut across organizational lines to determine interrelationships in the workflow and to assess complexities in the structure and in the environment of the organization. Their attention is drawn to changes in the environment that affect the organization and its units. Managers are aided in their analysis of the organization because the input-output model frees them of personal bias toward or attachment to the existing mode of operations. Furthermore, the classic functions of a manager, which are carried out in the distinct, unique environment of a given organization, are reflected in the systems approach. Table 1-2 summarizes this interrelationship. The remainder of this presentation of management principles is developed in the context of specific functions of the manager carried out in an overall organizational environment. Since the functions of the manager are shaped and modified by the particular organizational environment, the tools for analyzing the organization will be presented first, followed by detailed discussion of individual management functions.

Table 1-2 Relationship of Classic Management Functions and Systems Concepts

Systems Concept	*Predominant Management Function*
Input analysis	
Identification of constraints	
Assessment of client characteristics	Planning
Assessment of physical space	
Budget allocation analysis	
Throughput determination	
Development of policies, procedures, methods	Planning and controlling
Development of detailed departmental layout	
Specification of staffing pattern	Staffing
Methods of worker productivity enhancement	Controlling, leadership, and motivation
Output analysis	
Goal formulation	Planning
Statement of objectives	
Development of management by objectives plan	Planning and controlling
Feedback mechanisms	
Development of feedback processes	Controlling, communicating, and resolving conflict
Adjustment of inputs and outputs in light of feedback	Renewing planning cycle
Adjustment of internal throughputs	

MANAGEMENT FOR THE NINETIES: INTEGRATION OF CLINICAL PRACTICE AND MANAGEMENT SKILLS*

It is predicted that the decade of the 1990s will be the era of the consumer. The consumer will measure the value of health care services purchased by care outcomes. With the emphasis placed on outcomes, the successful health care organization of the 1990s will be *focused, fast, friendly,* and *flexible,* according to Kantor.[12] Achieving success will require an interdisciplinary cadre of highly skilled and enthusiastic managers. These managers must develop and test new strategies for care delivery that address (1) different levels of acuity; (2) a variety of care settings; (3) the health resources and technologies available to serve patients; (4) quality assurance; (5) the creation of staffing and scheduling patterns that increase productivity and reduce the impact of manpower shortages; (6) the use of sophisticated computerized information systems to coordinate the various disciplines in the patient management process; (7) the use of interactive and participative education programs (for staff and patients) that are useful in reducing staff turnover rates and attracting staff and patients; (8) the use of community resources to facilitate discharge planning even before preadmission testing and hospitalization; and (9) the use of clinical research in patient care management to motivate and challenge the staff and to identify measurable cost-effective patient outcomes.

How will the manager of the 90s meet all these challenges? First, the manager must acquire an extensive knowledge base in human relations management, business theory, planning, finance, productivity theory, risk management, marketing, and leadership, organizational, change, systems, and communication theory and be able to apply this knowledge base to the ever-evolving issues and trends in the health care environment. Acquisition of this knowledge base and of a management conceptual framework will help the manager perform successfully in the arena of power politics that exists in every health care organization.

Management Trends

Today's health care administrator or manager is no longer the senior therapist with the longest tenure of service but the therapist with the best ability to balance the requirements of business management and human resource management. It used to be generally accepted that management was goal-oriented and that the process for achieving goals included (1) planning, (2) directing, (3) organizing, (4) coordinating, and (5) controlling. Many books on administration

---

* *Source*: Reprinted from "Management for the Nineties: Integration of Clinical Practice and Management Skills" by Elizabeth Forbes in *The Pyramid*, Vol. 20, No. 3, pp. 11–12, with permission of American Physical Therapy Association, ©1990.

dedicated a chapter to each of these five management functions. A clear-cut definition was given for each of the five functions that addressed information or data collection, dealing with people, and decision-making strategies. Then a management revolution occurred as a result of Peters and Waterman's book *In Search of Excellence*,[13] which examined the characteristics of several successful businesses. Hospitals and other health care organizations started pondering some of the catchy slogans. "Staying close to the customer" suggested the importance of learning what patients need and providing those services or products. Another slogan, "bias for action," indicated that the delivery of those services or products should occur without undue delay. In addition, there seemed to be a direct correlation between business success and the characteristics of employees. The slogan "productivity through people" pointed to the necessity of motivating employees to give their all for the success of the organization and of allowing them to share the benefits of that success. Consequently, special attention was given to the education, orientation, and motivation of employees. By the close of 1989, hospitals and other health care organizations had become versed in incorporating programs of excellence and marketing and they began advertising their services and products like any other business.

Integrating Clinical Expertise

Health care managers provide the accountability framework needed by their organizations in order to compete successfully. However, health care managers also need to maintain their own clinical expertise in order to ensure their own credibility. The maintenance of expertise may be accomplished by participating in direct or indirect care activities and developing strategies for successfully implementing the clinical practice roles as well as the management role. One good strategy is to include clinical responsibilities in the job description. Other strategies are as follows:

- Select continuing education programs to attend.
- Set aside blocks of time for clinical practice.
- When identifying annual management goals, include clinical goals.
- In the quarterly progress summary, list management and clinical accomplishments.
- Get the support of the administration for the continuation of clinical practice.
- Evaluate quarterly the role functions, responsibilities, and accountability for both management and clinical practice.

Direct care activities that can help to maintain clinical expertise include these:

- providing primary care or secondary care to a small select group of patients
- addressing a complex patient problem
- addressing a complex discharge-planning situation
- administering special patient treatments
- developing and implementing a patient education program for an individual or group of patients
- writing a care plan for a complex patient problem

Useful indirect care activities include these:

- collaborating with other staff in developing care plans
- participating in interdisciplinary care conferences and interdepartmental activities
- participating in medical rounds and discharge planning
- participating in risk management and quality assurance activities
- providing consultation to other health care providers
- writing standards of care
- transferring protocols or standards of care and documentation criteria to a computer information system
- participating in research studies

There are several reasons why a manager might engage in direct care activities, including these:[14]

- It provides an opportunity to demonstrate clinical expertise.
- It helps the manager maintain certification.
- The manager can function as a role model.
- The manager is able to assess environmental working conditions.
- The manager is more likely to be accepted by the staff.
- It enhances the visibility and accessibility of the manager.
- The manager experiences the reality of the practice environment.

Management Characteristics Model

Since this is the era of the consumer, effective management strategies must start and end with the needs of patients and their health care expectations and health outcomes weighed against the technological delivery resources that are available. The manager of the 90s has the challenge of indentifying shared goals

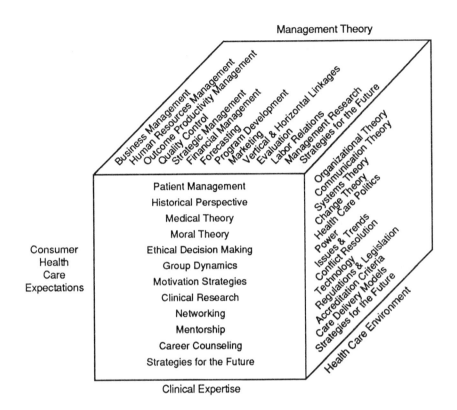

Figure 1-3 Characteristics of The Health Care Management Role

with the administration and staff and establishing mutual trust. The manager must also integrate the roles of therapist, business manager, and human relations manager. These roles require strategic planning, visionary thinking, and the establishment of vertical and horizontal linkages within the organization and between it and other organizations in the community. The characteristics of the management role are outlined in Figure 1-3.

NOTES

1. Luther Gulick and Lyndall F. Urwick, eds., *Papers on the Science of Administration* (New York: Institute of Public Administration, 1937).

2. Henri Fayol, *General and Industrial Administration* (Geneva, Switzerland: International Management Institute, 1929).

3. Chester Barnard, *The Functions of the Executive* (Cambridge, Mass.: Harvard University Press, 1968).

4. Louis D. Brandeis, "Scientific Management and Railroads," *The Engineering Magazine,* 1911.

5. James Mooney and A.C. Reiley, *The Principles of Organization* (New York: Harper, 1939).

6. Ludwig von Bertalanffy, "General Systems Theory: A New Approach to the Unity of Science," *Human Biology* (December 1951): 303–61.

7. Ludwig von Bertalanffy, "General Systems Theory: A Critical Review," *General Systems 7* (1962): 1–20.

8. Kenneth E. Boulding, "General Systems Theory: The Skeleton of Science," *Management Science 2* (1956): 197–208.

9. Norbert Weiner, *The Human Use of Human Beings: Cybernetics and Society* (Garden City, N.Y.: Doubleday Anchor, 1954).

10. Stanley H. Brewer, *Rhochrematics: A Scientific Approach to the Management of Material Flows* (Seattle: University of Washington Bureau of Business Research, 1960).

11. Joseph M. Notterman and Richard Trumbull, "Notes on Self-regulating Systems and Stress," *Behavioral Science 4* (October 1950): 324–27.

12. R.M. Kanter, *When Giants Learn to Dance* (New York: Simon and Schuster, 1989).

13. T. Peters and R. Waterman, *In Search of Excellence* (New York: Warner Books, 1982).

14. A.B. Hamric and J.A. Spross, *The Clinical Nurse Specialist in Theory and Practice* (Philadelphia: W.B. Saunders, 1989).

BIBLIOGRAPHY

Csikszentmihalyi, Mihaly. *Flow: The Psychology of Optimal Experience.* New York: Harper Perennial, 1991.

George, Claude S. *The History of Management Thought.* Englewood Cliffs, N.J.: Prentice-Hall, 1968.

Heyel, Carl. *The Encyclopedia of Management.* 2nd ed. New York: Van Nostrand, 1973.

Kielhofer, Gary. "The Human Being as an Open System." In *A Model of Human Occupation,* edited by Gary Kielhofer, 2–11. Baltimore: Williams & Wilkins, 1985.

Kielhofer, Gary. "General Systems Theory: Implications for the Theory and Action in Occupational Therapy," *American Journal of Occupational Therapy 32* (1978): 637–45.

Chapter 2

Planning

CHAPTER OBJECTIVES

1. Define the management function of planning.
2. Identify the characteristics of plans.
3. Identify the participants in the planning process.
4. Indicate the constraints on or boundaries of planning.
5. Identify the characteristics that make plans effective.
6. Define and differentiate among the terms *philosophy, goal, objective, functional objective, policy, procedure, method,* and *rule.*
7. Illustrate these terms through examples.

Planning is the process of making decisions in the present to bring about an outcome in the future. It involves determining appropriate goals and the means to achieve them, stating assumptions, developing premises, and reviewing alternate courses of action. It is the what-who-when-how of alternate courses of action and of possible future actions. In planning, the manager contemplates the state of affairs desired for the future.

CHARACTERISTICS OF PLANNING

Planning is the most fundamental management function and logically precedes all other functions. Unplanned action cannot be controlled properly, because there is no basis on which to measure progress; organizing becomes meaningless and ineffective because there is no specific goal around which to mobilize resources. Decisions may be made without planning, but they will lack effectiveness unless they are related to a goal.

Planning goes beyond mere judgments, since judgments involve the assessment of a situation but do not stipulate actions to be taken. Planning concerns actions to be taken with reference to a specific goal.

In planning, the ideal state is first identified. Then the plan to achieve that ideal is modified, refined, and brought to a practical level through a variety of derived elements, such as intermediate target statements, functional objectives, and operational goals. Planning includes the decision-making process, particularly in the commitment phase. Logical planning includes commitment in terms of time and actions to be taken. There is a hierarchy in the process that includes the relationship of derived plans to the master course, the linkage of short-range and long-range plans, and the coordination of division and department or unit plans with those of the organization as a whole. Finally, planning is characterized by a cyclic process in which some or many goals and specific objectives are recycled.

In a sense, some plans are never achieved completely; they are continuous. For example, the goal of health care institutions to provide quality patient care is a continuing one that invests the many derived plans with a fundamental purpose. This goal is recycled during each planning period.

PARTICIPANTS IN PLANNING

Top-level managers set the basic tone for planning, determine overall goals for the organization, and give direction on the content of policies and similar planning documents. This is not done in isolation, but is based on information provided through the feedback cycle, through reports and special studies, and through the direct participation of personnel in each department or division.

Department heads are normally responsible for the planning process in their areas of jurisdiction. They identify overall goals and policies for their department, and they develop immediate objectives, taking into account their department's particular work constraints. In some organizations, a special planning department is created, such as a program and development division or a research and development unit.

Occasionally, clients participate in the planning process; such participation is required in some federally funded programs. In health care planning, for example, both provider and consumer membership is designated at each level of the review process. Professional associations frequently involve their members in the planning process at local, regional, state, and national levels.

The Planning Process

Since planning is intended to focus attention on objectives and to offset uncertainty, there must be a clear statement of goals. Once the goals to be attained have been established, premising must be developed, that is, the assumptions must be identified, stated, and used consistently. Premising includes an analysis of planning constraints and a statement of the anticipated environment within which the plans will unfold. In a health care organization, the premises reflect the level of care, the specific setting (e.g., outpatient clinic, inpatient unit, or home care), the specific number of beds per service, the anticipated number and kinds of specialty services or clinics, morbidity and mortality data for the outreach territory, and the availability of related services.

The department head states the premises on which departmental plans are based, for example, the number of inpatient beds, the readmission rate, the projected length of stay, and the interrelationship of the workflow. The following is an example of specific planning premises or assumptions based on the operation of a physical therapy service:

1. Anticipated hours of operation
   a. 6 days per week
   b. 8-hour day; evening coverage for selected patients and clinics
2. Anticipated caseload
   a. Inpatients—68 per day
   b. Outpatients—15 per day
3. Diagnostic categories
   a. Hemiplegics
   b. Arthritics
   c. Amputees
   d. Fractures
   e. Sports injuries
4. Patient characteristics
   a. Adults
   b. Children
5. Level of care
   a. Acute
   b. Subacute
   c. Convalescent
   d. Chronic

Alternate approaches to reaching the desired state are developed, and the choices to be made are stated. Commitment to one of these choices constitutes the decision-making phase. Derivative plans then are formulated, and details of sequence and timing are identified. Planning includes periodic checking and review, which leads into the control process. Review and necessary revisions of plans, based on feedback, are the final steps in the cycle of planning.

PLANNING CONSTRAINTS OR BOUNDARIES

To constrain means to limit, to bind, to delineate freedom of action. Constraints in planning are factors that managers must take into account in order to make their plans feasible and realistic. Constraints, which are both internal and external, take a variety of forms. Analysis of the organizational environment by means of the clientele network, specifically the category of "controller," leads to ready identification of planning constraints. (See Chapter 16 for discussion of this concept.) The use of the input-output model also yields practical information about the constraints specific to an organization. The planning process itself imposes a constraint because of time factors. Sometimes a manager must settle for speed rather than accuracy in gathering the data needed for planning. The cost of data gathering and analysis is another constraint; if committees or special review groups are involved, the cost of their time must be considered.

The general resistance to change impedes the planning process so that standing plans take on the force of habit. Without a program for regular review of plans, they become static and rooted in tradition. Precedent becomes the rule, and the bureaucratic processes become entrenched. The phase in the life cycle of the organization also affects planning, as the degree of innovation that is appropriate varies with each phase.

The nature of the organization also shapes the planning process. The extent to which the organization's members participate in planning correlates with the predominant mode of authority. Highly normative organizations tend to include more member participation in their planning than do coercive ones. Ethics and values of the larger society, of the individual members, and, in health care, of the many professional organizations help shape the goal formulation and subsequent policies and practices. When health care is seen as a right and not a privilege, there may be a greater openness to innovation and a demand for outreach programs and flexible patterns of delivery of service.

Within the organization, interdepartmental relationships may be constraints. In highly specialized organizations with many services or departments, each unit manager must consider how other departments' needs and processes are interwoven with those of the given department. Effective planning includes an assessment of such factors. The manager sometimes must accept as inputs or constraints the procedures and policies of another department.

Capital investments must also be considered. When a major commitment that involves the physical layout of the facility or some major equipment purchase has been made, the degree of flexibility in changing the process is necessarily limited.

External factors to be considered in planning include the political climate, which varies in its openness to extensive programs in health care. The era of a

Great Society approach may be replaced by an era in which an attempt is made to return health care delivery to private rather than government sponsorship, or the emphasis may shift from the federal government to the state government level. The general state of labor relations and the degree to which unionization is allowed and even mandated in an industry may be imposed on the organization. The many regulations, laws, and directives constitute another set of constraints.

In health care organizations, the many legal and accrediting requirements are specific, pervasive constraints that affect every aspect of planning. Such requirements can be developed into a reference grid for the use of the manager, since compliance with these mandates is a binding element in the overall constraint on departmental functioning.

An alternate approach to the identification of constraints in any health care planning situation is the systematic recognition of the following major factors:

1. General Setting. The level and particular emphasis of care must be determined. For example, the goal of one institution may be acute care in specialized diagnostic categories; the goal of another may be the long-term care of the aged. The critical organizational relationships that stem from the general setting should be identified (e.g., the institution's degree of independence versus its adherence to corporate and affiliation agreements and contractual arrangements). Physical location may also be a constraining factor, although an earlier decision to develop the facility in a specific location may be part of the ideal plan. For example, the decision to develop a pattern of decentralized care in order to enhance the outreach program of a community mental health center will serve as a constraint on many derived plans, such as workflow and staffing patterns.

2. Legal and Accrediting Agency Mandates. Each health care institution is regulated by a federal or state agency that imposes specific requirements for the level of care and nature of services offered. For example, a hospital is licensed by the state only after it meets certain requirements; it is approved for participation in the Medicare and Medicaid programs only after it fulfills certain conditions. In addition, a hospital must comply with special regulations for medical care evaluation and health planning agency requirements for changes in bed capacity or services offered. It also must comply, at a minimum, with malpractice insurance regulations and related risk management programs as well as fire, safety, and zoning codes.

3. Characteristics of the Clients. The general patterns of mortality and morbidity for a given population must be considered, as well as related factors such as length of inpatient stay, frequency of outpatient services, emergency unit usage, and readmission rate. Patient sources of payment relate to the stability and predictability of cash flow. Specific eligibility for treat-

ment may be another factor, as in certain community mental health/mental retardation programs, services for veterans, or programs for other specific groups.

4. Practitioners and Employees. The licensure laws for health care practitioners and physicians, as well as the many federal and state laws pertaining to most classes of employees, govern the utilization of staff. These include the Labor Management Relations Act (Taft-Hartley Act), the Civil Rights Act, the Age Discrimination in Employment Act, the Unemployment Compensation and Workers' Compensation Acts, and the Occupational Safety and Health Act. The personnel practices mandated in the accrediting agency standards and guidelines of health agencies and professional associations also must be followed. Any contractual agreement resulting from the collective bargaining process must be taken into account. The specific bylaws and related rules and regulations for medical staff and allied health care practitioners are yet another constraint on plans involving employees and professional practitioners in any role.

CHARACTERISTICS OF EFFECTIVE PLANS

Effective plans have flexibility. Plans should have a built-in capacity to change, an adaptability. A plan could include a timetable sequence, for example, that allows extra time for unexpected events before the plan becomes off schedule.

The manager seeks to balance plans so that they are neither too idealistic nor too practical or limited. Plans that are too idealistic tend to produce frustration because they cannot be attained; they may become mere mottoes. On the other hand, plans that are too modest lack motivational value, and it may be difficult to muster support for them. Clarity and vagueness must also be balanced in formulating plans. These factors help make the goals realistic. A precise goal may be a motivational tool because it provides immediate satisfaction, but there also is merit in a degree of vagueness because with some plans, especially long-range ones, it may not be possible or desirable to state goals in precise terms. Vagueness can contribute to motivation since it permits the development of detailed plans by those more directly involved in the work. Finally, vagueness can provide the necessary latitude to compromise when this is required or is a general strategy in the development of plans throughout the organization.

Types of Plans

The planning process involves a variety of plans that develop logically from the highly abstract, as in a statement of philosophy or ideal goals, to the progressively concrete, as in operational goals and procedures. Management literature on planning consistently includes the concepts of goals and objectives as central to the planning process. The terms *goal* and *objective* frequently are used in an interchangeable manner, except in discussions of management by objectives (MBO). The MBO concept refers to specific, measurable, attainable plans for the unit, department, or organization. For the purposes of this discussion of plans, the concept of goal will be discussed in terms of overall purpose. The concept of objective will be discussed in terms of more measurable attainable plans, including unit or departmental objectives and functional objectives. Exhibit 2-1 lists the sequence of planning documents from planning state through controlling by means of operational goals.

PHILOSOPHY OR UNDERLYING PURPOSE

Individuals who share a common vision and set of values come together to create a formal organization for purposes that are consistent with and derived from their common values. The statement of philosophy or underlying purpose provides an overall frame of reference for organizational practice; it is the basis of the overall goals, objectives, policies, and derived plans (see Exhibit 2-2 for a sample statement of the philosophy and objectives of a rehabilitation department). Actual practice, as delineated in policies and procedures, should not violate the organization's underlying philosophy. As new members and clients are attracted to the organization and as the organization grows from the gestational to the youthful stage, the statement of principles may be made more explicit. A philosophy may take one of several forms, such as a preamble, a creed, a pledge, or a statement of principle.

Exhibit 2-1 Relationship of Types of Plans

```
      I.  Underlying Purpose/Overall Mission/Philosophy/Goal
     II.  Objectives
         III.  Functional Objectives
         IV.  Policies
             V.  Procedures
                 V.1      Methods
                 V.2      Rules
    VI.  Work Standards
   VII.  Performance Standards
  VIII.  Training Objectives
    IX.  Management by Objectives
     X.  Operational Goals
```

Exhibit 2-2 Rehabilitation Department Philosophy and Objectives

Philosophy	Rehabilitation is the process of restoring an individual to his or her fullest physical, vocational, economic, and social ability when disabled by injury, disease, or disuse. The Rehabilitation Department staff evaluates each patient and develops a unique plan of treatment coordinated with the patient, family, and the other members of the health care team.
Objectives	1. Maximize each patient's physical ability.
	2. Assist each patient to adapt to remaining limitations.
	3. Assist each patient in the transition from hospital to home or another institution.
	4. Recommend/provide appropriate follow-up care for each patient.
	5. Provide (a) patient and family education to assist recovery and (b) information on prevention of illness or injury.
	6. Provide instruction and information about rehabilitation to professional and community groups.
	7. Provide training to fellow employees on good body mechanics and safe work habits.
	8. Promote continuing education of staff to improve the quality of patient care.
	9. Provide an organized learning experience for students in physical therapy and occupational therapy.
	10. Monitor the quality and effectiveness of each service within the department on a regular basis.

Source: Courtesy of Carol Pisapia, Rehabilitation Coordinator, St. Vincent's Medical Center of Staten Island, New York.

In addition to reflecting the values of the immediate, specific group that formed the organization, a statement of philosophy may reflect, implicitly or explicitly, the values of the larger society. To one degree or another, for example, society as a whole now accepts the burden of providing for those who need medical care. The concept of health care as a right, regardless of ability to pay, gradually emerged as an explicit value in the 1960s. Emphasis on the rights of consumers and patients emerged in a similar evolutionary pattern in the 1970s. Because free enterprise is a benchmark of the democratic way of life, a trend toward marketing and competition in health care is a feature of the 1980s and 1990s.

Department managers in a health care organization are guided by several philosophical premises. These may differ from, and even be in opposition to, the managers' personal values. However, as members of the executive team, the managers are expected to accept these premises. One of the goals of providing orientation and motivation is to foster acceptance of the underlying purpose of the organization. Typical philosophical premises in health care include

- the basic philosophy of the group that sponsors and/or controls the health care institution (e.g., federal or state government agency, religious or fraternal organization, business concern)
- the American Hospital Association's guidelines on patient rights and similar issues
- guidelines of accrediting agencies, such as the Joint Commission on the Accreditation of Healthcare Organizations (Joint Commission), that emphasize continuity of care, patient rights, and so on
- guidelines, codes of ethics, and position statements of professional associations (e.g., American Physical Therapy Association, American Health Information Management Association, American Occupational Therapy Association)
- values of society in general, such as the current concern for privacy, equal access, employee safety, and consumer/client participation in decision making
- contemporary trends in the delivery of health care, such as the shift from inpatient acute care to outpatient care and community-based outreach centers; the establishment of independent practices by health professionals (e.g., nurses) who formerly provided care only under the direct supervision of physicians; the emergence of technical levels in several health professions and the acceptance of the care given by technicians

The following are excerpts from statements of philosophy. One medical record department has its philosophy stated in a preamble:

Given the basic right of patients to comprehensive, quality health care, the medical record department, as a service department, provides support and assistance within its jurisdiction to the staff and programs of this institution. A major function of this department is to facilitate continuity of patient care through the development and maintenance of the appropriate medical information systems which shall reflect all episodes of care given by the professional and technical staff in any of the components of this institution.

An educational institution adheres to the following statement of philosophy:

One of the critical elements in an effective approach to health care is the establishment of the spirit and practice of cooperative endeavor among practitioners. Recognizing this need, the Consortium for Interdisciplinary Health Studies seeks to foster the team approach to the delivery of health care.

The statement of educational philosophy of the American Health Information Management Association contains the following:

> Formal and informal continuing education is recognized as an essential component of professional development for health personnel. It is the task of the professional organization to assist and encourage employers and employees to participate in and support programs of continuing education.

The following is from the statement of philosophy of a physical therapy department:

> The physical therapy department as a component of the health care system is committed to providing quality patient care and community services in the most responsive and cost-effective manner possible. In addition, the department will participate in research and investigative studies and provide educational programs for hospital personnel and affiliating students from the various medical and health professions.

The philosphy of an occupational therapy private practice group is stated in these terms:

> The Occupational Therapy Consultants, Inc. believe that humans are open systems that both influence and are influenced by the environment. Therefore, individuals are motivated to pursue goal-directed activities that reflect their values, roles and interest. We use activities and environmental adaptations to provide positive reinforcement and a sense of mastery to our clients. We make "doing" possible.

The mission of this private practice group is as follows:

> Occupational Therapy Consultants, Inc. will seek referrals from medical and non-medical sources and offer high quality, cost-effective services to clients and their caregivers whose roles, habits and interests are limited by pathological, congenital or traumatic incidents. Services, direct and consultative, will be offered in schools, homes, factories and out-patient facilities.

OVERALL GOALS

The goals of the organization originate in the common vision and sense of mission embodied in the statement of purpose or the underlying philosophy.

They reflect the general purpose of the organization and provide the basis for subsequent management action. As statements of long-range organizational intent and purpose, goals are the ends toward which activity is directed. In a sense, a goal is never completely achieved but rather continues to exist as an ideal state to be attained.

Goals serve as a basis for grouping organizations, for example, educational organizations, health care institutions, and philanthropic or fraternal associations. Goals, like statements of philosophy, may be found in an organization's charter, articles of incorporation, statement of mission, or introduction to the official bylaws. Again like the statement of philosophy, the overall goals may not bear a specific label; they may be identified only through common understanding. The planning process is facilitated when the philosophy and the goals are formally stated. Derivative plans may then be developed in a consistent manner and with less risk of implementing policies and procedures that violate fundamental values.

OBJECTIVES

In the planning process, the manager makes the plans progressively more explicit. The move from the ideal, relatively intangible statements of mission and purpose or overall goal to the "real" plans is accomplished through the development of specific objectives that bring the goals to a practical, working level. Objectives are relatively tangible, concrete plans and are usually stated in terms of results to be achieved. The manager reviews the underlying purpose and basically answers the following question: What is my unit or department to accomplish specifically in light of these overall goals?

Achieving specific objectives tends to be a continuous process; the work of the department must satisfy these objectives over and over again. An overall goal such as "to promote the health and well-being of the community" can be accomplished only through a series of specific objectives that are met on a continuing basis. Objectives add the dimensions of quality, time, accuracy, and priorities to goals. The objectives are specific to each unit or department, while the overall goals for an organization remain the same for all units.

Objectives may be stated in a variety of ways, and different levels of detail may be used. For example, objectives may be expressed

- quantitatively: to maintain the profit margin of 6 percent during each fiscal year by an increase in sales volume sufficient to offset increased cost
- qualitatively: to make effective use of community involvement by the

establishment of an advisory committee with a majority of members drawn from the active clients who live in the immediate geographical community
- as services to be offered: to provide comprehensive personal patient care services with full consideration for the elements of good medical care (e.g., accessibility, quality, continuity, and efficiency)
- as values to be supported: to ensure privacy and confidentiality in all phases of patient care interaction and documentation

Objectives for the department as a whole may include elements essential for proper delineation of all other objectives. These may be stated as objectives for the organization and need not, therefore, be repeated in the subsequent departmental statement of objectives:

- compliance with legal, regulatory, and accrediting standards and with institutional bylaws
- risk management factors, including accuracy
- privacy and confidentiality in patient care transactions and documentation
- reference to inpatient as well as outpatient/ambulatory care and other programs sponsored by the organization, such as home care or satellite clinics

Because they are intended to give specificity to overall goals, objectives are the key to management planning. Therefore, objectives must be measurable whenever possible. They must provide for formal accountability in terms of achieving the results. Furthermore, they must be flexible so that they can be adapted to changing circumstances over time. Two additional planning concepts must be used with the statements of objectives in order to make them meaningful: the statement of functional objectives and the development of policies. These related plans are both important in fleshing out departmental objectives.

FUNCTIONAL OBJECTIVES

A functional objective is a statement that refines a general objective in terms of

- specific service to be provided
- type of output
- quantity and/or specificity of output
- frequency and/or specificity of output
- accuracy
- priorities

Some elements, such as accuracy indicators, may be defined for the department or unit as a whole. A general objective's priority may be implied by its delineation in a related functional objective.

Planning data for organizing and staffing functions may be obtained by inference from statements of objectives; for example, the functional objective statement may include the stipulation that all discharge summaries shall be typed. The workload (number of discharge summaries) may be calculated based on the number of discharges per year. A priority system for processing such summaries or a designated turnaround time for such processing provides the necessary parameters for calculating the number of workers needed to meet the objective on a continuing basis. The staffing patterns for day, evening, and night shifts may be developed, again, in a way to satisfy the priority designation and turnaround time contained in the functional objective.

The relationship of the general objective and the functional objectives that support it are clearly seen in the following example drawn from the plans for a transcription/word processing unit of a medical record department.

> *General Objective:* The medical record department will provide a system for dictation of selected medical reports by specified health care providers and for the transcription of these reports on a routine basis.
> *Functional Objectives:* More specifically, this system will provide for:
>   a) dictation services for attending medical staff, house officers, and allied medical staff as defined by the medical staff bylaws.
>   b) transcription of reports will be done within the following time frame:
>   1. discharge summaries within three working days of receipt of dictation
>   2. operative reports within 24 hours of dictation
>   3. consultation reports within 24 hours of dictation.

This example specifies the quantity of output and the time frame and implies the priority of the objective through the designation of the time frame. A statement of accuracy is not included, because it is included in the objectives for the department as a whole. This accuracy statement, which may fall under the overall objective of risk management/quality control, may be expressed as follows:

> The medical record department strives to carry out its responsibilities and activities within 100 percent accuracy; however, an acceptable level of accuracy will be established both for individual employees as well as for each subsystem of the department.

The following is an example of a general objective and functional objectives from a direct patient care service:

General Objective: The physical therapy department will provide evaluation and assessment procedures appropriate to the patient's condition as requested by the referring physician.

Functional Objectives: More specifically,

    a) evaluations will be completed within two working days following receipt of the referral

    b) a verbal summary of findings will be submitted to the physician following the completion of the evaluation

    c) a written summary of the evaluation will be noted in the patient's chart within 24 hours following the verbal report.

Excerpts from systems objectives and related functional objectives are given below. These reflect the objectives for the release of information unit of a medical record department.[1]

The Medical Records Department will provide a system for the timely and accurate processing of requests and for the release of information from the medical records maintained by this health care facility. Specifically, this release of information system shall be established

- to comply with all applicable state and federal laws, regulations, and accrediting standards
- to comply with the generally accepted principles of patients' rights, privacy, and confidentiality
- to comply with the Patient's Bill of Rights promulgated by the American Hospital Association, the American Psychiatric Association, the Joint Commission on Accreditation of Healthcare Organizations, federal and state regulations designating specific bill of rights statements, and the American Health Information Management Association's Code of Ethics.

The Medical Records Department will develop detailed procedures for the timely, accurate, and appropriate response to requests within these basic time frames:

- emergency requests: priority response
- in-person requests from
  the patient or the patient's
  designated representative:
  1. general requests: immediate initiation of
                                           preliminary procedure

2. requests for access
to a record:

finalized response within
[_____] working days of
initiation of preliminary
procedure
immediate initiation of
preliminary procedure

appointment made for review
of the record [_____] days
from receipt of approval for
review from the attending
physician

• in-person requests from
nonpatients:

immediate initiation of
preliminary procedure
appointment made for review
of the record [_____] working days from receipt of
approval for review from the
attending physician, if applicable

• written requests:

initial response within one
working day of receipt of the
request if further information,
authorization, or fees are
required

completed response within
[_____] working days after
receipt of the necessary
authorizations and/or fees

return of the request completed within one working
day if the request cannot be
completed (for example, if
the individual named in the
request was not a patient of
this facility)

• court orders and sub-
poenas:

within mandated time
frames

The Medical Records Department will maintain systems to

- notify Risk Management of inquiries and authorized disclosures naming the facility in potential litigation
- coordinate with Patient Billing the release of information for reimbursement purposes
- coordinate inservice training about release of information practices
  1. for Medical Records Department employees at hiring and at least yearly thereafter
  2. for employees of other departments as requested by appropriate department heads
- maintain quality control
  1. through monthly quality control reviews focusing on detecting and preventing errors
  2. through monthly quality control reviews focusing on ensuring the accuracy and timeliness of responses

POLICIES

Policies are the guides to thinking and action by which managers seek to delineate the areas within which decisions will be made and subsequent actions taken. Policies spell out the required, prohibited, or suggested courses of action. The limitations on actions are stated, defined, or at least clearly implied. Policies predecide issues and limit actions so that situations that occur repeatedly are handled in the same way. Because policies are intended to be overall guides, their language is broad.

A balance must be found when policies are formulated. These comprehensive guides to thinking and action should be sufficiently specific to provide the user with information about the actions to take, the actions to be avoided, and when and how to respond; at the same time, however, they should be flexible enough to accommodate changing conditions. They should reinforce and be consistent with the overall goals and objectives. In addition, they should conform to legal and accrediting mandates as well as to any other requirement imposed by internal or external authorities.

Policies are relatively permanent plans, a kind of cornerstone of other, more detailed plans. Yet they must be sufficiently flexible in intent to permit change in the derived plans without necessitating a change in the policy. For example, a commitment to a centralized word processing system might be made through a policy statement on medical record department functions. However, no specification is made as to brand of equipment, exclusive use of in-house staffing, or external agency contract. All remain options as long as the equipment selected and the staffing pattern determined meet the policy considerations of an adequate dictation-word processing function. In the dictation-word processing policy contained in this book, the essential features of the word processing system are delineated. It is easy to derive from this a decision-making matrix for the comparison and selection of one or another commercial transcription/word processing service. In this sense, a policy statement serves to perform or shape detailed decision making because the overall parameters are stated within the policy or are easily derived from it.[2]

Sources of Policy

Department or unit managers develop the policies specific to their assigned areas, but these policies must be consistent with those originated by top-level management. Policies sometimes are implied, as in a tacit agreement to permit an afternoon coffee break. An implied policy may make it difficult to enforce some other course of action, however, if the implied policy has become standard—in spite of its lack of official approval. Policies are shaped in some instances by the effect of exceptions granted; a series of exceptions may become the basis of a new policy, or at least a revision of an existing one. Certain policies may be imposed by outside groups, such as an accrediting agency or a labor union, through a negotiated contract.

Wording of Policies

Policies permit and require interpretation. Language indicators, such as "whenever possible" or "as circumstances permit," are expressions typically used to give policies the flexibility needed. Policy statements in a health care institution may concern such items as definitions of categories of patients and designations of responsibility. In a medical records department, policy statements may specify, for example, a standardized medical record format, the internal and external distribution of copies, the use of abbreviations, the processing of urgent requests, and those allowed to use the dictation system.

In order to decrease the sheer volume of policy statements, a glossary may be developed that includes the institutional definition of *patient* as well as definitions for terms and acronyms referring to members of the medical and professional staff and legal and accrediting bodies. Occasionally, a statement of rationale is included in a policy statement, but the manager should avoid excessive explanations; in general, the manager needs to couch policy directives in wording that predecides issues and permits actions.

Policies are somewhat futuristic in that they are meant to remain in force, with little change, for long periods of time. In an age of rapid social and technical change, it is helpful to think in broad terms, anticipating change. It also helps to set aside the normal biases that stem from describing the way things are now.

- Edit all policies to omit sexist references (e.g., physician as "he," nurses as "she"). This is easily done by using plural pronouns.
- Edit all policies to reflect the continued growth of the nursing profession and the various allied health professionals who continually seek an expanded scope of practice. Include nurse practitioners, physician assistants, physical therapists, pharmacists, and similar credentialed, licensed practitioners in policy statements where applicable.
- Focus on the broad range of patient care. The 1990s will be characterized by increasing alternate modes of health care delivery. Although the acute care hospital is central to patient care, outpatient care, urgent care centers, and short-stay units are increasingly a part of the health care setting.
- Think "high tech," especially as technology develops in areas such as computerization and optical disk storage.
- Seek to avoid contradictions within policies and between policies and their related procedures. The careful development of procedures, in addition to checking against policy statements, is an essential step.[3]

The wording in the following examples, drawn from a variety of settings, tends to be broad and elastic yet gives sufficient information to guide the user. The first example is a policy for the waiver of tuition for senior citizens:

> In recognition of their efforts over the years in support of education, the college will waive tuition for academic and continuing education courses for senior citizens who reside in the tricounty area. All residents at least 62 years of age who are not engaged in full time gainful employment are eligible under this tuition waiver policy. This policy will be subject to annual budgeted funds.

This example provides a general sense of why the college is granting this waiver: in recognition of senior citizen support over the years. The outer limits of its applicability are noted: both academic and continuing education programs are included. A definition of senior citizen is given, and the additional eligibility factors are stated. A final parameter is included to provide flexibility should circumstances change: namely, the limitation determined by the availability of budgeted funds. With this short policy, the necessary procedures can be developed for determining eligibility, and a relatively untrained worker can make the necessary determination.

The following policy guides the user in determining eligibility for certain credit courtesies.

For business customers, the open account is available only to government agencies, recognized educational institutions, and companies with a Dun and Bradstreet rating of "good" or higher.

The limits are set by delineating the eligible agencies, and the benchmark of a specific rating is given.

The following are typical policies for health care institutions. For employee promotion:

It is the policy of this hospital to promote from within the organization whenever qualified employees are available for vacancies. The following factors shall be considered in the selection of individual employees for promotion: length of service with the organization; above-average performance in present position; special preparation for promotion. Employees on their present job for a reasonable length of time, excluding probationary period, may request promotion during the customary period in which a job is open and posted as being available.

For admission of patients to a research unit:

Since the primary purpose of this unit is research in specialized areas of medicine, the primary consideration in selecting elective patients for admission to the research unit accommodations is given to the teaching and research value of the clinical findings. The research unit offers two types of service: inpatient and outpatient. The research unit reserves the right to assign patients to either service category, depending on the characteristics of the case and facilities available at the time.

For a medical records system:

The recordkeeping system shall be a unit record and a unit numbering system. Each patient shall be assigned a unit number on the first occasion of service in any component of this health care facility and shall retain that number for all subsequent visits. Recording of information from both inpatient and outpatient services shall be contained in the same medical record.

For a physical therapy department:

The Physical Therapy Department shall be open from 8:30 A.M. to 4:30 P.M. Monday through Friday, and on weekends and holidays as required to meet patient care needs.

And below is an example of a policy regarding professional credentials:

All occupational therapy personnel will be licensed and registered.

Each applicant will submit the names of two references and the personnel officer will telephone these individuals and check on the applicant's ability to problem solve and communicate with others and his or her work habits and commitment to patient service delivery.

The director of the occupational therapy department will check to see if the applicant has passed the national certification examination (AOTCB) and has a current state license.

Recent graduates or therapists from foreign countries may treat patients but they must be supervised by a licensed and certified occupational therapist who countersigns their patient care plans and progress notes.

Occupational therapists may not work more than six months under these conditions. If not registered and licensed within six months after they were hired, the individuals will be asked to leave since they did not fulfill the job requirements.

Additional sample policy statements are contained in Appendixes 2-A and 2-B.

PROCEDURES

A procedure is a guide to action. It is a series of related tasks, given in chronological order, that constitute the prescribed manner of performing the work. Essential information in any procedure includes the specific tasks that must be done, at what time and/or under what circumstances they must be done, and who (job title, not name of employee) is to do them. Procedures are developed for repetitive work in order to ensure uniformity of practice, to facilitate personnel training, and to permit the development of controls and checks in the workflow. Unlike policies, which are more general, procedures are highly specific and need little, if any, interpretation.

Procedures for a specific organizational unit are developed by the manager of that unit. As with other plans, departmental procedures must be coordinated with those of related departments as well as with those developed by higher management levels for all departments. For example, the procedures for patient transport to various specialized service units, such as nuclear medicine, physical therapy, or occupational therapy, are developed jointly by the nursing service and these related departments or services. In contrast, procedures relating to employee matters may well be dictated by top-level management for the organization as a whole with little, if any, procedural development done at the departmental or unit level.

See Appendixes 2-B and 2-C for examples of procedures.

Procedure Manual Format

There are three types of formats used in procedure manuals: narrative, abbreviated narrative, and playscript. The narrative format contains a series of statements in paragraph form, with special notes or explanations in subparagraphs or in footnotes (Exhibit 2-3). The abbreviated narrative format illustrates procedures through the use of key steps and key points (Exhibits 2-4 and 2-5).

When a procedure involves several workers or departments, the playscript format may be used to advantage. Each participant in the action is identified by job title, the step is given a sequence number, a key action word or words is/are stated, and action sentences are developed for the step. The playscript format is direct and specific and its focus is on "who does what and when." As each step in the procedure is analyzed and stated in terms of actor, step sequence, key action word, and action sentence, ambiguity and vagueness are avoided (Exhibit 2-6).

An alternate version of the playscript format stresses responsible party, step sequence, and action (Exhibits 2-7 and 2-8).

Yet another version includes a set of detailed steps for each key step in the playscript sequence (Exhibit 2-9).

Exhibit 2-3 Narrative Procedure Format: Procedure for Pulling Clinic Records

Most records for clinic appointments are pulled two days in advance of the appointment date. However, there are always a few late appointments scheduled for the next day for which charts were not available when the day shift file clerks prepared records for appointments. The night file clerk is responsible for locating the records needed for these appointments. Procedures are as follows:

1. Go to admitting office to obtain late appointment slips and "due to arrive for admission" slips.
2. Pull appointment slips from DUE TO ARRIVE file in the admitting office for the next day's date.
3. Check name index for register number. (*Note:* Sometimes a patient will not have a number when the appointment is scheduled but will obtain a number between the time of scheduling the appointment and the actual appointment date.)
4. Write the number on the appointment slip if you find a card in file.
5. Write "No Number" on the appointment slip if you do not find a card in file.
6. Separate the blue and the white carbon copies for the "No Number" slips and leave the blue copies in alphabetical order in the "No Number" file on the counter.

Exhibit 2-4 Abbreviated Narrative Procedure Format: Procedure for Terminal Digit Filing

Key Step	Key Points
1. Terminal digit filing system	1. Read from *right to left*, two digits at a time. EXPLANATION: Records are filed in sections by the last two digits to the right, then the middle two digits, then the last two digits to the left. Example: if the history number is 06-52-18 *find it this way:*

Look here last within the 18 section 06	Look here second within the 18 section 52	Look here first 18 18

The last two digits (terminals) are color coded. The colors for each digit always remain the same, and once they are learned they can be used in many combinations of numbers. They help you file more accurately and quickly.

Exhibit 2-5 Abbreviated Narrative Procedure Format: Procedure for Interdepartmental Coordination

Key Step	Key Points
1. Determine patient care need.	1. Review medical care record. 2. Perform appropriate evaluation procedures. 3. Complete related medical documentation, including information needed for consultation.
2. Contact appropriate department.	1. Make verbal contact via telephone. 2. Confirm through interdepartmental request form for joint conference.

Exhibit 2-6 Playscript Format

Actor	Step Sequence	Action Words	Action Sentence
File clerk	1	Verifies identification	Check patient identification as given in patient master file: full name, date of birth, number.
File clerk	2	Records identification	Enter patient identification on medical report in appropriate section on form.

Exhibit 2-7 Alternate Playscript Format: Example 1

Responsibility	Step Sequence	Action
Patient Master File Clerk	1	Check patient identification as given in patient master file: full name, date of birth, number.
Patient Master File Clerk	2	Enter patient identification on medical report in appropriate section on form.
Terminal Digit File Clerk	3	Obtain batches of medical reports from Patient Identification section.
Terminal Digit File Clerk	4	File each medical report in specific patient record in numeric order.

Leslie Matthies[4] identified the following action verbs as useful in conveying central, specific ideas for procedure statements in the playscript format:

sends	uses
shows	checks
issues	places
obtains	decides
records	receives
provides	forwards
prepares	requests

The physical format of the procedure manual is important. A procedure manual should be convenient in size, easy to read, and arranged logically. If the manual is too large or too heavy for everyday use or is difficult to read because of too many unbroken pages of type, workers tend to develop their own procedures rather than refer to the manual for the prescribed steps. The choice of a format that makes it easy to update the manual (e.g., loose-leaf binder) removes a major disadvantage or limitation regarding the manual's use: pages of obsolete procedures.

Development of the Procedure Manual

The manager who is developing a procedure manual must first determine its purpose and audience (e.g., to train new employees or to bring about uniformity of practice among current employees). The level of detail and the number and kinds of examples depend on the purpose and the audience. Clarity, brevity, and the use of simple commands or direct language improve comprehension. Action verbs that specify actions the worker must take help to clarify the instructions. Keeping the focus of the procedure specific and its scope limited permits the man-

Exhibit 2-8 Alternative Playscript Format: Example 2

Responsibility	Step Sequence	Action
Senior Physical Therapist	1	Receives patient referral form. Enters name, date, and time received in master file.
Senior Physical Therapist	2	Assigns patient to physical therapist for evaluation.
Staff Physical Therapist	3	Arranges treatment as scheduled for patient evaluation.
Secretary	4	Requests central transportation to deliver patient and hospital chart at designated time.

ager to develop a highly detailed description of the steps to be followed. The steps are listed in logical sequence, with definitions, support examples, and illustrations.

Methods improvement is a prerequisite for efficient, effective procedure development. Flow charts and flow process charts are useful adjuncts to the procedure manual because they require logical sequencing and make it possible to reduce the backtracking and bottlenecks in the workflow.

METHODS

The way in which each step of a procedure is to be performed is a method. Methods focus on such elements as the arrangement of the work area, the use of certain forms, or the operation of specific equipment. A method describes the best way of performing a task. The manager may develop methods detail as part of the training package for employee development, leaving the procedure manual free of such detail.

RULES

One of the simplest and most direct types of plans is a rule. A continuing or repeat use plan, a rule delineates a required or prohibited course of action. The purpose of rules is to predecide issues and specify the required course of action authoritatively and officially.

Like policies, rules guide thinking and channel behavior. Rules, however, are more precise and specific than policies and, technically, allow no discretion in their application. As a result, management must direct careful attention to the number of rules and their intent. If the management intent is to guide and direct

Exhibit 2-9 Alternative Playscript Format That Includes Key Steps and Detailed Steps: Example 3

Key Step	Sequence	Responsibility	Detailed Steps
Receive the incoming mail: a. U.S. mail b. interdepartmental mail	Step 1	Release of information clerk	• Pick up the mail from the central mail room located in room [___]. • The mail is ready for pickup at [___] A.M. • The department mailbox is Number [___].

Perform the initial processing	Step 2	Release of information clerk	• Sort the mail by general categories:
			  1. loose reports received via interoffice mail: Direct these immediately to the Storage and Retrieval unit
			  2. mail marked "Confidential": Direct these immediately to department director's secretary
			  3. U.S. mail not marked "Confidential"
			• Open all mail except that marked "Confidential."
			• Staple the envelope to the back of each letter.
			• Date-stamp each letter in the lower right-hand area.
			• Do not obscure any information, such as the signature or date.

Distribute the mail and redirect non-Medical Record Department mail	Step 3	Release of information clerk	Distribution:
			• Direct loose reports to the Storage and Retrieval unit.
			• Direct "Confidential" mail to the department director's secretary.
			• Direct non-Medical Record Department mail for
			  1. a staff physician to the physician's office (see the telephone directory for office room numbers)
			  2. the outpatient clinic to the clinic co-ordinator (see the telephone directory for the office room number)
			• If there is an obvious error by the sender, return the mail immediately to the sender (for example, if the request for information is for another area hospital).

behavior rather than require or prohibit certain actions, the rule in effect becomes a policy and should be issued as such.

Like procedures, rules guide action; unlike procedures, however, rules have no time sequence or chronology. Some rules are contained in procedures (e.g.,

"Extinguish all smoking material before entering patient care unit"). Other rules are independent of any procedure and stand alone (e.g., "No Smoking"). The wording of rules is direct and specific:

- Food removed from the cafeteria must be carried in covered containers.
- Books returned to the library after 4 P.M. will be considered as returned the following day, and a late fine will be charged.
- Children under the age of 12 must be accompanied at all times by an adult who is responsible for their conduct.

SPACE AND RENOVATION PLANNING

Space and renovation planning present particular planning considerations for the manager. The planning constraints, for example, flow from such diverse sources as technical architectural details to federal law and regulation concerning barrier-free design for ease of access by handicapped persons. Appendix 2-D provides some suggested guidelines to assist the manager in such technical planning.

NOTES

1. Joan Gratto Liebler, *Medical Records: Policies and Guidelines* (Gaithersburg, Md.: Aspen Publishers, 1991), 10:42.

2. Ibid, 10:64–71.

3. Ibid, 2:1–25.

4. Leslie H. Matthies, *The Playscript Procedure* (New York: Office Publications, 1961), 95.

Appendix 2-A

Medical Record Department Policies

DATE ISSUED: _____

DATE REVISED: _____

MEDICAL STAFF COMMITTEE APPROVAL
    NAME: _____
    TITLE: _____
    SIGNATURE: _____
    DATE: _____

CHIEF EXECUTIVE OFFICER APPROVAL
    NAME: _____
    SIGNATURE: _____
    DATE: _____

The medical record department is a support service of [*name of health care facility*] whose primary purpose is to contribute to the quality of patient care through the development and maintenance of a comprehensive, centralized medical record system. This system also provides health care data and services to support and promote the related goals and activities of the health care facility: education, training, research, community health, and overall facility management and decision making.

CENTRALIZED MEDICAL RECORD DEPARTMENT

The medical record department shall be centralized in one coordinated functional unit under the direct authority of a management level practitioner who is a

Source: Reprinted from *Medical Records: Policies and Guidelines* by J.G. Liebler, pp. 2:i–2:5, Aspen Publishers, Inc., ©1990.

specialist in health data management. This service shall be designated as the medical record department. The title of the organizational head of this department shall be director of medical records. This individual shall be designated as the official custodian of health information for the health care facility as a whole.

SCOPE OF SERVICE

The centralized medical record department shall provide functional support to all components of the health care facility and the various departments with respect to health information services. These functions include

- patient/client identification and numbering system;
- creation and monitoring of medical record documentation;
- quality assurance and utilization review and studies;
- risk management review and studies;
- release of information, coordination of patient access to data, and response to court subpoena and depositions;
- dictation/transcription system;
- statistical abstracts and indexes;
- special studies for medical staff committee reviews;
- financial reimbursement support data, including diagnosis and procedure coding;
- storage and retrieval system, including chart tracking system;
- assistance in complying with legal and regulatory provisions and accrediting agency standards concerning health care data;
- data security, privacy, and confidentiality processes;
- inservice education and training for professional and support staff;
- educational programs for students under contractual and/or affiliation agreements; and
- assistance in research studies.

HOURS OF OPERATION AND STAFFING

The major services of the department shall be made available on a continuous basis, seven days a week, 24 hours a day. These services include

- patient identification/numbering system;
- access to patient care data for direct patient care purposes;

- dictation system; and
- transcription of priority reports needed for immediate, direct patient care.

All other services shall be offered during the normal business hours of the facility, on an extended workday plan. The extended workday for the department is 7 A.M. to 6 P.M., Monday through Friday.

An appropriate combination of full-time and permanent part-time staff shall be trained to carry out the usual health information functions. In the rare event that no department employee is available to carry out an emergency request during the non-business day work period, the administrator on call shall have access to the department to arrange for retrieval of the critical information.

COMPLIANCE WITH REGULATIONS AND STANDARDS

Services and functions shall be developed and implemented in a manner consistent with five groups of regulations and standards:

1. legal and regulatory provisions affecting the facility:
   - state department of health licensure regulations
   - Medicare Conditions of Participation
   - federal-state provisions for Medicaid programs
   - professional review organization mandates
   - federal and state reimbursement and financing regulations
2. professional association and accrediting agency standards:
   - Joint Commission on Accreditation of Healthcare Organizations (or American Osteopathic Association)
   - American Health Information Management Association's *Code of Ethics, Guidelines on Data Quality,* and *Professional Practice Standards* (latest editions)
3. institutional and medical staff bylaws
4. institutional policies of related departments, with particular attention given to admissions, patient billing and finance, nursing, clinic and emergency, and other departments where coordination of administrative practice and processing of patient care data are essential
5. contractual provisions with related service providers and/or reimbursement agencies, such as health maintenance organizations and Blue Cross contractors, and transfer agreement provisions with other health care facilities such as home care, hospice care, rehabilitation centers, and long-term care facilities

CONFIDENTIALITY, PRIVACY, AND DATA SECURITY CONSIDERATIONS

Services and functions shall be developed and implemented in such a way that confidentiality, privacy, and data security considerations are respected and fostered at all stages of health care information gathering and processing. The following eight practices help ensure that facilities will abide by these considerations:

1. *Employee orientation and training.* This area shall include
   - mandatory completion of inservice program by all medical record employees;
   - cooperation from appropriate department managers, offering of inservice education to admissions, business office, computer department, clerical support staff in outpatient clinics, emergency department, and nursing department;
   - active participation in orientation of all new employees of the facility.
2. *Confidentiality statement.* All medical record employees shall be required to sign the confidentiality statement (Exhibit 2A-1). This shall be placed in the employee's permanent personnel file and reviewed and updated at least annually. It shall also be updated during any year there is a significant change in the job duties of the employee.
3. *Researchers and students.* Students in education programs and researchers with access to health care data shall receive appropriate orientation and shall sign the confidentiality statement as a condition of access to the health data.
4. *Contractual services.* Appropriate provision for data security and confidentiality shall be included in any contract for service from outside vendors such as word processing, statistical abstracting, microfilming, and temporary agency staffing.
5. *Centralized release of information.* All requests for release of information, regardless of the department originating or receiving the request, shall be processed in the central release of information unit of the medical record department. See release of information policy.
6. *Rules for data access and use.* Detailed rules shall be developed and enforced to limit the rules of health care data and to specify the conditions under which such data may be used. See storage and retrieval policy.
7. *Data security provisions/computer access.* Appropriate safeguards shall be adopted for computerized processes relating to health care information. See computerized data security policy.
8. *Limited access to department.*
   - The following individuals who may be permitted access to health care data shall carry out an approved review of material in a supervised, restricted area that is separate from the general work area of the department.

Exhibit 2A-1 Confidentiality Statement

I, [*name*], understand that in the performance of my duties as an employee of [*name of health care facility*] I am required to have access to and am involved in the processing of patient care data. I understand that I am obliged to maintain the confidentiality of these data at all times, both at work and off duty. I understand that a violation of these confidentiality considerations may result in disciplinary action, including termination. I further understand that I could be subject to legal action. I certify by my signature that I have participated in the orientation and training session given on [*date*] concerning the privacy and confidentiality considerations of patient care.

Date	Signature

Original to be placed in the employee's permanent personnel file.
Copy to be placed in orientation and training session file.

Source: Reprinted from *Medical Records: Policies and Guidelines* by J.G. Liebler, p. 2:2, Aspen Publishers, Inc., ©1990.

  —patients and patient representatives, including lawyers
  —third-party review auditors from reimbursement agencies
  —students (except health care administrators and medical record administrators and technicians under specific affiliation agreements)
- Visitors, including health care facility employees from other departments, shall not be permitted access to the general work area of the department except as specifically noted in designated procedures.
- Health care facility employees who are not directly and actively carrying out a necessary function (e.g., housekeeping or maintenance) shall not be admitted to the work area.
- Researchers carrying out an approved research review of data shall work in a designated area, separate from the general work area.

EDUCATION AND TRAINING

Department Employees

A systematic program of orientation, on-the-job training, specialized training, and regular inservice training shall be developed and implemented for medical record employees for the following purposes:

- reduce potential liability because of error
- create a positive, motivational climate

- enhance employee productivity and efficiency
- enhance employee opportunity for promotion

When inservice programs reflect critical issues (e.g., fire drills, safety practices, and confidentiality), participation shall be mandatory and the program shall be offered during work hours. A variety of other offerings may be given at times when an employee may need to commit personal time and for which participation will be optional.

Management and supervisory personnel shall participate regularly in professional association meetings, conferences, and workshops as approved by the director of medical records. Appropriate budgetary support of these activities shall be made available insofar as possible.

Participation in orientation, on-the-job training, inservice offerings, and other training related to job duties shall be documented for each individual. This documentation shall become a part of the employee's permanent personnel file, and a copy shall become a part of the department inservice log. Such evidence of orientation and inservice training shall be made available when requested as part of the accreditation and/or licensure survey of the facility. Review of progress through inservice and other training shall be a part of the employee evaluation process.

Medical and Professional Staff

Medical record personnel shall provide the necessary assistance in orientation and training programs for the medical and professional staff, with particular emphasis on health care data documentation, privacy and confidentiality, data security, and related matters.

Health Care Facility Personnel

Medical record personnel shall provide the necessary assistance in the orientation and training of health care facility personnel in the areas of confidentiality and privacy. As time and resources permit, other program offerings may be developed and offered as part of the facilitywide training efforts.

Affiliated Programs

Active participation in the education and training of students from approved affiliated institutions (e.g., allied health and health care administration) shall be fostered in accordance with the health care facility's goal of teaching. Details of such training activities shall be specified in appropriate letters of agreement or affiliation contracts, with the approval of the chief executive officer or designee.

QUALITY ASSURANCE AND PROFESSIONAL PRACTICE STANDARDS

An active program of quality assurance review focusing on medical record practices shall be undertaken by the director of medical records (Exhibit 2A-2). Major components shall include the following:

- an annual review of each function using the American Health Information Management Association's *Professional Practice Standards*
- employee evaluation and training according to institutional practices (e.g., annual evaluation with special evaluation at the time of transfer or promotion or at the conclusion of a probationary/training period)

Exhibit 2A-2 Work Sheet For Customizing General Policies

Policy Elements	*Special Considerations*
Department Name	• Determine the organizational title and use it consistently throughout.
Centralized Service and Scope of Service	• Determine which departments of the facility will be covered by the policies: determine which services will be undertaken by the department.
	• Give particular attention to the impact of services to be rendered to the outpatient and emergency departments. This should include chart analyses and review, coding, and all related functions.
Hours of Operation	• Coordinate with patient care delivery; make provisions for access to critical data for off-hours.
	• Check with personnel labor relations concerning shift designations, e.g., any contractual labor agreements to be considered.
Access to Department during Nonoperating Periods	• The administrator on call is an appropriate designee; clear this with administrative officers. The director of nursing is another alternative, but this would add one more duty to individuals charged with direct patient care.

Exhibit 2A-2   continued

Compliance with Standards	• Refer to the work sheet done earlier in which specific state, federal, and accrediting agency provisions were noted.
Medical Staff Bylaws	• The rules and regulations section is a key area: chart content policies are an addendum to this section. Refer also to the work sheet done earlier for other medical staff issues.
Contractual Provisions	• State these, and determine the requirements for providing which services to which departments; cross reference this to the release of information because patient care data are sometimes sent with the patient directly.
Confidentiality Provisions	• See the American Health Information Management Association's *Statement of Confidentiality* for employee use.
Researchers and Students	• There is an impact on the physical layout of the department when this provision is adopted. If the present layout cannot be changed immediately, insert the phrase *as far as possible* and seek to have the layout changed as soon as possible.
Education and Training	• Consider the provisions of the Fair Labor Standards Act if required training is to take place after an employee's work hours.
Cross References and Internal Consistency	• Coordinate with policies for release of information, storage and retrieval, and computerized data security.

Source: Reprinted from *Medical Records: Policies and Guidelines* by J.G. Liebler, pp 2:4–2:5, Aspen Publishers, Inc., ©1990.

Physical Therapy Section
Policies and Procedures*

Preamble

Physical therapy is the assessment of physical capabilities and the identification and discrimination of actual or potential functional limitations; the planning of an appropriate treatment program in conjunction with a duly licensed referring physician, dentist, or podiatrist; the provision and direct supervision of therapeutic exercise, manual therapy, hydrotherapy, mechanotherapy, thermotherapy, and electrotherapy. Such treatments, tests, and measurements shall be rendered pursuant to prescription or referral by the physician and in accordance with the physician's diagnosis.

I. Referrals
    A. All referrals must contain an applicable diagnosis and a treatment plan. Any precautions should be indicated.
    B. All referrals must by signed by a physician (dentist, podiatrist). Verbal orders may be taken by therapists only, and must be followed up by written, signed orders from the doctor.
    C. Referrals must be renewed at least every 30 days in writing.
    D. If there exists a need to have additional professional consultants for patients requiring rehabilitation, the appropriate professionals will be contacted by the Director of Rehabilitation Medicine.

II. Scheduling
    A. Any outpatient reporting to the department without prior appointment

*Source: Courtesy of Carol Pisapia, Rehabilitation Coordinator, St. Vincent's Medical Center of Staten Island, New York.

will be treated if the schedule permits. Otherwise, the patient will be scheduled for the first available appointment.

B. Any outpatient phoning for an appointment will be given the first available time.

C. The clerk-receptionist is responsible for scheduling the initial visit as per predetermined evaluation slots (in the Outpatient Department). In the gym, the therapists are to determine initial appointment times.

D. The therapists in the respective areas are responsible for scheduling patients after the initial evaluation. Such schedule shall be conveyed to the clerk responsible for giving the patient the appointment card.

E. Last copy of referral is to be forwarded to the Office Assistant to be recorded. Inpatients will be seen on the same day a referral is received (ideally) unless the referral is received after 2:30 P.M. and it is not possible to schedule an appointment thereafter.

F. Electro-diagnostic consultations will be scheduled by the Office Assistant according to the Director of Rehabilitation Medicine's schedule.

III. Records

A. All referrals not received on the official Rehabilitation Referral form will be attached to such form and pertinent information transferred to that form by the therapist.

B. The patient's medical record shall contain, in chronological order:
   1. The physician's dated and signed initial orders or referral and subsequent renewals for rehabilitation therapy services.
   2. Rehabilitation treatment services, dated and signed by the therapist, including:
      a. the initial evaluation and treatment plan based upon findings, the immediate and ultimate rehabilitation goals, and frequency of treatment;
      b. the types and number of treatments, as given;
      c. summary of any significant consultation with the physician or other personnel;
      d. the periodic assessments of the patient's progress and response to treatment and revisions of the treatment plan. Progress notes should be present when the patient's status changes, with a minimum of two per week (inpatients) or one per month (outpatients). A flow sheet is to be maintained in all outpatient charts to insure continuity of care should the primary therapist be absent;
      e. daily attendance record;
      f. a discharge summary including treatment results, reasons for discharge, and any follow-up recommendations for the patient's maintenance regime.

C. The original of all notes will be included in the patient's hospital chart on all inpatients and clinic patients. The duplicate will be kept for the physical therapy record for clinic outpatients. Otherwise the original will be kept as the permanent physical therapy record and the duplicate will be sent to the referring physician.

IV. Treatment Procedures

  A. Every patient to receive physical therapy will be evaluated by the therapist to establish a profile of the patient's status at that time which will serve as a baseline to evaluate effectiveness of treatment over a specified period of time.

  B. Since the physical therapist is legally responsible for any treatment which he or she renders, he or she is obligated to withhold any treatment ordered by the physician which he or she feels is contraindicated. The physician should be contacted in this case and the treatment plan discussed in this light.

  C. The therapist will develop a treatment plan based upon his or her evaluation, the physician's referral, and the patient's rehabilitation potential. This plan will state problems, plans related to each short- and long-term goal, and plans for patient and/or family education. The patient and/or his or her family should take an active part in formulating this plan through discussion of the patient's problems and potential and the capabilities of the service, whenever possible.

  D. The physical therapist may delegate the treatment of those patients whose program is within the job description and ability of the assistant to that assistant.

  E. Certain standard procedures may be carried out by the aides when instructed to do so by the physical therapist. Those are:
  1. application of hot packs, cold packs, and paraffin;
  2. supervision of progressive resistive exercise (after program is set up by therapist);
  3. supervision of practice of gait patterns and transfer activities;
  4. set up of treatment modalities prior to actual administration of the treatment by the therapist; and
  5. general supervision of patients receiving whirlpool after they have been evaluated.

  F. Any home exercises that are a part of the patient's treatment plan should be given to the patient in writing. When necessary (as in the case of a child or a severely involved adult), this program should be reviewed with a parent or other responsible individual.

  G. Any instructions given to a patient and/or his or her family regarding care procedures to be followed after discharge should be given to the patient and/or family in writing.

V. Criteria for Discontinuing Therapy
 A. Goals have been met.
 B. Patient fails to demonstrate progress in a reasonable amount of time.
 C. Inpatient goes to OR.
 D. Inpatient transferred to ICU, CCU, or PCU.
 E. Inpatient persistently refuses treatment—patient must be interviewed first.
 F. Outpatient may be discontinued after failure to attend two consecutive appointments without notification—patient called after first failed appointment.
 G. Physician discontinues therapy; a new referral signed by the physician is required to reinstitute the therapy program.

VI. Maintenance of Equipment and Treatment Area
 A. Each room is to have one chair and a step stool for each treatment plinth.
 B. The treatment table sheets are to be changed after each treatment. This includes the EMG treatment table.
 C. As soon as a treatment room is empty, the aide or volunteer is to rearrange the furniture to make it pleasant and neat for the next patient.
 D. When a patient is being treated, the room curtain is to be kept closed.
 E. Each patient should be provided any necessary assistance on and off the treatment table and in dressing activities by the aide, and/or therapist.
 F. Patients are to be positioned according to the therapist's direction and appropriately draped for treatment. The patient's garments, hair, and other items should be protected from soiling when possible.
 G. The whirlpool area is to be kept neat and orderly and the floor kept dry at all times.
 H. The gym area is to be kept relatively neat and clean throughout the day.
 I. All machinery should be cleaned periodically as per schedule posted. (See Infection Control Section for routine cleaning procedures and schedules.)
 J. Smoking is not allowed in any of the areas of the department.
 K. All windows are to be closed and air conditioners turned off at the end of the day.
 L. Any noted need for wheelchair maintenance will be referred to the Messenger/Transport Service.

VII. Transportation of Patients
 A. Transportation of all rehabilitation patients will be performed by the Messenger/Transport Service according to the daily schedule provided to them. It is the responsibility of the Rehabilitation Aide to prepare and submit the daily rehabilitation transportation schedule in consultation with the therapists.

B. When necessary (e.g., episodes of illness, etc.), the Rehabilitation Aide will be expected to transport patients. At such times:

1. The transporter will seek assistance when transferring the patient from bed to wheelchair or vice versa and if the patient is extremely obese, or spastic, or unmanageable.

2. When the transporter returns the patient to the nursing unit, the transporter is to assist the nursing personnel in returning the patient to the bed if requested.

3. Patients are to be suitably covered with a robe or blanket when being transported.

4. When patients are mentally disoriented, they are to be restrained to the wheelchair by a seat belt type arrangement and to the stretcher by straps and attended to at all times. This restraint is for safety while in motion with transporter.

Appendix 2-C

Medical Record Procedures

Exhibit 2C-1 Emergency Requests

Key Step	Sequence	Responsibility	Detailed Steps
Handle emergency requests as they arrive.	Immediate handling	Release of information specialist	• Follow the steps as for the emergency release of information by telephone.

Source: Reprinted from *Medical Records: Policies and Guidelines, Supplement 1*, by J.G. Liebler, p. 10:73, Aspen Publishers, Inc., ©1991.

Exhibit 2C-2 Request for Access to Record

Key Step	Sequence	Responsibility	Detailed Steps
Receive request for access to record.	Step 1	Release of information specialist	• Review the need for authorization. • Determine the fee; collect the fee. • Explain the basic process to the requestor: —need for physician approval —appointment to review —notification of confirmed time of review • Have the requestor complete the Request for Access form. • Bring the discussion with the requestor to a conclusion.
Determine patient status, enter the information in the release of information log, and obtain the record.	Step 2	Release of information specialist	• Follow the basic procedure for written requests.

Exhibit 2C-2 continued

Key Step	Sequence	Responsibility	Detailed Steps
Notify the attending physician to obtain approval or denial of the request.	Step 3	Release of information specialist	• Attach the Approval/Denial form to the medical record. Forward the record to the attending physician. • If the attending physician is no longer associated with this facility, forward the record to the medical director.
Process the Approval/ Denial form after receipt from the attending physician.	Step 4	Release of information specialist	• If approved, notify the requestor, and finalize the review appointment time. • If denied, notify the requestor by completing the special letter. • File the Approval/Denial form in the medical record.
Monitor the in-person review of the record.	As scheduled by appointment	Release of information specialist	• Remain with the reviewer at all times. • Do not interpret information. • Refer all questions to the attending physician. • Do not permit removal of any information. • Supply the reviewer with a special form for making entries in the medical record. • If the reviewer wishes to have copies made of selected materials, explain the copy process and fees. Remove the record from the review area, and make the copies; collect the fee. • Note on the Request for Access and Review form the items copied. • If a copy of the complete record is needed, explain the copying fee; obtain the fee, and provide the requestor with an approximate date on which copy will be available. (This is usually [____] working days.) • Bring the interview to a close. • Arrange for copying and mailing the record as in the basic procedures. • Update the release of information log.

Source: Reprinted from *Medical Records: Policies and Guidelines, Supplement 1,* by J.G. Liebler, p. 10:73, Aspen Publishers, Inc., ©1991.

Exhibit 2C-3 Receiving and Processing Subpoenas

Key Step	Sequence	Responsibility	Detailed Steps
Receive the subpoena, and complete the initial review.	Step 1	Release of information specialist	• Review the subpoena while the server is still present to determine —type of subpoena —name of person/organization upon whom the subpoena is being served —name and location of the court (or other official body in which the proceeding is being held) —date and time the witness must appear —specific documents being requested (if it is a subpoena duces tecum) —name of the plaintiff —name of the defendant —name, address, telephone number of the attorney who caused the subpoena to be issued —docket number —signature of the clerk of the court —seal of the court • Check for inclusion of —witness fees and/or —mileage fees as appropriate • Determine if notice has been given in the proper amount of time *Note to users:* Witness and mileage fees and the amount of notice given must be consistent with state law.

Check jurisdiction.	Step 2	Release of information specialist	• Review the location of the court and its jursidiction:
			—municipal court
			—county court
			—state district court
			—federal court
			—administrative agency
			  –state government
			  –federal government
			—medical examiner
			• If the issuing federal court is beyond the 100-mile jurisdiction, notify the requesting attorney, and prepare a certified copy of the record.

Exhibit 2C-3 continued

Key Step	Sequence	Responsibility	Detailed Steps
Process witness and mileage and witness fees.	Step 3	Release of information specialist	• Are witness fees paid in advance? —civil cases: **Yes** —criminal cases: **Not applicable** —worker's compensation: **See state law** —medical examiner: **No** —federal courts: **Not usually paid in advance; hospital-designated witness will follow hospital's reimbursement for travel directives.** • Complete the Fee Transmittal form. *Note to users:* Review applicable state law.
Log the subpoena in the subpoena and deposition log.	Step 4	Release of information specialist	• Enter each of these items in the subpoena and deposition log: —patient's name —date of birth —date of subpoena —docket number —name of court —name of requesting attorney —type of subpoena —information requested —amount of fee received

Source: Reprinted from *Medical Records: Policies and Guidelines Supplement 1,* by J.G. Liebler, p. 10:77–10:79, Aspen Publishers, Inc. ©1991.

Appendix 2-D

Space and Renovation Planning

SPACE AND RENOVATION PLANNING

Most health care practitioners will, at some time in their career, participate in planning a new department or renovating an old one. This process requires knowledge of all the possible present and future uses of the space as well as an ability to make "best guesses" regarding future needs. Making changes commonly requires two to five years of work with a variety of professionals and craft specialists. To help present all the issues, we will suppose that you are working in rehabilitation as a manager and that your department head announces your department will be renovated in two years. Your participation in the planning and renovation is mandated; you are expected to improve the design of your area and increase the productivity of your staff.

The main steps for planning renovations include preparation, idea gathering, idea verification, modification of ideas, and revision of plans. After plans are finalized, your responsibilities shift and you now focus on monitoring. You supervise your staff; ensure the safety of patients, personnel, and equipment; and encourage your staff to be flexible as they try to accomplish their work in the midst of construction workers, materials and supplies, and daily inconveniences. Once the construction is complete, your job shifts again and you now test out the finished products. Follow-up is also imperative so that problems are not overlooked or forgotten.

THE PLANNING TEAM

The composition of the planning team will depend on the funding and the total allocation of support for the project, the composition of the institution's staff, and the expertise of team members. Usually the team includes representatives from facilities planning and an architect. For example, if the area to be constructed is in a hospital, the team would include the hospital administrator, appropriate department heads, the medical chief of staff, the director of nursing, an attorney, and the business manager or an accountant. An interior designer and a safety officer may also be included. It is recommended that the architect has had experience in designing similar projects and is familiar with specific characteristics of the physical environment.

PREPARATION FOR PLANNING

Before the actual design and construction phase takes place, it is helpful to address a number of preplanning factors. The scope of the preplanning stage depends on the structure and function of the area to be designed. Any present or possible future need to expand services should also be discussed among the parties involved. For example, if the medical record department anticipates that after a year of operation an additional computerized data system will be required, the staff may want to know whether there is available space physically located near the department for expansion. Perhaps the department should include an additional area in the initial plans and utilize it as storage space or for another function until the time is needed to expand services. Issues like these must be addressed before construction is started. It is likely that the costs for renovation and expansion will be higher after construction is completed.

Depending on the type and structure of the facility, general factors to be considered by the planning team before construction begins include the present and projected population trends in the area and the need for the new services based on existing services and referral sources. Information about such factors may help to support space needs and design. Other preplanning factors which should be considered include

- program purposes and goals
- location
- cost estimates
- financial resources
- equipment
- plan development

Program Purposes and Goals

Before any construction begins, it is recommended that the department define the services that will be provided. By so doing, the space needs will be better understood. The department should establish objectives and set standards that can be used to monitor and evaluate the success of the program. For example, if long-term rehabilitation services will be provided, the department should include an area for activities of daily living. If the department expects a student affiliation program, an area for students should be part of the design.

Location

The accessibility of the department must be considered prior to construction. Rehabilitation departments should be located near an elevator for easier patient transportation. Preferably, the area should be on the main floor near parking. In considering the location, it is important to keep in mind that the department must be accessible to and usable by the physically handicapped. The usability of bathrooms, the width of doors, and wheelchair maneuverability are some of the factors that need to be discussed with the architect as he or she begins work on the design.

Estimates

Although the exact cost for the facility may not be predictable, an approximation of the bottomline costs may be required. The approximation should include space, equipment, and renovation expenses. Note that it is better to overestimate rather than underestimate what the final cost may be.

Financial Resources

Depending on the type of facility and the administrative structure, the manager may be requested to determine the financial resources available for construction. These resources might include state or city funding appropriations and federal or private grant support.

Equipment

Certain rehabilitation equipment (e.g., the whirlpool hubbard tank, hydraulic lift, and the shoulder wheel) is fixed equipment and must be attached to the wall beams. It is necessary to include the location of fixed equipment in the initial design of the facility. Any special specifications for equipment should also be brought to the attention of the architect. This is especially important in the case of electrical requirements. For example, certain electrical modalities (EMG, moist heating units) may require 220-volt outlets instead of the standard 110-volt outlets. Any special electrical requirements should be included in the architectural drawings prior to construction.

Plan Development

It is crucial to the success of the project to work with the architect in developing the diagrammatic scheme or drawings of the facility. Decide on major and minor needs and visualize the placement of services, furniture, and equipment. Before the plan is presented, it is helpful to prepare a preliminary drawing of the facility to show the relationship of the various areas in the department. This drawing can aid the architect in developing a working area that facilitates the maximum efficiency of traffic flow and minimizes crosswise traffic patterns. The preliminary plan should indicate how the various rooms will be divided with regard to the various functions that will be provided.

The steps in developing a plan are as follows:

1. Sketch your present space and use a measuring tape to measure it. Determine the size of rooms and equipment. If you are planning new space, take the time to visit other facilities in order to measure their rooms and spatial arrangements.
2. Think about your present space and list the positive and negative factors. Include staff members in this process. The more advice you get, the better your chance of discovering all of your needs during this preliminary stage of planning.
3. Solicit ideas from other departments.
4. Visit other facilities. Note the positive and negative aspects of their space. Verify your ideas with the individuals who use the space every day.
5. Conceptualize ideas one room at a time. Keep notes on your ideas and needs.
6. Initiate a meeting with the architect or engineer who is in charge of the project. If this person does not express an interest in meeting with you, state your need to get input into the project before plans are drawn up.
7. Discuss your department's needs clearly and follow up discussions with written communications to confirm agreements.
8. Once you receive a copy of the plans, operationalize them by marking outlines of the actual equipment and cabinets on the floor with masking tape or some other form of temporary marking. Compare past and future needs and uses. Do not be afraid to ask questions or voice your discomfort with certain ideas. (See Figure 2D-1 for examples of common blueprint symbols.)

The purpose of the preplanning phase is to devise a rough outline of the requirements for the space. This outline or sketch does not replace the actual design of the area.

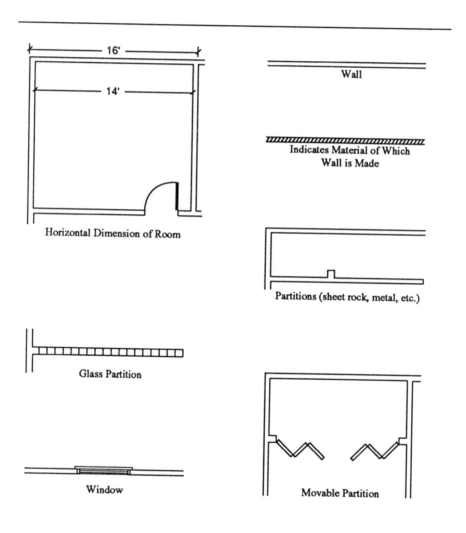

Figure 2D-1 General Blueprint Symbols. *Source:* The blueprint symbols were designed by Benjamin Hernandez, architecture student at the College of Staten Island, City University of New York.

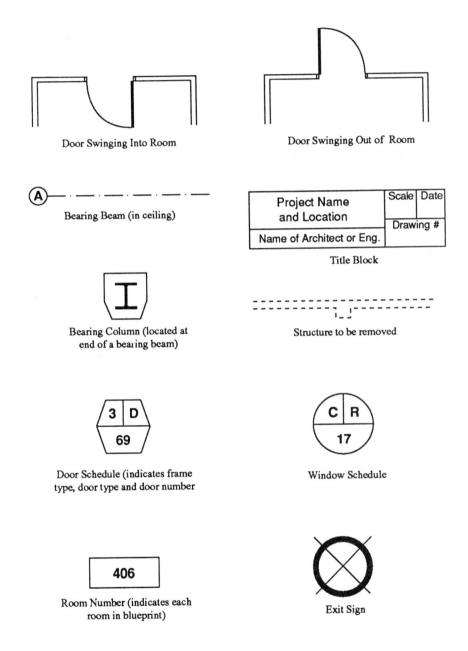

Door Swinging Into Room

Door Swinging Out of Room

Bearing Beam (in ceiling)

Title Block

Bearing Column (located at
end of a bearing beam)

Structure to be removed

Door Schedule (indicates frame
type, door type and door number

Window Schedule

Room Number (indicates each
room in blueprint)

Exit Sign

Figure 2D-1 continued

INVENTORY OF SPACE

The space that has been made available for the new facility or department must be carefully inventoried in order to determine how the space should be apportioned. The inventory of the space should include the following:

* square footage
* size of rooms
* location of rooms
* special equipment and facilities

The amount of space (or square footage) made available to the department will influence how the space is used. The size of a room, for example, might restrict the types of services that could be provided. For example, any room designated as a location for activities of daily living (ADL) should meet minimum space requirements. If a room does not meet the requirements for ADL, it may be suitable for another function.

The location of the department within the facility is an important factor and requires careful consideration. The rehabilitation areas should be located near the elevator and, if the department provides outpatient treatments, in close proximity to parking and to the main entrance to the institution. Certain equipment may need special preparation. Computer equipment and isokinetic devices may require special wiring and will need to be placed away from areas of heavy traffic. The size of a piece of equipment may also determine where it should be placed.

ARCHITECTURAL SPECIFICATIONS

In developing the architectural plans, the following must be considered:

* the function and organization of the various components
* the spatial requirements
* the workflow patterns

Function and Organization of Components

In designing or renovating an area within a facility, adequate consideration must be given to the specific functions to be located within that area. These functions should be given a full description, including a detailed explanation of how each activity is to be carried out in the space and how each activity relates to other functions. The description should also include any special requirements that may affect the design.

During this stage of the planning process, the bulk of the responsibility belongs to the facility staff, since they are the most familiar with the unique characteristics and features of the operational programs. Depending on the scope of the project, a medical services consultant may assist the staff in preparing the description of the functional components.

The purpose of describing the functions to be performed in the work area is to furnish the architect with adequate data to begin making space allocations. The organization of the functions provides a schematic outline that can be used in establishing the spatial requirements.

Spatial Requirements

The amount of space or square footage allocated for a given work area depends on a number of considerations. The types of services to be provided, the major pieces of equipment, the storage requirements, the shape of the area, the number of personnel that will work in the area, the number of clients or patients that will be seen, the reception and secretarial support systems, among other things, need to be taken into account when determining square footage. Of prime importance in determining the space requirements are the individual circumstances for a given situation. For example, there may be a preset amount of space allocated by the facility administration for the work area. The department would then have to decide how the space would be apportioned. Regardless of the situation, judgment and experience are crucial for the design of an appropriate and effective work area.

When determining if an allotted space is sufficient, a number of factors must be considered, including the nature of the equipment that must be housed. What is the dimension of each piece of equipment and how much space and personnel are needed to safely operate it? The vendor should be able to provide this information for any piece of equipment on order.

It should also be determined how many of the staff will require a private office. In most physical therapy and occupational therapy departments, the director, assistant director, and clinical education coordinator will each require a private office, but the staff therapists will be able to share one large office space. A private office is usually between 100 and 110 square feet. The size of the office for the therapists will depend on the number of therapists. For a staff of five physical therapists, an office space of 300 square feet should be sufficient.

The criteria used to determine square footage should come from more than one source (e.g., a consultant with experience in designing similar spaces, the appropriate professional organization, and current articles). The Joint Commission provides specific guidelines for each clinical service.[1] Magistro describes a report on space-planning criteria for physical therapy departments which was developed in the 1970s by the Tri-Service Physical Therapy Committee of the U.S. Armed Forces.[2] The Space requirements are based in large part on patient visits for physical therapy in military installations.

Whatever the source used to estimate square footage, it is important that the planning team carefully review the purpose of the department and the functions that will be carried out in the area. Pfister recommends utilizing a space factor in the range of 120 to 150 net assignable square feet (NASF) when estimating space needs for administrative functions in a medical record department.[3] Administrative functions include private offices and supporting clerical, reception, file, work, and storage areas. For example, a medical record department with 20 administrative, technical, and clerical staff members will require 2,400 to 3,000 NASF for administrative, record processing, and transcription. Pfister further suggests that the area be at the larger end of the scale so as to accommodate microfichery, computer terminals, and related technologies.

TECHNICAL CONSIDERATIONS

The manager confers with the architect and engineer to develop the detailed specifications relating to such technical aspects as:

- electrical lighting and power needs
- humidity control
- air conditioning and ventilation
- aisle space and door clearance requirements
- floor and wall thickness
- floor load
- noise control
- privacy needs for clients and personnel

The department manager has the responsibility to call attention to any special aspect of such technical specifications.

SYSTEMATIC LAYOUT PLANNING GRID

A manager may facilitate the planning process by developing a systematic planning grid. This customized layout planning grid is customized for each departmental function. The key activities of the unit, internal and external contacts, special architectural needs, and similar technical details are listed. The technical consideration associated with each aspect of planning is stated. Table 2D-1 displays such a layout grid for the word processing/transcription function of a medical record department

---

Table 2D-1 Layout Grid for Word Processing Function—Medical Records Department

Word Processing/Transcription

Number of Employees	Day_____ Evening_____ Night_____
Key Activities	Transcribe dictated reports Receive printouts from offsite transcription service Prepare and distribute originals and copies Coordinate wordflow with offsite transcription service
Contact with Clients and Patients	none
Contact with Professional Staff	Routine contact, usually by telephone, with physicians and other professionals who dictate reports

Technical Considerations

	Total work stations: _____ Special need: shared work space for three shifts Provide storage space for personal items for each worker No need for reception area for clients in the immediate work area Telephone at each workstation Supervisor's telephone has automatic redial capability
Interdepartmental Relationships	Coordination with chart processing: daily Coordination with release-of-information specialists for priority action (e.g., scheduled court or deposition appearance by ROI specialist; need for complete record)
Other Contacts	Daily contact with offsite transcription service
Privacy and Security Considerations	All material processed is confidential patient care documentation Night shift personnel work alone in this area of the building Computers and word processing equipment are "attractive" items for theft Holding bin for completed work designated as priority Word processing printer to receive offsite transmittal Placement of display screen so that material cannot be read by others Limited access to work area Special security alarms for safety of night shift personnel Equipment locks; antitheft devices on all equipment

Table 2D-1 continued

Noise Control	Production level word processing generates noise throughout the work periods; individual transcriptionists are generally protected from this noise because they use headphones; supervisor is exposed to this noise throughout workday.
Lighting	Close work; detailed clerical work processed throughout the workday
Electrical Needs	Word processing unit and convenience lighting at each workstation Outlets for computer terminal(s) and outlets for planned expansion (4 additional workstations) Place word processing unit in separate room or surround work unit with special noise reduction paneling Carpet the area Install sound-conditioning ceiling and walls Overhead ambient lighting: 100 foot candles Direct lighting at workstation: 100 foot candles Grounded outlets Power surge protection Minimum of three outlets per workstation No extension cords allowed
Telephone and Other Communication Devices	Needed for each workstation Need both internal and external access Workers wear headphones during most of the workday; cannot hear ringing phone; add visual signal Need to secure phones from unauthorized use
Temperature and Humidity	Personal comfort; enhanced productivity Equipment considerations, especially computers
Special Architectural Support or Weight-Bearing Considerations	Standard office equipment Both internal and external access lines on all phones Equip phones with flashing light Equip phones with lock feature Air conditioned work area Humidity control—40% to 50% 150 lbs. per sq. ft.
Work Surface Requirements	Sitting: most of work is done while sitting at desk Standing: sorting and distributing completed originals and copies Mobile: none needed
Square Footage (standard allotments)	Per employee Per supervisor Aisle space Sorting and receiving area and remote terminal area

MONITORING AND TESTING THE CONSTRUCTION

Once plans are finalized and equipment ordered, you must wait for the construction to begin. It is best not to have employees work in any area where construction is going on. Now construction is easier on the employees, the patients, and the contractors, since the new area can be segregated. If construction takes place while staff are working, you must enlist their support during this inconvenient time. Ask for a production schedule so that you can try to better organize staffing and service delivery. Protect fragile equipment from harm. Flexibility and adaptability will be needed as staff try to deal with noise, dust, strangers, and daily changes.

Monitor the installation of equipment and save instructions and guarantees.

Once construction is completed and the construction disorder is cleared away, you must test the results. Set up and test new machines and try out furniture, lights, and drawers. Report defective items to the architect.

THE AMERICANS WITH DISABILITIES ACT AND BARRIER-FREE DESIGNS

Accommodating handicapped persons to enable them to perform efficiently is both a humanitarian service and a legal requirement. It is estimated that at least 10 percent of the population have a significant physical handicap.

The American with Disabilities Act (ADA) provides a clear and comprehensive national mandate for the elimination of discrimination against the 43 million Americans who have physical or mental disabilities (see Exhibit 2D-1). The ADA's sweeping reforms make it the most significant expansion of civil rights in the United States in more than 25 years.[4]

The ADA seeks to alleviate discrimination against the disabled in employment and public accommodations and mandates that public transportation, telecommunications, and public services be accessible. The ADA also requires that newly constructed and renovated public transportation conveyances and commercial facilities be readily accessible to and usable by individuals with disabilities except where it can be shown that it is structurally impractical to meet this requirement.

Barrier-free design allows access to and free movement within a facility by persons with a wide range of disabilities. These disabilities include

- nonambulatory disabilities
- semiambulatory disabilities (e.g., the disabilities experienced by people on crutches, the grossly overweight, cardiac and pulmonary patients, stroke victims, amputees)

- disabilities involving coordination (e.g., cerebral palsy)
- sight disabilities
- hearing disabilities
- general disability (e.g., the disabilities associated with aging)
- temporary disabilities (e.g., disabilities associated with pregnancy)

Barrier-free design is required in both new and existing facilities of organizations that are federally sponsored or assisted by federal funds. Careful application of the criteria will be necessary if the needs of the handicapped are to be met without incurring expenses that are at great variance with the benefits received. The areas that the barrier-free design checklist covers include passenger arrival terminals, parking lots, walks, ramps, doors, entrances, corridors, public spaces, work areas, stairs, elevators, toilet facilities, drinking fountains, public telephones, controls (such as drapes, doors, windows, and light switches), identification signs, and warning or precaution areas.

Specific examples of barrier-free design include the following:

- eliminating revolving doors or providing standard doors as alternative entrances or exits
- installing time-delay doors
- placing doorknobs 36 inches from floor
- using entry and interior doors that are at least 32 inches wide
- making thresholds flush with floor
- providing ramps
- making corridors a minimum of 54 inches wide (wheelchairs need space to turn)
- providing restrooms with at least one wheelchair entry stall with grab rails
- putting controls on light switches, elevators, and fire and safety alarms that are within reach of wheelchair user
- making drapery, venetian blinds, or shade cords long enough to be reached by wheelchair user
- placing files so that access can be from front and side
- providing sturdy chairs
- providing chairs with casters for easy mobility
- providing reserved parking spaces

Exhibit 2D-1 Americans with Disabilities Act Fact Sheet

Title	Effective Date	Regulations	Enforcement/Remedies
Title I - Employment			
Employers with 15 or more employees may not discriminate against qualified individuals with disabilities. Employers must reasonably accommodate the disabilities of qualified applicants or employees, unless undue hardship would result.	July 26, 1992, for employers with 25 or more employees. July 26, 1994 for employers with 15 to 24 employees.	EEOC to issue regulations by July 26, 1991.	Individuals may file complaints with EEOC. Individuals may also file a private lawsuit. Remedies are same as available under Title VII of the Civil Rights Act of 1964. Court may order employer to hire or promote qualified individuals, reasonably accommodate their disabilities, and pay back wages and attorneys' fees
Title II - Public Services			
State and local governments may not discriminate against qualified individuals with disabilities. New construction and alterations to existing facilities must be accessible. Existing facilities must meet program accessibility requirements consistent with Section 504 of the Rehabilitation 1973.	January 26, 1992.	Attorney General to issue regulations except for public transportation by July 26, 1991. DOT to issue regulations for public transportation by July 26, 1991. Regulations must be consistent with MGRAD. ATBCB to supplement MGRAD by April 26, 1991.	Individuals may file complaints with DOT concerning public transportation and with other Federal agencies to be designated by the Attorney General concerning matters other than public transportation. Individuals may also file a private lawsuit. Remedies are the same as available. Act of under Section 505 of the Rehabilitation Act of 1973. Court may order entity to make facilities accessible, provide auxiliary aids or services, modify policies, and pay attorneys' fees.
New buses and rail vehicles must be accessible.	Ordered after August 25, 1990.		
One car per train must be accessible.	By July 26, 1995.	If final regulations not issued by July 26,1991, and building permit obtained prior to final regulations for new construction or alterations to transit facilities on which work begins within one year of receipt of the permit, then compliance with UFAS required. If final regulations not issued one year after MGRAD supplemented, then compliance with MGRAD required.	
Existing "key stations" in rapid rail, commuter rail, and light rail systems must be accessible.	By July 26, 1993. Extensions may be granted up to July 26, 2010, for commuter rail systems and July 26, 2020, for rapid and light rail systems for stations needing extraordinarily expensive structural changes.		

Exhibit 2D-1   continued

Title	Effective Date	Regulations	Enforcement/Remedies
Title II–Public Services (continued)			
Comparable paratransit must be provided to individuals who cannot use fixed route bus service to the extent that an undue financial burden is not imposed.	By January 26, 1992.	If final regulations not issued by July 26, 1991, Amtrak and commuter rail passenger cars must comply with MGRAD provisions for rail cars to the extent that they are in effect at the time the design of the cars is substantially completed.	
Amtrak passenger cars must have same number of accessible seats as would be available if every car in the train were accessible.	By July 26, 2000. Half of these seats must be available by July 26, 1995.		
All existing Amtrak stations must be accessible.	By July 26, 2010.		
Title III - Public Accommodations			
Public accommodations such as restaurants, hotels, theaters, doctors' offices, retail stores, museums, libraries, parks, private schools, and day care centers may not discriminate on the basis of disability.	January 26, 1992.	Attorney General to issue regulations except for privately operated transportation by July 26, 1991. DOT to issue regulations for privately operated transportation by July 26, 1991.	Individuals may file complaints with the Attorney General. Individuals may also file a private lawsuit.
Physical barriers in existing facilities must be removed if readily achievable (i.e., easily accomplishable and able to be carried out without much difficulty or expense). If not, alternative methods of providing services must be offered, if those methods are readily achievable.	January 26, 1992.	Regulations must be consistent with MGRAD. ATBCB to supplement MGRAD by April 26, 1991. If final regulations not issued by July 26, 1991, and building permit obtained for new construction or alterations to facilities on which work begins within one year of receipt of the permit, then compliance with UFAS required. If final regulations not issued one year after MGRAD supplemented, then compliance with supplemental MGRAD required.	Remedies are the same as available under Title II of the Civil Rights Act of 1964. Court may order an entity to make facilities accessible, provide auxiliary aids or services, modify policies and pay attorneys' fees.
New construction in public accommodations and commercial facilities must be accessible.	Facilities designed and constructed for first occupancy after January 26, 1993.		Lawsuits may not be filed against small businesses for violations occurring before July 26, 1992, or January 26, 1993 (depending on the size of the business and gross receipts), except for violations relating to new construction or alterations to facilities.

Exhibit 2D-1 continued

Title III-Public Accomodations (continued)

Requirement	Effective Date		Enforcement
Alterations to existing facilities must be accessible. When alterations to primary function areas are made, an accessible path of travel must be provided to the altered area, and the restrooms, telephone and drinking fountains serving the altered area must also be accessible, to the extent that the added accessibility costs are not disproportionate to the over-all alterations costs.	January 26, 1992.	If final regulations not issued by July 26, 1991, privately operated transit vehicles must comply with supplemental MGRAD to the extent that it is in effect at the time the design of the vehicles is substantially completed.	Court may award money damages and impose civil penalties in lawsuit filed by Attorney General but not in private lawsuit filed by individuals.
Elevators are not required in newly constructed or altered buildings under three stories or with less than 3,000 square feet per floor, unless the building is a shopping center, mall, or health provider's office. The Attorney General may determine that additional categories of such buildings require elevators.		On application by State or local government, Attorney General, in consultation with ATBCB, may certify that State or local building codes meet or exceed Federal accessibility requirements.	
New buses and other vehicles (except automobiles) operated by private entities in which vehicles are used must provide individuals with disabilities a level of service equivalent to that provided to the general public (depending on whether entity primarily engaged in business of transporting people, whether system is fixed route or demand responsive, and vehicle seating capacity).	Ordered after August 25, 1990.		
New over-the-road buses must be accessible.	Ordered after July 26, 1996 (July 26, 1997, for small companies). Date may be extended by one year after completion of a study. Structural changes to provide access to individuals who use wheelchairs and purchase of boarding assistance devices may not be required prior to these dates.		

Exhibit 2D-1   continued

Title	Effective Date	Regulations	Enforcement/Remedies
Title IV- Telecommunications			
Telephone companies must provide telecommunications relay services for hearing-impaired and speech-impaired persons 24 hours per day.	By July 26, 1993.	FCC to issue regulations by July 26, 1991.	Individuals may file complaints with the FCC.

Source: U.S. Agricultural and Transportation Barriers Compliance Board, Washington, D.C.

NOTES

1. Joint Commission on Accreditation of Healthcare Organizations, *Accreditation Manual for Hospitals* (Chicago: Joint Commission on Accreditation of Healthcare Organizations, 1990); idem, *Accreditation Manual for Long Term Care Facilities* (Chicago: Joint Commission on Accreditation of Healthcare Organizations, 1988).

2. C.M. Magistro, "Department Planning, Design and Construction," in *Physical Therapy Administration and Management*, 2d ed., edited by R. Hickok (Baltimore: Williams and Wilkins, 1982), 59–98.

3. J.P. Pfister, "Functional Space Justification," *Topics in Health Record Management* 6, no. 2 (1985): 27–33.

4. George Olson, "The Americans with Disability Act of 1990," *Rehabilitation Management*, August–September 1990, 23–100.

Chapter 3

Management by Objectives and Strategic Planning

CHAPTER OBJECTIVES

1. Define management by objectives (MBO).
2. Identify the participants in the MBO cycle.
3. Identify the phases in the MBO cycle.
4. Identify the characteristics of performance objectives in MBO.
5. Relate MBO to the use of operational goals.
6. Define strategic planning.
7. Describe the major steps in strategic planning.

MANAGEMENT BY OBJECTIVES

Management by objectives (MBO), or results management, is a process of planning, motivating, and controlling in which the resources of the organization are focused on achieving the key objectives stated in the organization's overall goals. MBO provides a framework within which the personnel and the resources of the organization are assessed continually in the light of specific goal attainment. The overall goals are emphasized, the impact of the work of a unit or division on total organizational effort is recognized, and the decisions to allocate organizational resources are made in a manner that optimizes overall performance. MBO is an integrative management concept, containing elements of the planning process, participative management, motivation, and control. It reflects the systems approach to management with its emphasis on a cycle of planning, effecting, and feedback, including assessment of change in the input-output cycle.

HISTORICAL DEVELOPMENT

Several parallel events in management history led to the development of MBO. These events include the work of behavioral scientists, who stressed the value of motivation and participation, and the application of MBO concepts to business and industrial long-range planning. Table 3-1 contains selected concepts in the development of MBO within the last two decades.

The manager in contemporary health care organizations should understand the MBO concept, since its use in health care management is increasing. A hospital, for example, may use this approach for its administrative reports as well as in its budget process. MBO may be required for research or special project grants; for example, the Department of Health, Education and Welfare (HEW) required MBO as the management process for developing the programs funded under its 1974 grants for trauma research.

ADVANTAGES OF MBO

Major reasons that have been identified for using MBO include the following:

Table 3-1 History of Management by Objectives

Date	Originator/Source	Key Concept, Term, or Point of Emphasis
1954	Peter Drucker *The Practice of Management*[1]	Introduction of the term *management by objectives*
1960	Douglas McGregor *The Human Side of Enterprise*[2]	Theory X and Theory Y of motivation; value of self-direction and self-control in working toward objectives
1961	Rensis Likert *New Patterns of Management*[3]	Behavioral science applied to management theory; emphasis on self-set goals and related self-set controls asmore effective than imposed goals and controls
1965	George S. Ordiome *Management by Objectives*[4]	Development of extensive written materials on MBO
1967	John Humble *Management by Objectives In Action*[5]	Development of detailed material for application of MBO
1960s		Long-range planning with adoption of MBO process in business and industry

- Rational organizational planning is more readily achieved; long-range plans become actualized through highly coordinated derived goals.
- Communication is facilitated through the management conference process; upward and downward communication flows in a systematic manner.
- Performance is monitored as an aspect of control; results of specific plans are examined in the performance review conferences, during which individual performance is assessed.
- Motivation is enhanced because of routine involvement of key participants.
- The authority-responsibility patterns are reinforced where the work to achieve the goal is performed; this clarity of authority and responsibility adds to both the motivational and the control aspects of the process.
- Training needs are identified and anticipated; the opportunity for individual development is provided.

MBO is adaptable to the budget process, as specific objectives can be linked to requests for allocation of money and personnel. Demonstrating objectives planned and objectives accomplished within a time frame corresponding to the budget cycle provides the manager with comparatively strong budget justification. MBO may be linked to the planning-programming-budgeting system process in this way.

The budget justification sometimes takes the form of MBO. The manager is required to relate budgeted costs to objectives to be achieved. The objectives for this documentation are similar to the objectives of the department (sometimes the wording is even the same). Progressive accomplishment throughout the year would be charted through traditional MBO statements (see Exhibit 3-1).

MBO can also be used in concert with the PERT network (see Chapter 10). As the activities needed to complete the many network events are delineated, the MBO components of objectives, target date, and responsibility are readily identified.

RELATIONSHIP TO PARTICIPATIVE MANAGEMENT

MBO emphasizes participative management, that is, the involvement of each individual affected, as far as practicable, in the planning process, in decision making, and in the assessment of results. Not only are the skills and abilities of these individuals assessed, but also the planning and decision-making process is opened so that they may become emotionally and mentally involved. It is more than involvement at the skill level; it is involvement of the self.

The purpose of participative management is to motivate the individuals to work toward the goals; it also helps elicit critical information from the supervisory and

Exhibit 3-1 Sample MBO Statement

Departmental Objective: (ongoing objective)
    Provision of all records requested for clinic use

Intermediate objectives:

a. Increase staffing in file area for morning shift.
    Estimated hours per week: 24
    Projected cost per week: $182.00

    Time frame: July through September

b. Prevent backlog in file area during vacation season
    Estimated hours per week: 65
    Projected staffing:
                overtime for 25 hours = $200.00
                temporary help for 40 hours = $320.00

    Time frame: July through September

c. Conversion to new work shifts in October to provide coverage from 7:00 A.M. through 8:00 P.M.

    Shifts to be seven hours each with some overlap to meet peak demands for clinic requests.

    Eliminate temporary help and overtime.

---

line workers. It enhances the acceptance of change, since the individuals affected by the change understand the reasons for it more fully. Participative management also encourages workers to accept responsibility for the activities, because they view the success of the plan as their own success; they help to determine the areas of responsibility rather than have responsibility imposed on them. The participative leadership style is the presumed authority relationship in the MBO process.

UNDERLYING MOTIVATIONAL ASSUMPTIONS

MBO may be linked with certain behavioral science assumptions about worker motivation. Self-motivation is stressed. Theory Y as described by Douglas McGregor reflects the management view of worker motivation that is consistent with MBO.[6] Basic tenets of the behavioral school of thought on motivation include the following:

- Employees want to know what is expected of them.
- Employees want to participate in and influence decisions affecting their performance.
- Employees want feedback on how they are performing.
- The performance of employees is affected positively by supervisor interest in their work.

PARTICIPANTS IN MBO

Who participates in MBO? Does MBO mean that the manager sits down with each and every employee? Do workers plan the details of the work within some overall boundary set by the manager? Is this a realistic approach to work? One could raise this objection: What manager has that kind of time? Furthermore, how can workers make management decisions? The level of MBO participation that is desirable varies; there is no absolute number of key participants. In some discussions of MBO, there is an implicit inclusion of all workers at all times. In others, the emphasis is on management pairs or small management-worker teams. The degree of participation and the point of participation in the MBO cycle depends on several factors.

The basic participants are, first of all, the management pair. A manager, at any level of the organization, and the manager's immediate assistant or supervisor constitute the first level of participants in the MBO process. These individual officeholders have the fundamental charge to develop goals and policies consistent with overall organizational goals and to carry them out. The concept of management pairs may easily be broadened to include other managers and supervisors who are concerned with the same derived objectives and the same workflow and who hold successive levels of authority and responsibility in the chain of command for a department. A review of the organization chart rapidly reveals potential key participants. Successive groups of supervisors or workers become involved as the plans are developed within each department or unit.

A health care organization may have an explicit goal of providing continuity of care. This goal invests all the departments with a fundamental charge to carry out activities to support continuity of care. An assistant administrator in charge of several departments, such as the admission unit, the medical record service, and patient information service, may call together the managers of these three departments to develop specific objectives for their departments to support continuity of care. Each of these managers in turn carries the MBO process into his or her department and develops the appropriate operational objectives with the supervisor or assistant director involved with activities that are central to this goal. In this pattern of participation, the MBO planning and feedback process is limited to those with clear management roles. The process may be carried another step by having these second- and third-level assistants and supervisors use the specific MBO cycle in their planning. It is at this level that immediate line workers become involved.

Factors that must be taken into account to determine the appropriate degree of worker involvement include the nature of the work, the degree of training of the workers, and the time frame for achieving the goals. Many of the same factors that determine the appropriate span of management (see Chapter 7) may be significant in determining the appropriate level of worker participation as well. Participation is restricted to those areas of work in which the workers have the knowledge and training to make meaningful contributions.

MBO CYCLE

There are three distinct phases in the MBO cycle: the planning phase, the performance review phase, and the feedback phase (which leads to a new planning phase). Table 3-2 summarizes the MBO cycle in terms of each phase, key activities for the phase, and the participants involved in each phase. To illustrate these phases, Table 3-3 presents an example of the MBO cycle as followed in an occupational therapy program.

Planning

The overall organizational goals are identified and stated. If this has been done in a prior planning phase, these goals are reaffirmed at the start of the MBO cycle. As noted earlier, many goals are recurring ones, such as maintaining accreditation of a hospital or an educational program, serving a distinct client group, or developing outreach programs. Specific departmental objectives are agreed upon within the framework of the overall objectives.

Selection of objectives is the basic activity on which the MBO process is built, and it must be given careful attention. A guiding principle for the choice of objectives is the rule of the critical few, also referred to as the Pareto principle. In essence, this concept reflects the probability that most of the key results will be generated by only a few of the activities, while most of the activities will generate only a few of the key results. Pareto estimated that the relationship was 20 percent to 80 percent in most situations; that is, 80 percent of the results would be derived from 20 percent of the objectives, while 80 percent of the objectives would generate only 20 percent of the key results. Priority of effort, then, may be given to those objectives identified as "the critical few."

Table 3-2 Summary of the MBO Cycle

Phase	Key Activities	Participants
Planning	Identifies and defines key organizational goals	Manager
	Identifies and defines key departmental goals that stem from overall goals	
	Identifies and defines performance measures (operational goals) for employees	
	Formulates and proposes goals for specific job	Subordinate
	Formulates and proposes measures for specific job	
	Participate in management conference	Manager and subordinates
	Achieve joint agreement on individual objectives and individual performance	
	Set up timetable for periodic meetings for performance review	
Performance review	Continue to participate in periodic management conferences	Manager and subordinates
	Adjust and refine objectives based on feedback, new constraints, and new inputs	
	Eliminate inappropriate goals	
	Readjust timetable as needed	
	Maintain ongoing comparison of proposed timetable and actual performance through use of control monitoring devices, such as visible control charts	
Feedback to new planning stage	Reviews overall organizational and departmental goals for the next planning period, such as the next fiscal year	Manager

The following examples illustrate the characteristics of properly formulated objectives. Quantifiers and the deadlines, as well as the designation of responsibility, are included.

- File clerk to complete audit of files to detect and correct misfiles in sections 00-38-76 to 00-99-76 by October 26.
- Director of Medical Record Department to recruit an assistant director specializing in medical care evaluation; to be done by December 15, for starting salary of not more than $30,500.
- Transcription unit supervisor to reduce backlog of discharge summaries by 50 percent by November 1. Reduce error rate per operative report by 10 percent by December 15.

Table 3-3 Example of an MBO Cycle

Date 9/17
Project: Reorganize program by December 31.

Phase	Key Activities	Participants
Planning	Review present program by 9/22	Director
	Prepare goals for patient dressing, bathing, and toileting activities by diagnostic categories by 9/30	Alice M., staff therapist
	Prepare goals for patient dressing, bathing, and toileting activities by patient functional ability by 9/30	Lenny R., staff therapist
	Compare goal statements and amended goals by 10/5	Director and staff
	Hold conference to discuss goals	Director and staff
	Finalize amendment of goals by 10/15	Director
Performance review	Introduce new program to patients; adjust goals and report during supervisory meetings	Director and staff
	Hold staff meetings every Friday for two months	Director and staff
Feedback	Confer with other department heads and supervisors regarding quality of new program by 11/15	Director
	Refine activities of daily living program as per suggestions and feedback; circulate among staff by 11/15	Director
	Meet with patients and families to access progress in individual cases and summarize findings by 11/15	Staff

The following examples, which correspond to those listed above, would be incorrect because they are too vague; they lack either a quantifying or qualifying element and there is no assigned deadline or responsibility.

Example 1: Reduce misfiles in permanent storage area.

Example 2: Hire an assistant to help with additional workload in medical record department.

Example 3: Reduce backlog and eliminate all typing errors in transcription unit.

Just as the statement of objectives must be realistic, the time frame for the accomplishment of objectives must be realistic. The time frame must be long enough to permit achievement of the objectives yet short enough to permit timely feedback and intervention. Through careful estimates of such factors as required training time, seasonal changes in workflow, the availability of personnel or supplies, and budgetary considerations, a timetable can be developed that leads to accomplishment of the objectives.

A natural time frame is given when MBO is linked to the annual budget period. This questioning process requires managers to rejustify the existence of the programs. Another easily identifiable time frame stems from deadlines imposed by outside agencies, such as a one-year provisional accreditation or the two-year full accreditation by the Joint Commission. If MBO is linked to a special project that is planned and controlled through a PERT network, the time frame coincides with the overall project target date, and the target dates for the completion of each set of activities correspond to events in the network. Within the overall time frame, management conferences are scheduled to assess progress and to adjust plans.

Performance Objectives

In the MBO process, the performance objectives developed are essentially operational goals or objectives. The objectives that are determined for an MBO sequence should be distinguished by three characteristics:

1. Specificity. Each objective should include a plan that shows the work to be done, the time frame within which it is to be accomplished, and a clear designation of the individual who is to accomplish the work.
2. Measurability. Each objective, as far as possible, should have quantitative indicators for the measurement of work accomplished. If an activity cannot be quantified, qualitative factors should be developed.
3. Attainability. Each objective should be realistic; it should be possible to carry out the activity within the time frame established.

Performance objectives have much in common with operational goals, which will be discussed here briefly, in conjunction with their use in management by objectives.

Operational Goals

In addition to the formal statements of objectives and desired functional statements of performance, a manager may wish to develop operational, or working, goals for internal departmental use only. Operational goals are also highly specific, measurable, and attainable; they must be sufficiently con-crete to relate the overall goals and objectives to specific actions. When the statement of objectives and the related functional objectives are sufficiently refined and stable, there may be no need for operational goals.

Operational goals may be seen as temporary measures that take into account the reality of changing, usually difficult, work situations. They reflect the impact of a high turnover rate, absenteeism, employees in a trainee status, physical renovation of the work area, or temporary emergency situations. Operational goals may become progressively more refined as progress is achieved in certain areas. In a training program, for example, the operational goals may be relatively lenient with respect to error tolerance or the time required for accomplishment of the work. As the trainee progresses to full employee status, the work standards and related operational goals become stricter, moving gradually toward the desired formal objectives. In MBO, when a situation is problematical, the performance objectives may have the flavor of operational goals; a plan is made to move, by specific tar-get dates, from the present situation to the desired goal. Thus, the time frame, the amount of work to be accomplished, and similar factors are stated in a realistic fashion, always in concert with the final goal—full compliance or full satisfaction of departmental goals.

Performance Review

The performance objectives determined in the MBO conference must be fair, based on all known relevant conditions, adjusted to the individual's capability, and adjusted to the specific constraints of the work situation. The objectives themselves do not vary from one performance meeting to another, but the points to be measured are subject to change because of variations in conditions during work cycles. The worker may be involved in special train-ing and, therefore, may be given a more modest output to attain at the begin-ning; later, the quantity or the quality may be set at a higher level. At another phase in the work cycle, some new constraint may be identified, such as equipment problems, unanticipated turnover in workers, or an unexpected surge in client demand; a consequent adjustment in quantity may be made.

The purpose of performance review is not only to monitor the performance but also to make adjustments as indicated by the situation. Successful use of MBO includes the allowance for a margin of error, that is, planning for mis-takes and accepting the human factor. This planning for contingencies gives realism to the objectives and is helpful in enhancing employee acceptance of the process.

Feedback

There will usually be at least several management conferences devoted to formulating the original plans, adjusting these plans during the performance review phase, and obtaining the necessary feedback. During the management conferences between workers and managers, specific planning takes place:

1. Appropriate objectives are identified through mutual agreement.
2. Time periods for achieving the objectives are established.
3. Responsibility in terms of results is defined.
4. Revisions and adjustments are made periodically.

The feedback process is structured and includes a review of the specific control documents that were developed to monitor progress, such as visible control charts, PERT network activity specification sheets, and training plans. Reasons for failure to meet objectives are documented; these factual data are assessed and plans are adjusted accordingly. The purpose of the interim feedback is to facilitate corrective action. There should be no punitive element to the conferences.

In addition to the periodic review of the work, an overall review is done at the end of the cycle, with the identification of objectives, constraints, and time frame for the next cycle.

FORMATS FOR MBO PLAN

The format for writing a detailed MBO plan varies; managers develop a format to suit their own needs unless a specific format is imposed by a higher authority in the organization. Exhibits 3-2 through 3-5 illustrate the essential components and relationships of the MBO plan. Regardless of what format is used, certain information should be included routinely in the MBO plan:

- department
- unit or subdivision
- overall objectives and the derived operational objectives
- the period covered in the MBO cycle
- key participants
- workflow factors and special constraints
- identification of training needs
- methods of evaluation to be used
- detailed time plan

Exhibit 3-2   MBO Plan: Example 1

Department	Medical Record Department
Unit/subdivision	Transcription unit
Overall objective	To develop and maintain a system of dictation and transcription for the timely and accurate processing of medical record entries.
Derived operational goals/specific objectives	To transcribe all priority reports within four hours of receipt. To transcribe all other reports within 24 hours of receipt.
Key participants	1. Director, Medical Record Department 2. Assistant Director 3. Transcription Unit Supervisor
Workflow factors	1. Assistant Director to check on problems stemming from delays in receipt of transcription belts from outpatient clinic area; to be done during June. 2. Transcription Unit Supervisor to have all equipment serviced by June; no new equipment budgeted for coming year.
Anticipated constraints	1. Vacancy anticipated owing to one employee's maternity leave August through January. 2. Vacation time mid-June through September. 3. Surge of transcription as residents change services and/or leave at end of June. 4. Uncertainty concerning budget; not usually approved until two to three months into budget cycle; uncertain allotment of money for overtime or additional temporary help, at least from July through September. 5. Close out of budget; use all available money from this budget for overtime or temporary help during late June.
Workers involved	See organization chart; all transcriptionists and Unit Supervisor; Assistant Director to give overall explanation of program; Unit Supervisor to work with each transcriptionist to identify special needs. Target date: first week in June.
Training needs	1. Only one worker trained to use automatic typewriter; train second worker. 2. All have completed basic terminology course, but need specialized terminology. 3. Assistant Director to develop 16-hour medical terminology course; to be given in two stages—June and September.

Exhibit 3-2   continued

Methods and standards for control	Continue to use present work standard of 800 lines per day, error-free; monitor overall unit output through visible control chart.

Detailed time plan	Meeting dates:
	    April 17
	    May 8
	    May 15
	    June 4

Exhibit 3-3   MBO Plan: Example 2

Department: Occupational Therapy
Unit: Rehabilitation

Overall Objective:	1. To offer quality occupational therapy to patients in the clinic and in the patient's room.
Derived Goals:	1. Pick up referrals within 24 hours. 2. Evaluate patients and report to physician within 72 hours of receipt of referral. 3. Treat all patients daily. 4. Participate in family and team conferences. 5. Teach home programs to family members. 6. Plan for patients' discharge.
Key Participants:	1. Director of OT 2. OT staff 3. Secretary
Workflow Factors:	1. Director to log all references and check on evaluation schedule. 2. Director to develop ADL schedule on ward. 3. Secretary to time/date all referrals. 4. Secretary to notify staff of pending discharges.
Anticipated Constraints:	1. Referrals may back up in physicians' offices. 2. Staff given short notice of discharges. 3. Family conferences scheduled during treatment times. 4. Secretary planning to resign next month. 5. Budget constraints force therapists to treat minimum of 4 patients per hour.
Workers Involved:	Director; 3 staff occupational therapists (OTR); 3 occupational therapy assistants (COTA); 1 secretary

Exhibit 3-3   continued

Training Needs:	1. Therapists must keep skills current.
	2. Therapists must attend continuing education programs.
Methods and Standards for Control:	1. Therapists must evaluate 2 patients per day.
	2. Therapists must treat 8 patients per day.
	3. Ongoing quality assurance program as detailed for hospital.

Exhibit 3-4   MBO Plan: Example 3–Yearly Cycle of Consultant Activity in Long-Term Care Facility

	Focus	Medical Record System	Chart Content
Jan. Feb. Mar.	Admissions	1. Patient care policies 2. Procedures: chart development at time of admission 3. In-house filing 4. In-service: patients' rights and consents	1. Patients' rights form 2. Consent forms 3. Face sheet completion 4. Admission physical 5. Initial progress note 6. Initial physician notes 7. Initial physician orders 8. Nurse's notes on admission
Apr. May June	Transfers	1. Transfer agreement 2. Patient care policies re transfers 3. Release of information 4. Exchange of information at time of transfers	1. Transfer orders 2. Completion of transfer form 3. Documentation: receiving a patient as a transfer; sending a patient as a transfer
July Aug. Sept.		1. Patient care policies re medical documentation 2. Chart review procedure; emphasis on in-house review 3. Adequacy of chart review list	1. Physician orders 2. Progress notes 3. Histories and physicals: at admission, annual
Oct. Nov. Dec.	Discharges	1. Processing charts at discharge 2. Coding and indexing 3. Statistical compilations 4. Permanent files	1. Discharge orders 2. Discharge summary 3. Final nurse's notes 4. Diagnoses 5. Death certificate

Exhibit 3-5   MBO Plan: Example 4

Department	Physical Therapy
Unit	Spinal Cord Unit
Overall Objective	To develop an educational handbook of patient care for respirator-dependent quadriplegics.
Derived Goals	To teach patients, families, and hospital personnel the care and progress of the respirator-dependent patient.
	To standardize information presented by the professional staff on the care of the patient throughout the period of hospitalization.
	To provide a quick reference for individuals involved in posthospitalization care of the respirator-dependent patient.
	To complete the handbook by May 4.
	To present completed handbook to Spinal Cord Unit Executive Committee on May 18.
Key Participants	1. Physicians
	2. Nurses
	3. Physical Therapists
	4. Occupational Therapists
	5. Speech Therapists
	6. Psychologists
	7. Social Workers
	8. Project Coordinator
Workflow Factors	1. Physicians to chair committee and also to provide medical information.
	2. Members of other disciplines to provide written procedures on the care and progress of the patient, including any equipment needed.
	3. Committee members to critique information presented by the various disciplines for clarity and understanding.
	4. Project coordinator to compose information presented at each meeting and prepare draft copy of the handbook.
	5. Final draft of the handbook to be presented to the Spinal Cord Unit Executive Committee for approval prior to printing.
Anticipated Constraints	1. Limited time available for committee personnel to be involved in the project.
	2. Committee members absent from meetings.

Exhibit 3-5   continued

	3. Committee member not meeting established timetable.
	4. Lack of adequate support staff for typing and collating information.
	5. Lack of sufficient funds to print completed handbook.
Workers Involved	1. Physicians
	2. Representatives of each discipline involved in the care of the respirator-dependent quadriplegic patient.
Training Needs	1. Member of each discipline involved in the care of the respirator-dependent quadriplegic patient will be responsible for educating respective staff personnel about the written procedures contained in the handbook.
	2. The social worker will be responsible for the distribution of the handbook to current patients in the Spinal Cord Unit and to newly admitted patients.
Methods and Standards for Control	1. Prior to discharge, the handbook to be reviewed by member of each discipline treating the patient to ensure all pertinent information has been included.
	2. Follow-up questionnaire to be sent to each patient six months after discharge.
	3. Questionnaire to be returned to the Project Coordinator for summarization prior to presentation to the respirator-dependent patient handbook committee.
Detailed Time Plan	Meeting dates
	January 5
	February 2
	March 2
	April 6

STRATEGIC PLANNING

Within the last ten years there has been growth in long-range planning. Today it is unusual that a company or industry does not have staff or a committee developing long-range plans. Almost all management decisions made, even the most basic, are long-range decisions. Whether concerned with the expansion of services, staff, or space, with developing a research program, or with instituting a student program, every decision takes months or years before it achieves its full effect. Each decision must be productive enough to pay off the investment, whether in terms of finances, services, or personnel. The effective manager must be skilled in making long-range decisions that lead to success.

It is often necessary for the manager to take chances. Success results from taking risks, taking action, and expending appropriate resources. In short, it depends on strategic planning.

What Strategic Planning Is Not

Before describing what strategic planning is, Drucker suggests that it is important for the manager to know what it is not. According to Drucker;

1. It is not a box of tricks, a bundle of techniques. It is analytical thinking and commitment of resources to action. Many techniques may be used in the process—but then again, none may be needed. Strategic planning is not the application of scientific methods to business decisions. It is the application of thought, analysis, imagination, and judgment. It is responsibility, rather than technique.
2. Strategic planning is not forecasting. It is not masterminding the future. Any attempt to do so is foolish; the future is unpredictable. Strategic planning is necessary precisely because we cannot forecast.
3. Strategic planning does not deal with future decisions. It deals with the futurity of present decisions. Decisions only exist in the present. We cannot ask what the organization should do tomorrow. The question is "what futurity do we have to build into our present thinking and doing, what time spans do we have to consider, and how can we use this information to make a rational decision now?"
4. Strategic planning is not an attempt to eliminate risk. We must understand the risks we take. We must be able to choose rationally among risk-taking courses of action rather than plunge into uncertainty on the bases of hunch, hearsay, or experience, no matter how meticulously this is measured and researched.[7]

What Is Strategic Planning?

Strategic planning is the process of determining the long-term objectives of organizations as a means of formulating strategies to accomplish these objectives. These activities and objectives lead to action today and require an appreciation of what the outcomes of strategic decisions will be in the future. Strategic planning should be viewed positively. An effective strategic plan can help the organization fulfill its mission by articulating a vision of its role, and its potential. (See Exhibit 3-6 for an example of a strategic plan.)

It is important to emphasize that there is no one acceptable way to engage in strategic planning. Each organization or department is unique, and any strategic plan must fit within the structure and function of the particular organization if it is to be successful.

Exhibit 3-6 Sample Strategic Plan

Department of Occupational Therapy
Seaview Community Hospital
Strategic Plan
August 30, 1991

I.   Mission Statement

The Department of Occupational Therapy is committed to providing the highest quality of care and service to all patients and clients referred for treatment. All therapists will maintain and upgrade their clinical skills through continuing education and development.

II.   Major Objectives
   A. Renovate existing space to accommodate a hand rehabilitation center.
   B. Recruit therapists with expertise in hand rehabilitation.
   C. Develop and implement a staff development program in hand rehabilitation.

III.   Action Plan
   A. Renovate existing space to accommodate a hand rehabilitation center.
   B. Recruit therapists with expertise in hand rehabilitation.
   C. Develop and implement a staff development program in hand rehabilitation.
   D. Publicize that the department is developing a hand rehabilitation center.

IV.   Resources Needed
   A. Funds for renovation of existing space
   B. Recruitment of hand therapists
   C. Consultant to assist department in developing a staff development plan
   D. Public relations for new program

V.   Possible Sources of Support
   A. Institution's capital expense could be met through state or federal budget allocations.
   B. Vacant therapy positions could be filled by hand specialists.
   C. Budget items could be transferred to continuing education line.
   D. Public service announcements could be placed on radio and television.

VI.   Monitoring
   A. Employees will be given a questionnaire to determine the extent of their satisfaction with the strategic plan and its success to date. Feedback may include suggestions for facilitating the implementation process.
   B. Status and progress reports on the recruitment of hand therapists, the staff development program, and the building renovations will be required.
   C. An annual review that includes the participation of all key personnel and support staff will be conducted.

Although there are a variety of ways of developing and implementing a strategic plan, there are factors that are characteristic of strategic planning in general. For example, each strategic plan should include

1. a mission statement
2. a definition of major objectives
3. an action plan
4. a description of resources needed
5. a procedure for monitoring performance
6. an evaluation system

Mission Statement

The mission statement should define the scope and focus of the organization's activities. It should be broad enough to encompass potential activities not currently being performed. The statement should allow for flexibility and creativity.

The mission statement can be as simple and straightforward as this:

> The Department of Occupational Therapy is committed to providing the highest quality of care and service to all patients and clients referred for treatment. All staff will maintain and upgrade their clinical skills through continuing education and development.

Definition of Major Objectives

In order to fulfill its mission, the organization must decide upon a set of major objectives. The objectives should reflect what is of greatest significance for the current and future direction of the organization. The efforts of the organization will be based on its major objectives and how they fit in with its structure, purpose, and goals.

The objectives should be developed by those who will participate in achieving them. Employees will strive harder to fulfill objectives if they have had a hand in setting them.

The objectives should be clearly stated and should be measurable quantitatively and/or qualitatively. One quantitative objective might be, for example, to increase the number of pediatric patients referred to the physical therapy department. On the other hand, staff satisfaction with a new department head or a new computer filing system for medical records would be considered a qualitative objective.

It is important during strategic planning to discard objectives that are no longer productive, or objectives that have already been achieved. For example, the medical record department might discard an objective relating to its former manual billing system since it recently instituted a computerized system.

Following are examples of possible major objectives:

- The Department of Occupational Therapy will develop a hand rehabilitation center that will specialize in posttraumatic injuries.
- The Department of Occupational Therapy will be staffed by therapists who are board-certified specialists in hand rehabilitation.
- The Department of Occupational Therapy will be recognized as a premier hand rehabilitation center.

Action Plan

The next stage of strategic planning is to develop an action plan that contains strategies and activities for achieving the objectives. This stage usually calls for an ability to develop new ways of doing things. Brainstorming is a common technique of searching for effective ways of achieving objectives, but intuition and luck are also necessary. The formulation of an action plan is complex, and there is usually no consensus on program strategies.

In the business arena, the action plan is referred to as the *competitive strategy*, especially as it relates to the financial objectives of the organization.

The plan should be action-oriented and should be allowed to develop over time. Few, if any, action plans can be devised overnight, and each plan should be given ample time to reach fruition. Each plan must also reflect the overall mission of the institution.

An action plan for the objective of creating a hand rehabilitation center within the department of occupational therapy might include these steps:

1. Renovate existing space to accommodate a hand rehabilitation center.
2. Recruit therapists with expertise in hand rehabilitation.
3. Develop and implement a staff development program in hand rehabilitation.
4. Through publicity, notify the hospital and local community that the department is developing a hand rehabilitation center.

Resources Needed

The resources that will be used to implement the strategic plan are, of course, essential. The statement of resources should include personnel, financial, equipment, and space requirements. The institution's policies and procedures will dictate how the resources will be described. The statement of resources should include a breakdown of activities and the necessary allocations. The strengths and the expected impact of the plan should also be presented.

To help justify the requested support, documentation might be presented that indicates how the activities relate to the institution's mission. Ideas on how to acquire federal or state grant support or private funding might also prove helpful, as might suggestions regarding the possible transfer of resources from another area within the department.

Resources needed to implement the action plan for creating a hand rehabilitation center, along with potential sources of support, might include the following:

Resource Needed	*Source of Support*
Funds for renovation of existing space	State or federal budget allocations
Hand Specialists	Hiring hand specialists to fill vacant therapy positions
Consultant to assist department in devising a staff development program	Transfer of budget items from equipment to continuing education line
Public relations for new program	Public service announcements on radio and television

Procedure for Monitoring Performance

In order to effectively control the implementation of the strategic plan, it is necessary to monitor the implementation process closely. The evaluation and monitoring system can utilize several approaches. The key point is to determine how well the action plan is progressing toward its objective. The assessment may lead to reconsideration and possible refinement of the objectives, modification of the activities, alteration of the allocation of resources, refinement of roles, and reassignment of individuals.

Measuring the effectiveness of the strategic plan can be done, for example, by having the staff fill out a questionnaire or survey form or by evaluating the extent to which objectives have been achieved over a given period of time. It is important that the supervisor look for signs that implementation of the plan is obstructed or occurring too slowly.

Procedures for monitoring performance may include the following:

- Survey Form. Employees are given a questionnaire to determine whether they are satisfied with the strategic plan and its success to date. Feedback may include suggestions for facilitating the implementation of the plan.
- Status Reports. These would include periodic reports on the recruitment of hand therapists, the staff development program, and the building renovations.

Evaluation System

It is important to recognize that a strategic plan entails innovation and the breaking of new ground. Therefore, there is a need to assess the effectiveness of the plan in achieving its objectives. An evaluation of the strategic plan should thus be performed at the end of each year. The annual review should address all relevant factors, including the action plan, the institutional objectives and resources, and the problems, successes, weaknesses, and strengths of the plan. Participants should include all key personnel as well as the support staff that will be affected by the plan.

The annual evaluation may include revisions or modifications of the plan. It is best to think in terms of "augmenting" the plan instead of "revising" it. For example, if current resources are not adequate, additional resources will need to be identified.

In summary, strategic planning is indispensable for guiding toward success. It is not mere forecasting but involves a commitment to current and future courses of action. An effective plan will be productive enough to pay off the investment of time and energy.

There are a diversity of methods that can be used to develop a strategic plan. Regardless of the method, the plan should relate to the institution's mission statement, define major objectives, spell out an action plan, indicate the resources needed, and suggest a procedure for monitoring the implementation process. An annual evaluation will help to ensure that the objectives of the plan are being met.

NOTES

1. Peter F. Drucker, *The Practice of Management* (New York: Harper & Row, 1954).

2. Douglas McGregor, *The Human Side of Enterprise* (New York: McGraw-Hill, 1960).

3. Rensis Likert, *New Patterns of Management* (New York: McGraw-Hill, 1961).

4. George S. Ordiorne, *Management by Objectives* (New York: Putnam, 1965).

5. John W. Humble, *Management by Objectives in Action* (New York: McGraw-Hill, 1970).

6. McGregor, *The Human Side of Enterprise*.

7. Peter F. Drucker, *Management: Tasks, Responsibilities, Practices* (New York: Harper & Row, 1985).

SUGGESTED READING

Camillus, John C. *Strategic Planning and Management Control*. Lexington, Mass: Lexington Books, 1986.

Capon, Noel, John U. Farley, and James Hulbert. *Complete Strategic Planning*. New York: Columbia University Press, 1987.

Steiner, George *Strategic Planning: What Every Manager Must Know*. New York: The Free Press, 1979.

Chapter 4

Budgeting

CHAPTER OBJECTIVES

1. Identify the requisites for successful budgeting.
2. Relate budget preparation and administration to the planning and controlling function of the manager.
3. Identify traditional budget periods.
4. Identify types of budgets.
5. Differentiate between traditional budgeting and the planning-programming-budgeting system (PPBS).
6. Identify the steps in the budget cycle.
7. Relate the dynamics of the budget approval process to the development of the budget.
8. Identify typical budget categories.
9. Identify the steps in budget controlling through analysis of budget variances.

Budget preparation and administration are major duties of the department head. Before dealing with the actual budget calculations, the manager must understand the basic concepts and principles of budgeting. The budget details presented here are treated from the perspective of the department head rather than the accountant, comptroller, or top-level administrator. In addition, this presentation is intended for the inexperienced manager; terms are defined and examples are given in detail to facilitate budget preparation and analysis by an inexperienced user. The first part of the discussion treats basic concepts such as budget periods, types of budgets, uniform code of accounts, approaches to budgeting, and the overall budget process. The second part of the discussion focuses on the details of the budget proper: the capital expenses, personnel budget, supplies, and related expenses.

Sound budgetary procedures are based on five requisites:

1. sound organizational structure so that the responsibility for budget preparation and administration is clear
2. a consistent, defined budget period
3. the development of adequate statistical data
4. a reporting system that reflects the organizational structure
5. a uniform code of accounts so that data are meaningful and consistent

USES OF THE BUDGET

Budgeting is both a planning and controlling tool. As a plan, the budget is a specific statement of the anticipated results, such as expected revenue to be earned and probable expenses to be incurred, in an operation for a future defined period. This plan is expressed in numerical terms, usually dollars. A statement of objectives in fiscal terms, the budget is a single-use plan that covers a specific period of time; it becomes the basis of future or continuing plans when the incremental approach to budgeting is used whereby the next budget is formulated through the addition of specific increments to the existing budget. It is a statement of what the organization intends to accomplish, not merely a forecast or a guess.

When the budget is properly administered, it becomes a tool of control and accountability in that it reflects the organizational structure, with each unit or department given a specific allocation of funds based on departmental goals and functions. The budget is an essential companion to the delegation of authority; the line manager who has the responsibility for developing the plans for the department or unit must be given the necessary resources to accomplish the approved plans. In turn, this manager accepts responsibility for assigning specific budget amounts to the personnel and material categories and monitoring the use of these resources. Because the budget permits a comparision of planned with actual performance, control is enhanced. The department head is responsible for those costs that are controllable, such as overtime authorization, supplies, and equipment purchases, but not for those that are arbitrarily assigned to the departmental budget, such as fringe benefits calculated as a flat percentage of personnel budget or administrative overhead calculated as a flat percentage of operating costs.

BUDGET PERIODS

A budget specifies the amount to be spent in a predetermined period. This budget period varies according to the purpose of the budget. The capital equipment or improvement budget may be developed for a long period, such as a three- or five- or ten-year period; the budget for supplies, expenses, and personnel costs may be developed for the immediate fiscal year. Given the various regulatory requirements for long-range planning and budgeting for capital improvements in health care organizations, these organizations commonly have such a combination of long- and short-term budget periods.

The usual accounting period within the overall budget framework is the fiscal year, which may or may not correspond to the calendar year. Any period equal to a full year may be chosen; this is an internal decision. Hospitals have commonly used the July to June cycle, which tends to reflect the movement of house staff at the end of the teaching year. The fiscal year may be broken into subunits of time corresponding to each of the 12 months or into 13 equal periods of 28 days each.

Periodic Moving Budget

Another approach to the definition of budget period is the periodic moving budget. In the moving budget, the basic forecast for the year is adjusted as specific periods are completed. As each period is completed, an equal time period is added:

1991	Jan	Feb.	Mar.	
	Apr.	May	June	
	July	Aug.	Sept.	
	Oct.	Nov.	Dec.	
1992	Jan.	Feb.	Mar.	(Added when the Jan.-Feb.-Mar. 1992 period is completed.)

The cycle of completion and addition may be shorter, as when the July-Aug.-Sept. period is added as soon as the Jan.-Feb.-Mar. period is completed. The periodic moving budget allows the manager to make use of the more up-to-date information that becomes available as each period closes and to thus make a more accurate prediction.

Milestone Budgeting

In milestone budgeting, the budget periods are tied to the subsidiary plans or projects. As these milestone events are accomplished, costs can be determined and budget allocations for the next segments of the project can be established. The budget periods are not uniform but depend on the projected time frame for the subsidiary plan.

TYPES OF BUDGETS

The budget may be developed to give emphasis to one of several aspects of the overall plan. The revenue and expense budget is the most common type of budget. It reflects anticipated revenues, such as those from sales, payment for services rendered, endowments, grants, and special funds, and it includes expenses, such as costs associated with personnel, capital equipment, or supplies. In the personnel or labor budget, projections are based on the number of personnel hours needed or types and kinds of skills needed rather than on wages and salaries, as in the personnel costs of the revenue and expense budget. A production budget expresses the information in terms of units of production, such as economic quantities to be produced or types and capacities of machines to be utilized.

The fixed budget presumes stable conditions; it is prepared on the basis of the best information available, such as past experience and forecasting. The plans, including cost and expense calculations, are made on the basis of this expected level of activity. The variable budget concept was developed because operating costs and level of activity may fluctuate. For example, a university may calculate its unit budgets according to credit hours generated, but student enrollment may be lower than anticipated; a hospital may use dollars per patient day or average census as its basis, but the daily census in the hospital may drop and remain low. Thus, costs and expenses are established for varying rates. As actual income and operating costs become known, the budget is adjusted The periodic moving budget is used with variable budgeting, as is the step budget.

The step budget is a form of variable budgeting in which a certain level of activity is assumed and the impact of deviations from this level of activity calculated. If the manager wishes to show several possibilities predicated on various factors, such as level of production or number of clients served, the step budget is used. These other levels may be greater or less than the basic estimate. For example, a step budget showing probable estimates plus pessimistic and optimistic allowances might be developed. The advantage of using the step budget is that it permits, even forces, the manager to examine the actions required in the event of a variation from the estimated revenue and expense. When a step budget is prepared, the fixed costs and revenues, that is, those that are not tied to volume of service, production levels, or other factors related to operational costs, are stated. Then, the variable revenues and costs are calculated according to the volume of service, operating costs, anticipated revenues, and similar factors.

The master budget is the central, composite budget for the total organization; all the major activities of the organization are coordinated in this central budget. The department budgets are the working, detailed budgets for each unit; they are highly specific so as to permit identification of each item as well as close coordination and monitoring of revenue and expense. In order to coordinate the several department or unit budgets into a master budget and in order to make budget processes consistent, a uniform code of accounts and specific cost centers must be developed.

The Uniform Code of Accounts

The standard classification of expenditures and other transactions made by an organization is the uniform code of accounts (also referred to as a uniform chart of accounts). Such a uniform code of accounts contains master codes and subdivisions to reflect such information as the specific transaction (e.g., personnel expense, travel expense, capital improvement) and the organizational unit within which the transaction occurred (e.g., purchasing department, dietary department, public relations unit). The delineation of the specific organizational unit facilitates responsibility reporting, as it is possible to relate specific expenditures to the manager in charge of that organizational unit.

The American Hospital Association, in conjunction with the American Association of Hospital Accountants, publishes a suggested code of accounts for hospitals, as well as related materials for financial management.[1] These account codes are used in the budget to group line items, such as a purchase requisition or a position authorization request. Account codes for a particular institution might include

200	Furniture
210	Capital Equipment
520	Equipment Rental
530	Equipment Maintenance and Service Contracts
580	Purchased Services (e.g., an outside contract with a coding and abstracting service)
600	Education and Travel
610	Dues and Subscriptions

Budget worksheets are coordinated with these account codes, with specific items listed, line by line, under each account code. *Line item* is a term commonly used to refer to such specifications. For example, the worksheet for budget preparation and, subsequently, the line items of the budget for the category of Dues and Subscriptions reflect the item in detail and the unit with which it is associated.

610.1	Hospital association dues	$ 120.00
610.2	Professional dues paid for Chief of Service	300.00
610.7	Accrediting agency regulations annual update subscription	90.00
610.8	Attendance at annual meeting of professional association	

	50% cost for Chief of Service	700.00
	25% cost for each staff assistant	350.00
610.9	In-service workshop for support staff (2-day seminar, in-house)	480.00

The code of accounts varies from one institution to another; the items and costs given here are for illustrative purposes only.

Cost Centers

An activity or group of activities for which costs are specified, such as housekeeping, maintenance and repairs, telephone service, and similar functions, is a cost center. Usually predetermined, cost centers generally parallel the department or service structure of the organization. For example, direct patient care cost centers, with their associated codes, may include

45	Physical Therapy
46	Occupational Therapy
47	Home Care Program
48	Social Services
49	Radiology

Administrative cost centers may include

50	Data Processing and Information Service
51	Health Records Service
52	Admissions Unit
53	Dietary
54	Laundry and Housekeeping

Additional cost centers reflect costs associated with the overall expense of operation:

1	Employee Health and Welfare Benefits
2	Depreciation: Buildings and Fixtures
3	Depreciation: Equipment
4	Payroll Processing

Responsibility Center

A unit of the organization headed by an individual who has authority over and who accepts responsibility for the unit is a responsibility center. These centers parallel the organizational structure as outlined in the organization chart. The departments or services are responsibility centers, each with its detailed budget. The cost center codes and responsibility centers normally parallel one another.

APPROACHES TO BUDGETING

The two major approaches to the budgeting process are incremental budgeting and the planning-programming-budgeting system (PPBS). In incremental budgeting, the financial data base of the past is increased by some given percentage. For example, the personnel portion of the budget may be increased by a flat 5 percent over the last budget period allotment, capital expenses by 7 percent, and supplies by 4 percent. There is an efficiency in this approach, since the projected calculations are relatively straightforward. There is also a danger, however, significant changes, shifting priorities, or pressing needs within some unit of the organization may be overlooked. As with incremental decision making, there is an implicit assumption that the original money and resource allocation was appropriately calculated and distributed among organizational units. Incremental budgets are object-oriented, that is, they are developed in terms of personnel, materials, maintenance, and supplies. Traditional budgeting is control-oriented, while PPBS is planning-oriented.

PPBS was mandated in the Department of Defense in the early 1960s by Secretary Robert McNamara. PPBS, as the name implies, emphasizes the budgeting process in systems terms. The outputs for specific programs are assessed, and resource allocation and funding are related directly to the program goals. It is also referred to as "zero-based" budgeting because past dollar allocations are not the basis of projection.

A major feature of PPBS is its departure from the traditional one-year budget cycle. Funding is projected for the period of time (frequently three or more years) needed to achieve the goals of the program. In the planning phase, the general objectives are stated and refined, the projected schedule of activities is established, and the outputs are specified. These refined objectives are grouped into programs, resulting in a hierarchy within the plans.

The alternate means of achieving the plans are assessed through cost-effectiveness analysis. Units of measure for the outputs are developed (e.g., number of clients to be served, length of hospital stay, geographical area to be covered). Costs and resulting benefits for each approach are calculated, and the best alternative in terms of cost-benefit is selected. In the PPBS approach, managers seek to increase the number of factors that can be used to provide top-level decision makers with sufficient information to make the final resource allocation. An adequate information system is, therefore, required; this is consistent with the classic systems approach, which includes an information feedback cycle.

The PPBS approach has several disadvantages. First, it is a time-consuming process, involving long-range planning, the development and comparison of alternatives in terms of cost-effectiveness, and the final budgeting. Second, not all goals can be stated precisely; not all worthy objectives can be quantified in specific measures, with a specific dollar cost attached. Third, there is the presumption that all alternatives are known and attainable. Fourth, in PPBS, the value, the legitimacy, and the actual survival of the program or organization is questioned. This, in turn, reopens conflict and exposes the accumulation of internal and external politics—the power plays, the bargaining, the trade-offs that have developed over time. The concern for program survival may intensify to the point that line managers may seek to withhold negative information and the feedback cycle may become distorted.

THE BUDGETARY PROCESS

Initial Preparation

The budgetary process is a cyclic one; the feedback obtained during one budget period becomes the basis of budget development for the next period. The budget process usually begins with the setting of overall limits by top management. The specific guidelines for budget preparation reflect the mandatory federal, state, and accrediting requirements as well as union contract provisions and the financial assets of the organization. The timetable and particular forms to be used in budget preparation are issued along with these guidelines.

Development of the unit budget is the specific responsibility of the department manager. In some instances, a department manager may wish to use the "grass roots" approach to budgeting; unit managers or supervisors prepare their budgets and submit them to the department manager for coordination into the overall department budget. The supervisors or unit managers must, of course, be given sufficient information and guidance to carry out this function. An alternate way of involving supervisors and subordinates is to ask for suggestions about equipment needs, special resources, or supplies. In highly normative organizations, such as a university, there may be an advisory or review committee composed of selected employees who make recommendations to line officials regarding budget allocations. In any event, the department head bears the responsibility for final preparation, justification, and control of the budget.

The Review and Approval Process

Competition, bargaining, and compromise in the allocation of scarce resources (personnel, money, and space) occur in the review and approval phase of the budget process. It is important for the manager to have the necessary facts to support budget requests; control records to demonstrate fluctuations in the workload, staffing needs, equipment usage, and goal attainment are essential sources of such information.

The internal approval process begins with a review of the department's budget by the department head's immediate budget officer. Compliance with guidelines is checked; justifications for requests for exceptions are reviewed. The organization's designated financial officer (usually the comptroller) may assist the chief executive officer in coordinating the department budgets into the master budget for the organization, but the chief executive officer is the final arbiter of resource allocation in many instances.

In the present political climate, there is increasing insistence on cost containment, and a cost containment committee may be involved in the budget review process. Current voluntary efforts contribute to the routinization of this aspect of budget review. Cost-containment committees vary in structure and mandate, but their tasks typically include advising, investigating, and even participating in the implementation of cost-containment measures. Such a committee should have the questioning attitude as its primary philosophical stance; data are scrutinized and compared in an effort to identify areas where cost can be contained.

The final approval for the total budget is given by the governing board. In practice, a subcommittee on budget works with the chief executive officer, and final, formal approval is then given by the full governing board, as mandated in the organizational bylaws and/or charter of incorporation.

The budgets of organizations that receive some or all of their funds from state or federal sources may be subject to an external approval process, for example, by the state legislature or the federal Bureau of the Budget. There is a certain predictable drama in the budget process, which becomes more evident in the external review process. There is a tacit rule that budgets are padded, because budget requests are likely to be cut. The manager attempts to achieve a modicum of flexibility in budget maneuvering through overaim. There is also a necessary aspect of accountability, however. The public more or less demands that federal or state officials take proper care of the public purse. Even as clients (the public) seek greater services, they want cost containment, especially through tax relief. Public officials, then, must in fact dramatize their concern for cost containment, partly by a highly specific review of budget requests and a refusal to approve budgets as submitted.

On the other hand, should an agency request a budget allocation that is the same as, or less than, that of a previous year, it might be seriously questioned whether the agency is doing its job. At best, the manager must recognize the subtle and overt political maneuvers that touch the budget process.

Implementation Phase

The final phase of budgeting is the implementation stage, when the approved budget allocation is spent. During this phase, revenues and expenses are regularly compared, for example, through periodic budget reconciliation. Should revenues fall short of the anticipated amount or should unexpected expenses arise, there may be a budget freeze or certain items may be cut. For example, overtime may be prohibited; personnel vacancies may not be filled, except for emergency situations; supplies or travel money may be eliminated.

There are specific internal procedures that must be followed to activate budgeted funds in the normal course of business. For example, the budget may contain an appropriation for certain supplies, but a companion requisition system must be used to effect the actual purchase of such supplies. When an individual worker is to be hired, a position authorization request may be used to activate that position as approved in the budget. Finally, during the budget year, preparation for the following budget period is made, bringing the manager full circle in the budget process (Exhibit 4-1).

CAPITAL EXPENSES

An organization owns and operates capital facilities of a permanent or semipermanent nature, such as land, buildings, machinery, and equipment. Capital budget items are those revenues and costs related to the capital facilities. These expenses may be centralized as a single administrative cost for the entire organization, or they may be specified for each budgetary unit. The manager at the departmental level is normally concerned primarily with capital improvements for the department, such as acquisition of additional space, renovation and repairs, special electrical wiring, and painting.

The second capital expense in the departmental budget is major equipment. The equipment budget usually includes fixed equipment that is not subject to removal or transfer and that has a relatively long life. Major equipment that is movable is also included. The distinction between major and minor equipment is usually made on the basis of the cost and life expectancy of the item; major equipment commonly includes any item over $300.00 that has a life expectancy of more than five years. As with other aspects of budgeting, however, a specific organization may use some other cost or life expectancy factor to define major equipment/capital equipment expense. Major fixed equipment includes the heating fixtures, built-in cabinets or shelves, and appliances; major movable equipment includes file cabinets, patient beds, typewriters, and oxygen tents.

When budgeting for major equipment expenses, the manager may calculate the acquisition cost and prorate this cost over the expected life of the equipment. Depreciation costs are a factor in equipment selection. In *Chart of Accounts,*[2] the American Hospital Association included a reference table for estimating the useful life of major equipment and a formula to calculate composite depreciation rates for each unit of equipment. An item that is more costly to acquire may be less expensive in the long run because of a lower operating cost, long life expectancy, or

Exhibit 4-1 Annual Budget Plan—Based on Fiscal Year July 1 to June 30

Activity	Current Year												Projected Year							
	Jul	Aug	Sep	Oct	Nov	Dec	Jan	Feb	Mar	Apr	May	Jun	Jul	Aug	Sep	Oct	Nov	Dec	Jan	Feb
1. Current budget executed; monthly reconciliation & adjustments made	↑←——————————————————————→																			
2. CEO & Controller develop forecasts; issue budget guidelines to departments							▮													
3. Dept. heads formulate budgets and submit								▮												
4. CEO & Controller develop master budget									▮											
5. Department revisions made and submitted										▮										
6. CEO & Controller finalize budget										▮										
7. Board of Trustee subcommittee review: further adjustments made and final approval given											▮									
8. TRANSITION: close out current year accounts												▨								
9. New fiscal year budget in effect OR tentative budget in effect, pending full approval and/or further revisions													↑———————→							

slower rate of depreciation. This information should be included on the supplemental information forms used to justify equipment selection.

The worksheet for capital expenses includes the account code number from the uniform code of accounts, item description, unit cost, quantity, and total cost (Exhibits 4-2 and 4-3).

SUPPLIES AND OTHER EXPENSES

The many consumable items that are needed for the day-to-day work of the department are listed under the category of supplies. It may be tempting at first to group all these items under "Miscellaneous," but the clear delineation and listing of such items in the appropriate budget category alerts the manager to the magnitude of these costs and facilitates control. Items considered consumable supplies typically include routine items such as pens, pencils, notepads, letterhead stationery, staples, scissors, rubber bands, and paper clips. Postage is included in this category unless it is absorbed as a central administrative line item.

A given department may have special consumable supplies that are essential to its operation. The direct patient care units incur expenses related to medical and surgical supplies. The clinical laboratory has a major expense in reagents. A medical record department has as a major expense the color-coded, preprinted folders used for patient records. Special forms approved and mandated for medical record docu-

Exhibit 4-2 Sample Worksheet for Capital Expenses—Medical Records

Department: Medical Records Fiscal Year: July 1, 1991–June 30, 1992				
Account Code	Account Title: Item Description	Quantity	Item Cost	Total
210.6	Secretarial Desk	1	$760.00	$760.00
210.7	Side Chairs	3	150.00	450.00

Exhibit 4-3 Sample Worksheet for Capital Expenses—Physical Therapy

Department: Physical Therapy Fiscal Year: July 1, 1991–June 30, 1992				
Account Code	Account Title: Item Description	Quantity	Item Cost	Total
210.3	Parallel Bars–10 foot	1	$2,500.00	$2,500.00
210.4	Shoulder Wheel–Deluxe Heavy Duty	1	550.00	550.00

mentation (e.g., the face sheet/identification sheet used in the admission unit, the preoperative anesthesia report form used in the surgical unit, the laboratory requisition/report form for laboratory studies) may be charged to each department as they are requisitioned and used. An alternative practice is to charge the medical record department or central forms design unit with the cost of all preprinted forms. When the emphasis in the budgeting process is on control, however, it is preferable to charge the unit using such supplies so that administrative control may be fixed.

Special expenses commonly incurred at the department level include the lease and rental of equipment, the purchase of technical reference books and periodicals, training and education costs, and travel and meeting expenses. Contractual services for a special activity (such as transcription, microfilming, statistical abstracting, and special laboratory studies) are included under the expense category.

The work sheet for budget requests for consumable supplies and expenses typically includes the required account number from the organization's uniform code of accounts, the item description, the item cost, and the total requested (Exhibits 4-4 and 4-5).

THE PERSONNEL BUDGET

Typically, personnel is the largest category of expense, accounting for as much as 85 percent of the total budget in many cases. Personnel costs include the wage and salary calculation for each position and for each worker, including anticipated raises (e.g., cost of living increases, merit increases) and adjustments resulting from a change in status (e.g., from probationary employee to full-time, permanent employee). The department manager normally calculates these costs; special justification for an increase in the number of positions or for adjustments to individual salaries or wages is also included.

Exhibit 4-4   Sample Worksheet for Supplies and Other Expenses—Medical Records

Department: Medical Records
Fiscal Year: July 1, 1991–June 30, 1992

Account Code	Account Title: Item Description	Quantity	Item Cost	Total
610.2	Annual Professional Dues Paid for Department Head	—	$120.00	$120.00
610.7	Accrediting Agency Regulations Annual Update Subscription	1	90.00	90.00
610.4	Drug Usage Manual, Current Edition	4	28.00	112.00

Exhibit 4-5 Sample Worksheet for Supplies and Other Expenses—Physical Therapy

Account Code	Account Title: Item Description	Quantity	Item Cost	Total
Department: Physical Therapy Fiscal Year: July 1, 1991–June 30, 1992				
322.2	Ultrasound Gel	2	$ 18.00	$ 36.00
322.3	T.E.N.S. Pads	10	12.00	120.00
600.4	Four-Day Education Seminar	—	$125/day	500.00

Also calculated and justified by the department manager are those costs associated with vacation relief, overtime pay, and temporary or seasonal help. Specific support information may be required for these budget requests, such as a calculation of the personnel hours required to give proper departmental coverage and a calculation of the hours not available to the organization because of vacation time and holidays. If there is a high employee turnover rate or a distinct pattern of absenteeism, historical information, such as the average time lost over the past year or several years as a result of these circumstances, may be cited as support information.

In calculating the costs for personnel needs, the manager deals with impersonal costs, that is, those associated with the position, regardless of the incumbent; such costs include the wage or salary range for the position and the number of full-time equivalent positions. In addition, there are other costs that are associated with the incumbent and change with the holder of the position; these costs include those associated with the number of hours scheduled for work each week, the number of years in the job category, the eligibility for merit increases, and the anniversary date for a scheduled increase in pay. The following factors must be considered in any budget calculation:

1. Minimum Wage. Federal law mandates a base pay rate for certain jobs. Some categories of temporary help may be exempt from this wage; the manager must seek the guidance of the personnel specialist for details of this provision.
2. Union Contract Stipulations. Each class of job and each incumbent must be reviewed in light of contractual mandates for basic wage as well as mandatory increases. Where there is more than one contract in effect, the provisions of each contract must be reviewed and applied as appropriate. Wage and salary increases on a straight percentage basis may be mandated. In some cases, the contract may state that either a given percentage or a flat dollar amount, whichever gives the greater increase, is to be awarded. A hiring rate may be indicated for employees on "new-hire" status; a

related job rate may be indicated, with the employee moving to the job rate at the end of the probationary period (Table 4-1).

3. Organizational Wage and Salary Scale. Except for the specific provisions of union contracts, the organizational wage and salary scale applies. Positions are listed by job category or class, and the individual employee's rate is calculated from this scale. Increases may be in terms of a percentage or in terms of step increases dependent on the number of years in the position.

4. Cost of Living Increase. The organizational guidelines and/or contract provisions establish cost of living increases. Frequently, this amount is given as a flat percentage increase added to the base rate of pay, although it may be given as a flat dollar amount added to the base rate of pay.

5. Merit Raise or Bonus Pay. These costs may be shown as an overall amount given to the department as a whole. The manager may not be able to assign dollar amounts to an individual worker at the beginning of a year, since the merit award may not be given until some time period has passed and the worker has earned the increase. Specific guidelines are given to the manager concerning the calculation of merit or bonus pay as part of the base rate of pay or as a one-time increase that does not become part of the employee's base rate of pay.

6. Special Adjustments. From time to time, a special adjustment may be made to the wage or salary structure. An organization that is adjusting its wage and salary structure to satisfy Equal Employment Opportunity Commission (EEOC) mandates may grant a one-time adjustment to a class of workers or an individual (e.g., women and/or minority workers) to bring their rate of pay in line with other workers' pay scales. When long-term employees' rates of pay "shrink" as compared with those of incoming workers, a special one-time adjustment may be made to keep the comparative wages of new versus long-term employees equitable.

The budget worksheet and/or budget display sheet (Exhibit 4-6) generally includes the following items, which progress logically from the factual information based on the present salary of the incumbents to the projected salary through the coming budget period:

Table 4-1 Sample Salary Structure (Clerical)

Pay Grade	Hiring Rate (weekly)	Job Rate (90 calendar days)
B	$280	$300
C	$300	$316
D	$310	$342

Exhibit 4-6　Personnel Budget: Medical Record Department, Fiscal Year July 1 to June 30

Grade Code	Position Title	PT/FT Day Eve.	Incumbent	Current Bi-weekly	Projected Annual Base	Anniv. Date	Projected Annual Increase	Projected Total Salary	Hours Per Pay Period Biweekly
3	Record Locator Clerk	FT-E	H. Reinhold	640	16,640	12-20-91	832	17,472	80
4	Release of Information Clerk	FT-D	T. Maloney	800	20,800	3-17-92	1,040	21,840	80
5	Coding/Abstracting Clerk	FT-D	P. Hart	1,040	27,040	8-6-92	1,352	28,080	80
6	Quality Assurance Assistant	FT-D	M. Caretto	1,120	29,120	5-30-92	1,456	30,576	80

1. Position code or grade code, obtained from the master position code sheet for the department and organization.
2. Position description: abbreviated job title or category.
3. Budgeted full-time equivalents (FTEs): the number of personnel hours per position divided by the hours per full-time workweek. Example (based on a 40-hour workweek):

Worker A	40 hours
Worker B	27 hours
Worker C	20 hours
Worker D	13 hours
	100 = 2.5 FTEs

4. Employee number, usually assigned by personnel division or payroll division for identification of payroll costs and employee records.
5. Employee name: name of incumbent. If position is vacant, this information is noted.
6. Actual FTEs: number of employed workers and number of vacancies (See Exhibit 4-7 for an example of calculating FTEs in the medical records department budget process).
7. Current rate of pay: hourly rate, biweekly rate, or job rate. The hourly rate is calculated by dividing the total salary by the number of work hours per budget period; the biweekly rate, by dividing the total salary by 26. The job rate is usually specified in the wage scale, especially as given in a union contract.
8. Projected annual base salary, calculated by multiplying the rate by the appropriate unit of time. This projected salary is specific to the incumbent. Should the incumbent separate from the organization with the replacement worker hired at entry-level pay, the annual base salary would be lower.
9. Incumbent's anniversary date, used to calculate cost of living or other raise associated with date of employment.
10. Projected annual increase because of cost of living increase, merit or bonus pay, or special adjustments.
11. Projected total salary: present salary plus projected annual increase.

DIRECT AND INDIRECT EXPENSES

A department budget also reflects costs under the categories of direct and indirect expenses. Direct expenses typically include salaries, services and contracts, dues and subscriptions, and equipment. Indirect expenses are charged to the departmental budget on a formula basis or some process of assessment. These indirect costs are associated with the organization as a whole and are pro-

Exhibit 4-7 Calculating FTEs for Medical Record Services

To calculate the number of employee hours needed to process the work in a given function, the manager first establishes the basic definition of a full time equivalent position. This calculation is based on the usual work week as defined by the facility:

one FTE = 40 hours/week

40 hours/week × 52 weeks = 2080 hours/year

The hours needed may be concentrated in one full time position or distributed between two or more part time workers to total 2080 hours/year. The latter method provides flexibility.

The second part of the staffing calculation consists of estimating the volume of work to be done.

Work standard: 24 minutes to process one chart

Volume per day: 30 charts needing DRG assignment

30 charts × 24 minutes = 720 minutes needed

One FTE = 480 minutes per work day

$$480 \overline{)720.0} \quad 1.5$$

Needed: 1.5 FTE to process 30 discharge charts per day

rated per department. Examples of indirect costs and their units of assessment are shown in Table 4-2.

BUDGET JUSTIFICATION

As mentioned earlier, support or explanatory documentation may be required for budget requests. If a particular type of equipment is requested, the manager is expected to explain why that particular model or brand is needed. The reasons may include compatibility with existing equipment, guaranteed service contracts, availability, or durability. Projected patient usage is another element of support data; the acquisition of a particular item may enhance patient care because of its safety features or it may attract more patients to the facility.

Sometimes the facility may need an item simply to remain competitive and thereby retain a given patient population. The budget justification may take the form of a cost comparison, such as that between rental/long-term lease of equipment and outright purchase plus maintenance costs. For a medical record department, a cost comparison between an in-house word processing/transcription unit and a contractual service might be included.

Development of Fee Schedule

In direct patient care services, the details of the fee schedule may be part of the budget support information. The income generated on the basis of the fee sched-

Table 4-2   Indirect Expenses Charged to Medical Record Service

Item	Amount	Basis of Calculation
Fringe benefits/health and welfare	$ 156,000	Percentage of salaries
Equipment depreciation	30,000	Depreciation schedule
Telephone costs (equipment)	8,000	Number of telephones
Maintenance and repairs	2,300	Number of work orders
Physical plant operation (e.g., heat, air conditioning)	42,000	Number of square feet
Building depreciation	6,000	Number of square feet

ule must, at the least, meet expenses. Profit-making institutions must determine their profit base and add this percentage to the established fee schedule. The criteria employed in developing a fee schedule that accurately compensates a department for the services it renders is used as part of the budget justification.

The following discussion describes two ways of developing a fee schedule for a physical therapy department. Many physical therapy departments have established fee schedules primarily on the basis of supply and demand, existing fee schedules in other departments in the community or surrounding area, actual time involved in administering a treatment, the number of modalities used, and cost of equipment. In order to establish an equitable fee schedule, many of these factors should be considered. However, it is also necessary to determine the total costs of providing the physical therapy services.

Time Unit System

One recommended method of establishing a fee for services is the time unit system developed by Jagger and May.[3] Their approach is based on the total cost of providing the services for a specific length of time. Patients pay for services according to the amount of time they spend in the department each day.

Before the fee schedule is established as proposed by Jagger and May, the cost of operating the total program, both direct and indirect costs, must be calculated. Direct costs usually include salaries, fringe benefits, therapeutic supplies, educational travel, and other expenses over which the Director of Physical Therapy has control. Indirect costs usually include charges to the department for services provided by the institution, such as utilities, mail and telephone services, housekeeping and general maintenance, as well as the cost of housing the department. Indirect costs are assigned in many ways, but they are generally computed on the basis of square footage. The hospital accountant or financial officer can assist the department head in gathering this information.

Once the total cost of operating the department has been established, the units of time available to recover that cost through charges to the patient must be determined. Regardless of how many hours per week a department is open, charges can be assessed only on the actual time the therapist has available for patient care. Therapists must also devote some time to support activities, such as attending clinics or rounds, writing notes in the patients' medical records, and meeting with other health care professionals. In addition, therapists provide nondirect patient care, such as supervising patients who may be practicing a skill on their own.

According to the 1990 Active Membership Profile Report published by the American Physical Therapy Association, clinical physical therapy staff (those not in a primary supervisory position) devoted 79.4% of their time to patient care, 20% to administration and supervision, and 7.4% to teaching.[4] Each facility must determine the percentages of available direct and indirect time. These figures vary among general hospitals, medical center teaching facilities, outpatient services, and private practice facilities.

The number of hours the percentages of direct and nondirect time represent for each therapist must be determined. On the basis of a 40-hour week, each therapist is theoretically available 2,080 maximum hours each year. However, vacation time, sick leave, attendance at educational seminars, and other similar activities reduce the total available hours per year. The maximum number and actual number of hours available per therapist for patient care are computed as follows:

1. Maximum number of hours available per therapist per year; weekend coverage not included (52 weeks × 40 hours per week = 2,080).
2. Actual available weeks per therapist per year (52 weeks minus 2 weeks vacation, 1 week sick leave, 1 week educational leave = 48).
3. Actual available hours per therapist per year (48 weeks × 40 hours per week = 1,920).
4. Hours available for direct patient services per therapist (1,920 hours × 60% time spent in direct patient service = 1,152).
5. Hours available for nondirect patient services (1,920 hours × 10% time spent in nondirect services = 192).

After determining personnel time available for direct and nondirect patient care, the manager calculates total FTEs for all personnel involved in the delivery of patient services, that is, full-time and part-time physical therapists and physical therapy assistants. Since the primary role of the physical therapy aides is to provide support services, they are excluded in determining available time units.

The number of time units per hour to be used as the base for the time unit system of fee setting is arbitrary. This unit of time can be 5 minutes, 10 minutes, 20 minutes, or any number of minutes as determined by the department. Most hospitals use 15 minutes as the basic time unit. If 15 minutes is used as the base time unit and there is a professional staff of physical therapists and physical therapy assistants of 6.5 FTEs, the total number of time units available for patient care is determined by multiplying the total available hours by 4:

1. Total time units available for direct patient care (1,152 hours × 6.5 FTE × 4 = 29,952).
2. Total time units available for nondirect patient care (192 hours × 6.5 FTE × 4 = 4,992).
3. Total available time units (29,952 + 4,992 = 34,944).

In many institutions, especially rehabilitation facilities, patients spend additional time practicing activities initially taught by the physical therapists. For example, the physical therapist may be involved with a patient for one hour on a one-to-one basis, and the patient may use the facility for two additional hours to practice activities. Since the patient is using the facility for direct instruction and for practice, it is proper to establish two fees: (1) a personnel time unit fee to cover the cost of all personnel involved in direct care, and (2) a facility time unit fee to cover the time spent in the department during direct and nondirect care time.

To establish the personnel time unit fee charge, the cost of the professional staff (FTEs) involved in providing direct patient care, including their portion of the fringe benefits, is subtracted from the total operating budget of the department (direct and indirect expenses). Next, the cost of professional staff (FTEs) providing direct patient care is divided by the number of time units available for direct patient care, thereby establishing the personnel time unit fee.

$$\frac{\text{Professional staff costs (FTEs)} + \text{fringe benefits}}{\text{Time units for direct care}} = \frac{\text{Personnel time}}{\text{unit fee}}$$

The facility time use fee is computed by dividing the adjusted cost of operating the department (minus the costs of the professional staff and their fringe benefits) by the total available time units.

$$\frac{\text{Adjusted operating cost of the department}}{\underset{\text{time units}}{\text{Total direct}} + \underset{\text{time units}}{\text{Total nondirect}}} = \frac{\text{Facility time}}{\text{unit fee}}$$

The charges to a patient can be seen in the following example. An amputee spends a total of three hours a day in the department: one hour of direct care and two additional hours practicing activities on his own (but still under the supervision of the physical therapy department staff). Using the 15-minute base as the time unit, the patient is charged for the following:

Personnel fee: 4 units
Facility fee: 12 units

The charges determined under the time unit system reflect the patient's use of resources in terms of time, supplies, and a share of the indirect costs.

Modality-based Fee Schedule

The modality-based method is frequently used in physical therapy and occupational therapy departments located within hospitals. In this method, the patient is charged for each modality provided. The modalities are equivalent to the different kinds of treatment or services provided

There are several ways to devise the charge for a modality. The charge could be based on the average time actually needed to perform the modality or the number and level of experience of staff required to carry it out. The advantage of this system is that it provides a clear itemization of the charges both to the patient and the insurance carrier. It is suggested that a maximum limit of charges be established to avoid an excessive fee if many modalities are provided.

The disadvantage of this system is its ambiguity. The average time for a particular modality may differ between patients and therapists. If a patient is receiving several modalities at the same time, the therapist must decide which modality the patient should be charged for. It is important to be as consistent as possible when using this method.

Table 4-3 is an example of a schedule of fees for various modalities (*note*: the maximum charge per visit is $90).

Cost Comparison

Budget justification also includes cost comparison. One example would be that of comparing costs of in-house or commercial storage of medical records. A sample worksheet for this type of cost comparison as shown in Exhibit 4-8.

Table 4-3 Modality-based Fee Schedule

Modality	Charge
Ultrasound	$20
Active Exercises	$30
Electrical Stimulation	$30
Crutch Walking	$30
PNF Exercises	$45
Initial Evaluation	$75
Nerve Conduction Velocity Study	$75
Splint for Upper Extremity	$60

Exhibit 4-8 Worksheet for Comparison of Storage Options

Factors	In-House Hard Copy	Commercial Storage Hard Copy	In-House Microfilm	Service Bureau Microfilm

Personnel
  • labor costs
  • training
Equipment and supplies
  • camera
  • processing equipment
  • supplies
Physical space
  • for equipment
  • for processing
  • for temporary holding
  • for permanent holding
Availability of data/records
  • during processing
  • after processing
  • access time
    —STAT/emergency
    —readmission
    —administrative use
  • additional cost for
    special access
Custom features
  • not allowed
  • done at additional cost
Project completion time
Confidentiality
  • during processing
  • after processing
Bonded/insured
Authentication certificate
  provided
Certificate of destruction
Quality controls
Volume discounts
Total cost per year of
  retention				

BUDGET VARIANCES

During the fiscal year, the manager receives periodic reports showing budgeted amounts versus amounts spent. This report may categorize such information under the headings of "over budget" or "under budget" for the period and for the year. The manager uses this information as a monitoring and control device. A particular unit's budget may include money for overtime that is assigned arbitrarily to budget quarters. A periodic report may show that the manager was over budget in that category for the quarter but not for the year. Such a report is an internal warning system that alerts the manager to that line item. Filed with higher level management, the variance report reflects the manager's awareness of the expenditure for the quarter and its relationship to the yearly amount as a whole. Should there be some unexpected cause for utilizing these overtime funds, such as high absenteeism because of employee illness or injury, this information is noted in the variance report.

Under budget indicators require similar explanations as part of the control process in budgeting. Explanations for under budget items are not required in every instance, but particular attention must be given to large sums that have not been spent because of delay factors in the outside environment. For example, the purchase of a large, expensive piece of equipment may be included in the budget for the fiscal year. If it is not available until the next fiscal year, the delay could throw a carefully planned budget out of balance; that is, funds are not expended in one year, and no funds are allotted for this purchase in the upcoming budget. The manager should anticipate such a situation and make arrangements for the transfer of funds in a timely way.

Direct patient care service budgets include projections of care to be rendered. Actual revenue generated per patient visit is compared with projected revenue. The explanations—over or under projections of care to be rendered—are made by the budget officer for the service. If patient care services are below those projected, plans for increasing services may be included with the explanation.

Example of Variance Analysis

Exhibit 4-9 displays a year-to-date summary of expenditures. The fiscal year in this sample runs from July through June. This report reflects year-to-date costs as posted through April 30, the close of the third quarter. The department manager reviews these figures to:

1. Verify accuracy of posting (making sure costs are posted and none are omitted due to error). The department daily ledgers are compared to this official listing prepared by the finance office.
2. Review specific object codes where the actual costs exceed the approved budgeted amounts. An item may be over budget for the period but not for the year. The manager would note these and prepare explanations.
3. Review specific object codes where actual costs are below the approved budgeted amounts. If the allotted money is not going to be spent in the approved category, the manager may seek approval to use these funds for some other need. Particular attention is given to an under budget category

in which a major expense has been, or soon will be, incurred but which has not yet been posted. Object code 138, Computer License Agreement, reflects a major cost yet to be posted, namely, the fourth quarter payment.

Exhibit 4-9 Summary of Expenditures, Year-to-Date

Cost Center 234		Budgeted	Actual	Over/under
Object Code	Supplies			
021	Printed forms, stationary, office supplies: Vendors	51,999.00	50,000.00	1,999.00
026	Books	400.00	304.80	95.00
027	Journals and magazine subscriptions	620.00	754.00	(134.00 –)
028	General stores, supplies–internal	2,400.00	1,987.00	413.00
035	Parking	-0-	30.00	(30.00 –)
044	Travel	1,700.00	1,483.00	217.00
051	Film rental	-0-	42.00	(42.00 –)
	Supplies–subtotal	57,119.00	54,600.80	2,518.00
Object Code	Services			
122	Contractual temps	850.00	600.00	250.00
131	Equipment rental	2,000.00	1,811.00	189.00
134	Outside contractual service	5,000.00	3,750.00	1,250.00
136	Equipment repair contracts	380.00	31.60	348.40
138	Computer license agreement	12,000.00	9,000.00	3,000.00
	Services–subtotal	20,230.00	15,192.60	5,037.40

NOTES

1. American Hospital Association, *Chart of Accounts* (Chicago: American Hospital Association, 1973).

2. Ibid.

3. Dilys M. Jagger and Bella T. May, "Time Unit System of Fee Setting," *Physical Therapy* 56 (May 1976): 536–40.

4. American Physical Therapy Association, *1990 Active Membership Profile Report* (1991).

5. Joan Gratto Liebler, *Medical Records: Policies and Guidelines* (Gaithersburg, Md.: Aspen Publishers, 1991), 9:10.

Appendix 4-A

Sample Operating Budget— Department of Physical Therapy

(July 1, 1991, through June 30, 1992)

I. Revenue and Income
   A. Inpatient Charges . . . . $ 550,000
   B. Outpatient Charges 310,000
   C. Research Grant Support 29,000
   D. Continuing Education Conference 3,200
   E. Supplies and Equipment Sales 11,500

                Total Revenue $ 903,700

II. Expenses
   Direct Expenses
   A. Salaries . . . . $ 260,000
   B. Consultant 2,500
   C. Honorarium 1,500
   D. Minor Equipment 6,000
   E. Equipment Rental 2,000
   F. Travel 2,500
   G. Telephone 5,000
   H. Supplies 6,000
   I. Postage 350
   J. Xerox Rental 11,000
   K. Advertisement 1,500
   L. Dues 800
   M. Books 350
   N. Equipment Maintenance and Service Contracts . . 2,000

             Total Direct Expenses $ 301,500

Indirect Expenses

A. Employee Benefits (23%)	$ 59,800
B. Administration	23,000
C. Equipment Depreciation	7,200
D. Physical Plant Operation	39,000
E. Maintenance and Repairs	2,000
F. Building Depreciation	6,000
G. Laundry/Linen	2,500
H. Housekeeping	4,900
Total Indirect Expenses	$ 144,400
Total Expenses	$ 445,900
Net Profit or Loss	$ 457,800

Appendix 4-B

Medical Record Department Budget

This budget is based on the following premises:

1. Fiscal year: July through June
2. Work week: 40 hours/week; 2080 hours/year per FTE
3. Cost of living increase: 5% of current base rate (See Table 4B-1 for detailed cost of living calculations by position title.)
4. Effective date of cost of living increase: January 1
5. Overtime rate: time and a half, based on current base for employee
6. Holiday pay: regular base rate (for employees who work on a scheduled holiday: double time, calculated on current base for each employee)
7. Temporary agency rate: average rate is $13.00/hr. for clerical worker, no fringe benefits given
8. Sick pay: calculated on each employee's current base
9. Fringe benefits: 29% of total wages and salaries for the department; 29% for each individual employee
10. Wage and salary calculations are displayed to show these details:

Factor	Example
Current annual base	$ 58,000
July–December of current	
calendar year—total earnings	29,000
January 1 cost of living increase (5%)	2,900
New annual base effective January 1	60,900
January–June of coming calendar	
year—total earnings	30,450
Total needed for full 12 month	
period of the fiscal year	29,000
	30,450
	59,450

134

Table 4B-1 Wages and Salaries by Position Title

Position Title	Current Base	July Through December	January 1 5% Increase	New Base	January Through June	Total For Fiscal Year
Director	$58,000	$29,000	$2,900	$60,900	$30,450	$59,450
Q/A Specialist	34,000	17,000	1,700	35,700	17,850	34,850
DRG Specialist	32,000	16,000	1,600	33,600	16,800	32,800
Release of Information Specialist	21,000	10,500	1,050	22,050	11,025	21,525
Secretary	18,100	9,050	905	19,005	9,503	18,533
Data Control Clerk	16,000	8,000	800	16,800	8,400	16,400
Medical Transcriptionist	22,000	11,000	1,100	23,100	11,550	22,550
Medical Transcriptionist	19,400	9,700	970	20,370	10,185	19,885
Medical Transcriptionist	18,500	9,250	925	19,425	9,713	18,963
Medical Transcriptionist	17,800	8,900	890	18,690	9,345	18,245
Release of Information Clerk	15,200	7,600	760	15,960	7,980	15,580
Registries Specialist	21,000	10,500	1,050	22,050	11,025	21,525
Medical Record Specialist II	17,900	8,950	895	18,795	9,475	18,425
Medical Record Specialist II	12,000	6,000	600	12,600	6,300	12,300
Messenger	10,400	5,200	520	10,920	5,460	10,660
Medical Record Specialist I	15,200	7,600	760	15,960	7,980	15,580
Medical Record Clerk I	13,900	6,950	695	14,595	7,298	14,248

Medical Record Department Budget

PERSONNEL COSTS
Object Code

01	Wages and Salaries	$ 371,539.00
02	Fringe Benefits	107,746.00
03	Vacation Relief Coverage	10,400.00
	Subtotal A	$ 489,685.00

EQUIPMENT
Object Code

10	Stenochairs (6 at $128 each)	$ 768.00
	Automatic Paper Shredder	429.00
	Stepstools (3 at $59 each)	177.00
	Multiterminal Wordprocessing System	74,000.00
	Subtotal B	$ 75,374.00

SUPPLIES
Object Code

021	Printed Forms, Stationary, Office Supplies: Vendors	$ 51,999.00
026	Books	400.00
027	Journals and Magazine Subscriptions	620.00
028	General Stores Supplies–Internal	2,400.00
035	Parking	-0-
044	Travel	1,700.00
051	Film Rental	-0-
	Subtotal C	$ 57,119.00

SERVICES
Object Code

122	Contractual Temporaries	$ 850.00
131	Equipment Rental	2,000.00
134	Outside Contractual Service	5,000.00
136	Equipment Repair Contracts	380.00
138	Computer License Agreement	12,000.00
	Subtotal D	$ 20,230.00

COST TRANSFERS
Object Code

150	Telephone	$ 3,840.00
151	Work Orders	-0-
152	Postage	360.00
153	Photocopy/Print Shop	200.00
154	TV-VCR Rental	-0-
158	Dietary	560.00
	Subtotal E	$ 4,960.00

SUMMARY

Personnel Costs	$489,685.00
Equipment	75,374.00
Supplies	57,119.00
Services	20,230.00
Cost Transfers	4,960.00
Total	$647,368.00

Chapter 5

Decision Making

CHAPTER OBJECTIVES

1. Define the management function of decision making.
2. Identify the participants in the decision-making process.
3. Evaluate a decision's importance.
4. Identify the classic steps in decision making.
5. Relate organizational constraints to decision making through identification of the barriers to rational choice.
6. Identify the bases for decision making.
7. Identify the tools for decision making.

In the planning process, the step involving the choice among alternatives is designated the decision-making phase. Decision making is choosing from among alternatives to determine the course of action. Alternatives may be limited or abundant; in any case, there must be at least two options, or there is no decision, only forced choice. Herbert Simon assigned this function a primary role; he defined decision making as the main function of a manager, the most important activity the manager performs.[1] Simon added that the best way to learn about an organization is to determine where decisions are made and by whom.[2]

PARTICIPANTS IN DECISION MAKING

The decision-making function belongs primarily to top-level management, but it involves interaction among several groups and individuals in the organization. Normally, no major decision is made by any one manager. The organizational hierarchy determines the pattern of participation in the decision-making process. Top-level managers make the pervasive, critical, nonprogrammed, root decisions, such as selection of organizational goals and major policy guidelines, although they may be assisted by technical staff advisers who develop the alternatives based on research and analysis. Line managers may also be consulted.

The organizational structure limits the decision-making ability of all other managers in terms of authority and responsibility for specific departments or units. Such middle managers make decisions for their own units or departments within the framework set by top management rulings. In addition, because middle managers usually have some specific technical competence, they are often key participants in decisions relating to these technical areas. Top management may defer to the technical competence of individual department heads, giving them a specific charge of making final decisions in their areas of expertise. The middle manager's decision mix, then, consists of routine, recurring decisions and nonrecurring decisions in an area of specialized technical competence. For example, the director of an occupational therapy department makes the routine decisions regarding vacation scheduling for department employees in accordance with overall organizational guidelines and makes certain nonprogrammed, critical decisions, such as the selection of equipment for the unit. These latter decisions are made on the basis of the director's specialized knowledge as an occupational therapist.

Rank and file employees are involved in decision making in both direct and indirect ways. Collective bargaining agreements may specify areas in which employees must be consulted. Sometimes their participation is limited to ratification of the contract, but their legitimate, legal claim to participation is recognized to the degree specified in the bargaining agreement. Employees are involved in the decision-making process in a continuous, although indirect, manner; all levels of management depend on the feedback provided by workers who actually perform the day-to-day activities. This feedback process may be formalized, with employees given formal recognition as participants in planning and decision making, as in the management by objectives cycle.

Clients of an organization sometimes participate in decision making. Like employees, clients may have a legitimate claim to participation because of a legislative mandate. For example, the legislation that creates and/or funds community mental health centers or health planning agencies often requires the presence of consumers and community members on advisory councils or even governing boards. Federal and state agencies are required to hold public hearings on certain issues, which fosters client participation in decision making. Members of professional associations also participate in the decision-making process. Although primarily limited to the role of ratifying decisions presented by an elected board and/or by an appointed executive officer, members of such associations can participate more actively should a group of members wish to press a claim.

The decision-making process in health care organizations has an additional dimension in that the medical staff participate in major determinations. Neither clients nor employees in the usual sense of the term, the medical staff have a tradition of involvement in hospital governance. The dual track of authority in health care organizations brings about a special situation for the chief executive officer and for line department heads who report to the administrative officer. Through the committee structure, the medical staff become involved directly in the operations of some departments. In the pharmacy, for example, decisions such as the use of brand names versus generic names in drug selection cannot be made by the pharmacist alone. The pharmacy and therapeutics committee of the medical staff must make the final decision. The day-to-day operations of the medical record department are the responsibility of the medical record administrator, but the medical record committee may have as a charge, stated in the bylaws, the review of the medical record system. Although the actions of the medical staff in these areas are generally limited to suggestions rather than mandates, a limit is imposed nonetheless on the decision-making power of these managers.

Chief executive officers in a health care institution hold a role similar to that of professional managers or hired administrators in an industrial or business corporation. They are not the owners, nor do they have strong kinship ties with the owners. In the case of a hospital under the control and sponsorship of a religious order or a philanthropic group, they may not be members of the sponsoring group. They must make decisions with continual reference to their unwritten mandate: What do the owners or those in authority wish them to decide? The complexities of the decision-making process become evident when the participants and their distinct roles are identified and when the difficulties imposed by the mixed authority constellation in health care organizations are recognized.

EVALUATING A DECISION'S IMPORTANCE

By its nature, decision making means commitment. The importance of a decision may be measured in terms of the resources and time being committed. Some decisions affect only small segments of the organization, while others involve the entire organization. Some decisions are irrevocable because they create new situations. The degree of flexibility that remains after the commitment has been made may also be used in evaluating the significance of a decision: Are the resulting conditions tightly circumscribed, with little flexibility permitted, or are several options still available in developing subsequent plans? Decisions regarding capital expenditures, major procedural systems, and the cost of the equipment that must be prorated over the projected life of the equipment are examples.

The degree of uncertainty—and therefore the degree of risk—associated with a decision is another dimension that must be evaluated in weighing its impact.

The greater the impact in terms of time, resources, and degree of risk, the more time, money, and effort must be directed toward making such decisions. Finally, in any organization, the impact on humans is a major factor. The environmental impact and social cost must be assessed.

STEPS IN DECISION MAKING

The decision-making process consists of several sequential steps: (1) agenda building, including problem definition; (2) the search for alternatives; (3) evaluation of the alternatives; (4) commitment (i.e., the choice among alternatives); and (5) continuing assessment of decisions, which leads back to agenda building.

Agenda Building

Like planning, decision making may be viewed as a cyclic process. The first step, agenda building, flows from the feedback process. Information is gathered, clarified, and analyzed. The problem is defined and priorities are assigned. This step is critical, because subsequent decisions may be meaningless and nonproductive unless the problem has been clarified. Indeed, the wrong problem may be solved, so to speak. Without problem clarification, a manager could implement a solution—possibly one that is costly in time, effort, and personnel—only to find recurring evidence and symptoms of the original problem, which remains unidentified and therefore unsolved.

For example, in a health center, there were long delays from the time of patient arrival until the time of treatment. The nursing and physician team felt under pressure because of patient complaints about the crowded waiting room and the long waits. The first effort to find a solution resulted in a triage system through which patients were assessed promptly and assigned priorities in the treatment process. In addition, considerable effort was made to improve the time allotments and sequencing of patients in the appointment system to help create a more orderly patient flow.

Having developed the triage system, changed the staffing pattern, and revamped the appointment system, the staff was faced with the same crowded waiting room. Why? During the second analysis, the true problem was identified. Because the transportation system in the local community was inadequate, patients tended to come to the center at the beginning of the day or at the end of the noon hour, when family members were free to bring them. There was no other convenient way to get to the center. Furthermore, patients did not understand the appointment system process, nor did they believe that they would be seen at the appointed time.

When the health center, with the assistance of its community board, developed an alternate neighborhood transportation system, the problem was solved. Patient education programs concerning the appointment system were prepared, further helping to alleviate the problem.

Several management processes provide the executive with critical information for use in agenda building and problem identification. Analysis of the institution through use of the input-output model, for example, creates a systematic awareness of change in the organizational environment. Specific feedback processes, such as periodic formal reports and quality control routines, provide specific information for problem identification.

Search for Alternatives

Having defined and analyzed the problem, the decision maker searches for alternatives. It is the manager's job both to identify existing alternatives and to create new and better ones. The manager must remain open to all possible solutions to problems, taking care not to reject nontraditional approaches automatically. Alternatives may be identified quickly from past experience, but these must be accepted with caution because they may not fit the present situation. Creativity is a necessary element. An organizational climate of openness in which the development of original ideas is considered a legitimate use of the manager's time and effort fosters this approach. Coordinated time should be arranged for the management team as a whole, such as periodic team retreats during which day-to-day operations are set aside and the group assesses organizational needs and seeks creative approaches to satisfy these needs.

Chester Barnard, in his classic work on the functions of managers, stressed the importance of identifying the strategic or limiting factors that constrain the realistic development of alternatives.[3] The decision maker should confine the search for alternatives to those that will overcome these elements. This selectivity tends to prevent a waste of time and energy in developing alternatives that are infeasible and ineffective. Limiting factors that constrain decision making in health care include legal and accrediting standards, ethics, and lack of capital and trained personnel. The limiting or strategic factors change from time to time. Barnard saw the strategic factor as the point at which choice applies.[4] The solutions are narrowed to include only those that fit the organizational goals and the availability of resources.

Evaluation of Alternatives

In order to evaluate alternatives, a manager must adopt an underlying philosophical stance and make a preliminary decision about the approach to decision making that will be taken. Depending on the philosophical stance, certain alternatives will be acceptable and others will be excluded automatically. Root and branch decision making, "satisficing," maximizing, and the use of Paretian optimality are among the fundamental types of (or approaches to) decision making that will partially determine the decisions that are actually reached.

Root and Branch Decision Making

Certain decisions are so basic to the organization's nature that their effects are pervasive and far-reaching in terms of organizational values, philosophy, goals, and overall policies. Such decisions, root decisions, invest the organization with its fundamental nature at its inception and carry it into periodic, comprehensive review of its fundamental purpose, often resulting in massive innovation. Thus, in the life cycle of an organization, root decisions may be associated with gestation, when the fundamental form and purpose of the organization are crystallized. They may occur in middle age, when new goals are developed and new organizational patterns are adopted. Finally, during old age and decline, a fundamental decision to dissolve the organization may be made. The pervasive effect of root decisions may be seen in the decision of a board of trustees to change a two-year college into a baccalaureate degree-granting institution or to convert a hospital into a multiple component health care center.

Charles Lindblom described root decisions and their opposite, branch or incremental decisions.[5] According to Lindblom, these incremental, limited, successive decisions do not involve a reevaluation of goals, policies, or underlying philosophy. Objectives and goals are recycled and policies are accepted without massive review and revision. Change is by degree. Only a small segment of the organization is affected.

Branch decision making is more conservative in its approach than is root decision making, with innovation inhibited. The stability of organizational life is enhanced, in many cases, when decision making is of the successive, incremental type, because the manager does not have the option of completely reviewing the organizational structure, functions, staffing patterns, equipment selection, and similar capital expenditures. Incrementalism also simplifies decision making because it tends to limit conflicts that might occur if the patterns of compromise, consensus, organizational territory, and subtle internal politics are disturbed. Incrementalism also may be the simple outcome of previous root decisions. On the other hand, the manager may overlook some excellent alternatives because they are not readily apparent in the chain of successive decisions. Incrementalism lacks the built-in safeguard of explicit, programmed review of values and philosophy.

Satisficing and Maximizing

"It might easily happen that what is second best is best, actually, because that which is actually best may be out of the question." This quotation, attributed to the philosopher-educator Cardinal Newman, expresses the idea contained in the concepts of satisficing and maximizing. In decision making, the one best solution may be determined by developing a set of criteria against which all alternatives are compared until one solution emerges as clearly preeminent. In the form of decision making known as *maximizing*, this one best solution is the only acceptable one.

In the form of decision making known as *satisficing*, a term used by Simon,[6] a set of minimal criteria is developed, and any alternative that fulfills the minimal criteria is acceptable. A course of action that is good enough is selected, with the conscious recognition that there may be better solutions. When the manager seeks several options, satisficing may be employed. As with incrementalism, satisficing obstructs absolute, rational, optimal decision making, yet it simplifies the process. In satisficing, the manager accepts the fact that not every decision need be made with the same degree of intensity.

The Pareto Principle or Paretian Optimality

Vilfredo Pareto (1848–1923) was an Italian economist and sociologist who postulated a criterion for decision making that is referred to as the Pareto principle or Paretian optimality.[7] He suggested that each person's needs be met as much as possible without any loss to another person. In this mode of decision making, certain alternatives are rejected because of the decrease in benefits for one or several groups. Decisions that result in a major gain for one individual with a concomitant major loss for another are avoided. The approach involves compromise and consensus, with each manager accepting the needs of other units of the organization as legitimate and the needs of the organization as a whole as paramount. The concessions and trade-offs in the budget process or in the labor negotiation process illustrate the balance required to satisfy the needs of many departments or groups without penalizing any one (or by penalizing all departments or groups in equal measure if penalization is unavoidable).

Commitment Phase

In the definition of decision making, the essential focus is choice—the specific selection from among alternatives. At some point, deliberation must be ended. If a manager does not make a decision in a timely way, someone else may make the decision. In some rare cases, managers find that alternatives are of equal merit. Should that occur, the manager can simply follow personal preference.

The commitment phase can be divided into stages: the pilot run and sequential implementation. A pilot run to test the chosen alternative helps reduce the risk attached to the decision. For example, a manufacturing company may offer a new product on trial and make further decisions based on the results. Rather than purchasing expensive equipment, managers may choose a leasing arrangement with an option to purchase. Pilot runs have two distinct limitations, however; they are costly in terms of time and money, and they are not always feasible.

In sequential implementation, managers make a basic determination and assess the results before they take the next step in the implementation process. The cycle is shortened; feedback is obtained and alternatives are reviewed and implemented after a relatively short time. During the implementation stage, the decisions must be communicated to those who will carry out the detailed plans that flow from it.

Continuing Assessment of Decisions

The final step in the decision-making process is the continuous analysis of the decision. Through the feedback process, a new agenda is generated and new alternatives are revealed. The steps in the control process provide a link back to the planning and decision-making functions.

BARRIERS TO RATIONAL CHOICE

Managers must recognize that there are barriers to rational choice and that it may not be possible to make the perfect decision because of these subtle barriers. One set of barriers stems from human nature itself—ignorance, prejudice, and resistance to change all influence decision making. If managers do not have the necessary information or if they have it but cannot make use of it because they lack proper training in analysis, their ability to make informed decisions is circumscribed. Prejudice (i.e., preconceived opinion) is another aspect of human nature that must be taken into account. Even with sufficient factual knowledge, the value elements in decisions are inescapable. Resistance to change constitutes a third such barrier; managers may continue to make decisions based on their own past experience.

Together, these barriers constitute an overall impediment: inadequate leadership. Leaders may fail to take risks, choosing the security of incremental change. They may stifle creative thinking in themselves and their subordinates. They may so limit their zone of acceptance that change becomes difficult and decisions by precedent become the only decisions possible. They may ignore feedback, thus reinforcing their own positions and making determinations based on limited facts that are colored by their own value premises.

The internal dynamics of the decision-making process have been studied by psychologists Irving L. Janis and Leon Mann.[*] They identified four situations in which the decision maker fails to reach the ideal of "vigilant information processing":

1. If the risks involved in continuing to do whatever has been done in the past appear low, the individual is likely to go on doing it and is unlikely to collect adequate information about possible alternatives.
2. If the risks of continuing to do whatever has been done in the past appear high and if the risks of an obvious alternative appear low, the decision maker is likely to choose the obvious alternative and again is unlikely to collect adequate information about other possibilities.
3. If all the obvious alternatives seem to involve risk and if the decision maker feels that there is little chance of coming up with a better alternative, the individual is likely to engage in "defensive avoidance" by denying that a problem exists, to exaggerate the advantage of the chosen alternative, or to try to get someone else to make the decision.
4. If the decision maker feels that there is a potentially satisfactory course of action and that this alternative may disappear if there is a delay to investigate other possibilities, the individual is likely to panic, trying to pursue the obvious alternative before it is too late.

Decision makers undertake "vigilant information processing" only if they feel that all the obvious choices are risky, that there may be a better choice that is not obvious, and that there is sufficient time to seek the best possible choice.

Other barriers to rational choice flow from the organizational structure. There may be so much organizational red tape that decision making is limited to decision by precedent. Department managers may lack sufficient authority to make decisions and may be required to submit to a committee process for some decisions. Decisions made in other departments may, in turn, affect their own, but they may have no influence in those areas. There may be a lack of sufficient coordination in decision making throughout the organization. Organizational politics (e.g., bargaining, forming alliances, and choosing "the right time") also subtly limit rational decision making.

Factors related to the social, political, and economic climate outside the organization also act as barriers. The many aspects of law and regulation governing health care set specific limits, for example. Finally, the degree of certainty under which decisions are made tends to impose limits on choice. Under conditions of high certainty, the risk involved in decision making is low and decisions may become routine. After they have been standardized through the use of policies, procedures, and rules, routine decisions may be made at lower levels of the organization. Conditions of relative uncertainty obviously increase risk, and managers attempt to evaluate alternatives in terms of probable payoff. The decision maker's efforts focus on reducing the risk and on developing, as far as possible, quantifiers with which to measure the probable payoff. Statistical analysis of data, market research, and forecasting are a few of the decision-making tools that may be employed in assessing comparative probability. Decisions made under great uncertainty involve the highest level of risk, and the burden for making such decisions belongs to the top echelons of the organization.

BASES FOR DECISION MAKING

Since effective decision making is critical to organizational survival, managers seek to overcome the barriers to rational choice. The bases for decision making range from intuition and serendipity to research and analysis. The manager's previous experience may be a valid basis for decisions, provided that there are no changes in the constraints, nor in the goals to be reached. Managers may draw from the experiences of other similar organizations. This "copy your neighbor" or "follow the leader" approach may provide managers with information they do not currently have. For example, another organization may have research information available, or a manager in another institution may have explored alternatives in great detail and done an analysis that others could profit from. A manager may take the philosophical attitude that it is not necessary to reinvent the wheel and that it is wise to learn from others; however, not only are these approaches based on an assumption that the managers being copied are correct in their decisions, but also they do not take into account the different constraints under which each manager operates.

The creative approach to decision making seeks to capitalize on intuition and serendipity, but the concrete analysis of information is necessary before final determinations are made. Experimentation, research, and analysis constitute the most effective base for selecting among alternatives.

DECISION-MAKING TOOLS AND TECHNIQUES

Managers have available the historical records, information about past performance, and summaries of their own and other managers' experience. In addition, managers may test alternatives through the use of decision-making tools and techniques.

Considered Opinion and Devil's Advocate

A manager may obtain the considered opinion of experts and use the technique of "the devil's advocate" to sharpen the arguments for and against an alternative. In the first instance, the manager asks staff experts or other members of the management team to assess the several alternatives and develop arguments for and against each; the resulting comparative assessment helps the decision maker to select a course of action.

When the devil's advocate technique is used, the decision maker assigns an individual or group the duty of developing statements of all the negative aspects or weaknesses of each alternative. Each alternative is then tested through frank discussion of weaknesses and error before the final decision is made. The underlying theory is that it is better to subject alternatives to strict, internal, organized criticism than to run the risk of having a hidden weakness or error exposed after a decision has been implemented. The devil's advocate does not make the decision but simply develops arguments to ensure that all aspects are considered.

The Factor Analysis Matrix

For the decision maker who must overcome personal preference to make an impartial decision, the matrix of comparative factors is an effective tool of analysis. As a first step, the decision maker develops the criteria under two major categories: essential elements (musts) and desired elements (wants).

The choices available are compared through the development of a table or matrix. The factors can be assigned relative weight, as in a point scale, and the alternative with the highest point value becomes the best option. Even without the weighting factors, the matrix remains useful as a technique of factual comparison. Table 5-1 illustrates the use of the must and want categories to compare equipment for departmental use. A similar process could be used to evaluate applicants for a job; personal bias can be set aside more easily and candidates compared on the basis of their qualifications for the position (Table 5-2 and Table 5-3).

Tbe Decision Tree

A managerial tool used to depict the possible directions that actions might take from various decision points, the decision tree forces the manager to ask the "what then" questions (i.e., to anticipate outcomes). Possible events are included, with a notation about the probabilities associated with each. The basic decisions are stated, with all the unfolding, probable events branching out from them. Decision trees enable managers to undertake disciplined speculation about the consequences, including the unpleasant or negative ones, of actions. Through the use of decision trees, managers are forced to delineate their reasoning, and the constraints imposed by probable future events on subsequent decisions become evident. Each decision tree reveals the probable new situation that results from a decision.

Table 5-1 Matrix of Comparison for Equipment Purchase

	Brand A	Brand B	Brand C
• Maximum cost	Acceptable	Acceptable	$4,000
• Compatibility with related equipment	Yes	Yes	No
• Minimum years of service	No	Yes	Yes
• Availability of service	Yes	Yes	Yes
• Renovation of existing space needed	No	Yes	No
○ Safety features	Yes	Yes	Yes
○ Trade-in value for present equipment	No	No	Yes
○ Available delivery date	Yes	No	Yes
○ Special training for use	No	Yes	Yes
○ Lease option	No	No	Yes

• = must;   ○ = want.

Table 5-2 Matrix for Evaluation of Job Applicants

	Applicant A	Applicant B	Applicant C
• Type at 60 wpm	40 wpm	50	60
• Transcription of medical reports			
at 800 lines/day	600	600	750
Previous experience in this type job	0	1 yr.	1 yr.
Previous experience in related clerical job	Telephone unit clerk	Same	
Yrs. in organization (organizational policy: preference for internal applicants)	3 yrs.	1 yr.	0
• Willing to accept salary of $19,100	Yes	Yes	Prefers higher; wants raise within six months
• Full time	Yes	Yes	
• 3 P.M. to 10 P.M. shift acceptable	Yes	Yes	Prefers day; plans to switch as soon as opening is available

It is possible to use a decision tree without including mathematical calculations of probability, although computers are commonly used to calculate the probability of events when such detailed information is available. Managers in business corporations with sufficient market data about profit, loss, patterns of consumer response, and national economic fluctuations include these data in the construction of a decision tree for the marketing of a new product, for example.

Table 5-3 Matrix for Selection of Relief Therapists

Factor	Applicant A	Group 1	Group 2
Willing to work weekends/ evenings	1 x month	Yes	Bi-monthly
Same person	Yes	No	Share 2 therapists
Experience	2 years	Extensive	Extensive
Continuity with staff	Yes	No	Limited
Salary	$35/hr	$30/hr	$50/hr
Response to calls	Within 48 hrs.	Within 4 hrs.	Within 2 hrs.
Reputation	Fine	Excellent	Excellent/master clinicians

The Director of OT met with the senior staff and decided that salary, continuity with staff, and response to calls were "must" areas. They decided to compromise on continuity with the staff and took a chance and hired Group 1 for a trial. They decided to give the group 60 days to work with them and to evaluate their level of performance for 30 days.

Managers who lack detailed information of this type can still use decision trees to advantage. In developing a decision tree, these managers use symbols to designate points of certainty and uncertainty. For example, events of certainty may be placed in rectangles; events of uncertainty, in ovals. This technique emphasizes the relative risk in each decision track. The goal to be reached is the continual reference point. The sequence of decisions that leads to the goal with the least uncertainty emerges as a distinct track, thereby facilitating the manager's decision. For decisions in which the manager has intense personal involvement, this approach is a valuable aid in overcoming emotional barriers to objective choice.

Operations Research

During World War II, operations research was developed when the military in Britain and in the United States faced massive logistical problems. Because there was not enough time to carry out research and trial runs, conditions were simulated using models that permitted greater experimentation. Management literature contains three terms, used interchangeably at times, that reflect this process of model building to analyze decision alternatives: *operational research, operations research*, and *management science. Operational research*, the earliest term used, was shortened to *operations research* as the processes were applied to business practices.

The use of operations research, with its extensive mathematical analyses and probability calculations, became broadly feasible with the development of computer technology. By definition, operations research is an applied science in which the scientific method is brought to bear on a problem, process, or operation. It is a technique for quantitative problem solving and decision making in which mathematical models are applied to management problems. Three major steps are included in operations research techniques:

1. Problem Formulation. The problem is stated and preconceived notions are set aside.
2. Construction of a Mathematical or Conceptual Model. This is usually done through equations or formulas representing and relating critical factors that are involved in the problem under analysis.
3. Manipulation of Variables. This is done to develop and assess alternatives in terms of designated criteria.

Simulation and Model Building

Simulation is the representation of a process or system by means of a model. A model is a logical, simplified representation of an aspect of reality. Models range from simple (e.g., physical models) to complex (e.g., models consisting of mathematical equations). Since legal, ethical, and economic constraints limit the manipulation of reality, experimentation may be carried out on the representation of reality (i.e., the model) rather than on reality itself. Through the development of models, managers attempt to gain additional information about the uncertainties in a situation; those elements are brought into focus and assessments are made concerning the degree of chance associated with them.

Managers use several models routinely. For example, they may use a physical model of the office layout, reducing in scale the dimensions of the office space and equipment. During an in-service training session, a manager in a health-related profession may use one or several physical models, such as a model of a body organ. An organization chart is a graphic model of departmental and authority relationships. A decision tree is a schematic model of plans or decisions. Analog and mathematical models are the most complex, with mathematical models the most abstract. Some models are developed through reasoning by analogy (analog model); a problem is approached indirectly by setting up an analogous situation, solving it, and making a similar application to the original problem. The model for one problem is converted into a form suitable for a different problem.

Stochastic Simulation

A model designed to include the element of randomness is called a stochastic simulation model. Stochastic is derived from the Greek word meaning guess or not certain. The Monte Carlo method is a form of stochastic simulation in which data are developed through the random number generator. Where the variables are uncertain, at least a sample of their values may be assigned through the development of a statistical pattern of distribution. In this way, managers may simulate such occurrences as employee absenteeism, patient arrivals, or equipment failures. The Monte Carlo technique involves factors of change and their effect on the process or system. Probability sampling is used extensively with simulation and model building.

Waiting Line and Queuing Theory

In any organization in which the demand for service fluctuates, managers must balance the cost of waiting lines with the cost of preventing waiting lines through increased service. Waiting lines or queues are a common everyday experience: customers in a grocery store, cars at a toll gate, airplanes stacked to land, patients in a clinic or emergency room, telephone requests for information. A characteristic of such queues is the randomness of demand. Waiting line or queuing theory is useful for analyzing those situations in which the units to be provided for the service are relatively predictable. The underlying premise is that delays are costly, yet too little activity on another occasion is also costly. For example, hospital emergency room resources are costly when not used; however, the cost in terms of patient pain, aggravation, and inconvenience must be taken into account if an emergency arises and there is a delay in treatment.

There are three basic components in waiting line analysis: arrivals, servicing, and queue discipline. The unit of arrival is defined (e.g., grocery orders to be rung up, planes to be landed, or patients to be examined). The pattern of arrival is studied to determine probabilities of arrival. Arrivals can be divided into three categories:

1. predetermined arrivals, such as scheduled airplane landings or scheduled patient appointments
2. random arrivals, such as emergency landings at an airport or patient arrivals at a walk-in clinic or emergency unit
3. combination of predetermined and random arrivals, such as arrivals at a clinic with both scheduled appointments and a walk-in system

Servicing is the focus of analysis of the workflow; the service is defined in terms of number of units and time needed for each pattern of distribution. Analysis of these data shows both random and constant factors that must be taken into account when procedures are developed. Various control processes are developed to smooth these internal activities. Queue discipline involves an analysis of the patterns or characteristics of the waiting line, such as the average minimum and maximum wait, the number of lines, and the manner in which units are selected for service (e.g., first come, first served; random selection; a triage system according to severity of problem or ease of processing; a priority and preference system). Through the analysis of such information, managers can make informed decisions to overcome the negative aspects of waiting lines (delay for patients) and the cost to the organization (idle equipment, over-staffing).

Gaming and Game Theory

Gaming is the simulation of competitive situations in which the element of uncertainty is introduced as a result of some other, often competing, decision maker's action. In the management field, games give reality to training situations and to the decision-making process. Unlike other forms of simulation, gaming uses human decisions, although they may be computer-assisted.

Game theory is a branch of mathematical analysis of conflict and strategy; it is associated with the concepts of zero sum games and minimax strategy. Both involve theoretical situations in which competitive conditions are central; they are based on the premises that each competitor acts rationally and seeks to max-imize gain, to minimize loss, and to outwit the other competitors. Game theory remains relatively undeveloped because of the complexities that arise once the number of contestants or rules is increased.

Gaming and game theory are separate, distinct concepts, although somewhat related. These techniques of operations research are costly means of testing alternatives, yet they are less expensive than a monumental mistake. By making dry runs possible, these methods clarify the size of the risks.

HEALTH CARE PRACTITIONERS AS DECISION MAKERS

The health care practitioner in a managerial role faces decision-making situations on a routine basis. There are three levels of decisions that the manager must make: decisions regarding day-to-day operations, decisions regarding the development of department resources, and decisions that affect the entire organ-ization and sometimes even society at large. Each of these levels of decision making affects the other levels.

Operational decisions are the bread and butter decisions that seem routine, yet they are the foundation of any department's operations. They include deci-sions about vendors, department scheduling, staffing patterns, patient safety procedures, department regulations, and program planning. For example, sup-pose George G., an occupational therapy manager, decided to use a more expen-sive vendor for ADL equipment because the products were superior to those of other vendors. Before finalizing his decision, George discussed it with his direct supervisor and the business manager of the hospital. George realized that the added cost would affect other parts of the organization and that product superiority had to be weighed against other organizational needs. George argued that the superior products would be cheaper in the long run because equipment maintenance would be minimized and patient safety would be protected.

Each manager must also make decisions that impact on department resources. The health care industry is currently expanding in cost while offering few areas of resource growth, and managers are struggling to direct resources to their patients. This requires the skillful use of formal and informal power.

Organizational decisions require the manager to concentrate on the department's relationship to the total organization. Many staff-level personnel are unable to appreciate the complex demands of the organization. They also have a parochial view of the organization's needs. The successful manager translates the needs of the organization into ideas that the department staff understands and appreciates. No group totally agrees with all organizational demands, but the manager should try to match the needs of personnel with the needs of the organization. To accomplish this delicate balancing act, the manager must have a comprehensive understanding of the organization's hierarchy, resources, and personnel.

CASE STUDIES

The elements of decision making are embodied in the following cases drawn from typical management situations in a health care setting.

Helen R. is an experienced home health administrator. An O.T.R. with a master's degree in business administration and five years of experience, she recently joined the staff of a nonprofit home health agency as its director of professional services. Her duties include the supervision of nurses, physical therapists, occupational therapists, and home health aides. She realized that several hurdles would have to be overcome if the full authority of the position were to be realized. For example, Helen observed that she would have to change the informal power structure of the agency if she wanted to fulfill her formal role.

The factors that Helen found were these:

1. The management of the agency consisted of the owner-director and his wife. Both had experience in operating a wholesale business, but neither had any experience in health care delivery.
2. Madeline B. managed the nursing and home health aide units. She was efficient and knowledgeable, but she seemed controlling

and tactless during supervisory meetings. Staff rarely remained with the agency for more than 11 months.

3. Madeline avoided Helen and never talked about patient care matters.

4. The agency contracted for physical therapy services from a private practice group. These practitioners were not employees of the agency.

5. Occupational therapy services were also obtained from private practice groups on a contract basis.

Helen confirmed her observations during the next two weeks. She listed her priorities: (1) to increase her visibility in the social system by establishing her credibility as an expert and (2) to fashion an appropriate role for the position of director of professional services.

Initially, Helen did not have the power to assume the duties of her role formally. The director and his wife not only seemed uninterested in helping her but also appeared not to understand why they had hired her, other than a general recognition that the agency "ought to have a director of professional services because several other agencies had such a position." Since Madeline enjoyed so much informal power, Helen would have to build her own role over a period of time.

To solidify her formal position, Helen developed a strategy. She would offer her expert opinions to the director and his wife. These would be cost-effective and at the same time would benefit her own position. Helen decided to avoid direct confrontation with Madeline until she had accrued more status in the organization. Helen's ability to select her issues marks her as an experienced manager. The decision to increase her status as she created more income for the agency was a creative use of opportunity and resources.

Helen accomplished her goal by role expansion. She hired three occupational therapists and two speech pathologists. She met with the director of the physical therapy practice group and selected her contract professionals carefully, hiring individuals who would support her in her role as director of professional services. The introduction of new services increased the agency's revenues. Because of the increase in patient referrals, Helen added a second nursing supervisor, making sure that this nursing supervisor also accepted Helen's role as overall director of professional services. Madeline's informal power was thus diluted by a series of formal and informal actions. Helen's decisions were calculated risks.

A second example offered here for analysis is presented in a summary form to highlight the decision-making elements:

1. Problem definition.
   a. Whether to retain John J., staff therapist, or lay him off.
   b. Background of the problem:
      (1) John is the senior therapist in the rehabilitation department of a municipal hospital. He has worked at the hospital for seven years.
      (2) John's work has been deteriorating over the past two years. He comes to work late, is slow to start, takes numerous breaks, and does not seem interested in his patients. Several employees have reported that he is alcoholic.
      (3) John has been absent from work without telephoning to report the reason. This has created bad feelings among the other staff, as it makes last-minute scheduling changes necessary.
      (4) John's supervisor has discussed his situation with him every other week for the past six months. She would like to offer him an extended leave at half pay until he is "better."
2. Search for alternatives. The supervisor made an appointment with the physician-director of rehabilitation services. Together, they searched for alternatives:
   a. Give employee formal notice of unsatisfactory performance, stipulating that, if he fails to improve, he will be placed on probation.
   b. Insist that employee enter a counseling program offered to employees.
   c. Demote employee, with a subsequent decrease in pay and benefits.
   d. Leave employee alone to work out his problems.
3. Evaluation of alternatives.
   a. Giving him notice seems drastic since he has senior status. This alternative could be used later if other measures fail.
   b. Counseling seems most promising, but what happens if employee refuses to enter the program?
   c. Demotion requires much documentation and does not address the real problem.
   d. Leaving employee alone has been tried, and the results were not successful.
4. Commitment: choice of alternative.
   a. Offer employee the option of seeking counseling. Stipulate that his work must improve or he must suffer the consequences. Give employee a written summary of conference.
   b. Other alternatives are eliminated at present time.
5. Assessment.
   a. Employee's performance will be monitored and appropriate documentation will be developed over a specified time frame.
   b. If employee's performance does not improve, supervisor must begin the decision-making cycle again, redefining the problem and assessing alternatives in the light of new information.

The following example illustrates the entire decision-making cycle, which starts with problem identification and concludes with the assessment phase.

> Karen J. read a newspaper article on pediatric AIDS. She was moved by the article and wondered if HIV positive children were enrolled in school where she worked. She wanted to help the children lead productive and satisfying lives.

1. Problem definition:
   a. Finding out if HIV-infected children were present in the school population, if they had an appropriate need for therapy, and if they should be treated by staff.
   b. Background of problem:
      (1) The board of education offered no programs or information about HIV-infected children to parents, teachers, therapists, or staff.
      (2) Several experienced staff members were threatening to quit if they were "forced" to treat HIV-infected children.
      (3) The staff failed a self-test on basic facts about HIV infection, universal precautions, and personal safety issues.
      (4) Karen spoke with her administrator about the problem and discovered that the school board had voted to continue to offer programs to each HIV-infected child as long as the staff understood the universal precautions and the child had bowel and bladder control and had no open sores.
      (5) Karen reviewed the codes of ethics of the professionals on her staff. The codes clearly stated that the professionals were to treat individuals in need as long as the individuals posed no danger to them.
2. Search for alternatives: Karen met with her supervisor and discussed alternatives.
   a. The assistance of several organizations that offered programs on pediatric AIDS could be enlisted.
   b. Karen could insist that staff members treat HIV-infected children or be dismissed.
   c. Staff members refusing care to appropriate referrals could be counselled outside of the department.
   d. Biweekly in-service meetings could be scheduled to expose staff members to more information about AIDS.
   e. Parents of HIV-infected children could discuss their children's needs in small meetings with resistant staff members.
   f. Professionals who treat HIV-infected children could teach staff members how to use universal precautions to avoid exposure to the infection.

3. Evaluation of alternatives.
   a. Organizations that offer educational materials and volunteer speakers were anxious to visit the department. Since the cost was minimal and the staff were willing to listen, this was viewed as an important first step.
   b. Given the shortage of physical and occupational therapists, this seemed like an unwelcome solution. Besides, the staff would still be ignorant about HIV infection and how the disease is spread.
   c. The shortage of staff and the assignment of patients by diagnosis was contrary to ethical practice.
   d. As noted, education and the sharing of feelings about HIV infection were proven ways to combat staff ignorance about the disease.
   e. These meetings might break down the therapists' preconceived notions about HIV-infected children and their caregivers, but the therapists would need to expend valuable time in meeting with and talking to the children and their family members.
   f. Other professionals prepared to share their precautionary techniques would need to be compensated for their teaching time. The cost for two professionals to visit on site and offer a full-day program was $1,000. Karen decided that this option was too costly and that universal precautions could be taught to her staff by the nursing staff for no cost.
4. Commitment.
   a. Karen decided to choose the least expensive alternative, which she felt had been proven successful by other groups. Individuals need time to grasp the facts about HIV infection and also to explore their own feelings about the disease, individuals who test positive, and children who are born with the disease. Although the education route seemed logical, it required a commitment of time and offered no guarantee that staff would agree to treat the children.
   b. Other alternatives were rejected at this time but they could be embraced later if the results from the present program were unsatisfactory.
5. Assessment.
   a. Karen selected a cost-effective solution that did not use sanctions.
   b. Given poor results, Karen could modify her plan and use punitive actions to get results.

CLINICAL REASONING

Recently, professional educators and master clinicians have been focusing on problem identification rather than on the specific techniques needed to solve patient problems. Contextual problem solving was identified by Donald Schon as a needed means to address the complexities of professional service delivery.[9] Schon suggests that professionals need to learn how to help clients or patients to frame their problems rather than rushing in to do something which may offer no real help.

Clinical reasoning is important for managers because it offers an orientation that promotes the integration of theory and practice. Physician, nursing, dental hygiene, and occupational therapy researchers are exploring how professionals make clinical decisions. Rather than rely on a single theory, practitioners generate hypotheses about their patients. These hypotheses are either supported by additional data gathering and experience or are refined and changed. Reliance on cause-effect reasoning is expanded, so practitioners are encouraged to think contextually.

Occupational therapy researchers hypothesize that therapists use three types of approaches in dealing with patients: procedural, interactive, and conditional. The procedural approach focuses on using knowledge and skill to treat the specific clinical conditions. This approach requires thorough understanding of interventions and techniques. The practitioner asks, "What is the clinical problem to be solved and what procedures should I use to treat it?[10] The interactive approach focuses on the relationship between the practitioner and the patient. In talking about feelings and problems, trust and rapport are established. Here the therapist asks, "Who is this person and how should I interact with him or her?"[11] Finally, in the conditional approach, the practitioner "puts it all together,"[12] moving easily between the other two approaches and attempting to tailor the treatment to best serve the patient's needs. Balancing knowledge, experience, facts, and circumstances, intuitive thinking is considered essential in this process.[13] Managers can use clinical reasoning to increase interest in quality care, promote research, and generate new knowledge. The complexity of delivery of allied health services can then be described factually for physicians, family members, government and civic officials, and fiscal intermediaries.

NOTES

1. Herbert Simon, *Administrative Behavior* (New York: MacMillan, 1957), preface and chap. 1.

2. Ibid.

3. Chester Barnard, *The Functions of the Executive* (Cambridge, Mass: Harvard University Press, 1968), 202.

4. Ibid., 205.

5. Charles Lindblom, "The Science of Muddling Through," *Public Administration Review*, Spring 1959, 79–88.

6. Herbert Simon, *Models of Man* (New York: John Wiley & Sons, 1957), 207.

7. Vilfredo Pareto, *Mind and Society* (New York: Harcourt, Brace, & Co., 1935).

8. Irving L. Janis and Leon Mann, *A Psychological Analysis of Conflict, Choice and Commitment* (New York: The Free Press, 1978).

9. Donald Schon, *Educating the Reflective Practitioner* (San Francisco: Jossey-Bass, 1987).

10. M. Fleming, *The Therapist with the Three-Track Mind* (Rockville, Md.: AOTA Practice Symposium, 1989), 72.

11. Ibid.

12. Ibid.

13. P. Bermer and S. Tenner, "Clinical Judgement: How Expert Nurses Use Intuition," *American Journal of Nursing* (1987): 23–31.

Chapter 6

Organizing

CHAPTER OBJECTIVES

1. Define the management function of organizing.
2. Identify the basic steps in the process of organizing.
3. Define key concepts: hierarchy, chain of command, splintered authority, concurring authority.
4. Cite factors that shape the span of management.
5. Differentiate between line and staff relationships.
6. Identify basic line and staff relationships.
7. Recognize the dual pyramid arrangement in health care patterns of authority.
8. Identify the basic patterns of departmentation.
9. Relate temporary departmentation and matrix organization to the need for organizational flexibility.
10. Identify the principles for constructing an organizational chart.
11. Identify the elements of job description development.
12. Identify the uses of the job description.

Organizing is the process of grouping the necessary responsibilities and activities into workable units, determining the lines of authority and communication, and developing patterns of coordination. It is the conscious development of role structures of superior and subordinate, line and staff. The organizational process stems from the following underlying premises:

- There is a common goal toward which work effort is directed.
- The goal is spelled out in detailed plans.
- There is need for clear authority-responsibility relationships.
- Power and authority elements must be reconciled so that individual inter-actions within the organization are productive and goal-directed.

- Conflict is inevitable but may be reduced through clarity of organizational relationships.
- Individual needs must be reconciled with and subordinated to the organizational needs.
- Unity of command must prevail.
- Authority must be delegated.

THE PROCESS OF ORGANIZING

The immediately identifiable aspects of the organizational process include clear delineation of the goal in terms of scope, function, and priorities. For example, will a health care institution focus on acute care for inpatients or comprehensive care, including outpatient care, even home care? Will the organization expand its services through decentralized locations and active outreach programs?

The development of a specific organizational structure must be considered. What degree of specialization will be sought? Specialization is a major feature of health care organizations; it is dictated and shaped in part by the specific licensure mandates for each health profession. The manager must assess the question of line and staff officers and units. A major organizational question concerns the division of work. What will be the pattern of departmentation? The development of the organization chart, the job descriptions, and the statements of interdepartmental and intradepartmental workflow systems must be assessed and implemented as part of the management function of organizing. Finally, the changes in the internal and external organizational environment must be monitored so that the organizational structure can be adjusted accordingly.

In summary, the basic steps of organizing are these:

1. goal recognition and statement
2. review of organizational environment
3. determination of structure needed to reach the goal (e.g., degree of centralization, basis of departmentation, committee use, line and staff relationships)
4. determination of authority relationships and development of the organizational chart, job descriptions, and related support documents

FUNDAMENTAL CONCEPTS AND PRINCIPLES

Relationships in formal organizations are highly structured in terms of authority and responsibility. The resulting hierarchy, that is, the arrangement of individuals into a graded series of superiors and subordinates, authority holders, and rank and file members, constitutes one of the most obvious characteristics of formal organizations. A pyramid-shaped organization tends to result from the development of a hierarchy (Figure 6-1).

The flow of authority and responsibility that can be observed in the hierarchy constitutes a distinct chain of command, also referred to as the *scalar principle:* the chain of direct authority from superior to subordinate. Unity of command can be expected to prevail. Unity of command is the uninterrupted line of authority from superior to subordinate so that each individual reports to one and only one superior. A clear chain of command shows who reports to whom, who is responsible for the actions of an individual, who has authority over each worker.

The authority delegated to any individual must be equal to the responsibility assigned. This principle of parity—that responsibility cannot be greater than the authority given—ensures that individuals can carry out their assigned duties without provoking conflict over their right to do so. In developing policies and documents that support the organizational chart, managers must avoid contradicting this principle. At the same time, managers cannot so completely dele-

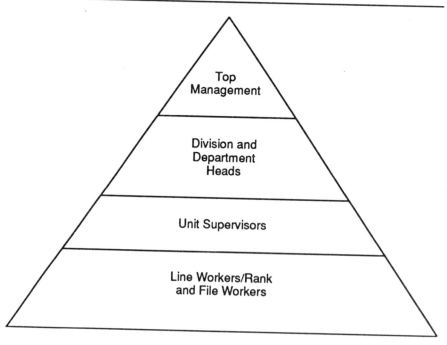

Figure 6-1 Pyramidal Hierarchy

gate authority that they become free of responsibility. This is reflected in the principle of the absoluteness of responsibility; authority may (and must) be delegated, but ultimate responsibility is retained by the manager. This, in turn, is the basis of the manager's right to exercise the necessary controls and require accountability.

Normally, managers have adequate authority to carry out the required activities of their divisions or units without recourse to the authority possessed by other managers. Two situations occur, however, in which the authority of a single manager is not sufficient for unilateral decision making or action. Occasionally, because the work must be coordinated and because there are necessary limits on each manager's authority, a problem cannot be solved or a decision made without pooling the authority of two or more managers. These problems of splintered authority are overcome in three ways: (1) the managers may simply pool their authority and make the decision or solve the problem; (2) the problem may be referred to a higher level of authority until it reaches a single manager with sufficient authority; or (3) reorganization may be done so that recurring situations of splintered authority are eliminated. Such recurring situations sometimes require adjustment in the delegation of authority.

Concurring authority is sometimes given to related departments to ensure uniformity of practice. For example, the packaging department of a manufacturing company cannot change specifications without the agreement of the production division. A data processing manager in a health care setting may be given concurring authority on any form design changes, although this is the primary responsibility of the medical record practitioner, in order to foster compatibility throughout the information processing function. Concurring authority, as a control and coordinating measure, can be a normal part of the routine check and balance system. Splintered authority and concurring authority are the natural consequences of the division of labor and specialization that make it necessary to coordinate the authority delegated to different managers.

THE SPAN OF MANAGEMENT

If authority is to be delegated appropriately, consideration must be given to the number of subordinates a manager may supervise effectively. Four terms are used to refer to this concept: *span of management, span of control, span of supervision,* and *span of authority.* Stated another way, the span of management is the number of immediate subordinates who report to any one manager. It is essential to recognize that the number of individuals whose activities can be properly coordinated and controlled by one manager is limited.

There is no ideal span of management, although a span of 4 or 5 subordinates at higher levels and a span of 8 to 12 at the lower levels have been suggested.

Modifying factors shape the appropriate span of management for any authority holder, however. These factors include the following:

- Type of Work. Routine, repetitive, and homogeneous work allows a larger span of management.
- Degree of Training of the Worker. Those who are well trained and well motivated do not need as much supervision as a trainee group; the more highly trained the group, the larger the span of management may be.
- Organizational Stability. When the organization as a whole, as well as the specific department, is stable, the span of control can be wider; when there are rapid changes, high turnover, and general organizational instability, a narrower span of control may be needed.
- Geographical Location. When the work units are dispersed over a scattered physical layout, sometimes even involving separate geographical locations, closer supervision is necessary to control and coordinate the work.
- Flow of Work. If much coordination of workflow is needed, there is a companion need for greater supervision and a narrow span of control.
- Supervisor's Qualifications. As the amount of training and experience of the supervisor increases, the span of control for that supervisor may increase also.
- Availability of Staff Specialists. When staff specialists and selected support services, such as a training or personnel development department, are available, a supervisor's span of management may be widened.
- Value System of the Organization. In highly coercive organizations, a supervisor may have a large span of management, since there is a pervasive system to help ensure conformity, even to the extent of severe punishment for deviation from the rules. In a highly normative organization, however, there may be an emphasis on participation in planning and decision making and a resultant complexity in the communication process; thus, a smaller span of management may be appropriate. In health care organizations, traditionally normative settings with respect to the professional worker, the span of management may be large because the health care professional is a specialist within an area and does not always require close supervision.

As an example, the span of management in an occupational therapy department is shown in Figure 6-2. The relationship of other units in the division, as well as the relationship of the division to other divisions in the organization, can be seen. Figures 6-3 and 6-4 illustrate other organizational arrangements.

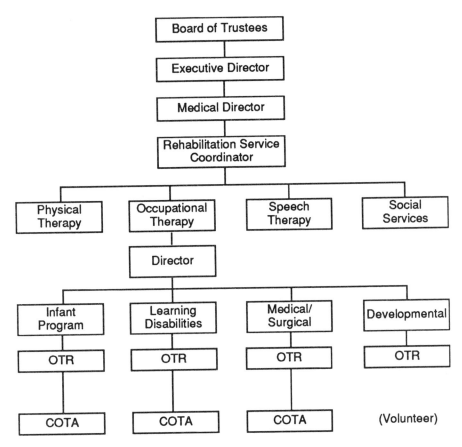

Note: OTR = Occupational Therapist Registered; COTA = Certified Occupational Therapy Assistant.

Figure 6-2 Organizational Chart of Bentwood Hospital for Children

LINE AND STAFF RELATIONSHIPS

The terms *line* and *staff* are key words in any discussion of organizing. In common usage, *staff* refers to the groups of employees who perform the work of a given department or unit. The director of nursing speaks of the nursing staff, the chief dietitian discusses the dietary staff, and the physicians who practice in a hospital are referred to as the medical staff.

In management literature, a differentiation is made between line and staff departments or officers. *Line* refers only to those that have direct responsibility for accomplishing the objectives of the organization, and *staff* refers to those that help the line units achieve the objectives. In a health care organization, direct patient care units are considered to perform line functions, and all other units are listed as staff services. The problem with this distinction becomes apparent when it must be applied to such units as the dietary, purchasing, or housekeeping departments; are these functions any less essential to the operation of a health care organization than a direct patient care unit? Some authors prefer to list such units as service departments, reserving the term *staff* for a specific authority relationship.

The concept of line and staff was inherited by management theorists from the military of the 18th and 19th centuries. An examination of a typical military encounter during this era makes it easier to conceptualize the notions of line and staff. The soldiers literally formed a line; the immediate commanding officers were those who commanded the line, that is, line officers. The actual fighting of the battle was the duty of these troops and officers. In turn, these troops and

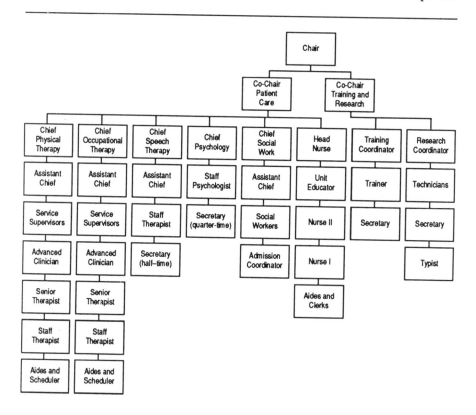

Figure 6-3 Department of Rehabilitation Medicine Organizational Chart. *Source:* Courtesy of Joanne Cassidy, MEd, OTR/L, Chief Occupational Therapist, Department of Rehabilitation Medicine, Thomas Jefferson University Hospital.

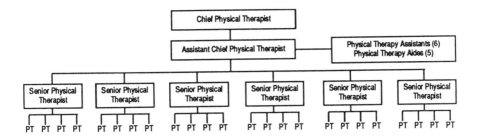

PT = Physical Therapist

Note: Each physical therapy team has assigned to it a cross section of disabilities and may include patients who are paraplegic, quadriplegic, hemiplegic, arthritic, or amputees or have multiple sclerosis, spina bifida, cerebral palsy, and so on. One physical therapy assistant is assigned to each team. The five aides are assigned various duties (i.e., transporting patients or helping out in the hydrotherapy room, the therapeutic exercise rooms, the functional therapy room, etc.). Their specific assignments for the shift are made by the assistant chief physical therapist.

Figure 6-4 Physical Therapy Department Organizational Chart

---

officers were assisted by staff officers and other units that provided logistical support, supplies, and information. The idea carried over as formal bureaucratic organizational theory developed in the 19th century.

The Relationship of Line and Staff Authority

The term *staff* also connotes a certain kind of authority relationship. Again, the original usage of the term was derived from the military, in which the staff assistant pattern was developed as a means of relieving commanders of details that could be handled by others. The staff officer was an "assistant to" the commander, and this assistant's authority was an extension of line authority.

Line authority is based on a direct chain of command from the top level of authority through each successive level of the organization. A manager with line authority has direct authority and responsibility for the work of a unit; the line manager alone has the right to command others to act. A staff assistant provides advice, counsel, or technical support that may be accepted, altered, or rejected by the line officer.

Functional authority is the right of individuals to exercise a limited form of authority over the specialized functions for which they are responsible, regardless of who exercises line authority over the employees performing the activities. For example, the data processing staff is responsible for developing and implementing a specific computerized data collection system. The unit manager has functional authority over processing input documents, although these documents may be originated and completed by workers in other units, such as the admission office, business office, nursing service, or medical record service. A personnel officer may be charged with monitoring organizational compliance with affirmative action programs or labor union contracts; the advice of such an officer could not be rejected or altered arbitrarily by a line officer.

A staff officer or manager may hold a staff position. Such an individual may be the designated officer in charge of a support department, such as the legal or personnel department. Yet, this manager may also have charge of one or several workers within the unit and would exercise line authority within that unit. Organization charts, job descriptions, and similar documents should contain clear statements as to the nature of each position: whether it is a line or staff position, what kind of authority it possesses, and what its area of responsibility is.

Line and Staff Interaction

Various types of staff arrangements may be developed to channel line and staff interaction. As noted earlier, one basic mode of interaction is to designate a staff member as the personal assistant to an individual holding office in the upper levels of the organization. This position should not be confused with that of an assistant department head or assistant manager, who generally shares in direct line authority. Managers in the upper levels of the organization may have several assistants, each carrying out highly specialized tasks. When there is only one position of assistant, this individual's work may be general, varied, and determined by the needs of the superior officer. The style of interaction may be highly personal, as when the staff assistant is seen as an alter ego of the line officer. When such a staff member indicates a point of view, a desired action, or a preferred decision, other members of the organization recognize that this individual is reflecting the opinion and wishes of the line officer.

A full department that gives specialized assistance and support frequently has a general staff. The relationship between staff and line personnel is less intimate than the assistant relationship. The work tends to be technical and highly specialized (e.g., the work of logistical staff in the military). Table 6-1 contains a comparison of seven basic line-staff relationships.

A third aspect of line and staff relationship is the organizational arrangement of the specialized staff. Specialized staff members (or departments in a large institution) give highly specialized counsel, such as that provided by engineers, architects, accountants, lawyers, and auditors. Finally, as noted, departments can be arranged in terms of direct line entities, assisted by support or service units.

Table 6-1 Seven Basic Line-Staff Relationships Compared

No. Type	Relationship of staff unit employees to head of operating unit.	Relationship of head of operating unit to staff unit and members of staff unit working in his department.	Relationship of staff unit to employees of operating unit.
1. Advisory	May only volunteer suggestions...but may not necessarily have to wait to be invited.	May or may not have to avail himself of suggestions.	Do not give or receive instructions.
2. Service as requested	Similar to (1) but involves services, and the staff unit must be invited into the department.	Same as toward any outside contractor. The "boss" of the staff personnel is their own staff unit head.	Through operating unit's supervisors issue such requests as required to make service effective.
3. Staff services supplied on a programmed basis	Somewhat stronger than (2). Services are rendered on a programmed basis approved by higher authority and cannot be refused by operating head.	The direct chain of command of the staff personnel is to the staff unit head. Operating unit head must work through head of staff unit if dissatisfied with mode of operations.	Same as (2).
4. Auxiliary services routinely supplied	Services are a routine part of operations, not on an "invited" or specifically programmed basis.	Same as (3).	Staff-service personnel can insist on regular procedures being followed. Routine communications flow directly between staff and operating personnel except in cases of sharp disagreement.
5. Central staff and counterpart staff unit in operating department	Advisory and suggestive only... but does not have to wait to be invited.	May or may not have to avail himself of advice and suggestions of central staff unit. Through his own chain of command, head of operating unit is "boss" of the staff unit in his department.	"Functional" relationship between central unit and employees of staff unit in operating department...on matters of professional standards, mode of operation, etc., "suggestions" from central unit have strong force and are to be disregarded only under special circumstances and with approval of head of operating unit.
6. Personnel assigned to operating unit by staff unit	Assigned personnel are under administrative command of head of operating unit as to deployment on job, discipline, hours of work, etc., but their "boss" is the head of the staff unit.	In administrative command of the assigned personnel... head of staff unit may, with notice to head of operating unit, withdraw them from the job if he can supply replacements.	Relationships are those of any employees under direct supervision of head of operating unit. They carry on their own activities and work through normal channels within departments.

Table 6-1 continued

No. Type	Relationship of staff unit employees to head of operating unit.	Relationship of head of operating unit to staff unit and members of staff unit working in his department.	Relationship of staff unit to employees of operating unit.
7. A staff unit which is part of an operating organization unit	Supply information and advise and recommend...Decisions are made by operating head, and he issues instructions to operating personnel.	Direct relationship, through chain of command.	Same as (6). Staff personnel do not issue direct instructions to operating personnel except under unusual circumstances (e.g., a safety man or quality inspector shutting down an operation where emergency does not permit normal working through channels).

Source: Reprinted from The Encyclopedia of Management by C. Heyel, p. 796, with permission of Business Research Publications, Inc., © 1982.

THE DUAL PYRAMID FORM OF ORGANIZATION IN HEALTH CARE

Health care institutions are characterized by a dual pyramid form of organization because of the traditional relationship of the medical staff to the administrative staff. The ultimate authority and responsibility for the management of the institution is vested in the governing board. In accordance with the stipulations of licensure and accrediting agencies, the board appoints a chief executive officer (administrator) and a chief of medical staff, resulting in two lines of authority. The chief executive officer is responsible for effectively managing the administrative components of the institution and delegates authority to each department head in the administrative component. Within the administrative units, there is a typical pyramidal organization with a unified chain of command.

The physicians and dentists are organized under a specific set of bylaws for the governance of the medical and dental staff. With governing board approval, the chief of the medical staff appoints the chief of each clinical service. Physicians and dentists apply for clinical privileges through the medical staff credentials committee and receive appointment from the governing board. A second pyramid results from this organization of the medical staff into clinical services, with each having a chief of service who reports to the chief of the medical staff.

In an effort to consolidate authority and clarify responsibility, the top administrative levels of a health care organization may be expanded to include a central officer to whom both the administrator and the chief of the medical staff report. In some institutions, however, there may be no permanent medical staff position that corresponds to the position of administrator on the organizational chart. The elected president of the medical staff may fill this role when there is no organizational slot for a medical director per se. It is important to determine the precise meaning of titles as they are used in a specific health care setting. The following are titles commonly used:

- **Chief of Staff.** This is the officer of the medical staff to whom the chiefs of medical and clinical services report. The chief of staff is appointed by the governing board.
- **Chief of Service.** Each chief of service is the physician-director of a specific clinical service (e.g., chief of surgery) and is the line officer for physicians who are appointed to that specific service.
- **Department Chairperson.** The chairperson of a department is the director of a specific clinical service in an academic institution, such as a teaching hospital. (This title may be used as an alternate to chief of service in this type of setting.)
- **Medical Director.** This is a full-time position in a line authority structure. It is sometimes seen as the counterpart of the chief executive officer for the medical staff.
- **President of the Medical Staff.** The president is the presiding officer for the medical staff and is usually elected for a year. In the absence of a full-time medical director, this individual serves as coordinating officer for the medical staff.

Although all authority flows from the governing board, there are two distinct chains of command, one in the administrative structure and one in the medical sector. Furthermore, in matters of direct patient care, the attending physician exercises professional authority; thus, a single employee not only may be subject to more than one line of authority but also may have professional authority. Line officers in the administrative unit may find that their authority is limited in some areas because of the specific jurisdiction of the medical staff committees, such as the pharmacy and therapeutics committee. The director of the physical therapy department, for example, may report to a committee of physicians of the active medical staff, which limits the authority mandate of this line manager. Because of the dual pyramid structure, much coordination is needed.

BASIC DEPARTMENTATION

The development of departments is a natural adjunct to the specialization and division of labor that are characteristic of formal organizations. Departmentation overcomes the limitation imposed by the span of management. The organization, through its departments and similar subdivisions, can expand almost indefinitely in size. Departmentation facilitates the coordination process, since there is a logical grouping of closely related activities. Basic departmentation may be developed according to any one of several patterns:

1. By function. Because it is logical, efficient, and natural, the most widely used form of departmentation groups all related activities or jobs together. This permits managers to take advantage of specialization and to concern themselves with only one major focus of activity. Hospital departments are usually developed according to function (e.g., the business office and the medical record, personnel, housekeeping, maintenance, and dietary departments).
2. By product. All activities needed in the development, production, and marketing of a product may be grouped for purposes of coordination and control. This pattern of departmentation is used in business and industry where one or a few closely related products are grouped. It facilitates the use of research funds, the use of specialized skills and knowledge, and the development of cost control data for each product line. Functional departmentation may be an adjunct of product departmentation.
3. By territory. In business, the marketing process may be developed according to geographical boundaries. In service organizations, a decentralized pattern based on customer or client groupings may be appropriate. In some health care organizations, territorial departmentation is used because funding stipulations designate specific catchment areas or require coverage of certain population centers. Local needs, such as participation of clients and prompt settlement of difficulties, may be accommodated more easily through departmentation by territory. Grouping by geographical territory is a common element in outreach programs and home care services, as it fosters efficient movement of personnel to client locations.
4. By customer. Departmentation may be based on client needs. Specialty clinics in health care tend to follow this pattern. Government programs frequently focus on a specific client need, partly in response to the lobbying of interest groups. Specific examples of customer departmentation include special maternal and infant care programs, the Veterans Administration, and programs for migrant workers. A university may have components such as day, evening, and weekend divisions, as well as continuing education programs, to accommodate the needs and interests of differing student populations.
5. By time. Activities may be grouped according to the time of day they are performed. This pattern, which is usually based on the use of shifts, is common in manufacturing and similar organizations in which the activities of a relatively large group of semi-skilled or technical workers are repetitive and continue around the clock. Organizations that provide essential services

throughout the day and night use this pattern, usually in conjunction with functional departmentation.

6. By process. Technological considerations and specialized equipment usage may lead to departmentation by process. This is similar to functional departmentation in that all the activities involving one major process or some set of specialized equipment are grouped. In health care organizations, the formation of radiology and clinical laboratory departments is an example of departmentation by process as well as by function.

7. By number. Departmentation may be done by assigning certain duties to undifferentiated workers under specific supervision. This form of departmentation is used when many workers are needed to carry out an activity. Its use is relatively limited in modern organizations, but it was traditional in early societies, such as tribes, clans, and armies. Organizing by sheer number may be used in such activities as house-to-house soliciting campaigns and membership drives. Unskilled labor crews may be organized in this pattern.

Orphan Activities

Certain activities may not merit grouping into a separate department, and there may be no compelling reason to place them in any specific location in the organization. Yet, these orphan activities must be coordinated and interlocked with all others. The "most use" criterion is followed to resolve the question of organizational placement. The major department that most often uses or needs the service absorbs it. Other units that need the service obtain it from the major department to which it has been assigned.

Patient transportation in a hospital involves such a set of activities. These services are used by the physical therapy, occupational therapy, and radiology departments, among others, but overall coordination is assigned to the inpatient nursing units because one central placement is needed for these groups of workers. As another example, in small nursing homes one worker often performs several activities on a limited basis, such as general maintenance activities, running errands, and transporting patients to appointments with private physicians. The individual with these responsibilities may report to a central manager, such as the director of nursing, since the director or a delegate is present on all shifts. This arrangement provides coordination and control of the activities.

Deadly Parallel Arrangements

In an alternative organizational pattern, the higher levels of management establish dual organizational units for the purposes of control and/or competition. As a control device, the parallel arrangement permits comparison of costs, productivity, and similar parameters. Competition may be enhanced, if this is desired as a means of motivation, because productivity and performance can be compared.

FLEXIBILITY IN ORGANIZATIONAL STRUCTURE

Managers, in their role as change agents, continually seek ways to respond to change in the external and internal organizational environment. It may be necessary to adjust traditional organizational patterns because of advances in modern technology, the increase in workers' technical and professional training, the need to offset employee alienation, and the need to overcome the problems inherent in decentralized, widely dispersed units.

In general, functional departmentation has predominated, and there has been a strong emphasis on unity of command. When technical advice or assistance was needed, staff roles were developed to assist the line managers. When intraorganizational communication and cooperation among several units were needed, the committee structure was employed. Three alternative temporary or permanent organizational patterns allow managers to retain the benefits of these traditional practices and to reduce some of their disadvantages: (1) the matrix approach, (2) temporary departmentation, and (3) the task force (see Chapter 8). These approaches may supplement the traditional organizational structure or, in the case of the matrix approach, supplant it.

Matrix Organization

Matrix organization, a design that involves both functional and product departmentation, is used predominantly to provide a flexible and adaptable organizational structure for specific projects in, for example, research, engineering, or product development. This pattern is also called *grid* or *lattice work organization* and *project* or *product management*. The matrix of organizational relationships involves a chief for the technical aspects, an administrative officer for the managerial aspects, and a project coordinator as the final authority. This dual authority structure is a predominant characteristic of the matrix organization and stands in distinct contrast to the unity of command in the traditional organizational pattern.

Workers essentially are borrowed from functional units and temporarily assigned to the project unit. Rather than designating line and staff interactions, the developers of the matrix pattern seek to create a web of relationships among technical and managerial workers. Multiple reporting systems are developed and communication lines are interwoven throughout the matrix.

Participants in the matrix organizational pattern tend to be highly trained, self-motivated individuals with a relatively independent mode of working. These functional personnel are grouped together according to the needs dictated by the phase of the project that has been undertaken. In the matrix arrangement, workers receive direction from the technical or the administrative chief as appropriate, but it is assumed that they have the ability to develop the necessary communication and work patterns without specific direction in every aspect. The project coordinator has the traditional responsibilities of guiding the technical and administrative groups and of developing the basic channels of communication and lines of coordination; however, there may be none of the detailed stipulations that are commonly associated with the highly bureaucratic traditional organizational pattern. In the health care organization, a matrix organization frees nurses, physical therapists, occupational therapists, and other direct patient care professionals from some of the relatively rigid elements of formal organization.

Temporary Departmentation

The temporary department or unit reflects a management decision to create an organizational division with a predetermined lifetime to meet some temporary need. This lifetime may be imposed by an inherent, self-limiting element, such as funding through a defense contract or private research grant. Although the predominant organizational structure may be modified periodically, there is an implicit assumption that the basic unit will remain substantially unchanged for the life of the organization. The use of the term *temporary* may be somewhat misleading: temporary departmentation usually reflects an organizational pattern that will exist for more than a few months, since an activity limited to only a few months' duration would be placed under the category of special project or task force rather than temporary departmentation. Several years may be involved, although there is no set rule.

The development of a new product, i.e., the calculation of comparative cost data, product development, and marketing, may be placed under a temporary department assigned to carry out the necessary research development and marketing within a specific time period. A team of workers with the necessary specialized knowledge may be assembled under the jurisdiction of the temporary department, deadlines set, necessary accounting processes developed, and related functions delineated.

In businesses and institutions with defense contracts or research grants, temporary departmentation provides the necessary organizational structure without interference with the establishment's normal efforts. Equipment is purchased and workers hired with special funds designated for that purpose. These workers are not necessarily subject to the same pay scale, fringe benefits, union contracts, and similar regulations as are regular employees. The manager must make it clear to these workers that their jobs are temporary, limited to the life of the contract or grant. There should also be a clear understanding about worker movement into the main organizational unit: Is this employee eligible for such movement with or without having accrued seniority and similar benefits? Patients who receive full or partial subsidy for their care in a health care institution under a special research grant or project should be informed about the limited scope of the project, and their options for continuity of care after the life of the project should be explained.

THE ORGANIZATIONAL CHART

The management tool used for depicting organizational relationships is the organizational chart. It is a diagrammatic form, a visual arrangement, that depicts the following aspects of an institution:

1. major functions, usually by department
2. relationships of functions or departments
3. channels of supervision
4. lines of authority and of communication
5. positions (by job title) within departments or units (see Figures 6-2–6-4)

There are numerous reasons for using organizational charts:

- Since an organizational chart maps major lines of decision making and authority, managers can review it to identify any inconsistencies and complexities in the organizational structure. The diagrammatic representation makes it easier to determine and correct these inconsistencies and complexities.
- An organizational chart may be used to orient employees, since it shows where each job fits in relation to supervisors and to other jobs in the department. It shows the relationship of the department to the organization as a whole.
- The chart is a useful tool in managerial audits. Managers can review such factors as the span of management, mixed lines of authority, and splintered authority; they can also check that individual job titles are on the chart so it is clear to whom each employee reports. In addition, managers can compare current practice with the original plan of job assignments to determine if any discrepancies exist.

Certain limitations are inherent in the rather static structure presented by organizational charts, and these limitations can offset some of the advantages of using the charts:

- Only formal lines of authority and communication are shown; important lines of informal communication and significant informal relationships cannot be shown.
- The chart may become obsolete if not updated at least once a year (or more frequently if there is a major change in the organizational pattern).
- Individuals without proper training in interpretation may confuse authority relationship with status. Managers whose positions are placed physically higher in the graphic representation may be perceived as having authority over those whose positions are lower on the chart. The emphasis must be placed on the direct authority relationships and the chain of command.
- The chart cannot be properly interpreted without reference to support information, such as that usually contained in the organizational manual and related job descriptions.

Types of Charts

There are two major kinds of organizational charts: master and supplementary. The master chart depicts the entire organization, although not in great detail, and normally shows all departments and major positions of authority. A detailed listing of formal positions or job titles is not given in the master chart, however. Each supplementary chart depicts a section, department, or unit, including the specific details of its organizational pattern. An organization has as many supplementary charts as it has departments or units.

The supplementary chart of a department usually reflects the master chart and shows the direct chain of command from highest authority to that derived by the department head. The master chart usually shows the major functions, while the supplementary charts depict each individual job title and the number of positions in each section, as well as full-time or part-time status. Additional information, such as cost centers, major codes, or similar identifying information, sometimes appears on the charts.

General Arrangements and Conventions

The conventional organizational chart is a line or scalar chart showing each layer of the organization in sequence (Figure 6-5). In another arrangement, the flow of authority may be depicted from left to right, starting with major officials on the extreme left and with each successive division to the right of the preceding unit. The advantage of this form stems from its similarity to normal reading patterns. A circular arrangement, in which the authority flows from the center

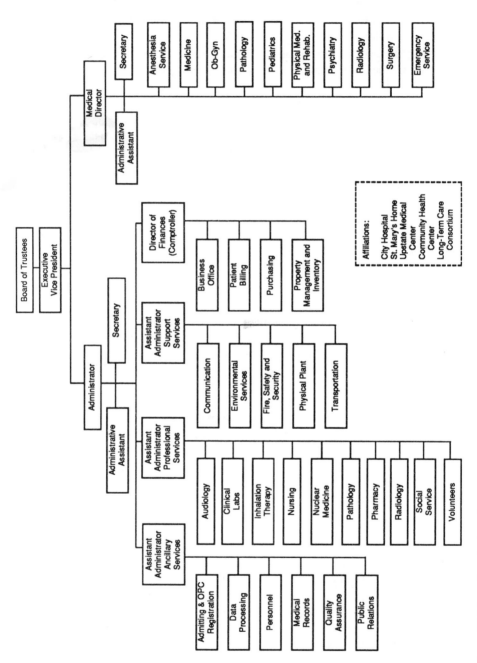

Figure 6-5 Master Organizational Chart of a Hospital

outward, is sometimes used; its advantage is that it shows the authority flow reaching out and permeating all levels, not just flowing from top to bottom.

Certain general conventions are followed when an organizational chart is drawn. Ordinarily line authority and line relationships are indicated by solid lines, and staff positions are indicated by broken or dotted lines. In Figure 6-6, the position of medical record consultant has a staff relationship to the administrator, which is, accordingly, shown by a broken line. Sometimes the staff relationship is indicated by a small *s* with a slash mark setting it off from the job title.

Occasionally, a special relationship is indicated by surrounding an entire unit or even another organization with broken lines and leaving it unconnected to any line or staff unit. Such a unit is included in the organizational chart to call attention to the existence of a related, auxiliary, or affiliated organization. This technique is used in Figure 6-5 to indicate the relationship of the teaching institutions affiliated with the hospital.

Preparing the Organizational Chart

If the chart is prepared during a planning or reorganization stage, the first step is to list all the major functions and the jobs associated with them. The major groupings by function then are brought together as specific units, for example, all jobs dealing with the file area or with patient identification systems, all jobs dealing with physical medicine and rehabilitation, or all jobs dealing with data processing and computer activities. If there is a question about the proper placement of one or several functions, managers can derive significant information by asking the following questions:

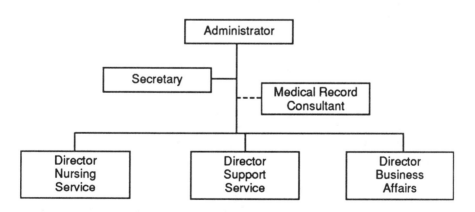

Figure 6-6 Special Relationships: Consultant in Advisory Role

- If there is a problem, who must be involved to effect a solution?
- Do the supervisors at each level have the necessary authority to carry out their functions?
- If a change in systems and procedures is needed, who must agree to the changes?
- If critical information must be channeled through the organization, who is responsible for its transmission throughout each unit of the organization?

As an aid in developing the organizational chart, it is useful to prepare a simple tabulation showing the following information:

1. job title
2. reporting line: supervised by whom (title)
3. full time or part time
4. day, evening, or night shift
5. line or staff position

The inclusion of the incumbent's name is optional for this work sheet preparation, although names may be useful in a subsequent managerial audit of the department in which the manager is comparing present practice with the original plan. The use of names as the basic means of developing the chart could be misleading, however, as it may block managers' thinking, causing them to describe organizational relationships as they are rather than as they should be. It may be best to show names only on a staffing chart that is prepared after the organization chart has been developed.

After obtaining the necessary information about work relationships, shifts, supervisory needs, and span of management factors, managers develop the final chart, using the general conventions for depicting organizational relationships. A support narrative or a section of the organization's manual can be developed to give additional information.

THE JOB DESCRIPTION

The duties associated with each job should be determined by the needs of the department. Frequently, jobs evolve as duties become assigned to an employee. These jobs are accumulations of tasks rather than products of prior planning. Some form of control is necessary to keep assignments within intended limits. In order to provide this control of the various work assignments, the duties and responsibilities of each job should be set forth in written form. This helps to ensure that employees' concepts of their duties will be consistent with those of the manager and with the needs of the department.

In every formal organization, there are job descriptions to cover all jobs. In order to fill the various positions with the appropriate employees, it is necessary to match the jobs available in the department with the individuals. This can only be done with the help of job descriptions, which are written objective statements defining duties and functions. Each job description includes responsibilities, experience, organizational relationships, working conditions, and other essential factors of the position.

Job Analysis

The process of preparing a job description is time consuming but invaluable. A job analysis must be undertaken in order to collect complete data on the content and requirements of each job so that objective standards can be established. This process may be carried out by the manager, the employee, or consultants. Various methods may be employed, including the use of observation, interviews, questionnaires, checklists, a daily log, or a combination of these tools.

When a job analysis is done, the employees must understand that their performance is not being evaluated; it is the job that is being analyzed. Otherwise, the employees may be uncooperative for fear that their jobs will be downgraded, with a resultant loss in salary. Each employee should be encouraged to contribute personal thoughts and concerns about the job. Involving the employees is helpful in the collection of data. Everyone should be fully informed of the purpose of the analysis and the methods to be used.

Job Description Format

The format of a job description should present the information in an orderly manner. Since there is no standard format, job descriptions vary with the type of facility and with the size and scope of the department. The following format is suggested as a guide:

- Job Title. The job should be identified by a title that clarifies the position. The inclusion in the job title of such words as *director, supervisor, senior, staff,* or *clerk* can help to indicate the duties and skill level of the job.
- Immediate Supervisor. The position and title of the immediate supervisor should be clearly identified.
- Job Summary. A short statement of the major activities of the job should indicate the purpose and scope of the job in specific terms. This section serves principally to identify the job and differentiate the duties that are performed from those of other jobs.

- Job Duties. The major part of the job description should state what the employee does and how the duties are accomplished. The description of duties should also indicate the degree of supervision received or given.
- Job Specifications. A written record of minimum hiring requirements for a particular job comes from the job analysis procedure. The items covered in the specifications may be divided into two groups:
  1. The skill requirements include the mental and manual skills, plus the personal traits and qualities, needed to perform the job effectively:
     - minimum educational requirements
     - licensure or registration requirements
     - experience expressed in objective and quantitative terms, such as years
     - specific knowledge requirements or advanced educational requirements
     - manual skills required in terms of the quality, quantity, or nature of the work to be performed
     - communication skills, both oral and written
  2. The physical demands of a job may include the following:
     - physical effort required to perform the job and the length of time involved in performing a given activity
     - working conditions and general physical environment in which the job is to be performed
     - job hazards and their probability of occurrence

Exhibit 6-1 is a typical job description for a clerical position.

In some institutions, the job specifications are organized as a separate record, because the information is not used for the same purpose as the information contained in the job description. The specifications receive the most usage in connection with the recruitment and selection of employees, since this part of the job description defines the qualifications that are needed to perform the job. Job evaluations and the establishment of different wage and salary schedules are other functions that depend on the data contained in the job specifications.

Uses and Purposes of Job Descriptions*

Compliance with Legal, Contractual, and Accrediting Requirements

The following outline summarizes the relationship of the job description to the other personnel management functions.

Exhibit 6-1 Excerpts from Typical Job Description: Clerical Position

---

Job Summary

This is a clerical position in the health records service of an acute care facility affiliated with a medical school and a research institution. This full-time, day shift position is under the direct supervision of the Assistant Health Records Administrator; incumbent performs duties with relative independence, referring exceptions to policy and procedure to supervisory personnel with the department.

Job Duties

1. Receives visitors to the department; processes their requests by routing them to appropriate supervisors; assists requestor as needed; schedules appointments.
2. Answers departmental telephones and routes calls or takes messages.
3. Takes dictation from transcribing machine and from rough draft and transcribes according to prescribed format.

Job Specification

1. Fluency in English language, both oral and written expression.
2. Ability to type final copy, from both dictation and handwritten copy, error-free, minimum of 50 words per minute (electric typewriter).
3. Minimum of high school degree or its equivalent and at least one year of secretarial experience or successful completion of postsecondary secretarial school.

Note flexibility in requirement 3; this fosters a nondiscriminatory approach to hiring, giving flexibility to the manner in which an individual may qualify for the position.

Job analysis and job classification

- wage and salary scale
- exempt/nonexempt status under the Fair Labor Standards Act
- collective bargaining unit inclusion
- transfer and promotion pattern

Recruitment

- advertising
- preliminary screening
- testing

Selection

- information for prospective employee
- focus of interview

Source: Reprinted from Joan Gratto Liebler, "Job Descriptions: Development and Use," in *Health Care Supervisor* 1:2, pp. 25–30, Aspen Publishers, Inc., © 1983.

- determination of physical fitness for job as described

Orientation and training: tailored to job qualifications

Evaluation

- performance evaluation
- basis for error correction and retraining
- reference point in grievance hearings

Job Rating and Classification

Before employees are selected and hired, the organization develops a job classification. This classification is based on the results of the job rating process. In job rating, each set of functions within each unit of the organization is analyzed using some set of common denominators. In health care, these variables include complexity of duties; error impact; contacts with patients, families, and other individuals both within and outside of the organization; degree of supervision received and nature of duties ranging from unskilled to highly technical and professional. Mental and physical demands as well as working conditions may also be assessed because these variables may make a job different from a seemingly similar position in the organization.

When developing a job description, it is useful to compare the draft of the description with the job rating scale specific to the organization. From this "dry run," changes in actual wording may result so that the final expression of job duties and related conditions matches the categories or factors to be assessed. Without such a correlation between the job rating scale and the job description's wording, inequities could be fostered. Similar jobs could receive different ratings based on a lack of proper wording in a particular job description.

Ideally, the overall job rating process contains safeguards against discrepancies; ideally, the personnel manager makes such job rating information available to unit managers. It is still the duty and prerogative of line managers to take active steps in these matters and anticipate the job rating process.

In addition to the overall job classification, the wage and salary and fringe benefit package will be predicated on information gained in the job description or job rating process. Another key to success in developing useful job descriptions is to assess the written document for its adequacy in conveying information about the factors used in job rating and wage and salary considerations.

Two additional outcomes of the job classification that concern the manager are the determinations made for exempt and nonexempt positions under the Fair Labor Standards Act (FLSA) and the applicability of a union contract in terms of jobs included in a particular bargaining union. In both of these cases, information about supervisory activity is critical. Thus there is another benchmark against which to measure the adequacy of the job description: Does it contain sufficient information to justify inclusion—or exclusion—of a job in terms of overtime pay and related FLSA provisions? Is the nature of the job clearly delineated in terms of rating as skilled or unskilled, technical or professional, for purposes of union contract applicability?

Recruitment

Certain steps in the recruitment process involve information derived from the job description. Internal job posting may involve the placement of the complete job description in a specified location, such as on an employee bulletin board. Potential transfer employees essentially participate in a self-selection or rejection process as they read this job description. They can take the opportunity to assess such practical aspects of a job as shift work or weekend coverage requirements in terms of their availability to work such hours.

The physical, mental, or technical demands of the job also may sway the potential transfer employee to reconsider applying for a position. Then, too, the job description may have the effect of encouraging applicants. Does the job description contain enough information to help prospective employees make such a preliminary determination?

Those involved in the preliminary selection interviews, usually members of the personnel department, need sufficient information about all the jobs in the institution to carry out initial screening. The unit managers must convey, through the job description, key points of information about duties, responsibilities, and qualifications. It is important to note that the unit manager is the individual most familiar with the work of the unit. This information must be conveyed in a way that it can be understood by persons who are not involved in the unit or department on a daily basis.

Awareness of the wide audience who will use the job descriptions will help the manager write them in understandable form. The unit manager may find it useful to try out the wording of a job description on another manager. Does the wording convey enough information for this person, familiar with the health care setting but not necessarily familiar with the details of the specific department, to form a basic idea of the job?

The Final Selection Process

A major use of the job description occurs during the selection process as the candidate is matched to the job. During the selection interview, information about the duties, responsibilities, and qualifications is conveyed. One sensitive overlay to the selection process, which includes all aspects of the interview, testing, and physical examination, is the strict avoidance of discriminatory practices, even inadvertent discrimination.

When the job, as summarized in the job description, is the focus of the interview, it is easier to avoid the pitfalls of interviewing that could suggest discriminatory practices. Thus with a job description that spells out such expectations as weekend coverage, shift work availability, and similar requirements, the manager and prospective employee can deal with that set of expectations without the manager probing in any way into such questions as days of religious observance, arrangements for child care, and other topics that are off limits for direct inquiry. The emphasis is on the job as it is described.

Job qualifications and mental, physical, and technical demands become the objective measures of candidate suitability when they are derived from job duties. These in turn foster a positive climate of compliance with nondiscriminatory practices.

For example, if the job duties include frequent routine interaction with patients in need of emergency care and the patient population involved is non-English speaking, a qualification of fluency in a specific language is not discriminatory. If the unit manager can tie each qualification to one or more job duties, the likelihood of discriminatory practices in the employment selection process is diminished. Sometimes it may seem that one is stating the obvious, such as ability to read, write, speak English (or some other language) with ease, hear, see, and lift—so why spell these out?

Another method to use in making a dry run of the job description that helps the manager determine the level of detail needed under the foregoing conditions is working with the personnel manager using a sample of applications that have been received over some period of time. How does the manager's job description hold up? On what basis would the manager hire, or not hire, a particular individual in light of the job description as it is written?

Employee Development and Retention

At each point of employee development, activities focus on the work to be done within each job. Orientation and training programs take on greater meaning as they are tailored to specific job duties and qualifications. Training outcomes can be stated in terms of the trainee's ability to perform the duties. This is another step toward objective evaluation of candidates.

Job descriptions also provide a focus for performance evaluations. Has the worker accomplished the duties and responsibilities made known in the job description? Error correction, retraining, and, if necessary, disciplinary action are carried out in the context of the job for which the individual was hired. In cases of grievance, emphasis will be given to the worker's accomplishment of the job duties, with the presumption that these have been made known to the worker. A comprehensive, up-to-date job description is a valuable management document in such cases.

Finally, in cases of illness or injury under review by such agencies as Workers' Compensation or the Occupational Safety and Health Administration (OSHA), the basic determination of job relatedness is made using the job description. Below is a summary of uses of the job description. How would the manager's current descriptions hold up when scrutinized in relation to each of these applications?

Summary of Uses of the Job Description

The job description

- fosters or contributes to overall compliance with legal, regulatory, con-tractual, and accrediting mandates;
- serves as a basis for job rating, job classification, and wage and salary administration;
- serves as a basis for determining exemption or inclusion under provi-sions of the Fair Labor Standards Act and collective bargaining agree-ments;
- provides information to prospective employees and to employer repre-sent-atives during the recruitment and selection process;
- serves as a basis for orientation and training programs at the time of ini-tial selection, transfer, or promotion;
- serves as a basis for performance evaluation, error correction, retraining requirements, and grievance determinations; and
- provides information to determine eligibility for claims under Workers' Compensation, OSHA, and similar programs.

Jobs, like the organizational structure of a hospital, are dynamic in nature. Changes in the size and nature of the organization, the introduction of new equipment, or the employment of new treatment techniques—to mention only a few factors—have a definite influence on the duties and requirements of jobs. Thus, the manager and the employees of a department must review the descrip-tion of each job on a periodic, regular schedule (at least once a year). The doc-ument should be dated when it is first prepared, redated when it is reviewed, and again redated when it is revised. An up-to-date accurate job description is essential when the personnel department recruits applicants for a job or when the manager hires new employees, appraises the performance of existing employees, and attempts to establish an equitable wage and salary pattern with-in the department.

See Exhibits 6-2 to 6-8 for examples of job descriptions and job duty delineations.

Exhibit 6-2 Job Description for Release of Information Specialist

JOB TITLE: Release of Information Specialist
RESPONSIBLE TO: Director, Medical Records Department

RESPONSIBILITIES

Under the general direction of the director, Medical Records Department, this specialist is responsible for processing requests for release of information from the official medical records of this facility. All work is carried out in accordance with the department's approved policies and procedures.

JOB SETTING AND CONDITIONS

This is an advanced-level clerical position in the Medical Records Department of this [*n*]-bed facility. The position is full time, day shift. Normal working days and hours are Monday through Friday, 8:30 A.M. to 4:30 P.M., with a paid 45-minute lunch period. Adjustments to the normal schedule are required when the employee travels to and from court or other site of legal proceedings to give testimony in response to subpoenas and court orders.

JOB DUTIES

In accordance with department policies and procedures, this specialist carries out these 13 major and closely related duties and responsibilities:

1. Process requests for release of information from the official records maintained by this facility
2. Receives and processes all incoming written requests for such release
3. Receives visitors to the unit to process these requests and inquiries
4. Answers the unit telephone to process these requests and inquiries
5. Reviews each request to determine
   a. need for authorization
   b. adequacy of authorization
6. Prepares responses appropriate to each request
7. Calculates, collects, and transmits fees associated with the release of information
8. Photocopies material from the original medical record and prepares abstract summaries
9. Accepts, processes, and responds to subpoenas and court orders
10. Maintains the release of information log used to track the status of each request
11. Operates the office equipment normally used in the routines of daily work, such as photocopy and facsimile equipment, computers and word processors, and adding machines
12. Promotes public relations through prompt and courteous service
13. Fosters respect for patient privacy by maintaining confidentiality in all phases of the work

EDUCATION AND EXPERIENCE

- The trainee should have a high school diploma or the equivalent.
- The trainee should have had advanced clerical training, which includes typing and

Exhibit 6-2 continued

computer skills, basic filing and bookkeeping, basic office procedures, and basic medical record terminology and practice.

- The trainee should have had relevant experience in clerical duties sufficient for individual development to the level of independent functioning with minimal direction.
- A trainee is acceptable provided the individual meets the established work standards within [n] weeks of completion of the mandatory training program for this job.

SKILLS

- fluent in English
- able to type final copy, error free, within prescribed deadlines
- able to maintain alphabetical and numerical files with no errors
- able to maintain fee collection system with no errors

PHYSICAL AND MENTAL DEMANDS

- ability to withstand the pressure of continual deadlines and receipt of work with variable requirements
- ability to concentrate and maintain accuracy in spite of frequent interruptions
- ability to be courteous, tactful, and cooperative throughout the working day
- ability to use judgment in carrying out all phases of the work
- ability to maintain confidentiality with regard to all phases of the work
- acute visual and auditory senses
- ability to communicate clearly in English in both oral and written forms of expression
- ability to sit for long periods; move about the facility; stoop and lift light loads such as packets of mail, medical records, and packages
- ability to use standard office equipment including computers and word processors, photocopy and facsimile machines, and reader-printers

SPECIAL REQUIREMENTS

- Ability to drive a car to and from area courts and law offices in the [n-county] area for the purpose of responding to subpoenas and depositions.
- Ability to maintain flexible working hours when required to travel to and from, and participate in, legal proceedings requiring the presentation of medical records and/or the provision of testimony.

DATE:

REVISIONS:

Source: Reprinted from *Medical Records: Policies and Guidelines, Supplement 1*, by J.G. Liebler, pp. 10:90, Aspen Publishers, Inc., © 1991

Exhibit 6-3 Job Description for Coordinator of Rehabilitation

---

Statement of Purpose

Coordinates and supervises operation of the rehabilitation department, which includes physical therapy, occupational therapy, and electrodiagnostics.

Major Tasks, Duties, and Responsibilities

Coordinates delivery of physical and occupational therapy services for inpatients and out-patients.

Assures prompt, efficient, and high-quality care according to professional standards

Maintains department cleanliness and safety.

Conducts new employee orientation and annual performance appraisals.

Reviews and revises the department policy and procedure manual as needed.

Prepares operating budget and plans expenditures accordingly.

Plans capital budget in keeping with the needs of the department.

Directs staff and equipment allocation, on a daily basis, to ensure the effectiveness of department services.

On a regular basis, informs the medical director and associate director of issues affecting delivery of service.

Maintains records pertinent to personnel and the operation of the department.

Has a working knowledge of current standards of care in regulatory codes and accrediting agencies.

Represents the department at hospitalwide committees and management meetings.

Prepares the annual report and plans objectives for the future.

Educational Requirements

Entry-level degree (bachelor's or master's) in physical therapy or occupational therapy from a program accredited by the appropriate professional associations.

Qualifications or Special Skills Required

Licensed (or eligible) to practice in New York State.

Basic management and supervisory skills required.

Experience

Four years of clinical practice and two years of supervisory/management experience.

Source: Courtesy of St. Vincent's Medical Center, Staten Island, N.Y.

Exhibit 6-4 Job Description for Senior Physical Therapist

Statement of Purpose

To assist the coordinator and assistant coordinator in the orientation and supervision of staff physical therapists and supportive personnel, in addition to providing direct patient care.

Major Tasks, Duties, and Responsibilities

Includes all the duties of the staff physical therapist.

Supervises staff physical therapists in the planning and execution of patient care in the respective areas of rotation, i.e., gym, outpatient, bedside.

Offers constructive criticism, in consultation with the coordinator, to staff therapists to promote growth and motivation.

Supervises assigned treatment areas or special programs within the department.

Assists the coordinator and assistant coordinator in monitoring department operations to ensure optimum patient care, safe and pleasant working conditions, and efficiency.

Demonstrates advanced clinical skill in one or more special areas and disseminates that skill to other staff.

Assists the coordinator in orientation of new employees.

Provides physical therapy services, as needed, at Carmel Richmond Nursing Home.

Educational Requirements

Entry-level degree (bachelor's or master's) from a program accredited by the American Physical Therapy Association.

Qualifications or Special Skills Required

Licensed (or eligible) to practice in New York State.

Advanced clinical or basic supervisory skills required.

Physical skills involve daily heavy lifting and long periods of standing.

Experience

Two years of clinical practice.

Source: Courtesy of St. Vincent's Medical Center, Staten Island, N.Y.

Exhibit 6-5 Job Description for Staff Physical Therapist

Statement of Purpose

Upon medical referral, organizes and conducts physical therapy programs in the hospital to restore function and prevent disability following disease or injury; applies high standards of quality care according to the overall objectives of the rehabilitation department.

Major Tasks, Duties, and Responsibilities

Reviews the patient's medical record and interprets tests and measurements to assess pathophysiological, pathomechanical, and developmental deficits of human systems to determine treatment and assist in diagnosis and prognosis.

Establishes appropriate short- and long-term goals with input from the patient and family.

Provides appropriate treatment, including, but not limited to, heat, cold, light, air, water, sound, electricity, massage, mobilization, and therapeutic exercise with or without assistive devices (wheelchair, crutches, prosthetics/orthotics).

Provides accurate and timely documentation of the evaluation and plan of care.

Communicates with medical/allied health personnel regarding patient's progress, needs, and discharge plans.

Assesses the patient's progress and response to treatment and revises the plan of care as needed.

Supervises rehabilitation aides, physical therapy students, and volunteers.

Participates in department in-service training and employee education programs.

Participates in professional conferences, seminars, and continuing education.

Understands the impact of regulatory and accrediting agencies on the standards of patient care.

Educational Requirements

Entry-level degree (bachelor's or master's) from a program accredited by the American Physical Therapy Association.

Qualifications or Special Skills Required

Licensed (or eligible) to practice in New York State.
Physical skills involve daily heavy lifting and long periods of standing.

Experience

Preferred, not required.

Source: Courtesy of St. Vincent's Medical Center, Staten Island, N.Y.

Exhibit 6-6 Job Description for Physical Therapist Assistant

Statement of Purpose

Performs various patient-related activities, such as treatment with exercise or modalities, as directed by a physical therapist.

Major Tasks, Duties, and Responsibilities

Administers physical therapy care programs or portions thereof as planned and directed by a physical therapist.

Maintains open communication with the physical therapist regarding patient's response to treatment.

Communicates with medical/allied health personnel regarding patient's progress, needs, and discharge planning.

Acts as an assistant to the physical therapist when the physical therapist is performing tests, evaluation, and complex procedures.

Documents patient's response to treatment in the medical record.

Maintains a neat and organized appearance in all areas of the department; puts equipment back in assigned places.

Educational Requirements/Experience

Either completion of a two-year college program accredited by the American Physical Therapy Association or experience satisfactory to the New York State Board for Physical Therapy as leading to state licensure.

Qualifications or Special Skills Required

Licensed (or eligible) to practice in New York State.

Physical skills require daily heavy lifting and long periods of standing.

Source: Courtesy of St. Vincent's Medical Center, Staten Island, N.Y.

Exhibit 6-7 Job Description for Senior Specialist-Occupational Therapist III

Immediate Supervisor: Reports directly to the Director of Occupational Therapy. In addition, receives medical supervision from rehabilitation physicians and residents. Must relate to other professionals, such as those in nursing, physical therapy, health records administration, speech therapy, and social work.

Job Summary: Treats spinal-cord-injured and respirator-dependent spinal-cord-injured patients. Supervises occupational therapy staff and aides. Teaches home programs to family members and caregivers. Participates in spinal cord research project. Prepares report on spinal cord unit for CARF.

Exhibit 6-7 continued

Job Duties: Evaluates all new admissions and establishes treatment goals and program. Approves all adaptive equipment orders and staff home visits. Directs student training and volunteer programs. Treats complex cases and supervises all staff, reviewing documentation, treatment techniques, and follow-up. Represents occupational therapy at monthly research committee meetings. Serves on Strategic Planning Committee. Orients all OTR staff and supervises orientation of COTAs and aides.

Job Specifications: Must be a licensed occupational therapist with passing grade in American Occupational Therapy Certification Board examination and have a minimum of three years of experience with spinal-cord-injured patients. Master's degree preferred. Must demonstrate knowledge and skill in evaluating and treating spinal-cord-injured and ventilator-dependent patients. Must have knowledge of adaptive equipment and some experience with environmental control systems. Must have good communication skills, including good writing skills.

Exhibit 6-8 Occupational Therapy Department Job Duties

Staff Therapist (Grade 81)

1. Patient care: evaluates patients
2. Patient care: plans and implements treatments
3. Patient care: educates patients
4. Patient care: maintains documentation that is thorough, timely, and meets department standards
5. Patient care: communicates with and evaluates
6. Manages schedule, maintains clinic/office space, meets productivity expectations (average 12 treatments per day, back-to-work average 15 treatments per day)
7. Quality assurance: participates in chart review process
8. Utilizes and communicates with support staff appropriately
9. Teaching: attends and participates in in-services, supervises students (Level I), participates in resident evaluation
10. Represents and promotes OT within the university and community

Senior Therapist (Grade 82)

1. Patient care: evaluates patients
2. Patient care: plans and implements treatments
3. Patient care: provides patient and family education
4. Patient care: maintains documentation that is thorough and timely
5. Manages schedule, maintains clinic/office space, meets productivity expectations (average 12 treatments per day, back-to-work average 15 treatments per day)
6. Serves on section committee (i.e., volunteers, departmental in-services, interviews, quality assurance)

Exhibit 6-8 continued

7. Quality assurance: participates in chart review process
8. Utilizes and communicates with support staff appropriately
9. Teaching: serves as role model/mentor for new staff, attends and participates in in-services, supervises students (Level I and II), participates in resident evaluation
10. Represents and promotes OT within the university and community

Unit Supervisors (Grade 83)

1. Manages schedule, supervises support staff, evaluates residents, etc.
2. Staff supervision: orients staff to service, provides day-to-day monitoring and feedback, reviews billing sheets, gives appraisal at end of service
3. Patient care: develops and implements programs, maintains caseload, follows documentation guidelines, meets productivity expectations (50 treatments per week), coordinates OT with other services
4. Quality assurance: monitors unit performance, performs chart reviews and staff audits according to schedule, supports quality assurance activities
5. Teaching: attends and participates in in-services, instructs residents and medical students, supervises OT students, lectures to OT students
6. Research: designs, implements, or participates in clinical research
7. Promotes OT within the university and the community

Advanced Clinician (Grade 83)

1. Patient care: evaluates, plans, and implements patient services for a specific patient population
2. Documentation: maintains complete and up-to-date records
3. Quality assurance: participates in quality assurance program
4. Teaching: attends and participates in in-services
5. Teaching: instructs staff through cotreatment, individual instruction, and mentoring
6. Teaching: instructs OT students on affiliation (Level I and II) and in OT school education program
7. Research: designs, implements, or participates in clinical research projects
8. Manages schedule, maintains productivity (60 treatments per week), utilizes support staff appropriately
9. Promotes OT within the university and community
10. Orients residents to OT's role in specialty area

Assistant Chief (Grade 84)

1. Patient care: maintains half-time patient load, maintains productivity average of 5-6 patient treatments per day
2. Quality assurance: coordinates section quality assurance program
3. Coordinates OT student program, including scheduling affiliates and clerkships, orients and supports student supervisors, problem solves
4. Teaching: schedules section in in-services, coordinates OT in in-services with Rehab in-service committee, works with individual staff members on development, instructs medical students

Exhibit 6-8 continued

5. Research: designs, implements, or participates in clinical research
6. Promotes OT within the university and community

Chief (Grade 85)

1. Personnel: is responsible for recruitment, orientation, supervision, evaluation, and retention of staff
2. Patient care: is responsible for program development, supervision, continuous quality improvement, program evaluation; monitors and maintains compliance with CARF and Joint Commission standards
3. Administration: is responsible for management of budget, productivity, supplies, space; submits reports as necessary
4. Education: oversees in-service and staff development, oversees orientation and evaluation of residents, oversees student program (Level I and II), oversees medical student training, instructs at College of Allied Health Sciences
5. Research: promotes use of current research information and tools, encourages/facilitates development and participation in clinical research activities

Source: Courtesy of Joanne Cassidy, MEd, OTR/L, Chief Occupational Therapist, Department of Rehabilitation Medicine, Thomas Jefferson University Hospital, Philadelphia, Pa.

CONSULTANTS

There are situations when an organization needs to confer with an external professional consultant. Time constraints, lack of special expertise, and regulatory requirements are some of the factors that may precipitate the need for a consultant. The role of the consultant and the extent of the arrangement will depend on the type and scope of the project. Most projects requiring consultants are one-time efforts with limitations. However, a consultant may be requested to confer periodically with the organization over an extended period of time. For example, a consultant may have assisted in preparing a research or training grant proposal. If the proposal is funded, the consultant may assist in monitoring and evaluating the project for several years during and following its implementation.

Role and Function

The function of a consultant is to provide advice on a specified task, problem, or procedure. Some consultants work independently whereas others are members of a consulting firm or organization. Consultants can often make valuable recommendations that could improve care and services or increase cost-effectiveness.

There are many areas in which consultants can serve a health care organization, including the following:

- legal counseling
- space and facility planning
- financial planning
- grants and research
- curriculum development
- strategic planning
- fund raising

Selection of Consultants

The need for the consultant must be clearly defined before the selection process begins. The selection committee will develop the criteria and necessary qualifications required for the position. The committee may also identify potentially qualified individuals or firms. Prospective consultants will be invited for a site visit to discuss the proposal. A track record of success is highly desirable.

Development of the Contract

To ensure success, it is important that the contract with the consultant include a definitive outline of what is to be done, when it will be done, and who is to perform the assigned tasks. The fees and remuneration for the services should be negotiated and clearly stated in the contract. A specified time to complete each task or the total project should also be included in the contract. The consequences of a failure to comply with the agreed terms of the contract should also be delineated. The contract should be approved by legal counsel and then signed by the appropriate official from each party involved. A final, summative, written report is a required part of the contract.

Chapter 7

Committees

CHAPTER OBJECTIVES

1. Define what a committee is.
2. Differentiate among committees, plural executives, and task forces.
3. Identify the purposes and uses of committees.
4. Recognize the limitations and disadvantages of the committee structure.
5. Identify means for improving committee effectiveness.
6. Identify the role and functions of the committee chairperson.
7. Understand the importance of minutes and formal proceedings.

Committees have become a fact of life in modern organizations. The democratic tradition in American society, the committee system's history of success in organizations, and the legal and accrediting authority mandates for such activity contribute to the widespread use of committees in health care organizations. Committee participation is an expected part of the daily routine of the chief of service, department head, or manager. The committee structure complements the overall organizational structure, because it can be used to overcome problems stemming from specialization and departmentation. The weakness of specialization is the potential loss of broad organizational vision on the part of the individual manager; however, coordination of action and assessment of the overall organizational impact of a decision may be facilitated when a committee brings together a number of specialists for organized deliberation.

Health care organizations need committees to help consolidate the dual authority tracks within the medical authority structure and the administrative/support structure. The joint conference committee, consisting of representatives from the medical staff, the board of trustees, and the administration, is commonly used for this purpose. Functions of health care organizations typically monitored and assessed by committees include pharmacy and therapeutics, infection control, patient care evaluation, surgical case review, medical records, quality assurance, and utilization review. Table 7-1 summarizes typical committee participation by various health care professionals.

Table 7-1 Examples of Committee Participation

Department Head	Utilization Review	Medical Records	Risk Management	Quality Assurance
Occupational Therapy	*	*	X	X
Physical Therapy	*	*	X	X
Medical Technology		*	X	X
Dietary		*	X	X
Health Records	*	X	X	X
Nursing	X	X	X	X
Social Service	X	X	*	X

Note: * = rotating membership with other department heads; X = permanent ex officio membership.

THE NATURE OF COMMITTEES

A committee may be defined as a group of persons in an organization who function collectively on an organized basis to perform some administrative activity. A committee is more than an informal group that meets to discuss an issue and share ideas, even if such a group meets regularly. The manager who informally calls together a team of subordinates or other managers to talk over an idea or problem is not dealing with a committee. The emphasis in the committee concept is the creation of a structure that has an organized basis for its activity and interaction and that is accountable for its function. The predominant characteristic of the committee is group deliberation on a recurring basis done in the context of a specific grant of authority.

Committees may be temporary or permanent. The temporary, or ad hoc, committee is created to deal with one issue, such as the implementation of the problem-oriented medical record or cost-containment compliance, and its work is limited to that issue. If the problem assigned to an ad hoc committee becomes a recurring one, it may be handled by an existing committee, it may be referred to an existing department, or a new standing committee may be created to deal with it.

Standing committees, which are relatively permanent, focus on recurring matters. The individual members change, but the committee is continuing with respect to the number of members, the distribution of representatives, and its basic charge. Typical standing committees in health care organizations include those responsible for dealing with credentials, infection control, patient care policies, medical records, and quality assurance. A department may have specific standing committees, such as departmental quality assurance, safety control, or professional development committees.

A committee may have either line or staff authority. If the committee has authority to bind subordinates who are responsible to it, it is part of the line unit structure. For example, a governing board may have an executive committee that gives directives to the chief executive officer of the institution and thus exercises line authority. A grievance committee, whose decision is binding because of a policy or union contract, exercises line authority in producing its determinations; managers are not free to act contrary to such decisions. If, on the other hand, the committee has an advisory relationship to line managers, it is a staff unit.

In actual practice, the distinction between line and staff authority of a committee is sometimes blurred. A credentials committee of the medical staff may have limited line authority in that, except for unusual cases, the next levels of authority are bound by the recommendations it makes. A union contract governing faculty at a medical school or university may require that a faculty committee review each case of promotion and tenure and make a recommendation to the line officer, the dean, who in turn must add a recommendation, with the final decision made by the board of trustees. Participation in the decision process by several layers in the hierarchy is mandatory in such cases. In that sense, the credentials committee of the medical staff, as well as the promotion and tenure committee of a college, may be viewed as a line committee with limited but explicit input into decisions concerning professional colleagues. Their decisions are not final, but their recommendations are well protected by custom and, in some cases, by law.

The Plural Executive

Although most committees are nonmanagerial in nature, there is a structural variation in which a committee is created that has line authority and undertakes some or all of the traditional functions of a manager. These committees are created as a result of policy decisions. A familiar example in the health care setting is the executive board of a national professional association. Established through the bylaws of the organization, the executive board typically consists of the elected officers and has the authority to act on behalf of the membership in prescribed areas. The board of trustees in a hospital is also a plural executive, although it is almost universal practice to appoint a chief executive officer and assign management functions to that officer.

The plural executive may be established by law, as in federal regulatory agencies (e.g., the Federal Communications Commission and the Securities and Exchange Commission) or in special federal agencies (e.g., the Tennessee Valley Authority). The law creating such agencies stipulates that there be a regulatory board (usually) of 5 to 11 members who have line authority as a board. The board varies greatly in the amount of power held and authority exercised.

Although the board has formal authority, the center of true power in the organization may shift from the executive board to the appointed chief executive officer, who reports to the executive board.

The individual officeholders who constitute the plural executive must rely greatly on an appointed officer, such as the executive director, and on the staff chosen by that officer. While the executive officer is in a continuing position, the plural executive group may meet infrequently, and its membership may change as frequently as every year. Furthermore, the members of the plural executive unit tend to remain less visible, as they give directives to the executive, who issues these under the office's title. This common practice often obscures the authority constellation proper to the plural executive and may even reduce it to one of symbolic rather than actual authority and power.

The Task Force

A temporary organizational unit, the task force is created to carry out a specific project or assignment and present its findings to some person or committee that has line authority. It has as its focus highly specific work that requires technical expertise. The task force analyzes the question, completes the research, and makes its recommendations, which may take the form of a complete plan of action. Unlike committees, which remain in existence until specifically dissolved, the task force automatically ceases functioning when its assigned task is completed.

Members of a task force are chosen on the basis of technical competence and specialized training to form a composite, interdisciplinary team. They are not selected to represent a special group interest, and not every department or organizational unit is represented. A task force rarely, if ever, has line authority. Its findings sometimes are referred to a committee that deliberates issues of a basic policy nature; the work of the task force complements that of committees by providing technical research and preparing background information. The group may be created as a result of committee deliberations; for example, the executive committee or the board of trustees of a health care institution may wish to expand its services or to develop an entirely new physical complex. These technical problems could be referred to a task force for study; when the work of the task force is done, the executive committee or board takes appropriate action.

A task force sometimes is created for its symbolic value—a common political use. The various presidential commissions of the last decades are examples of the use of task forces to call attention to an important issue (e.g., civil rights, space technology, and care of the aged). In order to provide an arena that is relatively free from vested interests and particular biases, a task force rather than an administrative agency or department personnel may be assigned the responsibility of studying an issue.

THE PURPOSES AND USES OF COMMITTEES

Committees are created to fulfill various specific needs. The following purposes and uses of committees include the advantages that accrue to an organization as a result of effective committee structure development.

To Gain the Advantage of Group Deliberation

Many management problems are so complex that their impact on the organization as a whole is best assessed through group deliberation and decision making. Decisions may have a long-range effect, and no single manager has the knowledge necessary to see all the ramifications of a problem. In a committee structure, no one manager bears the burden of a decision that will have far-reaching consequences. Probing of the facts and their implications is likely to be more thorough if the knowledge, experience, and judgment of several individuals are brought to bear on the problem in a coordinated manner. The stimulation of shared thinking may lead to a better decision than could be reached by an individual. Finally, group deliberations may be mandatory in some organizations because of the stipulations in a union contract, an accrediting agency, or a regulatory body.

To Offset Decentralization and Consolidate Authority

In the process of organizing, each manager is given only a portion of the organization's authority. Normally, each manager receives sufficient authority to carry out the responsibilities of the branch or unit of the organization over which that individual has charge. When the organizational structure is consolidated, efforts are made to avoid splintered authority. Yet, because of the limits placed on the manager's authority, not every problem a manager faces can be solved, nor every plan implemented. It is necessary to consolidate organizational authority through specific coordinating efforts, and committees provide an additional organizational structure that can be used for this purpose.

The creation of a special purpose committee to deal with a project or problem involving several units of an institution is an acceptable means of augmenting the normal organizational structure. If the problem is a recurring one, the structure itself should be adjusted to consolidate authority in a formal manner. For nonrecurring special problems, however, special purpose committees are appropriate.

Coordination among units in a highly decentralized organization may be fostered through committees. The focus under these circumstances is on the need for consistency of action and coordination of detailed plans among several units, which are often separated geographically. The health systems agency and the statewide health coordinating committee in health care planning are examples of committees created specifically for the purpose of coordinating activity among units with wide geographical distribution and multiple categories of membership.

To Counterbalance Authority

The check and balance system in an organization is subject to many pressures. When individuals in decentralized locations surrender authority to higher levels in the hierarchy, there is an attendant desire to monitor those higher levels. For example, in order to avoid a concentration of power in an executive director, a professional organization or a union with nationwide membership may create an executive committee with power to finalize all decisions, to approve the budget and authorize payments over a stated amount, and to act as sole decision-making body in many areas.

In a situation in which there has been significant fraud or deception or extreme authoritarianism, an officer may be retained temporarily to avoid a public scandal that would have negative effects for the organization. To limit the actions of such an individual during the transition period, the authority of the office is stripped away and placed in a special group that acts as a line committee in place of the official, who retains only the title and selected symbols of office. This committee functions until the officer is safely removed in a politically acceptable manner and a successor is chosen. The committee structure can be costly in economic terms, but an organization may be willing to pay the price to offset concentrated power and to obtain a diffused authority pattern in certain circumstances.

To Provide Representation of Interest Groups

Occasionally, certain groups have a vested interest in an organization and seek representation in its decision-making arenas, including committee participation. Wanting to protect the value of their degrees, alumni of a college seek positions on the board of trustees or on advisory committees to specific programs. Community members concerned with both long- and short-range plans of a health care organization seek input into patient care policies and community health programs through committee participation.

The organization, in turn, is interested in obtaining the support of specific groups and extends to them an opportunity to participate in its deliberations, often through the committee structure. A college may seek alumni representation to consolidate financial support from that group. A hospital or health center may seek community representatives for its advisory committee so that it can better determine local sentiment, assess probable responses to changes in the pattern of services offered, gain tangible financial support, and create good will toward the institution.

To Protect Due Process

In disciplinary matters, an organization may seek to reflect the larger societal value of due process, even when there is no legal or contractual requirement to do so. An increase in litigation has added an almost legal flavor to processes in which an individual's performance is evaluated. A committee of the individual's peers, even if the peer group does not have line authority, may be constituted to make a recommendation to the line officer or governing board. Examples of this approach include the promotion and tenure committee of a university, the ethics committee of a professional association, or the credentials committee of a medical staff. A union contract may specify the composition and function of a grievance committee to ensure that it includes line workers as well as management officials.

To Promote Coordination and Cooperation

When individuals affected by a decision have participated in making that decision, they are more likely to accept it and abide by it. Participants in group deliberations develop a fuller understanding of each unit's role. The communication process is facilitated, since the managers affected by the decision have had an opportunity to present their positions, the constraints under which their departments function, and their special needs, as well as to express disagreements. All members can evaluate the overall plan, review their own functions, and become familiar with the tasks assigned to other units that depend on their unit's output or, in turn, constrain the work assigned to their unit. In its final decision or recommendation, the committee states the assignments for each unit, and these are known to all. This is especially valuable when the success of the work depends on the full understanding and acceptance of the decision and plan of execution.

To Avoid Action

A manager who wishes to avoid or postpone an action indefinitely may create a committee to study the question or may refer it to a panel that has a long agenda and sends its findings to yet another committee for action. If members are selected carefully or if the assignment to an existing committee is made strategically, action will be slow. The issue may die for lack of interest or may become moot because of a decision made in some other arena or because of the departure from the organization of the individuals concerned. Although this intentional delaying tactic can be misused by a manager, it may also be a positive strategy; for example, delay through committee deliberation may be a form of "buying" time for issues to become less emotionally charged.

To Train Members

Committee participation may be used as part of the executive training process. Exposure to multiple facets of a decision, the defense of various positions, and the development of insight into the problems and considerations of other managers' decisions are part of this training experience. The potential manager is assessed by other members of the executive team during this interaction, and appropriate coaching and counseling may be given to the management trainee.

LIMITATIONS AND DISADVANTAGES OF COMMITTEES

Humorous and disparaging comments sometimes reflect the limitations and disadvantages of committee use: "A camel is a horse that was designed by a committee," or "There are no great individuals in this organization, only great committees."

Committee interaction, with its emphasis on deliberation and group participation, is slow. The committee structure, therefore, is not the proper arena for making decisions that must be made quickly. The time consumed, including the hours spent in formal meetings, is also costly. In highly decentralized organizations or professional associations, travel and lodging costs alone may run as high as $5,000 for a meeting of only a few members. The cost of an individual member's attendance (separate from travel and related costs) is calculated by establishing an average hourly rate per member and multiplying the meeting time by this rate. For example, an executive committee in which ten department heads participate meets a minimum of 2½ hours once a week. Their salaries are calculated and an hourly rate obtained. At an average of $50 per hour per member, a typical meeting of such a group costs at least $1250, not including preparation, follow-up time, or the cost of staff support and services. The results of committee action should offset the costs in time, money, and overall effort.

Because of time pressures, committee deliberations may be cut short, thus removing the major advantages of the committee structure (i.e., group participation and presentation of multiple viewpoints). The committee may be indecisive because there is insufficient time to deliberate, or the discussion may become vague and tangential, leading to adjournment without action. Members' lack of preparation prevents full discussion of issues. Being present and on time is only part of a committee member's responsibility; member preparation is a critical factor.

There are several pitfalls to be avoided in regard to preparation. Material may be prepared and distributed in a timely manner, but the committee members may fail to brief themselves prior to the meeting. A member of a subcommittee may fail to carry out an assignment that is critical for the panel's further action. Staff aides or the chairperson may be late in preparing items so that committee members arrive to find large quantities of critical material at their places and are expected to reach decisions without the time to develop an informed opinion.

Absenteeism or tardiness may obstruct the committee's work. If a quorum is required, absence or lateness (or early departure) of several members may upset the critical balance. When the discussion of an agenda item is dependent on a particular member's presence, this part of the meeting must be delayed or postponed if that member is absent or late. Furthermore, time spent waiting for members to arrive to provide a quorum or to discuss a particular agenda item generates cost with no offsetting productivity.

Obstructionist behavior in committee meetings can limit debate. On the one hand, a member who continually declines to give an opinion and who continually votes "abstain" muddies the outcome. The committee may be seen as lacking in decisiveness, and its recommendations may be set aside more easily. On the other hand, an individual or a few members may try to dominate the committee. When unanimity or at least major consensus is required, such members may refuse to give in or may insist on their own suggestions for compromise. The committee, in order to act, must accept this dominance by a few. A ready solution to this problem is the encouragement of minority reports. Some open discussion of group dynamics may also foster solutions to this type of roadblock.

Even with much good will and a high degree of commitment on the part of members, certain aspects of committee dynamics tend to limit the group's effectiveness. In seeking common ground for agreement and in dealing with small group pressures to be polite and maintain mutual respect, diluted decisions or compromise to the point of the least common denominator may characterize committee decisions.

Furthermore, a committee never can take the place of individual managers who accept specific responsibilities and exhibit leadership. Managers must accept the responsibility for certain decisions, even when they are unpopular. It may be especially important to have a specific individual held responsible for decisions in conflict situations. The proverbial buck stops at the highest level of officers, and one manager must be the first among equals when it is a decision in that manager's area of jurisdiction.

ENHANCEMENT OF COMMITTEE EFFECTIVENESS

Committees, in spite of their limitations, are valuable for organizational deliberations. Their effectiveness may be enhanced by

- viewing committee activity as important and legitimate
- providing the necessary logistical support
- assigning clear-cut responsibilities and specific functions to the committee
- considering committee size, composition, and selection of members carefully
- selecting the committee chairperson carefully
- maintaining adequate documentation and follow-up activity
- creating task forces as an alternative to the proliferation of committees
- ensuring that members are sensitive to group dynamics and organizational conflict

Legitimization of Committee Activity

The top management of an organization must create a climate in which the work of committee members is valued. The evaluation system for merit raises and promotions should include the assessment of individuals' work on committee assignments. Committee membership should be viewed positively by members rather than merely tolerated as a duty. Job descriptions should include committee assignment as a necessary component of the work. When staffing patterns are established, work hours should be allotted for essential committee participation. Committee structure should be streamlined so that action is purposeful and members can see the results of their work. Training specifically for effective committee involvement should be part of the overall training program for members rather than left to chance.

Logistical Support

All necessary staff assistance should be given to the committee chairperson and members. Staff assistants may prepare specific material, devise research questions, gather necessary support data, and carry out follow-up activities. Clerical support should be provided for recording and transcribing minutes and related documents. Adequate space is made available for meetings. Top management may enhance committee workings by requiring that committee meetings be scheduled regularly and that membership be drawn from several organizational components. Setting aside a certain block of time for interdepartmental meetings and proscribing intradepartmental sessions during that period facilitates the coordination of schedules. If it is deemed preferable, committee meetings may be scheduled for longer periods of time at less frequent intervals.

Scope, Function, and Authority

When a committee is created, its purpose and function, as well as its scope of activity, must be presented clearly. Will its purpose be merely to deliberate? Will it deliberate and make a recommendation or will its decision be a binding one? What subjects will it consider? For example, will the medical care evaluation committee concern itself only with assessments of the topics of quality assurance that are mandated by outside review agencies or will it expand its function to organizationwide quality assurance and education? Will utilization review remain a separate function? Will the medical record committee focus only on the records of inpatients or on the records of all patients who receive care in the institution regardless of patient category (e.g., inpatient, outpatient, group practice).

The scope of the committee's work is shaped by its authority. If the credentials committee of the medical staff only makes recommendations to the governing board, while the board retains final authority to make staff appointments, this should be stated in the bylaws creating the panel and setting forth its mandates. The committee's accountability also needs delineation. To whom does it make its reports? How frequently? Is coordination required with certain administrative components or with other committees?

Committee Size and Composition

No absolute figure can be given as the optimum size of a committee. Since open, free deliberation is a major reason for a committee, the size of the group should be small enough to permit discussion. On the other hand, it should be large enough to represent various interest groups. The organization's bylaws and charter may stipulate a required committee's composition, which, in turn, will affect the committee's size. Some hospital policies, for example, state that all chiefs of service are members of the executive committee; therefore, the size of the committee is determined by the organization's department structure.

The need for a quorum to undertake official committee action presents special problems if members' schedules simply do not allow them to attend meetings on a predictable basis. Committee size may be increased in order to ensure a quorum so that business may be conducted.

Committee composition is one of the most important factors in the success of a group's work. Whether they volunteer, are appointed, or are elected, members should possess certain personal qualities; they should be able to

- express themselves in a group
- keep to the point
- discuss issues in a practical rather than theoretical way
- give information that advances the thinking of the group about the topic rather than about themselves
- assess a topic in an orderly yet flexible way
- suppress the natural desire to speak for the sake of being heard or of saying what they think the leader or some powerful member wants to hear

The members also should have sufficient authority to commit the unit or group that they represent to the course of action adopted by the committee. If an individual is appointed to a committee to represent a busy executive, that person should have the power to cast a vote that binds the executive who deputized the member. Deputizing is not without its hazards, but they may be avoided by careful review and discussion between the executive and the representative before the meeting.

Generally, committee members should be of approximately equal rank and status in the organization in order to permit the free exchange of ideas. The presence of ex officio members, who may be viewed as more powerful than the elected members, may deter free discussion. Individuals who attend meetings as staff assistants should respect the limits placed on their participation. There should be a clear understanding that the duties of secretary of the committee are those of the individual appointed or elected from within the group; other persons present to carry out the clerical aspects of secretarial work, such as taking down the raw proceedings from which minutes will be extracted, should not be asked to participate in the discussion and should not volunteer information or opinions as they are not official members. If a parliamentarian who is not a member of the committee attends the meetings, this individual should confine any interaction with the committee to points of parliamentary procedure and should withhold all opinions, agreements, and disagreements concerning the issues under discussion. A group that appoints or elects a committee should have confidence that only those individuals duly appointed or elected will make decisions and recommendations on its behalf.

While diverse points of view should be represented in deliberations, not every participant must be a full-time committee member. Individuals can be invited to attend a meeting or a portion of one in order to answer questions from the committee, share information, or present a point of view. Like staff assistants, individuals who attend meetings as guests should respect the limits of their participation.

In summary, committee size and composition are matters of individual organizational determination. Committees should be large enough to represent various interest groups and ensure adequate group deliberation, but small enough to ensure that the deliberation will be effective.

THE COMMITTEE CHAIRPERSON

Selection and Duties

The position of chairperson of a committee may be filled in several ways. One is direct appointment by the individual with the mandate and the authority to do so. The bylaws of an organization may direct the president of the medical staff to appoint a committee chairperson. The manager of a department may be the chairperson of a related committee as a matter of course, the director of the utilization review program may be the appointed chairperson of the utilization review committee, and the individual who holds the line position responsible for safety will probably automatically become the chairperson of the safety committee.

Managers may appoint themselves chairpersons of committees that they constitute and over which they wish to exercise control, or they may offset powerful members by appointing as chairperson an individual sympathetic to their position. Selection of committee chairpersons may or may not be left to the group's membership. In committees where members are elected from the panel as a whole and where there is an accepted egalitarianism in the group, this is a common practice. The group conveys the idea that all those selected for membership have equal ability and that equal confidence is placed in all of them. Conversely, the group also could convey the idea that the committee is not very important so it does not matter who is chairperson. A group that elects the members of a committee may select the chairperson as a separate action by a special vote or may direct that the individual who receives the highest number of votes automatically assumes the chairpersonship.

Occasionally, the office is simply rotated among members of the committee in order to avoid a power struggle. When a specific activity of a standing committee requires extensive and recurring follow-up work and staff assistance is limited, the work of the chairperson is divided by rotation; since the burden of staff support must be shared by the chairperson's department or unit, this approach spreads the support work over several organizational units. When the committee's work is viewed as mere compliance with bureaucratic red tape and the work is not valued by its members nor by the group as a whole, the position of chairperson is sometimes downplayed by this rotation process. Finally, individual members may volunteer to accept the assignment as chairperson because of a sense of duty, because of a desire to advance themselves or protect some potentially threatened interest, or because the committee deals with an issue within their field of expertise.

An able, well-qualified individual sometimes refuses to accept the position of chairperson because it would limit his or her ability to participate in deliberations. Eligibility factors sometimes determine the choice of a chairperson. Prerequisites might include prior membership on the committee, tenure as a faculty member, ten years of service as a full-time employee, or a certain technical or professional degree.

A committee chairperson's duties include arranging for logistical support, chairing meetings, and monitoring follow-up assignments. The logistical duties include

- coordinating the schedules of committee members
- correlating committee activities with the work of related committees or departments
- checking for compliance with mandated deadlines and actions
- obtaining meeting space
- issuing meeting notices as to time, date, place, and agenda
- coordinating and distributing support information before meetings
- preparing the agenda, including sequencing items according to priority

Chairing the Meeting

The chairperson sets the tone of meetings, controls the agenda to a major extent, guides deliberation on the issues, and provides or denies opportunities for committee members to express themselves. The degree of formality or informality is indicated not only by the manner in which the chairperson conducts the business of the meeting but also by an explicit statement. At the outset, the chairperson makes known the rules of debate, for example, whether there will be general discussion followed by a formal vote and whether strict adherence to parliamentary procedures will be required throughout the meeting.

It is the duty of the chairperson to conduct the meeting efficiently by starting the session on time, following the agenda, and providing sufficient time for deliberation. Subtle leadership skills must be brought to bear as the chairperson referees the members' deliberations. The process of group deliberation and participation must be protected and promoted. The chairperson must artfully provide time for individuals to be heard, which is far more than merely letting each person have a turn to speak. Group cohesion must be fostered even when there are differences of opinion.

The agenda is usually prepared by the chairperson. It is intended to guide the proceedings, but the chairperson may take an item out of sequence if the course of discussion creates a natural opening for the deliberation of related agenda items. The chairperson keeps the meeting flowing by moving from one agenda item to another at appropriate times, calling the group's attention to work accomplished and work yet to be done.

The chairperson must seek to prevent polarization, overhasty decisions, or the eruption of blatant conflict. It is the chairperson's duty to prevent the group from moving into discussion of nonrelated topics or returning to issues that have already been settled. The chairperson periodically integrates the discussion by summarizing major points, calling for motions, and appointing subcommittees or individuals to carry out special assignments.

Follow-up Activity

The final duty of the chairperson is follow-up. The chairperson participates in the preparation of minutes either directly by formulating them or indirectly by reviewing and approving them as prepared by the committee secretary. Periodic reports must be made to administrative officials. In addition, the chairperson must write letters to invite special guests, consult technical staff, hold informal sessions with members between meetings, and attend subcommittee meetings or those of related committees; all these duties fall within the category of follow-up.

The chairperson must periodically review the work of the committee. Is this work satisfactory given the committee's basic charge? Is the committee fulfilling its designated function? The minutes of several recent months may be examined and specific follow-up inquiries made to individuals and subcommittees concerning the progress of work assigned; agenda items that were set aside or those not discussed for lack of time should be brought to the committee's attention again. All unfinished business should be monitored. Exhibit 7-1 is a form a committee chairperson may use to facilitate this follow-up. Exhibit 7-2 provides an example of a tabulated form for recording minutes.

MINUTES AND PROCEEDINGS

Sound practice requires that an organization maintain official documentation of business transacted. Minutes serve as the permanent factual record of

Exhibit 7-1 Follow-up of Committee Action

				Committee_____	
				Year_____	
Agenda Item Topic	*Meeting Date Deliberated*	*Description*	*Responsibility Assigned to*	*Next Action Due*	*Date Action Completed*
Outpatient Clinic Records	May 15	1. Develop chart review list.	Medical Record Administrator	July 20	
Suspension of Privileges for Admitting Patients	June 11	1. Review legal aspects of pro-cedure for suspending physician privileges.	Chief of Medical Staff	July 20	
		2. Update pro-cedures in light of legal aspects.	Chief of Medical Staff	October 17	

Exhibit 7-2 Excerpts from Utilization Review Committee Minutes

			Date_____
Agency No. Patient Initial	Start of Care	Discharge Date	Findings and Remarks
512-02 F.C.	10/25/90	current	RN, PT, OT: Good records; progress documented by all disciplines. RN evaluation had excellent needs assessment and nursing plan. PT evidenced ongoing teaching and good carry over. OT documentation not always legible, but patient progress in ADL was obvious to reviewer. Team cooperation evident throughout record.
513-07 A.B.	12/20/91	current	RN; Aide; ST; OT; PT: No list of medications. Two nursing supervision notes missing; doctors' orders not current. Nursing supervision is evident but aide notes are incomplete. Communication among all disciplines is weak. Why no social service referral? Recommend review of case with all disciplines; needs discharge plan.

committee proceedings. An explicit statement in bylaws or policies may state that the minutes shall be maintained, including a record of attendance; that they shall reflect the transactions, conclusions, and recommendations of each meeting adequately; and that they shall be kept in a permanent file. Some other time frame for retention that reflects the legal and statutory requirements for the organization may be stated. Committee manuals should contain such information.

Properly formulated, minutes summarize business transacted, including matters that require follow-up action, matters on which there is substantial agreement or disagreement, and issues that remain open for committee deliberation. Minutes are sometimes transmitted to individuals who are not currently members, as determined by the policies on distribution and by legal and accrediting requirements. The historical record provided in the minutes gives new members an overall sense of committee activity. A surveyor checking for compliance with utilization review requirements may request the minutes of the utilization review committee over the past year. Representatives of the Joint Commission may call for minutes and proceedings of the medical staff committees to help in determining whether the staff is fulfilling its medicoadministrative responsibilities.

In legal proceedings, the admissibility of committee minutes and proceedings as evidence rests on the premise that these records were made in the normal course of business at the time of the actions or events, or within a reasonable time thereafter. Thus, minutes of the official business of the organization's committees must be prepared, reviewed, and distributed in a timely manner (i.e., close to the time of the actual proceedings). They are reviewed formally at the next meeting to obtain general agreement that their content reflects the business transacted. Should a lawsuit be instituted regarding the possible negligence, malpractice, denial of privileges, or discipline of a practitioner, the minutes of such proceedings might, in some instances, be admissible as legal evidence; the laws on this point vary from state to state.

It could be argued that minutes do not reflect all the business transacted by the committee. The counterargument is a question: Why not? The effort spent on proper documentation in the normal course of business is a legitimate use of organizational time and staff. It has also been argued that minutes could be altered to reflect business that, in fact, was not transacted, but this is true of any form of documentation. Review of minutes by all members is one way to safeguard accuracy. Managers can only go forward guided by their own ethical code as well as by the organizational and societal presumption that the work was carried out "in good faith."

Preparation of Minutes

Minutes are prepared in two stages. First, either the proceedings are transcribed in their entirety by clerical staff or a summary of key points is compiled by a staff assistant. Then, the official secretary to the committee (if there is such an officer) or the committee chairperson formulates the official minutes from the transcript or summary. If there is no clerical assistant or staff aide, the chairperson (or member-secretary) uses self-compiled notes to formulate the minutes. Any required approval is obtained, and the minutes are sent out according to a prescribed distribution list. The distribution process may be simplified by developing a standing list of the names and titles of members, administrative officers to whom certain minutes are sent because of their organizational jurisdiction, and/or the chairpersons of related committees. The chairperson then needs only to check the names of those who are to receive a particular set of minutes. It is useful to include the statement *Standard Distribution* and also to list any additional individuals to whom minutes were sent as a point of information. The inclusion of a list of support material or enclosures makes the minutes more complete.

Exhibit 7-3 illustrates a format that makes it possible to scan the pages of a volume of minutes and focus on specific topics. The topic key should be placed in the right-hand margin; if the left-hand margin is used for the topic key, it may be placed too deeply in a bound or semibound margin for ready reference. Inclusion of the dates on which there was previous discussion gives the user an easy means of reference to related information. This format generates an index of committee topics, and members have the benefit of ready reference to past deliberations of a related nature.

Content of Minutes

Minutes are more than a mere listing of committee actions in chronological order. The topics discussed are normally grouped, a process facilitated by adherence to a formal agenda. In relatively informal meetings, however, the discussion may be diffuse and less focused on discrete topics than is a discussion in a meeting conducted under strict parliamentary procedure.

The minutes should reflect what is done, not what is said. Adequate minutes as a matter of course contain such information as

Exhibit 7-3   Sample Format for Minutes

The committee directed its attention to new guidelines concerning the content of discharge summaries. A random sample of discharge summaries dictated during recent months was compared with the guidelines to determine areas of noncompliance and areas of strength.	DISCHARGE SUMMARIES 2/23/90 9/23/91

- the name of the committee
- the date, time, and place of the meeting
- whether it is a regular or special meeting
- the names of members present (specify ex officio if appropriate)
- the names of members absent (include a notation of excused absence if appropriate)
- the names of guests, including title or department as an additional indicator of reason for attending

The opening paragraph of the minutes, which is relatively standardized, normally includes

- the name of the presiding officer
- the establishment of quorum, if this is done routinely or at the request of a member
- a routine review of the minutes of the previous meeting, noting whether they were reviewed as read or only as distributed and whether any corrections were made

The proceedings are summarized. The names of those who made formal motions are given, but the names of those who seconded the motions need not be recorded. All main motions, whether adopted or rejected, are included.

The bulk of the business may be reflected in general discussion only. There are five basic dispositions of agenda items, and each should be listed with its disposition:

1. Item is discussed and a formal motion is made; formal wording of motion is given. Votes for and against, as well as abstentions, are recorded. Notation is made whether motion is adopted or rejected.
2. Item is discussed and there is general consensus. No formal motion is made. Summary statement of general discussion is entered with notation that there was general agreement with action taken.
3. Item is discussed and tabled informally or set aside for discussion at another time because members need more information. Reason for setting it aside may be stated; indeed, it is useful to give this information for later reference.
4. Item is discussed, with subsequent formal motion to table it permanently.
5. Item is not discussed. This is not stated directly; item is simply carried as old business.

A useful practice for providing background information for new members of a committee or for review of past committee action is to include a rationale statement for each motion that is made. Although this is not required, such a statement provides a succinct summary of the underlying reasons for an action:

> It was moved and seconded that chart review will be carried out by medical record department personnel for all patients in the long-term care/rehabilitation unit whose length of stay exceeds 14 days. This review will be made on a weekly basis for each patient.
>
> *Rationale:* Because of the extended length of stay for this category of patients (an average of 47 days in this facility), the detection and subsequent correction of medical record documentation deficiencies should be carried out during the patients' stay.

Both the positive and negative discussion of each topic may be summarized. If there is a specific follow-up action to be taken and a committee member is assigned this task, the name of the individual should be included in the minutes. If a subcommittee is created, the names of its members are given. In the minutes of a formal meeting, points of order and appeals, whether sustained or lost, are noted.

At the conclusion of the minutes, the name of the individual who compiled them is given. The legend *minutes compiled by* may be used instead of the somewhat archaic phrase *respectfully submitted.* If minutes are approved or reviewed by the chairperson before distribution, this is stated. The minutes should be signed by the person who compiled them (e.g., the committee secretary) and the person who approved them for distribution. If the committee does not have an official secretary, the chairperson's name and signature are entered.

Minutes and proceedings reflecting patient care often are summarized in tabular form. Exhibits 7-4 to 7-7 include samples of such documentation.

Exhibit 7-4 Department of Rehabilitation Interdisciplinary Monitoring and Evaluation Standard

Aspect of Program: Assessment of patient education, patient training, and discharge planning needs.

Standard: Comprehensive inpatient rehabilitation services include education, training, and discharge planning for persons served and their families.

Threshold: 80%

Indicator:	Total Monitored	No. of Yeses	No. of Noes	Percent Compliance
1. The patient will receive an initial documented physician's assessment within 24 hours of admission that includes patient/family education and training needs and discharge planning needs.				
2. The patient will receive an initial documented nursing assessment within 24 hours of admission that includes patient/family education and training needs and discharge planning needs.				

Exhibit 7-4 *continued*

Indicator:	Total Monitored	No. of Yeses	No. of Noes	Percent Compliance
3. The patient will receive an initial OT assessment within 24 hours of admission (with documentation) within 72 hours that includes patient/family education and training needs and discharge planning needs.				
4. The patient will receive an initial PT assessment within 24 hours of admission (with documentation) within 72 hours that includes the goal of patient/family education and training and discharge planning.				

Source: Developed by the QA/QI Committee, Department of Rehabilitation Medicine, Thomas Jefferson University Hospital, Philadelphia, PA. Reprinted by permission.

Exhibit 7-5 Occupational Therapy Department Quality Assurance Report—Chart Audit

(charts reviewed Jan. & Feb. 1991)		Date: 3/4/91
Criteria	Standard	Outcome
1. Contact Note	100%	34% *
2. Date	100%	100%
Discipline	100%	100%
Time	100%	0% *
3. SOAP Format	100%	100%
4. ADL Status Doc.	95%	100%
5. UE Status Doc.	95%	100%
6. Legibility	100%	94%
7. D/C recom.	95%	67% *
8. Stated Weekly Goals	95%	60% *
9. Green Sheets Included	100%	100%

*Follow-up section required.

Source: Developed by the QA/QI Committee, Department of Rehabilitation Medicine, Thomas Jefferson University Hospital, Philadelphia, PA. Reprinted by permission.

Exhibit 7-6 Rehabilitation Inpatient Unit Monitoring and Evaluation of Falls Risk Program

Standard: All rehabilitation patients will remain free from injury. The Department of Rehabilitation will take action to reduce unsupervised falls risk through the development and utilization of a falls assessment.

Indicator:	Monitored	No. of Yeses	Percent Compliance
1. The patient has wristband code for falls risk	24	20	83%
2. The patient has knowledge of falls risk and intervention	24	16	66%
3. Chart review:			
a. The patient has a falls risk assessment by a physician	10	10	100%
b. There will be daily falls risk assessment by the nurse	24	22	92%

Note: Improvements noted in all areas. Indicators chosen to examine the compliance of team members with falls risk assessment program. Patient knowledge and understanding indicators may suggest need to increase.

Source: Developed by Shirlee Drayton-Hargrove, RN, MSN for QA/QI Committee, Department of Rehabilitation Medicine, Thomas Jefferson University Hospital, Philadelphia, PA. Reprinted by permission.

Exhibit 7-7 Occupational Therapy Program Evaluation

								1/91 - 3/91
Program Objectives	*Weight*	*Population*	*Measure*	*Time*	*Goal (national avg.)*	*Results*	*Performance*	*Performance Index*
Maximize Rate of Improvement in Self-Care	25	All Patients	Total FIM	adm to dc	0.26	0.29	1.11	27.9
Maximize Feeding	10	All Patients	FIM Feeding	dc	6.1	6.8	1.11	11.1
Grooming	10	All Patients	FIM Grooming	dc	5.7	7	1.23	12.3
Bathing	10	All Patients	FIM Bathing	dc	4.8	6.1	1.27	12.7
Dress UE	10	All Patients	FIM UE Dress	dc	5.5	6.8	1.23	12.3
Dress LE	10	All Patients	FIM LE Dress	dc	4.8	6.3	1.31	13.1
Maximize Rate of Improvement in Mobility	15	All Patients	FIM Mobility	adm to dc	0.16	0.18	1.13	16.95
Maximize Increase in Tub Transfer	10	All Patients	FIM Tub Transf.	adm to dc	1.7	1.7	1	10

TOTAL PERFORMANCE 116.35% OF NATIONAL AVERAGE

Source: Developed by Joanne C. Cassidy, M.Ed, OTR/L, Chief Occupational Therapist, for the QA/QI Committee, Department of Rehabilitation Medicine, Thomas Jefferson University Hospital, Philadelphia, PA. Reprinted by permission.

Chapter 8

Adaptation, Motivation, and Conflict Management

CHAPTER OBJECTIVES

1. Recognize the necessity of integrating the individual into the organization.
2. Identify the techniques that foster integration of the individual into the organization.
3. Identify the patterns of behavior through which workers express their attitude toward the organization.
4. Define the management function of motivation.
5. Identify the theories of motivation.
6. Identify the significance of the study of conflict in the organizational setting.
7. Understand the origins of conflict situations.
8. Develop strategies for analyzing each type of conflict.
9. Learn to deal with personal, small group, and organizational conflict.
10. Analyze organizational conflict in terms of its causes, participants, and processes.
11. Identify strategies for dealing with conflict in organizations.

ADAPTATION AND MOTIVATION

In order to get work done efficiently and effectively, managers must motivate workers and assist in their adaptation to organizational demands. Individuals must fit into the organizational framework. There is a close tie between motivation and adaptation activities and the controlling function of the manager. The worker who fits into the organization and who values an

Note: Significant portions of this chapter were contributed by Joanne C. Cassidy, M.Ed., OTR/L, Chief of Occupational Therapy, Thomas Jefferson University Hospital, Department of Rehabilitation Medicine.

assigned role is likely to be motivated more easily. In turn, the need to control activity through disciplinary action is reduced.

Adaptation to Organizational Life

Two specific factors that result from organizational structure may be cited to illustrate the need for an explicit management process to help integrate the individual into the organization:

1. the need to offset the effect of decentralization
2. the need to coordinate the many individual functions that result from departmentation and specialization

Overall goals and policies are made at the highest level of the hierarchy, but the work is carried out at every level. Occasionally, conflicting directives are issued from the central authority.

Additionally, the number of individuals who enter the organization and the different manner in which these individuals react to the complexities of organizational life must be taken into consideration. These individuals not only have different values, different personalities, and different life experiences, but they also belong to many other organizations, some of which may have values that compete and even conflict with the values embodied in the workplace. Some of the patterns of accommodation to organizational life may be functional for the organization but dysfunctional for the individual. Potential conflict must be offset, and the personality mixes of workers and clients must be melded into smooth interpersonal relationships.

Techniques for Fostering Integration

Events and conditions should be anticipated as fully as possible, and the courses of action to be taken for designated categories of events and conditions should be described. Authorization of the course of action applicable to any category may be permissive; it may spell out several series of steps among which the employee shall choose. In order to prevent undesirable actions from arising, penalties should be established for those who commit them. The policy manual, the procedure manual, the employee handbook, the medical staff bylaws, and the licensure laws for the various health professionals are all routine management tools for guiding behavior and fostering integration.

Work Rules

Rule formation generally has been accepted as a management prerogative in the control function. Work rules are related to motivational processes because they contribute to a stable organizational environment. They serve several functions in an organization:

- They create order and discipline so that the behavior of workers is goal-oriented.
- They help unify the organization by channeling and limiting behavior.
- They give members confidence that the behavior of other members will be predictable and uniform.
- They make behavior routine so that managers are free to give attention to nonroutine problems.
- They prevent harm, discomfort, and annoyance to clients.
- They help ensure compliance with legislation that affects the institution as a whole.

The organization has a positive duty to protect both clients and workers with regard to health, sanitation, and safety. In addition, it must seek to prevent behavior that has the potential of alienating or offending clients. Because they deal with patients and their families in stressful situations, health care organizations have specific obligations in this area.

Sanctions

Both positive and negative sanctions can be used to induce compliance. Bonus pay, merit increases, and special time off with pay are positive sanctions; demotion, suspension, and written reprimands are negative sanctions. An essential element in any system of sanctions is the development of adequate feedback mechanisms and correction where needed. Employee evaluation and training processes can provide feedback and correction on a routine basis.

Selection

Kaufman stressed that the recruitment and selection process can be used to influence the degree to which employees tend to conform and become integrated into the workplace.[1] The more selective an organization is, the more effective the involvement of the members tends to be. Their commitment to organizational values is deeper, and they need fewer external controls.

In recruiting members, the highly selective organization should try to appeal to an audience composed of individuals who are well disposed toward the values of the organization—even at this preselection stage. Recruitment information may indicate implicitly or explicitly the need to conform.

Training

Kaufman also noted that highly structured orientation training can ensure the technical readiness of new employees and increase the likelihood they will conform.[2] For example, their technical skills can be modified so that they perform the work according to the specific procedures unique to the organization. Orientation programs have been developed in hospitals in order to familiarize professionally trained individuals (e.g., technologists) with particular routines. Businesses use the rotating management internship to foster integration of newly graduated management majors.

Identification with the Organization

The process of developing in employees a strong sense of identification with the organization is enhanced by the internal transfer and promotion process, which can also add to their ability to adjust and broaden themselves.[3] The development of a sense of identification is good for the organization but it can also be good for each individual. Any continuity, any structure possessed by the person's work life is provided by the organization. The organization becomes, as it were, a major source of personal identity, and through the promotion process a stable career path can be developed.

The Work Group

An employee's particular mindset is continually reinforced by his or her work group. Through the work group, the individual is assimilated into the organization—or is perhaps prevented from being properly assimilated. In addition to the formal prescriptions regarding work activities, informal patterns of behavior arise among members of the group. The individual learns the unwritten rules as well as interpretations of the written rules. The informal organization of the work group also satisfies an essential human need—the need to belong. Nonconformity with group norms could lead to expulsion from the group, which would eliminate a vital source of information and communication as well as an arena in which to air conflicts that stem from the formal organizational role demands.

PATTERNS OF ACCOMMODATION

Individuals adjust to highly organized settings in a variety of ways. Presthus suggested that the bureaucratic situation evokes three types of accommodation: (1) upward mobility, (2) indifference, and (3) ambivalence.[4]

Upward Mobility

An individual who identifies deeply with the organization and derives strength from his or her involvement is upwardly mobile. This strong identification not only evokes a sense of loyalty and affirmation but also provides a constant point of reference. Presthus noted that, because the upwardly mobile employee accepts organization's demand for complete conformity, he or she can overlook the contradictions between the routine operations of the organization and its official myths.

Indifference

Unlike the upwardly mobile employee, an employee who is indifferent refuses to compete for organizational rewards. Although alienated by the structural conditions of big organizations, the indifferent employee has come to terms with the work environment. Presthus noted the use of general psychological withdrawal as a means of reducing conflict. In particular, the individual redirects interest toward off-the-job satisfactions. Work is not the individual's whole life, and his or her off-the-job activities are rarely job-related. Presthus noted that indifferent employees are often the most satisfied members of the organization, since their aspirations are based on a realistic appraisal of opportunities.

Ambivalence

The employee who neither rejects the promise of power nor plays the games required to get power in the organization demonstrates ambivalence. This individual has high aspirations, but lacks the interpersonal skills of the upwardly mobile. The ambivalent employee does not honor the status system and tends to have difficulty with superiors, who are aware that their relationship with the employee is based on formal authority, not on esteem. The ambivalent employee is often a specialist caught between the world of specialized skills and the organizational hierarchy. He or she is usually sensitive to change and can be a catalytic agent in bringing about change.

THEORIES OF MOTIVATION

On the one hand, the manager seeks to develop a work force that fits the organization; on the other hand, the manager must remain aware of the basic needs of the workers. The art of motivating is built on this recognition of human need.

Motivation is the degree of readiness or the desire within an individual to pursue some goal. The function of motivating or actuating is essentially a matter of leading the workers to understand and accept the organizational goals and to contribute effectively to meeting these goals. In motivating or actuating, the manager seeks to increase the zone of acceptance within the individual and to create an organizational environment that enhances the individual's will to work. As self-motivation increases, the need for coercive controls and punishment decreases.

Bases of Motivation

Needs are the internal, felt wants of an individual (they are also referred to as *drives* and *desires*). Incentives are external factors that an individual perceives as possible satisfiers of felt needs. A review of management history reveals shifting emphases in the understanding of motivation.

Maslow's Hierarchy of Needs

Maslow's theory of motivation is predicated on the premise that every action is motivated by an unsatisfied need. Purposeful behavior is motivated by a multiplicity of interests and motivators and therefore, varies with circumstances and with individuals. Once a need has been satisfied, another level of need must be appealed to in order to motivate workers, for a satisfied need is no longer a motivator. Maslow's hierarchy of needs consists of the following scale[5]:

1. physiological needs
2. safety and security needs
3. the need to belong and to engage in social activity
4. the need for esteem and status
5. the need for self-fulfillment

Herzberg's Two-Factor Theory

Herzberg approached the theory of motivation by identifying two factors or elements that are operative in motivation: satisfiers and dissatisfiers. There are, according to Herzberg, many factors in organizational life that satisfy or dissatisfy, including company policy, supervisors, working conditions, and interpersonal relationships among work group members. If these are perceived as negative or lacking, they are dissatisfiers. If they are present and perceived as "good," they are satisfiers; they are not motivators, however. Herzberg identifies the following as examples of motivators: opportunity for advancement and promotion, greater responsibility, and opportunity for growth and interesting work. His concept of motivators tends to parallel Maslow's concept of higher-level needs—those of esteem and status and self-fulfillment.[6]

Relationship of Maslow to Herzberg

If you know the motives (needs) of individuals you want to influence (according to Maslow), then you should be able to determine what goals (Herzberg) you should provide in the environment to motivate those individuals. Hersey and Blanchard postulate that this is possible because it has been found that money and benefits tend to satisfy needs at the physiological and security levels; interpersonal relations and supervision are examples of factors that satisfy social needs; and increased responsibility, challenging work, and growth and development are motivators at the esteem and self-actualization levels.[7]

McGregor's Theory X and Theory Y

McGregor set forth a series of assumptions that compare the traditional view of workers (Theory X) with his own view of industrial behavior (Theory Y). The manager who holds Theory X believes that employees have an inherent dislike for work and assumes that they have little ambition, will avoid work if possible, and want security above all else. In contrast, the manager who holds Theory Y assumes that work is as natural as play or rest; that the average worker, under the right conditions, seeks to accept responsibility; and that workers will exercise self-direction and self-control in the service of objectives to which they are committed.[8]

Contemporary Emphasis in Motivation Theory

Developed primarily by Japanese managers in the late 1960s and 1970s, Theory Z is a contemporary approach to management and motivation that focuses on increased productivity and job satisfaction among workers. The cultural climate in which this pattern of management developed, that of Japan, emphasizes close linkage of work and the worker's life. The term *Theory Z* was coined by William Ouchi, who described in detail the elements of this motivational approach[9]:

1. lifelong careers with the same organization
2. group decision making
3. quality circles to foster worker involvement in decisions and control processes
4. lateral movement throughout most of the divisions of the organization

Although this approach to management is not universal, the focus on increasing productivity and motivating workers through participative management has become widely influential.

HIGH-PERFORMANCE MANAGEMENT

An effective manager motivates workers through the provision of adequate support and resources. The high-performance equation suggested by J. R. Schermerhorn, Jr., in his article "Improving Health Care Productivity through High-Performance Managerial Development"[10] offers an approach for middle managers to improve productivity by promoting a better use of human resources. The High-Performance Equation (performance = ability × support × effort) broadens the managerial perspective by focusing on the factors of ability, support, and motivation. According to Schermerhorn, for high levels of performance, people must have the right abilities and support, and must be motivated to exert the necessary work effort.[11] When these factors are maximized, higher performance is consistantly achieved. The successful manager identifies the importance of these elements and utilizes these elements for increased productivity.[12]

The Requisite Abilities

In order for individuals to achieve high performance in their work they must have the necessary abilities. Through employee selection, the manager must choose individuals with the necessary skills to match the job requirements and duties for that position. It is important to recognize that the manager must be able to provide on-going training to maintain and further develop the employee's skills. For example, this can be made available for the employee through a continuing education fund or tuition reimbursement mechanism.

As health care professionals, we are aware of the importance of continued education. However, the financial assistance and time off to attend these courses and workshops are not always supported by the respective institution. A manager must be able to demonstrate the importance of these educational programs and the return on investment for the institution. Worker participation in such programs contributes to high performance and increased productivity.

The Requisite Support

According to Schermerhorn, "Even the most capable employee will not achieve *high* performance unless proper support for the required work activities is available."[13] To provide this support, the manager must create and maintain a work environment that permits each employee's abilities and skills to be fully utilized. For example, the manager should ensure each employee has up-to-date equipment, an environment conducive to work, and proper guidance and direction. In addition, departmental goals should be attainable, interference from unrelated work activities should be minimal, and fringe benefits and remuneration should be competitive. The effective manager, working in concert with upper management, helps to provide the requisite resources to achieve high performance from his or her employees.

Effort and the Competency Factor

Schermerhorn looks at the issue of competency as "something that all too often is neglected as a motivational resource . . . when an individual feels competent in their work, they can be expected to work harder."[14] The manager can help employees be more competent in their work by ensuring that they have the necessary skills and support for the jobs they are performing. The work environment should help to facilitate the successful completion of the work assigned. The effective manager will organize work assignments in such a way as to match employees' skills and abilities with the tasks that need to be completed. According to Schermerhorn, "When people have the necessary abilities and the proper support to do their jobs, it is likely that feelings of personal competency will motivate them to work harder and do these jobs well."[15]

Strategies for High-Performance Management

To incorporate the concepts of high-performance management, the manager should identify strategies on how to influence the three high-performance factors: abilities, support, and competency. Schermerhorn recommends that the manager develop action agendas from which realistic, people-oriented productivity strategies can be developed. The following action agendas were adapted from the article by Schermerhorn and have implications for managers of physical therapy, occupational therapy, and medical record departments.[16]

Agenda: Focusing on Ability

Action Objective: Staff all employee positions with people capable of completing the necessary work.
   Action Strategies:

- Assess and delineate all work in the work unit and develop job descriptions with job specifications.
- Communicate achievable performance goals to all employees in all areas of the work unit. This communication should be done on a regularly scheduled basis.
- Keep informed of training and development needs for employees in all areas of the work unit.
- Communicate formally and informally with higher management regarding staff limitations and capabilities as well as suggested promotions, transfers, and replacements.
- Establish a positive image of the department to ensure that capable people want to work in it.
- When a position becomes available, view it as an opportunity to adjust the job description and to recruit new, qualified candidates.
- Be informed on relevant labor markets, including wage and salary levels and fringe benefits. Communicate this information to higher management.

Agenda: Focusing on Support

Action Objective: Assist employees in obtaining the support they require to fully utilize their skills.
   Action Strategies:

- Specify task directions for all employees.
- Provide regular and constructive feedback to all persons on the job.
- Eliminate or modify unnecessary or inconsistent rules, procedures, and policies.
- Treat employees fairly and consistently in applying all rules and policies.
- Meet regularly with employees to discuss their work and what resources are needed to do their work well.
- Be persistent in trying to provide the best possible resources (equipment, budgets, facilities, and technologies).
- Act in ways that help create a pleasant, socially satisfying, and dynamic work environment.

Agenda: Focusing on Effort

Action Objective: Encourage employees to work hard at their jobs.
Action Strategies:

- Do everything possible to maximize ability and support as positive performance factors in the work unit.
- Work with all employees in setting performance objectives and standards for evaluating the results.
- Provide rewards and reinforcements for high-performance achievements whenever possible.
- Use praise and public recognition regularly as rewards for high productivity for a job well done.
- Train all supervisors in the work unit to be competent in dealing with their subordinates.
- Communicate with higher management about performance accomplishments in the work unit.
- Be a visible, confident, and enthusiastic leader in the workplace, not just the work unit.
- Be a role model of high performance.

In summary, high-performance management is a useful and practical approach for all health care managers at all levels. The elements of the high-performance equation provide a means to develop strategies to increase production and better utilize human resources. As Schermerhorn concludes, "The equation can be used as a framework for educating others about their supervisory responsibilities, and for creating a self-renewing and productivity-oriented, team development process."[17]

CONFLICT

Conflict is an inevitable component of cooperative action, and the effects of conflict are felt by all participants in organizational life. Indeed, in a sense organizational life largely consists of carefully orchestrated conflict, so much so that one of the classic functions of a manager is to ensure coordination, which includes promoting cooperation and minimizing conflict.

Dictionary definitions of conflict use terms such as *variance, incompatibility, disagreement, inner divergence,* and *disturbance.* Conflict is basically a state of external and internal tension that results when two or more demands are made on an individual, group, or organization.

The Study of Conflict

The manager and health care practitioner must understand the phenomenon of conflict within organizations so that they can make it acceptable, predictable, and therefore manageable. Conflict must be accepted as an inevitable part of all group effort. The causes of conflict are located primarily in the organizational structure, with its system of authority, roles, and specialization. The clash of personal styles of interaction can be analyzed so as to deal more effectively with such clashes.

Conflict can be accepted as an element of change, a positive catalyst for continual challenge to the organization. Aggression may be accepted and channeled to foster survival. If conflict is not channeled and controlled, it may have negative effects that impede the growth of both the individual and the organization.

In certain situations, conflict may clarify relationships, effect change, and define organizational territories or jurisdictions. When there has been an integrative solution, resulting from open review of all points of view, agreement is strengthened and morale heightened. Conflict tends to energize an organization, forcing it to keep alert, to plan and anticipate change, and to serve clients in more effective ways.

Personal Conflict

According to Freud, who viewed the mind as an open system, incoming energy creates an imbalance and upsets the individual's equilibrium. The resulting inner tensions generate psychic energy that produces conflict. The greater the inequities in energy, the greater the tension. The person experiences the anxiety of conflict. Once the opposing forces are resolved, equilibrium is restored.

Jung believed that conflicting tendencies formed the basis of life because polar elements both attract and repel each other. Personality polarities include introversion versus extroversion, thinking versus feeling, and love versus hate. The stable personality recognizes the polar forces and works to integrate both sides.

Because people have polar forces, one-sided solutions to conflicts must be avoided. Unfortunately, it is common to label conflict as a battle—one force competing with another for the same resources. This military analogy reinforces the idea that there must be a winner and a loser. "Fighting" to win is a primitive way to resolve conflicts, because the loser will work to regain lost resources. Since the losing side is not represented in the resolution, the loser's needs will become important once again, and the conflict will require additional attention.

Developmental Perspective

Erikson expanded Freud's theory of personality development, dividing a life span into eight stages. Each stage is an arena for personal conflict. Individuals can work through each stage or carry unresolved issues into the next stage of life. Because the effective resolution of the conflict at each stage requires a balance among polar forces, some conflicts are longstanding and reappear throughout a person's life. The stages are as follows[18]:

1. trust vs. mistrust
2. autonomy vs. shame
3. initiative vs. guilt
4. industry vs. inferiority
5. identity vs. role diffusion
6. intimacy vs. isolation
7. generativity vs. stagnation
8. ego identity vs. despair

Maturity requires work at every stage. Freud, Jung, and Erikson all agree that unresolved conflicts remain with the person, appearing again and again throughout life in a variety of forms.

Conflict and Learning

Other theorists study conflict from an external vantage point. Two of these theorists, Miller and Dollard, developed an explanation of conflict that is based on psychoanalytic theory. They theorized that personal conflict emerges from unconscious emotions that are incongruous with other feelings.[19]

Learning theorists identify four types of conflict:

1. approach-approach conflict, in which "the individual is confronted with two desirable but incompatible goals"[20]
2. approach-avoidance conflict, in which "a single object, person, or situation has both attracting and repelling attributes"[21]
3. double approach-avoidance conflict, in which there are alternative possibilities, each possessing positive and negative characteristics[22]
4. avoidance-avoidance conflict, in which "the individual must choose between two undesirable courses of action"[23]

Resolution of Personal Conflict

There are a number of ways to resolve personal conflict. Lewin developed a method (force field analysis) to unify conflicting forces.[24] The person who is experiencing conflict generates objective data to acquire an overview of the situation and resolve the conflict. The six stages of the process are as follows:

1. Schedule a period of uninterrupted time to study the personal conflict.
2. List all the forces pushing in one direction. Repeat the process for all the forces pushing in the opposite direction.
3. Read over the list and label the forces as positive or negative.
4. Take another sheet of paper and divide the paper in half. Put the positive forces on one side and the negative forces on the other side. Look over the list and refine the labeling system by dividing the positive forces into very positive (++), positive (+), and barely positive (−+) forces. Divide the negative forces into very negative (−−), negative (−), and barely negative (+−) forces.
5. Recopy the list and group the forces into similar categories (e.g., all very positive forces in one area, all positive forces in another, etc.).
6. Put the list away for a period of time, even if only for an hour or so. Bring the list out and weigh the positive and negative forces. Determine which categories balance and which categories create the difference needed to make a decision.

Small-Group Conflict

A small group consists of two or more individuals who share some goal or purpose. The shared goal generates interdependence, and the individuals in the group communicate with each other and modify their behavior in light of the behavior of others.[25] Every small group is unique and has a collective personality that depends on all the individuals in the group. Thus, if one member is happy, sad, or absent, the composition of the collective personality changes. The collective group experience is called the *group culture*.[26] Group life is not always pleasant. At times, group members experience emotions that create anxiety, and these emotions can build up and create group conflict. Group conflict is commonplace and endemic to group life.

Origin

Today, opportunities for a solitary existence are limited. In fact, because of increased population, sophisticated means of travel and communication, and advances in technology, people's lives are more interdependent than ever. The push to satisfy the personal desires of the group members must be tempered by the pull to fulfill societal obligations. The *I* struggles with the demands of *we*. Conflict arises when personal needs are overrun by the group needs.

Theoretical Perspectives

Group conflict can be explained from several theoretical perspectives: (1) psychoanalytical, (2) developmental, and (3) systems. Each perspective offers a unique focus for the study of conflict.

Psychoanalytical Approach. Those who adhere to the psychoanalytical approach believe that each group struggles between task and emotional needs. The conflict can be pictured as a wheel divided into two halves. If the group's energy shifts, the wheel is unbalanced. The group then must move to establish a new balance. The shifts are based on both conscious and unconscious desires that emerge from infancy. Tension arises from unmet needs on either level. The most productive goals satisfy the emotional and task needs of members. A goal that concerns only tasks or only emotions cannot be completely fulfilling. Work requires a balance so that task and emotional needs are addressed equally.

Developmental Approach. Developmental group theorists conclude that groups go through stages of development. Tuchman presented the following model[27]:

1. A group initially concerns itself with orientation, which is accomplished by testing.[28]
2. The second stage is characterized by conflict and polarization around interpersonal issues. The individual members resist the group's influence and task requirements.
3. In the third stage, the members develop a cohesive feeling, and new standards and roles are adopted.
4. Finally, the group members are able to use their roles to achieve the goals of the group. Roles become flexible, and group energy is devoted to the tasks that need to be done.

Systems Approach. Lewin developed a systems approach for explaining group behavior. He addressed the forces that shape individual and group behavior and stressed the importance of subjective interpretations of live events. Actions cannot be viewed as isolated events, because each individual is part of a social system.[29]

The system is divided into regions that are differentiated from the background, valences (degree of attraction to a goal) that promote or retard movement, barriers that impede movement in the life space, and forces that are either internal or external pressures to move. Conflict can be viewed as forces or barriers that impede or promote movement toward a valence or goal.

The system seeks balance or equilibrium. Lewin's focus on the entire social system and his view of the importance of understanding everyone's subjective experience are useful. Change can be viewed as an event that upsets the equilibrium of the system. The group is an open system, receiving input from the environment. The group needs feedback or information that is fed into the system to keep the system on course.

Resolution of Small-Group Conflict

The first step in resolving group conflict is to identify the underlying causes and categorize the conflict as a resource, ideological, or personal identity conflict.

Unconscious Resolution Methods. There are several unconscious means to protect the ego from anxiety-producing events. These strategies are called defense mechanisms:

- Repression is a method of pushing unpleasant thoughts or feelings into the unconscious. The person may feel a vague pull when reminded of them, but the cause is hidden from consciousness.
- Rationalization is a substitution process by which acceptable thoughts or feelings are substituted for unacceptable ones.
- Denial is a refusal to admit that a conflict or problem exists. It is a form of repression, because the unpleasant thoughts and emotions are negated.
- Projection is a method of moving the cause of anxiety from the inner world to a person or event in the external world.

These defense mechanisms create communication barriers, because they make it difficult to share deep-seated emotions and thoughts. Unconscious thoughts obviously cannot be tapped as easily as conscious thoughts and emotions.

Conscious Resolution Methods

There are two conscious strategies to promote conflict resolution: compromise and integration. Compromise requires interaction and an agreement to work together. It is a mutual agreement to solve the differences by concessions on both sides. Since each side gives up something, there is no loser. Individuals who are familiar with competition may consider compromise a surrender that opens them up to dangerous concessions. This view is a short-sighted and pessimistic view of compromise.

Compromise can be a creative solution to the cause of the conflict. Group members share ideas and together they alter their concerns. This sharing is one of the benefits of group interaction.

Integration is the most difficult method of resolving conflicts. Instead of making concessions in a compromise, individuals unite their differences in the solution. Successful integration requires group members who are willing to express their task and emotional needs, are able to prioritize issues and concerns, are willing to work on a method to integrate polar desires and needs, and are committed to longstanding conflict resolution. This method requires a great deal of work, but it usually resolves conflict successfully.

Cultural Aspects of Conflict Resolution

Conflicts emerge from differences among people, and differences are based on values. A value is an attitude, belief, or feeling that is learned. Family, peers, religious affiliates, and school personnel all shape values. People orient themselves to daily life by weighing input from the environment on an internal value scale. Values help people to function efficiently in the world, but they may become so automatic that they close a person's mind to new ideas or approaches to situations.

Values shape individual responses to confrontation and fighting. Some people are silent; some, aggressive; some, assertive; and some, active on selected issues. The group members must develop norms to handle decision making, fighting, and conflict in a positive manner.

ORGANIZATIONAL CONFLICT

Managers can assess organizational conflicts by using a theoretical model, since it frees them from the bias created by their own immediate involvement in the conflict. By analyzing conflict in a relatively objective manner, a manager can deal with it more positively and more easily. The following is a basic model for such an analysis:

1. The basic conflict
   a. Overt level
   b. The hidden agenda
   c. The source of conflict
2. The participants
   a. Immediate and primary participants
   b. Secondary participants
   c. The audience
3. The provision of an arena
4. The development of rules
5. Strategies for dealing with organizational conflict

Exhibit 8-1 is an example of the use of this model.

Exhibit 8-1   Conflict Model with Example

The Basic Conflict	
Overt issue	Habitual lateness and/or absenteeism of employee
Hidden agenda	Growing employee resistance to managerial authority
Sources	Human need vs. organizational need
	Organizational structure
Participants	
Immediate	Unit supervisor and employee
Secondary	Chief of service, personnel director
Audience	Other employees with similar problem with work schedule, other managers with similar employee disciplinary problems, and higher levels of management who monitor organizational climate
Arena	Grievance procedure
Rules	Work rules re attendance, procedures for filing grievances
Strategy	Limitation of conflict to unit members

The Basic Conflict

Overt Level

As a starting point, the manager analyzing a conflict describes the obvious problem. This process of naming the conflict elements provides focus and clarifies the issues that are at stake. Examples include

- habitual lateness by an employee
- delays in transport of patients from inpatient services to physical therapy or occupational therapy services
- lack of clarity about job responsibilities
- delays in treating patients, causing patients to wait unduly for their appointments

The Hidden Agenda

While the overt issue may be the true and only substance of the conflict, there is sometimes another area of conflict that constitutes a hidden agenda.

This hidden agenda may be the true conflict, or it may be an adjunct issue. The process of naming the conflict and describing its elements helps bring to light any hidden agenda that may exist.

Conflict issues are buried for several reasons. They may be too explosive to deal with openly, or subconscious protective mechanisms may prevent a threatening subject from surfacing until the individual in question has a safe structure and the necessary support to deal with it. Within an institution, the climate may not be appropriate for accepting conflict, or organizational resources may be insufficient to deal with it.

The subtleties of intraorganizational power struggles cause certain aspects of conflict to remain hidden. Individuals may choose to obscure the real issue as a means of testing their strength, of determining points of opposition before plunging ahead with an issue, or of checking the intensity of opposition. Periodic sparring over issues that never seem to be resolved is a clue to the existence of a hidden agenda. For example, the hospital budget issue of billing a medical group practice for certain administrative services may surface each year for temporary resolution. The root of the problem is not the allocation of money; it is the creation of a new institutional structure. As a consequence, organizational control of outpatient services is at stake.

The Sources of Conflict

The definition of a conflict should indicate its primary sources: competition for resources, authority relationships, extraorganizational pressures, and so on. As discussed earlier, organizational conflicts are ultimately due to the individuals who participate in organizational activities.

The Nature of the Organization. Organizations with multiple goals face competing and sometimes mutually exclusive demands for available resources. A hospital, for example, must safeguard against malpractice claims through active risk control management, yet it must also contain costs. The rules, regulations, and requirements imposed by the many controllers of the organization identified in the clientele network may be a source of conflict. Shifting client demand and changes in the degree of client participation in the organization lead to conflict when an increase in the allocation of resources for one group is a loss for another. The authority structure is another clue to potential conflict; members of coercive organizations are more frequently in conflict with the organization than are members of normative institutions.

The Organizational Climate. An emphasis on competition as a means of enhancing productivity, as in the use of the "deadly parallel" organizational structure or the use of a reward system that emphasizes competition among individuals or departments, may cause conflict. The intentional overlap and blurred jurisdiction of units can produce continual jockeying for organizational territory. Competition for scarce resources may be sharp, with resulting conflict, coalitions, and compromises. The subtleties of an institution's power struggles, the shifting balance of power (e.g., a growing union movement), and the need to demonstrate power constitute another facet of organizational climate. Denial of conflict is a potential source of trouble, since it removes a safe outlet for the resolution of conflict before it becomes a serious problem.

The Organizational Structure. The complex authority structure in health care organizations (i.e., a dual track of authority coupled with an increasing professionalism among the many specialized workers) creates situations of potential conflict. Professional practitioners, such as nurses, physical therapists, clinical psychologists, and social workers, are trained to assess patient needs and to take actions within the scope of licensure or certification; however, their ability to make decisions is limited by the hierarchical organizational structure. This problem is compounded when the individual practitioner has a legal duty to act or refrain from acting that is directly opposite to the hierarchical system, such as when a nurse refrains from giving a medication that would be harmful to the patient even when the physician has (inadvertently) ordered such a dosage.

Physicians, in holding staff appointments, find themselves required to shift regularly from their roles as independent practitioners when functioning outside the health care facility to more limited roles as members of the organizational hierarchy. This regular role shift may also be required of the physical therapist, nurse practitioner, or occupational therapist who functions as an independent agent in private practice and at the same time participates in the patient care process as a staff member of a health care institution.

Conflict may also arise from specialization within the organizational structure when individuals attempt to carry out their assigned activities. For example, the social worker might seek to place a patient in a long-term care facility, but the utilization review coordinator must impose strict guidelines in terms of days of care allotted under certain payment contracts. The medical record practitioner must develop a system of record control, although many users of records find it more practical to retain records in restricted areas of their own. The purchasing agent must comply with certain regulations on deadlines, budget restrictions, and auditing procedures in spite of individual needs. Specialization within the complexities of bureaucratization leads to frustration, misunderstanding, and conflict.

Superior-subordinate relationships constitute another area of potential conflict. The organization chart is, in fact, a suppression chart that specifies which positions have authority over and literally suppress other individual jobs or units. The legitimacy of a leader's claim to office is continually assessed. The power, prestige, and rewards built into the hierarchical system all represent gain for some and related loss for others. The erosion of traditional territory associated with line management results from activities clearly intended to remove some authority from line managers. These activities include client or worker involvement in decision making.

The process of management by objectives, in which the workers are directly involved in setting and assessing objectives, commands much attention for its motivational value; streamlined processes, such as central number assignments or patient bed assignments, have much merit as systems improvements; a central pool of patient aides, assistants, and transporters is an alternative to assignment by department. Yet each of these processes erodes the distinct territory of one or several managers, whose ability to make decisions is affected by such changes. Increased specialization in some technical areas leads to a more frequent use of functional specialists. Although the line manager retains authority, the specialist must be included in the planning and decision-making process; the line manager is no longer the sole agent.

Unions may invade managerial territory in several areas relating to personnel management and direct work assignment. In the collective bargaining process, the nature of the work, who will do it, and how much will be done may be issues. Union gains may be management losses.

Individual vs. Organizational Needs. Human needs and values must be welded into the organizational framework. A large number of clients and workers enter the organization, and they have different values, experience, motives, and expectations. The degree to which each individual internalizes the values of the organization and accepts a primary identity derived from the institution varies greatly. Individuals who do not participate directly in the accomplishment of organizational goals or in the institutional authority structure tend to identify less with the organization and view its demands less favorably than those who participate more fully in direct, goal-oriented activities.

Solutions to Previous Conflicts. New problems may arise from solutions to previous conflicts. The use of compromise as a strategy in dealing with conflict tends to leave all participants somewhat dissatisfied. At the next opportunity, one or more participants may seek to reopen the issue in order to regain what was lost, particularly if the loss was acute. The loser may build up resources and enter into an active state of aggression when such resources have been accumulated, such as a nation defeated after a war (e.g., Germany after World War I). When there is a consistent denial pattern, the conflict may "go underground" for a time, then emerge again with greater force. Again, managers should realistically examine the negative consequences of conflict resolutions in order to minimize their recurrence.

The Participants

The immediate participants in the conflict can be identified readily as the individuals or groups caught in the open exchange. The secondary participants are the individuals called in to take an active role, such as persons at the next level of the hierarchy. A manager may consult with a senior official to whom the individual involved in the conflict reports or with a staff adviser, such as a labor relations specialist. A unit manager may be required in some instances to refer conflict to the next level for resolution, as in some grievance procedures. In the case of a unionized employee, a representative of the union, such as a shop steward, may be involved. A "neutral" may be called in by both parties in a labor dispute (e.g., a mediator or an arbitrator). Occasionally, a manager may consult informally with certain "marginal" individuals, such as those in the department or organization who have an overlapping role set, a supervisor whose domain spans several activities, a client who is also on an advisory committee, or another department head who has faced similar situations. Because they link groups, these individuals are sought out in order to test a potential solution or to obtain information and even advice.

A third category of participants may be classified as the audience. This category may include the following:

- The Clients. If the conflict is overt and severe, the organization may turn to other organizations for the necessary services in order to avoid the conflict. On the other hand, uncertainty may cause tension within this group, and clients may become active participants. A client group alienated from the institution may develop its own system to meet its needs.
- The Public at Large. This group may seek action through recourse to some government agency, and an agency's intervention into the conflict may take the form of additional regulation of the organization. The conflict may be brought into the public arena; for example, a labor dispute may be taken to court. The net effect of intervention by some agent on behalf of the public at large is the opening or broadening of the conflict, which removes it from the immediate control of the original parties to the dispute.
- A Potential Rival or Enemy. While one group and its opponents are absorbed in conflict, a third group whose energies are not drained by conflict may seek to expand its services and attract the clients of the groups locked in the dispute.
- Individuals or Groups with Similar Complaints. Some observers may seek to press a similar claim if "the right side" wins. In the case of employee unrest, a labor organizer may consider more active unioniza-

tion attempts. The Independent practitioners who seek greater autonomy in the practice of health care may monitor changes in organizational bylaws or state licensure regulations and find gains made by one individual or group of practitioners the catalyst needed to obtain similar gains. In malpractice cases, jury awards are monitored and publicized. As the basis for a certain kind of claim is expanded through a trend in court decisions, more individuals may advance their cases. Without extensive publicity of the benchmark cases, this basis of claim might not have arisen. A worker who sees another worker win a concession from the manager about some work rule will more readily press a similar claim.

- The Opportunist. Some individual or group may seek to enter the conflict as champion or savior. Such action may be undertaken by individuals seeking to raise themselves to leadership positions.

In many cases, members of the audience not only cheer and jeer, but also become active participants, thus expanding the conflict in terms of the number of individuals or groups who must be satisfied in any solution.

Conflict should be resolved at as low an organizational level as possible. The facts are better known by the immediate participants, who are able to communicate directly. Also, because the number of participants is limited, agreement on a solution may be more easily obtained. Top levels of management should be involved only rarely in conflicts within the organization, because their involvement might give undue weight to the problem, establish precedent, and force the setting of policy that escalates resolutions to a higher level. The resources of top management should generally be reserved for critical issues.

The Provision of an Arena

The development of a safe, predictable, accessible arena tends to create a sense of security and to keep the problems from becoming diffuse. The aggrieved know where to turn and what to do in order to seek redress. The provision of an acceptable arena is also efficient. The individuals involved give their attention to it in a highly structured manner, and it establishes clear boundaries to the conflict. It is legitimate to bring issues of conflict to this place, through this structure, at these designated times. The court system and legislative debate are such arenas in the larger society. In organizations, arenas include the structured grievance process for employees (Exhibit 8-2), the appeals process for the professional staff member seeking staff appointment, or the complaint department for customers. Committees in which multiple input is invited are also common arenas for the resolution of conflict.

Exhibit 8-2 Excerpts from Grievance Procedure

Any grievance which may arise between the parties concerning the application, meaning, or interpretation of this Agreement shall be resolved in the following manner:

Step 1: An employee having a grievance and his Union delegate shall discuss it with his immediate supervisor within five (5) working days after it arose or should have been made known to the employee. The Hospital shall give its response through the supervisor to the employee and to this Union delegate within five (5) working days after the presentation of the grievance. In the event no appeal is taken to the next step (Step 2) the decision rendered in this step shall be final.

Step 2: If the grievance is not settled in Step 1, the grievance may, within five (5) working days after the answer in Step 1, be presented in Step 2. When grievances are presented in Step 2, they shall be reduced to writing on grievance forms provided by the Hospital (which shall then be assigned a number by the Personnel Services at the Union's request), signed by the grievant and his or her Union representative, and presented to the Department Head and the Department of Personnel Services. A grievance so presented in Step 2 shall be answered in writing within five (5) working days after its presentation.

The Development of Rules

Rules serve to limit the energy expended on the conflict process. The provision of rules has a face-saving and legitimizing effect; it is permissible to disagree, equal time is guaranteed, and each point of view is aired. The rules also provide a basis for the intervention of a referee or neutral. The rules may be developed to allow a cooling-off period so that the issues can be put in perspective. The time frame given by the rules reduces uneasiness, since participants are assured of a legitimate opportunity to present the issues. Conflict remains under control.

Strategies for Dealing with Organizational Conflict

Two strategies for dealing with conflict are opposite in nature: limitation and purposeful expansion. The limitation of conflict as a strategy was developed by E.E. Schattschneider, who noted the contagiousness of conflict. An organization runs the risk of losing control as conflict is widened, and it is unlikely that both sides will be reinforced equally. Conflict is best kept private, limited, and therefore controllable.[30]

An underlying purpose of the intentional expansion of conflict is to demonstrate its immediate effect on the clients or the public, who in turn will bring pressure on the opposing party to end the dispute. The immediate involvement of the client group is sought in the hope that it will act as a catalytic factor, forcing quick resolution. For example, a teachers' union may go on strike at the beginning of a school year, a coal miners' union may strike during the winter, and traffic officers may conduct a slowdown or job action during the height of the Fourth of July traffic to the shore.

The routinization of conflict is a third strategy. Another aspect of this strategy may be seen in the symbolic value of the short strike that is a kind of catharsis, an annual or biennial event. Other strategies include concepts noted in other discussions, for example, cooptation, strategic leniency, preformed decisions, and the selection of individuals who fit the organization.

In addition to such conscious strategies, a manager should make use of the general principles of sound organization. When used properly, these principles bring about stability and reduce conflict. Known policies and rules, sufficient orientation and training of members, proper authority-responsibility designations, and clear chains of command and communication: these practices foster cooperation and mutual expectation, with the attendant reduction of undue conflict. Finally, awareness of "burnout" and programs to prevent it can contribute to the reduction of conflict and enhance motivation. Such programs are discussed in the next chapter.

NOTES

1. H. Kaufman, *The Forest Ranger: A Study in Administrative Behavior* (Baltimore: Johns Hopkins University Press, 1967), 128.

2. Ibid., 170.

3. Ibid., 178.

4. R. Presthus, *The Organizational Society* (New York: Random House, 1962), 166, 178–226, passim 286.

5. A. Maslow, *Motivation and Personality* (New York: Harper & Row, 1954).

6. F. Herzberg, *The Motivation to Work* (New York: Wiley, 1959).

7. Hersey and Blanchard, *Management of Organizational Behavior*, (Englewood Cliffs, N.J.: Prentice Hall, 1982), 60.

8. D. McGregor, *The Human Side of Enterprise* (New York: McGraw-Hill, 1960).

9. William Ouchi, *Theory Z: How American Business Can Meet the Japanese Challenge* (Reading, Mass.: Addison-Wesley, 1981).

10. J.R. Schermerhorn, Jr., "Improving Health Care Productivity through High-Performance Managerial Development," *Health Care Management Review* 12 (1987): 49–55.

11. Ibid.

12. Ibid.

13. Ibid.

14. Ibid.

15. Ibid.

16. Ibid.

17. Ibid.

18. E. Erikson, "Eight Ages of Man," in *Readings in Child Behavior and Development,* edited by C. S. Lavatelli and F. Stendler (New York: Harcourt Brace Jovanovich, 1972), 19–30.

19. C.S. Hall and G. Lindzey, *Theories of Personality* (New York: Wiley, 1957), 442.

20. G.A. Kimble and N. Garmezy, *Principles of General Psychology* (New York: Ronald Press, 1962), 485.

21. Ibid., 486

22. Ibid.

23. Ibid., 487

24. K. Lewin, *Resolving Social Conflicts* (New York: Harper & Row, 1948).

25. E.E. Sampson and M.S. Martas, *Group Process for the Health Professional* (New York: Wiley, 1977), 22.

26. W.R. Bion, *Experiences in Groups* (New York: Basic Books, 1959), 59–60.

27. B.W. Tuchman, "Developmental Sequence in Small Groups," *Psychological Bulletin*, 1965, 384–99.

28. Ibid.

29. Lewin, *Resolving Social Conflicts.*

30. E.E. Schattschneider, *The Semisovereign People* (New York: Holt, Rinehart & Winston, 1960), 1–18.

Chapter 9

Recruitment and Retention of Staff

Ellen L. Kolodner and Maureen Freda

CHAPTER OBJECTIVES

1. Identify recruiting strategies.
2. Identify factors influencing job stability.
3. Identify factors influencing job turnover.
4. Identify patterns leading to job dissatisfaction and burnout.
5. Identify retention strategies.

INTRODUCTION

The purpose of this chapter is to discuss a key role of the allied health manager—the recruitment and retention of staff. Program plans and supplies are rendered virtually useless without the personnel to deliver the services.

During the past decade, recruiting and retaining allied health personnel has become the greatest challenge managers face. The shortage of personnel in all allied health fields is critical. Projections through the year 2000 indicate a shortfall of at least 30 percent in all allied health fields, including physical therapy, laboratory sciences, occupational therapy, and diagnostic imaging. Indeed, a study published in *Hospitals* estimates that by the year 2000 the demand for occupational therapy services will increase by 52 percent. In recent years, the American Hospital Association placed the shortage of allied health professionals on its list of critical priorities which the health care industry and the nation must address in order to survive into the next century.[1]

WHY IS THERE A SHORTAGE?

The shortage of allied health personnel cannot be traced to any one single cause. Rather, it can be attributed to complication factors of both supply and

246

demand. The National Association of Rehabilitation Facilities (NARF) has identified several demand-related reasons for the staff shortage, including an increase in the aging population, dramatic advances in medical technology that have resulted in a tremendous increase in people surviving traumatic accidents and devastating illnesses, and an unprecedented growth in the number of rehabilitation facilities. These trends have, in turn, resulted in an increased use of rehabilitation beds and an increased demand for allied health personnel and services.[2]

The supply of allied health professionals has been negatively impacted by decreases in the population of college-aged youth in the United States and a perceived expansion of the job options available to women and minorities. The success of social movements of the 1960s has resulted in potential female allied health professionals selecting other career paths. Allied health fields have traditionally been women's fields; today women are interested in pursuing careers with more status, power, and money than the allied health professions seem able to offer.

Thus, allied health educational programs have experienced a decrease in the number of applicants and enrollees in their programs and have been unable to meet the rising personnel demand. NARF also cites retention difficulties, low wages, and increased caseloads due to employer cost-containment strategies as additional factors that contribute to the supply shortage.

RECRUITMENT

Recruitment has two major phases: attracting applicants (recruiting in the narrow sense) and convincing them to come on board (hiring). Each phase has unique components that must be attended to in order for the entire process to be successful.

Phase 1: Attracting Applicants

Health organizations currently utilize a wide variety of recruiting strategies. These strategies can be categorized as direct and indirect. Indirect recruitment programs may be conducted in collaboration with volunteer resources departments, community outreach programs, public relations departments, consumer advocacy groups, or local professional organizations.

Direct Recruiting

Direct recruiting methods are those face-to-face or media-based activities that connect an organization directly with potential employees. Often, particularly in large facilities, the implementation of direct strategies is done in conjunction with a human resources department. However, department managers and staff, as well as human resources personnel, may all be involved in the implementation of any of these tactics. The specific timelines, duties, and responsibilities of all involved parties should be delineated prior to using any of these methods. Some examples of direct recruiting strategies are as follows:

- Advertise specific job openings in trade papers that are mailed directly to the homes of credentialed professionals in the field. These types of publications typically resemble newspapers and are published by private publishing houses or by professional trade associations such as the American Occupational Therapy Association and the American Speech and Language Association. The publishers usually maintain large mailing lists of professionals, students, and employers in the field and may be aggressive in pursuing notifications of job openings. Placement of job ads in these publications is a costly proposition, but use of this strategy does offer direct access to a large applicant pool.

- Advertise job openings in the want ads section of local newspapers. These types of ads are often less costly than trade paper ads and reach a wider section of the general public. Although these ads will reach a more limited professional readership, they may be seen by individuals who would be likely to apprise potential applicants of job openings.

- Send personalized letters to students or credentialed professionals at their schools or homes. Many professional associations and trade unions have established guidelines under which they will, for a fee, provide the names and addresses of their members. Some associations can provide you with lists that are targeted at a specific practice specialty or geographic location. Although you cannot usually obtain mailing lists of all senior students in a professional education program, it is possible to mail open letters to students and address them thus: "Senior Student [the profession], ABC College," etc. It is wise to contact the education program prior to mailing the letters to ascertain whether there would be a willingness to distribute the letters.

- Participate in job recruitment fairs. These fairs may be conducted on local, regional, or national levels and may be located at college campuses or convention centers or be held in conjunction with professional meetings. Be certain to come prepared with an eye-catching display and brochures. Frequently, organizations employ sophisticated marketing strategies in these highly visible, highly competitive arenas. The best representatives to send to recruitment fairs are usually individuals who are familiar with current employment opportunities in a number of departments in the same facility and can answer a wide range of questions concerning location, programs, and benefits.

- Advertise and interview for specific job openings at local, regional, and national professional meetings and conferences. Identify recruiting activities as a primary outcome goal of attendance. Be prepared to sacrifice educational benefits of conference attendance for recruiting and networking activities.
- Offer incentive bonuses to employees who recruit new employees. Incentive bonuses can take such diverse forms as cash, day-care credits at an onsite day-care center, additional time off, and professional books.
- Sponsor open-house events that showcase new programs and invite clinicians to your facility. Consider working with your facility's public relations department to promote the event and maximize your exposure in the community.
- Interview each student who is on a part-time or full-time clinical rotation and discuss current or future employment opportunities at your facility. Even if the student is not ready to consider employment or you do not have any current openings, this is an invaluable opportunity to lay the groundwork for future recruiting efforts.
- Offer education grants or scholarships for basic professional education. In this kind of incentive program, a student receives money to help finance his or her professional education or clinical training, and in return the student "owes" the institution a prescribed amount of time as an employee.

Indirect Recruiting

Indirect recruiting activities are those activities that do not immediately yield employees but that greatly increase the potential applicant pool. Such activities, for example, increase the visibility of the facility, profession, or department and decrease the stigma of working in the health care arena.

Indirect recruiting activities may include the following:

- Keep the name of your institution in the forefront of the field and in the public's eye. Encourage staff to publish articles describing their clinical programs or research in professional and lay journals and periodicals. Consider capturing some of the more visually appealing activities of the department on film and submitting these pictorial images to local papers or professional trade publications.
- Train students at your facility. Most allied health training programs require students to spend a portion of their education in field-based training. Develop a student training program and aggressively market it to professional programs in your field. Be sure to delineate the learning objectives that can be accomplished at your site and to describe the special

skills your staff possess as well as the demographics (patient population, specialized treatment programs, specific state-of-the-art equipment, etc.) of your facility. Consider offering a stipend for training at your site. Do not limit yourself to educational programs in your immediate geographic area; develop networks to facilitate student relocation. The easier you make it for students to relocate and train at your facility, the more likely they are to consider future employment at your site.

- Develop a relationship with a local high school and encourage students to volunteer in your department. Facilitate staff participation in high school career days to promote the profession and make additional direct contacts with students.

- Conduct health promotion programs such as free cholesterol screenings or energy conservation clinics in conjunction with a local health fair or celebration (e.g., National Physical Therapy Month). These programs can be conducted at your facility or in a public arena such as a shopping mall, train station, or airport. Be sure that your display and handouts prominently proclaim the name of your facility.

- Lecture at local professional educational programs or forums. Prepare a list of topics about which you and your staff possess expert knowledge; offer to present lectures on these topics to local professional schools, chapters of professional organizations, and professional special interest groups.

- Encourage staff to assume leadership roles in professional and civic organizations. By creating images of your profession and your facility as replete with committed, interested, energetic people, you can positively influence individuals to consider both your profession and your facility as viable career options.

- Develop an ongoing relationship with a local disability advocacy group. Select a project that your staff can work on in conjunction with members of the community-based group. Be certain to obtain publicity for some of the activities.

- Collaborate on a research project with faculty at a local allied health educational program. Expanding the knowledge base of your profession and participating in developing and evaluating "cutting edge" programs will enhance your visibility and image in the eyes of potential employees.

Phase 2: Hiring

Once you have succeeded in enticing a job applicant to your facility, you are ready to enter Phase 2 of the recruitment process—hiring the candidate.

This phase encompasses interviewing the candidate, evaluating the candidate, proffering the job offer, and solidifying the employment contract. Each component is equally important to the successful completion of the recruitment process.

The Job Interview

The interview provides a critical opportunity for both the potential employee and the manager to determine whether to pursue the job search process any further. The value of a pleasant, informative interview cannot be underestimated. Both parties should utilize this time to assess the personalities, expectations, and opportunities involved. The manager may choose to conduct the interview alone or in conjunction with members of the human resources department or members of his or her own staff. During the interview, it is critical that the following issues be clarified:

1. job requirements and expectations
2. department and institution characteristics (including patient and staff demographics)
3. department and institution strengths
4. management's unique vision of health care delivery
5. mission of the institution
6. applicant's technical level of skill
7. opportunities for advancement within the department and institution
8. applicant's career goals
9. salary expectations
10. applicant's personal and professional assets and liabilities as they relate to the worker role
11. "fit" between the institution and the individual
12. benefits

It is the responsibility of the manager to ensure that the above issues are discussed satisfactorily. In addition to the verbal interview, the manager should use this opportunity to "showcase" the department and the facility by taking the applicant on a tour and introducing him or her to key individuals. The manager might also consider providing the applicant with written materials that describe the job and highlight the assets of the facility.

It is the responsibility of the applicant to be certain that none of his or her questions go unanswered. But it is the responsibility of the manager to be certain that all potential arenas for questions are reviewed so that the applicant may use the onsite interview time wisely.

Making the Job Offer

After the interview, the manager must evaluate the applicant and determine whether to offer him or her the position. Applicants should be judged on the basis of their skills, adaptability, and responses to the questions which were set forth during the interview, as well as on the basis of feedback from references. The match between the individual and the organization can often be ascertained as a result of objective answers received during a routine reference check.

Business etiquette recommends that applicants be notified of a manager's decision to make a definite job offer within a two-week period. Applicants are also expected to respond to an offer in a similar time frame. Salary and benefits packages should be negotiated at the time of the actual job offer.

RETENTION: KEEPING YOUR STAFF

Once an employee has been hired, the manager's challenge has only begun. The critical shortage of personnel, combined with the high costs of recruitment and training make retention one of the most critical issues in allied health employment today. Hospitals in particular are experiencing severe staffing problems due to expanded career opportunities within the community. Therapists can achieve increased flexibility and higher hourly compensation in contractual or private practice situations.

Turnover of staff is not only disruptive to clinical care but has been related to staff morale and group productivity.[3] Several authors have linked turnover to a decrease in efficiency as well as the quantity and quality of care.[4] Staff turnover has also been shown to be extremely costly. Replacement costs include the expenses incurred as a result of recruitment activities and orientating and training new employees as well as out-of-pocket expenditures such as paid-out vacation time and payments to PRN staff. In 1977 the average cost of replacing a rehabilitation staff member was $600, in 1983 the figure had risen to approximately $2,300, and by 1988 the estimates ran from the low of $2,400 to a high of $25,000.[5] Current estimates of the cost of replacing a staff member are as high as 50 percent of the first year's salary.

In order to effectively retain staff, you will need to understand why employees might choose to stay at a particular place of employment and why they might choose to leave. You will also need to know how to gauge their level of job satisfaction and how to combat dissatisfaction.

WHY DO ALLIED HEALTH PROFESSIONALS STAY AT THEIR JOBS?

A multitude of job factors have been identified as contributing to an individual's decision to remain at a particular job. Studies of occupational therapists, physical therapists, and nurses have revealed that there are significant differences in the reasons cited for remaining at a job depending upon the number of years the individual has been in practice.[6] Among the reasons cited are both professional and personal factors (see Table 9-1).

The strongest motivators for occupational therapists appear to be benefits (salary and vacation time), opportunities for professional growth, and peer relationships. In addition, 92 percent of the occupational therapy clinicians identified direct patient care as the most rewarding aspect of their job. The studies of nurses identified autonomy, recognition, respect, group cohesiveness, and professional growth as the key "job satisfiers."[7] The physical therapists also identified "attaining a sense of achievement" as an important contributing factor to therapists remaining at their current place of employment.[8]

In order to devise effective staff retention strategies, you must understand the factors that motivate therapists to change jobs. The study of rehabilitation occupational therapists mentioned above also identified factors of importance to therapists in deciding to leave a job.[9] Again, the results revealed a difference in motivators related to number of years of practice.

As Table 9-2 indicates, salary and status (promotions) are of the greatest import to occupational therapists regardless of the number of years of experience. Additionally, the most frequently cited cause of dissatisfaction was paperwork; 77 percent of the sample identified paperwork as the most stressful part of their jobs. The group with 1–3 years of experience appear to be the most vulnerable to the offer of higher salary (92 percent of that group named this factor).

The nursing study showed that nurses employed 6–12 months had the highest turnover intensions and felt neglected the most often.[10] The group with 1–3 years of experience were most affected by overall work satisfaction factors,

Table 9-1 Why Therapists and Nurses Stay at Their Jobs

Years in Practice	*Factors*
Less than 1 year	Professional growth opportunities Fair salary Good peer relationships
1–3 years	Professional growth opportunities Choice of where to work in department Satisfying caseload
4–6 years	Professional growth opportunities Interdisciplinary team work Good relationship with department director
7–10 years	Professional growth opportunities

Table 9-2   Factors That Influence the Decision of Occupational Therapists To Change Jobs

	1 Year's Experience	1–3 Years' Experience	4–6 Years' Experience	7–10 Years' Experience
First child	X	X	X	
Spouse relocated		X	X	X
Wanted to live in another geographic area		X	X	
High caseload	X	X		X
High productivity		X		
High paperwork		X	X	
Low continued education	X		X	
High staff:patient ratio		X		X
Low salary increase			X	
Interpersonal conflict		X		X
Low input in department decisions				X
Disillusioned with management		X	X	X

including autonomy and growth need satisfaction. Career satisfaction, including the ability to see one's job as significant, was seen as important to those with 3–6 years of experience. Nurses in this study who worked over 6 years had the least turnover intentions and seemed to be least affected by potential for growth. This study concluded that the environment should meet the employees' work-related needs. Ullrich states, "Individuals experience satisfaction when they have achieved . . . those things to which they aspire."[11] He concludes that management practices that better support the work of nurses may have a positive impact on turnover.

Preventing Staff Turnover*

Step 1: Evaluating Current Job Satisfaction

The next step in addressing the issue of retaining staff is to evaluate each individual staff member's level of job satisfaction. Guarding against dissatisfaction in the workplace is as critical to retaining staff as motivating staff. Job dissatisfaction and chronic job-related stress have been correlated with a syndrome popularly referred to as "burnout." Regardless of how costly it is to replace a staff member, the effect of a "burned out" staff member on other staff members can be even more costly. Much has been written in the literature about the

---

* The author would like to acknowledge the contributions of Linda Apter Mates, MSS, OTR/L in the development of materials related to burnout.

prevalence of burnout among health care professionals.[12] The work environments and job responsibilities of allied health personnel are among those that
evidence the highest percentage of causative factors for burnout. These factors,
which include high caseloads, limited training or staff development opportunities, inadequate salaries, frequent staff meetings, and high paperwork demands,
closely correlate with the factors identified in Table 9-2. Therefore, it is incumbent upon a manager to be familiar with the components of the work environment that are potential stressors and to be on the lookout for the symptoms of
burnout. Similarly, intervention strategies to prevent the syndrome can be
devised to address each potential stressor.

Burnout is characterized by feelings of emotional exhaustion in which the
worker develops depersonalizing attitudes toward service recipients and experiences feelings of reduced personal accomplishment.[13] These feelings of
decreased personal accomplishment can lead an employee to seek to change
jobs. Burnout does not happen overnight. It is a progressive disorder. Four classic stages have been identified[14]:

Stage 1: Enthusiasm
Stage 2: Stagnation
Stage 3: Frustration
Stage 4: Apathy

Each stage has specific characteristics that are its hallmark. In Stage 1, the
employee is highly energized and is willing to engage in a multitude of job-related
activities. Few requests are seen as too demanding. In Stage 2, the employee begins
to take a close look at his personal needs and examine whether or not these needs
are being met by the job. Management requests are evaluated carefully before a
response is formulated. Only those job-related requests that are seen as being of
direct benefit to the employee are acted on. In Stage 3, the employee feels uneasy
about the job situation and questions his or her effectiveness and the value of the
job. The employee exudes an air of dissatisfaction and is at times argumentative
with management. In the final stage, the employee lacks investment in the job and
begins to take steps to avoid work. Few requests are met with a positive response.

An alternative way to view these stages is to consider each stage as having both
a negative and a positive aspect.[15] For example, despite all of the positive characteristics of the first stage (including the employee's enthusiasm), the "seeds of the
individual's discontent" are perhaps being sown. Conversely, although Stages 2, 3,
and 4 appear to constitute a negative trend, the potential for positive change is
inherent in them. As a manager, this perspective can prove to be useful in that it
offers a method for recognizing potential problems before they become intractable
and provides a format for designing management interventions. Reformulated, the
stages would look like this:

Stage 1: Enthusiasm/Overinvestment
Stage 2: Stagnation/Stabilization
Stage 3: Frustration/Productive Anger
Stage 4: Apathy/No Investment

An employee who is in Stage 1 still appears to be highly motivated and productive in the professional arena. However, upon closer examination one might find that this individual is spending a disproportionate amount of time involved with work. This "overinvestment" can lead to an unhealthy imbalance among work activities, rest, and leisure activities.[16]

A therapist in Stage 2 may question the value of his or her individual contribution to a particular patient's course of rehabilitation. Or the therapist may appear to be unwilling to participate in research or learn new treatment approaches. This questioning can be viewed as a sign that the employee is struggling to solidify skills and knowledge and to bolster a developing belief in his or her own efficacy as a therapist.

Behavior in Stage 3 almost always appears negativistic. The employee will frequently complain about the value of the profession, the institution, other staff, benefits, the caseload, and so on. Sick time will be used frequently and the employee may complain of boredom. Underlying the ennui and depression, however, is an edge of anger that can be harnessed to promote productive change if the complainer can be challenged to attempt to rectify the perceived problems.

Individuals in Stage 4 appear disinterested in the activities of the workplace. They frequently avoid job responsibilities and carry out job functions in a rote manner; even the most dramatic improvements in patients rarely generate a response. Staff who disintegrate to this level of performance can be viewed as uninvested rather than apathetic. Thus their behavior can be seen as having the potential to be reenergized (perhaps in a new environment) rather than being symptomatic of a personality flaw.

Step 2: Analyzing the Job

Analyzing a job for the purposes of avoiding burnout differs from traditional job analysis in that it does not require the manager to examine the job description or the cognitive or musculoskeletal demands. Rather, it requires the employee and the manager to jointly examine eight areas of work of the work environment where an employee might manifest symptoms of one of the four stages of burnout. By examining these areas, a personal burnout profile can be developed. Exhibit 9-1 is a questionnaire that may be used to develop an individual burnout profile across each of the four stages.

The eight key areas are these:

Exhibit 9-1 Personal Burnout Profile

Components	Stage 1 Enthusiasm/ Overinvestment	Stage 2 Stagnation/ Stabilization	Stage 3 Frustration/ Productive Anger	Stage 4 Apathy/ No Investment
Personal Characteristics	Do I invest my whole self in my work?	Am I beginning to question whether I like my job and whether it meets my personal needs?	Am I not only question- ing the value of my job but also the value of the entire profession?	Am I feeling totally disinterested in my job?
	Do I set extremely high goals for myself?	Am I beginning to see that there are limit- ations in my work en- vironment?	Do I blame myself when a patient does not improve or returns to treatment?	Do I avoid work by using all of my sick time?
				Am I disinterested in patient progress?
Program Development And Implementation	Do I work toward increasing my reper toireof activities and/orattempt to create new program ideas?	Do I find myself using the same modalities over and over again?	Is my stress so great that I no longer feel creative?	Do I always let the patients choose their activity, even when another modality may be more therapeutic?
	Do I verbally discuss with my patient the purpose of an activity and the progress which I have observed?	Do I focus on only one or two aspects of patient performance?	Do I look at product versus process?	Am I disinterested in mypatient's response to themodality selected?
Use of Theory	Am I interested in learning about new theories and actively applying them to my practice?	Do I prefer to use the theory base with which I am most comfortable?	Do I find new theories to be a waste of time and mere professional jargon?	Do I find myself using no theoretical base at all?
		Do I try to apply new concepts to my work?		
Interdisciplinary Relationships	Do I attempt to en- gageother disci- plines in theactivity process?	Do I get annoyed when other disciplines ask to observe my treatment sessions?	Do I feel competitive with other team mem- bers and avoid talking to them outside of required meetings?	Do I feel like there is noneed to deal with my team about un- resolved issues be- cause "nothing" helps?
	Do I work to increase communication among team mem- bers and to effective- ly resolve conflicts?	Do I feel that my do- main is being stepped on by other team members?	Do I find myself ex- pressing anger about the team to the other members of my department?	

Exhibit 9-1   continued

Components	Stage 1 Enthusiasm/ Overinvestment	Stage 2 Stagnation/ Stabilization	Stage 3 Frustration/ Productive Anger	Stage 4 Apathy/ No Investment
Education of Others/ Social Activism	Do I enjoy the opportunity to educate others about what I do?	Do I get tired of always having to explain my practice?	Am I beginning to resent the need to always educate others, especially team members?	Do I avoid having to explain what I do?
	Am I an active advocate for social change?	Am I only an advocate when it is convenient?	Is there an angry edge to my activism?	Do I rarely participate in social reform activities?
Fiscal Constraints	Do I find it easy to adapt to a low budget by finding creative ways to use limited supplies?	Am I becoming tired of the constant need to adapt my programs to supply/budget constraints?	Do I find myself frequently complaining to others about our limited budget and supplies?	Have I given in to our low budget by limiting my program to only those supplies that are readily available?
Response to Supervision and Increased Responsibilities	Do I look forward to supervision and the opportunity to improve my job performance?	Do I become anxious when my supervisor suggests a change or that I take on additional responsibilities?	Do I resent changes implemented within the department and frequently discuss my resentment with my peers?	Do I avoid work because of "what" will happen next?
Professional Development	Do I actively pursue workshops, seminars, and courses to improve my skills?	Do I find that out of work I always choose to pursue activities other than continuing education?	Do I find suggestions to pursue continuing education to be an imposition?	Am I totally disinterested in professional activities and continuing education?
	Do I put a lot of energy into my professional organizations?	Am I questioning the value of the profession and its organization?	Will I pursue these activities only on work time?	

Source: Reprinted with permission from *Occupational Therapy Forum*, September, 1987.

1. personal characteristics
2. program development and implementation
3. use of theory
4. interdisciplinary relationships
5. education of others and social activism
6. fiscal constraints
7. response to supervision and increased responsibilities
8. professional development

Personal characteristics are the unique attributes of an individual that might predispose him or her to respond to work demands in a particular manner. Such traits as investment in one's job, amount of spontaneous patient contact, and expectations of self and of treatment outcomes are included in this component.

For example, in Stage 1, employees sometimes overinvest in the job, use unstructured time to interact with patients, and set extremely high expectations for themselves and their patients. They may also overidentify with their patients and personalize criticism.

In Stage 2, employees tend to question whether their personal and professional needs are being met, realistically appraise their own limits and those of the workplace, and avoid learning new skills while striving to solidify basic professional skills.

Stage 3 individuals might spend their unstructured worktime complaining to other staff about the job or work environment and their own dissatisfaction. They may also mobilize their defenses, engage in a job search, and leave.

Stage 4 individuals avoid work and spend their unstructured worktime in personal pursuits such as handicrafts or reading novels.

Program development and implementation involves envisioning, planning, and implementing a wide variety of work-related programs. It includes expanding the professional domain of practice to respond to emerging needs in the work arena. Programs might be developed that address the needs of new patient populations, use new technology, or adapt traditional modalities in an innovative manner. It is important that there be a willingness to adjust daily practices in response to patient and staff values; personal, patient, and management priorities; and institutional role delineations.

The use of *theory* to guide professional action has been identified as a desired characteristic of allied health practitioners. This characteristic is assessed by examining the extent to which employees have developed the skill of identifying the rationale underlying their decisions and actions. For example, employees should show a willingness to explain their actions to patients, an ability to critique their own actions in light of actual outcomes, and an interest in learning new theoretical perspectives.

Interdisciplinary approaches to treatment have become the norm in the health care arena. Effective allied health professionals must interface with members of at least two other disciplines on a daily basis in an institutional environment. In the community, they are often responsible for initiating interaction with other professionals involved in the treatment of the same case in order to ensure high-quality care. To analyze an employee's interdisciplinary relationships, examine whether the employee coordinates activities with other members of the interdisciplinary team, collaborates with staff outside his or her own discipline, includes ideas that emanate from patients and families in program plans, shows an ability to resolve conflicts, and delineates practice boundaries.

The training, domain of practice, and unique contributions of each allied health profession are not familiar to many people. Often, unless a member of the immediate family has received services from an allied health provider or has entered the field, a patient or significant other may have no knowledge of an allied health practitioner's credentials and responsibilities. As a result of this general lack of knowledge, occupational therapists, physical therapists, radiographers, and so on, frequently find themselves in a position of having to explain not only the rationale for a procedure but also why they are uniquely qualified to perform it. *Education of others and social activism* are thus considered professional job functions. Social activism has been included with general education, since many of the clients of allied health professionals are the victims of stereotyping and stigma. They are often inarticulate in educating others about their special needs and it is encumbent upon allied health professionals to educate the public at large about the rights and needs of these individuals and advocate for their inclusion in the larger social world. In analyzing the job functions of education and social activism, evaluate the proficiency of employees at explaining the function of their profession and the methods and expected outcomes of specific treatment programs to patients, families, insurance representatives, and other members of the health care arena. Also examine their attitudes toward advocacy and whether they engage in advocacy activities.

In response to a general hue and cry that health care costs are unreasonable, the health care industry has initiated a variety of cost-containment measures. It is important to examine an employee's ability to adapt to a changing fiscal environment and act within current *fiscal constraints*. A willingness to explore the community to find new resources, creative management within the boundaries of a limited budget, and effective use of donated supplies are some of the things to look for.

Career development is best accomplished through an interactive process with a more experienced professional. The employee's *response to supervision* encompasses such reactions as the employee's response to negative or positive feedback concerning his or her job performance as well as the employee's response to proposed changes in job functions (e.g., increased responsibility). Does the employee welcome the feedback and take action (as would be evidenced in Stage 1)? Does the employee respond with some defensiveness but then use the support of the supervisor to make some changes (Stage 2)? Or does the employee sabotage supervisory problem-solving interventions and attempt to rally his or her peers to challenge the authority of the management to change job responsibilities (Stage 3)?

The final category is *professional development*—the extent to which the employee pursues professional growth. Factors that might be examined under this category include use of personal time to attend continuing education courses and professional meetings or participate in social change efforts, whether these activities are identified independently or by the supervisor, and whether the employee attends staff development programs only when they are discipline-specific or when attendance is required.

RETENTION STRATEGIES

Department managers, line supervisors, and employees can all engage in activities to promote job satisfaction and retain qualified staff. The primary responsibility lies with the supervisor and department director; however, there are some self-help activities that employees can perform. The types of interventions chosen depend on the outcome of the personal burnout assessment. Self-help interventions designed to address specific issues pertinent to each of the burnout stages can be found in Table 9-3.

Table 9-3 Self-Help Interventions

Enthusiasm/ Overinvestment	Stagnation/ Stabilization	Frustration/ Productive Anger	Apathy No Investment
Self-assessment of life style A. Sleep B. Diet C. Exercise D. Relaxation/meditation E. Use of leisure time F. "Private time" G. Leave work at work	Upgrade skills A. Continuing education B. Pursue advanced degree C. Self-improvement courses D. Modality courses	Participate in more energy expending leisure time activities Develop support network	Realistically evaluate options Recognize positive effect of career or job change
Acknowledge vulnerabilities A. Learn how to say "no" B. Learn how to ask for help C. Ventilate appropriately	Develop support network Utilize health distancing behaviors	Realistically evaluate options Recognize positive effect of career or job change	Seek professional career counseling services
Utilize time management techniques	Rotate modalities regularly Identify work stressors A. Separate work stress from personal stress B. Clarify which stressors are within personal power to change	Seek professional career counseling services Identify needs and motivations for being a helper Allow self to find humor, fun in work environment	
	Utilize supervision A. To share concerns B. Problem solve viable solutions		
	Recognize own skills and interests and explore ways to incorporate them into work sphere		
	Identify needs and motivations for being a helper		
	Allow self to find humor, fun in work environment		

The Supervisor's Role in Retaining Staff

Line supervisors are often the individuals who are directly responsible for overseeing the daily activities and professional development of employees. It is the line supervisor who would participate in the assessment of an employee's potential for burnout and the subsequent development and implementation of a plan for prevention. Therefore, the supervisor plays a key role in ensuring that qualified staff are retained. Table 9-4 identifies three types of supervisory interventions that can be used to promote retention and prevent burnout: role modeling, anticipatory guidance, and feedback. All three are used most effectively within the context of an individual supervisory session. The strategies are correlated with the four stages of burnout.

The Manager's Role in Retaining Staff

A manager can employ a wide variety of intervention strategies to promote staff retention. Management approaches can be effective in retaining staff if they are responsive to the actual needs, values, and personal and professional goals of staff. Additionally, they must be concrete and visible to staff and address the key factors that affect the decision to stay at a job. Table 9-5 pairs these contributory factors with concrete, although somewhat general, recommendations for management intervention. Specific interventions can only be determined within the context of a specific department. An effective manager will evaluate each staff member as well as the department as a whole and institute the appropriate strategies, keeping in mind the information presented earlier in the chapter regarding differences related to years of professional experience.

CONCLUSION

In summary, recruitment and retention have become key factors in the effective management of allied health professional programs. To achieve success in recruitment, the manager must utilize both direct and indirect recruiting methods and be skilled in all phases of the hiring process. Retaining staff requires that a manager be cognizant of the factors that motivate allied health professionals to stay at a particular job as well as those unique factors that compel them to seek employment elsewhere. Identifying job stressors and diagnosing an individual employee's burnout potential can enable a supervisor or manager to intervene in an effective, timely fashion and prevent staff turnover.

Table 9-4 Supervisory Interventions

	Enthusiasm/ Overinvestment	Stagnation/ Stabilization	Frustration/ Productive Anger	Apathy/ No Investment
Anticipatory Guidance	Identify potential work stressors and environmental limitations Set realistic goals and limits re: workload Set clear time frames re: expectations for change A. Patient progress B. Treatment programs C. Personal achievement Help employee recognize own limits and stress threshhold Facilitate use of time management techniques Encourage development of collaborative relationships	Focus on treatment process rather than individual patient progress or product Set clear time frames re: expectations for change A. Patient progress B. Treatment programs C. Personal achievement Encourage participation in continuing education opportunities Coordinate in-services on topics such as burnout, stress and time management, theory, networking, etc. Encourage regular use of vacation time and lunch breaks	Provide support for exploration of alternative employment opportunities Use of "Win-Win" conflict resolution strategies Breakdown large tasks into small components with manageable time frame	
Feedback	Help employee to recognize own limits and stress threshhold Provide clear expectations for effective job performance	Focus on individual's positive and unique contributions to department, institution, and/or profession Urge development of intra- and interdepartmental networks	Required use of vacation time and lunch breaks Acknowledge validity of feelings Actively promote collaborative problem solving	Alter work environment to create discomfort, thereby leading to change
Role Modeling	Utilize time management techniques Set realistic expectations for self and "label them" for staff Share personal perspective on work stressors and environmental limitations			

Source: Courtesy of Linda Apter Mates, MSS, OTR/L.

Table 9-5 Retention Strategies for Implementation by Managers

Factors	Strategies
Manageable paperwork	Critically review required paperwork
Continuing education	Make opportunities available to staff to increase their clinical knowledge Assist staff with professional growth Provide middle managers with management training and other advanced training opportunities Assist staff in the development of strong clinical reasoning skills
High-productivity expectations	Assist staff in understanding quantity and quality balance Reexamine productivity expectations in light of any acuity changes Rotate staff when feasible
Competitive salary	Complete annual salary surveys in your geographic area Stay competitive at all levels
Staff:patient ratio	Keep an eye on patient load, being mindful of acuity levels Develop a PRN pool Rotate staff Encourage job sharing
Professional growth	Create clinical ladders in department Support professional presentations Support clinical research Give time for special projects that will benefit both the staff member and the department Be a mentor where appropriate Give staff members opportunities and responsibilities in recognition of professional growth (even in the absence of promotions) Encourage multidisciplinary programming Rotate staff to promote development of broad range of skills
Peer relationships	Encourage teamwork Provide opportunities for staff to share knowledge with each other Set time aside for departmental social gatherings involving all levels of staff Plan special events (e.g., retreats, parties) Act as role model and demonstrate how important it is to really like what one does Conduct occasional team-building sessions involving entire department or other departments as well
Managerial responsiveness	Maintain open door policy Be available for problem solving and discussion of sensitive issues Offer opportunities for ventilation of concerns and complaints Follow through on all staff-identified items of concern Keep lines of communication open at all levels Keep department informed through effective use of regular staff meetings and dialogue Take an interest in staff members as individuals Use participatory management style Involve staff members in decision making and goal setting Form task forces to gather staff feedback on issues Provide opportunities for staff to share program development ideas
Recognition	Commend staff members' efforts publicly Promote department using institutional venues (e.g., newsletters, memos, employee-of-the-month awards) Let employees know they are valued Serve as strong advocate for department and profession

NOTES

1. B. England, "Manpower Shortages in Rehabilitation Hospitals." (Paper delivered at the Fiftieth Annual Assembly of the American Academy of Physical Medicine and Rehabilitation, November 1988, Seattle).

2. Ibid.

3. G. Wolf, "Nursing Turnover: Some Causes and Solutions." *Nursing Outlook* April 1981, 233–235.

4. M. Abelson, "Strategic Management of Turnover: A Model for the Health Care Administrator," *Health Care Management Review* 11, no. 2 (1986): 61–71; Wolf, "Nursing Turnover"; A. Hinshaw, C. Schmeltzer, and J. Atwood, "Innovative Retention Strategies for Nursing Staff, *Journal of Nursing Administration* 17, no. 6 (1987): 8–16.

5. S. Sills, "Shortage + Turnover + Orientation = Escalating Manpower Costs" (Paper presented at the Fiftieth Annual Assembly of the American Congress of Rehabilitation Medicine, October 1988, Seattle.

6. Maureen Freda, "Influential Factors for Occupational Therapists Deciding to Remain at Their Jobs," Master's thesis, Thomas Jefferson University, 1990; R. Ullrich, "Herzburg Revisited: Factors in Job Dissatisfaction," *Journal of Nursing Administration*, October 1978: 19–24; Hinshaw, Schmeltzer, and Atwood, "Innovative Strategies for Nursing Staff"; J.W. Seybolt, "Dealing with Premature Employee Turnover," *Journal of Nursing Administration* 16, no. 2 (1979): 25–32; M. Barnes and C. Crutchfield, "Job Satisfaction—Dissatisfaction," *Physical Therapy* 57, no. 1 (1977): 35–41.

7. Ullrich, "Herzburg Revisited"; Hinshaw, Schmeltzer, and Atwood, "Innovative Strategies for Nursing Staff."

8. Barnes and Crutchfield, "Job Satisfaction—Dissatisfaction."

9. Freda, "Influential Factors for Occupational Therapists Deciding to Remain at Their Jobs."

10. Ullrich, "Herzburg Revisited."

11. Ibid.

12. Joan C. Rogers and Susan C. Dodson, "Burnout in Occupational Therapists," *American Journal of Occupational Therapy* 42, no. 12 (1988): 787–92; Chestina Brollier et al., "A Pilot Study of Job Burnout Among Hospital-Based Occupational Therapists, *Occupational Therapy Journal of Research* 6, no. 5 (1986): 285–99; C. Cherniss, *Staff Burnout: Job Stress in the Human Services* (Beverly Hills, Calif.: Sage, 1980); Herbert J. Freudenberger, "The Staff Burn-out Syndrome in Alternative Institutions," *Psychotherapy: Theory, Research, and Practice* 12, no. 1 (1975): 73–82; Jennifer Sturgess and Anne Poulsen, "The Prevalence of Burnout in Occupational Therapists," *Occupational Therapy in Mental Health* 3, no. 4 (1983): 47–60; Joan Arches, "Social Structure, Burnout, and Job Satisfaction," *Social Work* 36, no. 3 (1991): 202–06.

13. Chestina Brollier et al., "OTR Burnout: A Comparison by Clinical Practice and Direct Service Time," *Occupational Therapy in Mental Health* 7, no. 1 (1987): 39–54; Ayala Pines and Christina Maslach, "Characteristics of Staff Burnout in Mental Health Settings," *Hospital and Community Psychiatry* 29, no. 4 (1978): 233–37.

14. Pines and Maslach, "Characteristics of Staff Burnout in Mental Health Settings"; Herbert J. Freudenberger, *Burn-out: The High Cost of High Achievement* (New York: Anchor Press, 1980).

15. Linda Apter and Ellen Kolodner, "Professional Burnout—Are You a Candidate?" *OT Forum* 11, no. 37 (1987).

16. Gary Kielhofner, ed., *A Model of Human Occupation* (Baltimore, Md.: Williams & Wilkins, 1985).

SUGGESTED READING

Abelson, M. "Strategic Management of Turnover: A Model for the Health Service Administrator." *Health Care Management Review* 11, no. 2 (1986): 61–71.

Bailey, Dianna. "Reasons for Attrition from Occupational Therapy." *American Journal of Occupational Therapy* 44, no. 1 (1990): 23–29.

Bailey, Dianna. "Ways to Retain or Reactivate Occupational Therapists." *American Journal of Occupational Therapy* 44, no. 1 (1990): 31–37.

Bordieri, James E. "Job Satisfaction of Occupational Therapists: Supervisors and Managers Versus Direct Service Staff." *Occupational Therapy Journal of Research* 8, no. 3 (1988): 155–163.

Brollier, Chestina. "Managerial Leadership and Staff OTR Job Satisfaction." *Occupational Therapy Journal of Research* 5 (1985): 170–184.

Brollier, Chestina. "A Multivariate Predictive Study of Staff OTR Job Satisfaction: Some Results of Importance to Psychosocial Occupational Therapy." *Occupational Therapy in Mental Health* 5, no. 2 (1985): 13–27.

Brollier, Chestina et al. "Managing Occupational Therapy Burnout." *Occupational Therapy in Health Care* 3, no. 2 (1986):129–143.

Davis, Gerald L. and James E. Bordieri. "Perceived Autonomy and Job Satisfaction in Occupational Therapists." *American Journal of Occupational Therapy* 42, no. 9 (1988):591–95.

Davis-Sacks, Mary Lou, Srinika Jayarante, and Wayne A. Chess. "A Comparison of the Effects of Social Support on the Incidence of Burnout." *Social Work* (May–June 1985): 240–44.

Edelwich, Jerry and Archie Brodsky. *Burnout: Stages of Disillusionment in the Helping Professionals.* New York: Human Services Press, 1980.

Ewalt, Patricia L. "Trends Affecting Recruitment and Retention of Social Work Staff in Human Services Agencies." *Social Work* 36, no. 3 (1991): 214–17.

Freda, Maureen."Retaining Occupational Therapists: Influential Factors." *American Journal of Occupational Therapy*: in press.

Huey, F. and S. Hartley. "What Keeps Nurses in Nursing?" *American Journal of Nursing* (1988): 181–88.

Jayarante, Srinika and Wayne A. Chess. "Job Satisfaction, Burnout, and Turnover: A National Study." *Social Work* (September–October 1984): 448–553.

Lehmann, L. "Occupational Therapists' Attitudes Toward Role Autonomy." *American Journal of Occupational Therapy* 27 (1973): 384–87.

Lynch, S. "Recruitment or Retention?" *AOTA Administrative and Management Special Interest Section Newsletter* 5, no. 3 (1989): 5.

National Association of Rehabilitation Facilities. "Memo to Members." (1988).

Ruben, B. "Keeping OTs on Staff." *OT Week* (March 15, 1990): 20–21.

Sabol, Peggy and Letty Sargant. "Unsolicited Professional Survey Looks at How OTs Select Their Jobs." *OT Week* (March 30, 1989): 4.

Taunton, R., S. Krampitz, and C. Woods. "Manager Impact on Retention of Hospital Staff: Part 1." *Journal of Nursing Administration* 19, no. 3 (1989): 14–18.

Taunton, R., S. Krampitz, and C. Woods. "Manager Impact on Retention of Hospital Staff: Part 2." *Journal of Nursing Administration* 19, no. 4 (1989): 15–19.

Tilke, Brenda. "Administrators, OTs Can Reduce Stress, Potential Burnout Factors." *Advance for Occupational Therapists* (April 23, 1990): 20.

Townsend, Kim R. and Marlys M. Mitchell. "Effectiveness of Recruitment and Information Techniques in Occupational Therapy." *American Journal of Occupational Therapy* 36 (1982): 524–29.

Chapter 10

Authority, Leadership, and Supervision

CHAPTER OBJECTIVES

1. Differentiate among the terms *power, influence,* and *authority.*
2. Recognize the importance of authority for organizational stability.
3. Identify the sources of power, influence, and authority.
4. Relate the sources of power, influence, and authority to the organizational position of the line manager.
5. Recognize the limits placed on the use of power and authority in organizational settings.
6. Identify the styles of leadership.
7. Identify the mentoring process.
8. Identify the relationship of leadership to the supervisory activities of issuing orders and directives, taking disciplinary action, and developing training activities.

The manager gives an order or directive, and there is compliance; why did the employee obey? Is it correct to use the term *obey* to describe this compliance? What bases of authority are operative in superior-subordinate transactions? What are the limits of a manager's authority? What if a particular supervisor is seen as a weak manager? Are there any remedies to problems related to weak or ineffective management leadership? Of what value to the organization is the authority structure? What are the consequences to organizational life if there is not a general, untested compliance most of the time? When such actions of compliance are described, which term is the proper point of reference: *power, authority,* or *influence*? Are these terms mutually exclusive or are they synonymous when used in the context of organizational relationships? These questions arise when discussion of authority in organizations is undertaken.

Organizational behavior is controlled behavior, directed toward goal attainment. The authority structure is created to ensure compliance with organizational norms, to suppress spontaneous or random behavior, and to induce purposeful behavior. No matter how the work within the organization is divided, no matter what degree of specialization, departmentation, centralization, or decentralization is formalized, there must be some measure of legitimate authority if the organization is to be effective. The concept of formal authority is supported by the two related concepts of power and influence. These concepts may be separated for analytical purposes; in actual practice, however, the three concepts are intertwined.

THE CONCEPT OF POWER

Power is the ability to obtain compliance by means of coercion, to have one's own will carried out despite resistance. Power is force or naked strength; it is a mental hold over another. Like authority and influence, power aims at compliance, but it does not seek consensus or agreement as a condition of that compliance.

Power is always relational. An individual who has power over another person can narrow that person's range of choice and obtain compliance. The power holder does not necessarily force the compliance by physical acts but may operate in more subtle ways, such as an implicit threat to carry out sanctions. Latent power is frequently as effective as a show of power. Power attaches to people, not to official positions. The formal authority holder (i.e., the person who has the official title, organizational position, and grant of authority) may or may not have power in addition to this formal grant of authority.

An imbalance in superior-subordinate relationships can occur when a nonofficeholder has more power than the official officeholder. This can even be seen in family life. For example, when a two-year-old shows signs of an incipient temper tantrum in the middle of the annual family gathering, the power balance clearly is in favor of the child if the tantrum pattern has developed. The child does not have to carry out the explosive behavior; the mere threat of doing so brings about some desired behavior from the parent caught in the situation. In the privacy of the home, however, the parent-child power balance shifts.

Workers have power over line supervisors and managers. A worker with specific technical knowledge can withhold that key information from a manager or can develop a relationship that is personally favorable. The information may not actually be withheld; the mere possibility that the manager cannot rely on an individual is enough to shift the balance, at least temporarily, in favor of the worker. Groups of workers can control a manager when it is well known that the manager is responsible for meeting a deadline or quota; the manager's ability to do this is dependent on the cooperation of the workers. The normal, steady output may be reached routinely, but that extra push needed to go over the quota or to reach a special level of output rests more with the workers than with the manager. Strikes by workers are classic examples of mobilized power, but the power shifts back in favor of management if striking workers are terminated during a strike.

When an individual can supply something that a person values and cannot obtain elsewhere in a regular manner, or when the individual can deprive this person of something valued, then there is a power relationship. This implicit or explicit power relationship may or may not be perceived by one or both parties.

THE CONCEPT OF INFLUENCE

Like power, influence is the capacity to produce effects on others or to obtain compliance, but it differs from power in the manner in which compliance is evoked. Power is coercive; influence is accepted voluntarily. Influence is the capacity to obtain compliance without relying on formal actions, rules, or force. In relationships of influence, not only compliance but also consensus and agreement are sought; persuasion rather than latent or overt force is the major factor in influence. Influence supplements power, and it is sometimes difficult to distinguish latent power from influence in a situation. Does the individual comply because of a relationship of influence or because of the latent power factor? Together, power and influence supplement formal authority.

THE CONCEPT OF FORMAL AUTHORITY

Authority may be termed legitimate power. It is the right to issue orders, to direct action, and to command or exact compliance. It is the right given to a manager to employ resources, make commitments, and exercise control. By a grant of formal authority, the manager is entitled, empowered, and authorized to act; thus, the manager incurs a responsibility to act. Authority may be expressed by direct command or instruction or, more commonly, by suggestion. Through the authority delegation, coordination is secured in the organization.

The authority mandate is delineated and reinforced in several ways, such as organization charts, job descriptions, procedure manuals, and work rules. Although the exercise of authority in many situations tends to be similar to transactions of influence, authority differs from influence in that authority is clearly vested in the formal chain of command. Individuals are given a specific grant of authority as a result of organizational position. Power and influence may be exercised by an individual authority holder, but they may also be exercised by individuals who do not have a specific grant of authority.

Authority is both complemented and supplemented by power on the one hand and influence on the other. It is within the realm of formal authority to exact compliance by the threat of firing a person; however, this may be such a rare occurrence in an organization that such a threat is really an exercise of power more than an exercise of authority. On the other hand, formal aspects of authority may be so well developed that the major transactions remain at the influence level, with the influence based largely on the holding of formal office. The infrequent use of formal authoritative directives to evoke compliance may indicate organizational health. For the remainder of this discussion, no further distinction between power, influence, and authority will be made.

THE IMPORTANCE OF AUTHORITY

When a subordinate refuses to accept the orders of a superior, the superior has several choices, each carrying potentially negative consequences for the attainment of organizational goals. The superior could accept the insubordination, withdraw the order, and seek to find others to carry out the directive. This action would probably further weaken authority, however, because the superior would be perceived as lacking the subtle blend of power and authority to exact compliance on a predictable basis. A chain reaction of insubordination could occur. If other workers are asked to carry out a directive that had been refused by a worker, resentment could build up with negative consequences. If the order is withdrawn completely, the work will not be accomplished.

The manager who decides to enforce compliance may suspend or fire the insubordinate worker. The superior still must find a worker to carry out the directive. If there is a chain reaction of insubordination, it may become impractical to suspend or fire the entire work force. The situation moves from one of authority to one of power. Therefore, managers must identify and widen their bases of authority to help ensure a stable work climate.

SOURCES OF POWER, INFLUENCE, AND AUTHORITY

The manager's organizational relationships flow along the continuum of power, influence, and authority, varying in emphasis at different times and in different situations. In order to understand more fully the dynamics of the power-influence-authority triad, it is useful to examine the sources or bases of authority in formal organizations. The wider the base of authority, the stronger the manager's position; with a wide base of authority, the manager can work in the realm of influence and need not rely only on the formal grant of authority that flows from organizational position.

The sources of formal authority have been studied by several theorists in the disciplines of social psychology, management, and political science. A review of the literature suggests several sources or bases of authority: (a) acceptance or consent, (b) patterns of formal organization, (c) cultural expectations, (d) technical competence and expertise, and (e) characteristics of authority holders. The limits or weaknesses of each theory are offset by the approach taken in another.

The Consent Theory of Authority

The concept that authority involves a subordinate's acceptance of a superior's decision is the basis for the acceptance or consent theory of formal authority. A superior has authority only insofar as the subordinate accepts it. This theory implies that members of the organization have a choice concerning compliance, when often they do not. It remains important to recognize the concepts of acceptance and consent in order to identify the centers of more subtle and diffuse resistance to authority, even when there is no overt and massive insubordination.

The zone of indifference and the zone of acceptance are two similar concepts in the acceptance or consent theory of authority. Chester Barnard used the term *zone of indifference* to describe that area in which an individual accepts orders without conscious questioning.[1] Barnard noted that the manager establishes an overall setting by means of preliminary education, prior persuasive efforts, and known inducements for compliance; the order then lies within the range that is more or less anticipated by the subordinate, who accepts it without conscious questioning or resistance because it is consistent with the overall organizational framework. Herbert Simon used the term *zone of acceptance* to reflect the same authority relationship. The zone of acceptance, according to Simon, is an area established by subordinates within which they are willing to accept the decisions made for them by their superior.[2] Simon noted that this zone is modified by the positive and negative sanctions in the authority relationship, as well as by such factors of community of purpose, habit, and leadership.

Coupled with these factors is the concept of the rule of anticipated reactions, which Simon included in his discussion of zone of acceptance.[3] The subordinate seeks to act in a manner that is acceptable to the superior, even when there has been no explicit command. The authority system, including anticipated review of actions, is so well developed that the superior needs only to review actions rather than issue commands. The past organizational history in which positive and negative sanctions were enforced is recalled; the expectation of the review of actions is fostered so that the subordinate's zone of acceptance is expanded.

Another approach to the concept of authority as a relationship between organizational leaders and their followers is described by Robert Presthus, who posited a transactional view of authority in which there is a reciprocity among individuals at different levels in the hierarchy.[4] Compliance with authority is in some way rewarding to the individual, and this individual, therefore, plays an active role in defining and accepting authority. Everyone has formal authority in that each has a formal role in the organization. There is, Presthus stated, an implicit bargaining and exchange of authority, each individual deferring to the other.

The notion of reciprocal expectations in authority relationships is further supported in Edgar Schein's discussion of the psychological contract.[5] As in Barnard's concept of the zone of indifference and in Simon's rule of anticipated reactions, the premise of member acceptance of organizational authority and its attendant control system is basic to the psychological contract. The workers' acceptance of authority constitutes a realm of upward influence; in turn, the workers expect the authority holders to honor the implicit restrictions on their grant of authority. The workers expect the authority holders to refrain from ordering actions that are inconsistent with the general climate of the given organization and from taking advantage of the workers' acceptance of authority. The workers also expect as part of this psychological contract the rewards of compliance (i.e., positive sanctions readily given and negative sanctions kept at a minimum).

The Theory of Formal Organizational Authority

In his classic study of bureaucracies, Max Weber discussed three forms of authority: charismatic, traditional, and rational-legal. Charisma, as defined by Weber, is a "certain quality of an individual personality by virtue of which he is set apart from ordinary men and treated as endowed with supernatural, superhuman, or at least specifically exceptional qualities."[6] The social, religious, and political groups that form around charismatic leaders tend to lack formal role structure. The routines of bureaucratic structure are not developed and may even be disdained by the group. Charismatic authority figures function as revolutionary forces against established systems of leadership and authority. Charismatic authority is not bound by explicit rules; the authority remains invested in the key charismatic individual. Personal devotion to and an almost irrational faith in the leader bind the members of the group to each other and to the leader.

Since charismatic authority is linked to the individual leader, the organization's survival is similarly linked. If the organization is to endure, it must take on some of the characteristics of formal organizations, including a formalized authority pattern. In this area, two developments are possible. The charismatic leadership may evolve into a traditional system of authority, or it may develop into the rational-legal system of formal authority. In traditionalism, a pattern of succession is developed. A successor may be designated by the leader or hereditary/kinship succession may be established; then a system of transferring the leadership to the legitimate designated individual or heir must be developed. This, in turn, leads to a system of roles and formal authority. Weber uses the term *routinization of charisma* to describe this transformation of charismatic authority into traditional and then into rational-legal authority.

Rational-legal authority is the authority predicated in formal organizations. It is generally assumed that formal organizations come into being and derive legitimacy from an overall social and legal system. Individuals accept authority within the formal organizational structure because the rights and duties of members of the organization are consistent with the more abstract rules that individuals in the larger society accept as legitimate and rational.

Within the formal organization, a system of roles and authority relationships is carefully constructed to enable the organization to survive and move toward its formal goal on a continuing, stable basis. Authority has its basis in the organizational position, not in any individual. Weber described in detail the major characteristics of bureaucratic structures; the following characteristics relate to the rational-legal authority structure[7]:

1. There is the principle of fixed and official jurisdictional areas, which are generally ordered by rules, that is, by laws or administrative regulations.
   a. The regular activities required for the purposes of the bureaucratically governed structure are distributed in a fixed way as official duties.
   b. The authority to give the commands required for the discharge of thes e duties is distributed in a stable way and is strictly delimited in a fixed way as official duties.
   c. Methodical provision is made for the regular and continuous fulfillment of these duties and for the execution of the corresponding rights; only persons who have generally regulated qualifications to serve are employed.
2. The principles of office hierarchy and of levels of graded authority mean a firmly ordered system of superiority and subordination in which there is supervision of the lower offices by the higher ones.

The theory of formal organizational authority rests on this rational-legal system of formal office, impersonality of the officeholder, and a system of rules and regulations to constrain the grant of authority. Delegation of formal authority from top management to each successive level of management is the basis for formal organizational authority. Authority is derived from official position and is circumscribed by the limits imposed by the hierarchical order.

Cultural Expectations

Both the consent theory of authority and the theory of formal organizational authority include an implicit assumption that individuals in a society are culturally induced to accept authority. Furthermore, the acceptable use of authority in organizations is defined in part by the larger societal mores as well as by union contract, corporate law, and state and federal law and regulation.

Acceptance of the status system in a society is learned as part of the general socialization process. General deference to authority is ingrained early in the psychosocial development of the child, and social roles with their sanctions are accepted and reinforced throughout adult life. The role of employee carries with it both formal and informal sanctions; insubordination is not generally condoned. Even as a group cheers the occasional rebel, there is an attendant discomfort because something is out of order in the relationship. When the insubordination of an individual begins to threaten the economic security of the group, there is counterpressure on that individual to bring about reacceptance of authority. Fear of authority may bring about a similar response of renewed acceptance of authority and counterpressure on any dissidents.

The expected zone of acceptance or zone of indifference varies with different social roles. These variables are rarely spelled out in great detail; they are learned as much through the pervasive cultural formation process as through the formal orientation process in any one organization. There is a kind of group mind that includes the general realization that a particular behavior pattern is part of a given role, and the entire role set reinforces this general acceptance of authority.

Technical Competence and Expertise

Three terms reflect the organizational authority that is derived from or based on the technical competence and expertise of the individual, regardless of what office or position the individual holds in the organization. These terms are *functional authority, the law of the situation,* and *the authority of facts.*

Functional authority is the limited right that line or staff members (or departments) may exercise over specified activities for which they are responsible (see "Line and Staff Relationships" in Chapter 6). Functional authority is given to the line or staff member as an exception to the principle of unity of command. For the purposes of this discussion on the sources of authority, it is useful to emphasize the special character of functional authority: It is given to a line or staff member primarily because that individual has specialized knowledge and technical competence. For example, the personnel manager normally assists all other department heads in matters of employee relations although this manager has no authority to intervene directly in manager-employee relations. The situation changes when there is a legally binding collective bargaining agreement; the personnel manager, with special training in labor relations, may be given functional authority over all matters stemming from the union contract because of specialized knowledge. Another example is that of data processing staff who, because of technical competence, are given authority to make final decisions over certain aspects of data collection. The authority is granted because of the technical competence of the staff members.

Mary Parker Follett, a pioneer in management thought, introduced the terms *law of the situation* and *authority of facts*.[8] Follett described the ideal authority relationship as that stemming from the situation as a whole. Each participant in the organization, who is assumed to have the necessary qualifications for the position held, has authority tied to position. Orders become depersonalized in that each participant in the process studies and accepts the factors in the situation as a whole. Follett stated that one *person* should not give orders to another *person* but that both should agree to take their orders from the situation.[9] She developed this concept further; both the employer and the employee should study the situation and should apply their specialized knowledge and technical competence through the principles of scientific management. The emphasis shifts, in Follett's approach, from authority derived from official position or office to authority derived from the situation. The individual who has the most knowledge and competence to make the decision and issue the order in a particular situation has the authority to do so. The staff assistant or a key employee potentially has as much authority in a particular situation as does a holder of hierarchical office.

Closely tied to the concept of the law of the situation is that of authority of facts. Follett stressed that, in modern organizations, individuals exercise authority and leadership because of their expert knowledge.[10] Again, the leadership and authority shift from the hierarchical position to the situation. The one with the knowledge demanded by the situation tends to exercise effective authority.

In both of these concepts, there is an emphasis on the depersonalization of orders. At the same time, the source of the authority is highly personal in that knowledge and competence for the exercise of authority belong to an individual. Underlying the concepts of functional authority, law of the situation, and authority of facts is the theme that authority is derived from the technical competence and knowledge of individuals in the organization who do not necessarily hold formal office in the line hierarchy.

Characteristics of Authority Holders

Authority rests in individuals. The talents and traits of the individual may become the source of authority, as in the case of the charismatic leader. A person holding power may use this as a base for gaining legitimate authority; a group may invest the person of power with legitimate authority as a protective measure and seek to impose the limits and customs of authority. They may also accept the power holder as formal officeholder as a means of accepting the situation without further conflict. Technical competence and knowledge are also personal characteristics that become the basis of authority in certain situations.

The Manager's Use of Sources of Authority

In practice, managers should recognize all the potential sources of authority and should weigh the contribution of each theory to obtain as complete a picture of the authority nexus as possible. They should assess their own grant of authority and try to determine which elements tend to strengthen their authority and which tend to erode it.

The base of authority shifts from time to time. For example, an individual is offered the position of department head of the medical record service because of that individual's competence in the administration of medical record systems; this specialized knowledge and technical competence is the first pillar of authority. When the individual accepts the position, the formal authority mandate of that official position is added. This authority, in turn, is shaped by the prevailing organizational climate, which includes a wide or narrow zone of acceptance on the part of employees. The personal traits of the authority holder complete the authority base for that office.

The individual with a participative management style may emphasize those aspects of authority that widen the zone of acceptance. The setting itself may dictate the predominant authority base, as in the law of the situation; in a highly technical setting, those with the most technical knowledge use this knowledge as the base of authority. Although there is a tendency to downplay internal politics in organizations such as health care institutions, some individual managers may use power as a major source of authority. Astute managers regularly assess the several bases of authority available to them in order to enhance the authority relationships and thereby contribute more effectively to the achievement of organizational goals.

RESTRICTIONS ON THE USE OF AUTHORITY

Several factors restrict the use of authority. Some constraints stem from internal factors, such as the limits placed on authority at each organizational level; others stem from external factors such as laws, regulations, and ethical considerations. The following is a systematic summary of these factors:

1. Organizational Position. Each holder of authority receives a limited delegation of authority consistent with the position held in the organization. An individual has no legitimate formal authority beyond that accorded to the organizational position.
2. Legal and Contractual Mandates. Authority is limited by the federal, state, and municipal laws and regulations relating to safety, work hours, licensure, and scope of practice; by internal corporate charter and bylaws; and by union contract.

3. Social Limitations. The social codes, mores, and values of the overall society include both implicit and explicit limits on the behavior of individuals. Authority holders are expected to act in a manner consistent with the predominant value system of the society. These social limitations are major factors in shaping the zone of acceptance and the general cultural deference of individuals who are members of organizations.

4. Physical Limits. An authority holder cannot force a person to do something that is simply beyond that person's physical capabilities, nor can an authority holder escape the natural limits of the physical environment, such as climate or physical laws.

5. Technological Constraints. The advances and the limitations of the state of the art must be considered in the exercise of authority; no amount of power or authority can bring about a result that is beyond the technical ability of the individuals.

6. Economic Constraints. The scarcity of needed resources limits the behavior of formal authority holders.

7. Zone of Acceptance of Organization Members. Both authority and power have their limits in that the net cost of using either must be calculated. When a weak manager is faced with a strong employee group, as in a strong union setting, the cost of using even legitimate authority may be too high; the authority grant is actually diminished.

Although many employees do not have complete freedom to choose what they will or will not do, they may resist authority in subtle ways, such as adherence to job duties exactly as stated in the job description, passive resistance, and failure to take initiative in any area not specifically designated by the supervisor. The manager must move into a distinct leadership position to develop a wide zone of acceptance, as leadership becomes an essential adjunct to the exercise of authority.

LEADERSHIP

Professionals frequently describe a leader as a powerful person who made it to the top of his or her field. The successful allied health professional does not seem to share familiar and common habits with the average practitioner. We imagine the person as a romantic figure that is not human. In reality, Drucker describes leadership as "mundane, unromantic and boring. Its essence is performance."[11] Yet, leadership is vital for the future growth and development of allied health professions. This section is designed to address the leadership qualities that everyone has buried within. Rather than define leadership as distant and unusual, this section describes it as a set of characteristics that emerges from individuals who are able to get things done within an organization.

Leaders are not born, they develop. In fact, leaders are not extraordinary except that they can match organizational goals to the abilities and interests of their work groups. This talent is mercurial and one finds that some leaders are effective in one set of circumstances but not in others. Leadership is not based on impossible characteristics possessed by few; rather, it is a collection of abilities.

Definition of Leadership

A leader is a person who can organize tasks and make things happen. Using the unique interests and needs of every member of the work group, effective leaders inspire goal-directed behavior that is consistent and efficient. The leader cajoles, rewards, punishes, organizes, stimulates, strengthens, communicates, and motivates. There is no set standard for leadership behavior as individuals must match their own characteristics to the needs of the organization.

The personal characteristics of leaders are a strong self-image, a vision of the future, a firm belief in the goals of the organization, the ability to influence the behavior of subordinates, and the ability to relate to and influence individuals in parallel or superior positions of authority.

Leadership exists both informally and formally. Informal leadership is exerted in many settings, including formal organizations. Within any formal organization, there are subunits and even paraorganizations, such as a collective bargaining unit, that are led by individuals who do not hold formal hierarchical office. Leadership is implied, even explicitly included, in the role of the manager whose function is to achieve organizational objectives by coordinating, motivating, and directing the work group. For the remainder of this discussion on formal leadership, the presumption is made that the manager is a leader in addition to being a holder of formal authority. Philip Selznick stressed leadership as an attribute of the manager, pointing out that leadership is needed to make critical decisions. The institutional leader is the unique possessor of a systems perspective, and this quality, Selznick noted, distinguishes a leader from the individual who is adept in interpersonal relationships.[12]

Leadership Qualities

In order to influence and induce others to strive toward a goal, the leader must possess not only a deep vision of that goal, but also the ability to render the goal meaningful to the group. The knowledge, insight, and skill of the leader are greater than those of other members of the group. At an obvious level, the leader leads but does not drag, coerce, or push the group; the group members are steadily induced to move toward the goal. They are influenced in a pervasive way so that the overall goal becomes their own goal. The leader does not achieve the work alone but instead successfully coordinates the work of the group. The leader inspires confidence through both emotional and knowledge ties with the followers.

Leadership Functions

In formal organizations, the leader has certain functions that are tied to the organizational need for leadership. The leader is expected to influence, persuade, and control the group. As the individual with vision, the leader is expected to take calculated risks and to be a catalytic agent in the change process.

The leader carries out important functions on behalf of group members through the role of representative; for example, employees look to their unit or department head to speak for them and to seek to obtain advantages for them. The leader may be cast in several roles by followers, especially at the symbolic level, and may even be seen as the father figure who shields the individual from difficulties. The leader may also be the scapegoat; as the management representative closest to the rank and file worker, the leader-manager bears the brunt of anger when the organizational situation is less than optimal.

The leader is presumed to embody the values of the group. As such, the leader becomes the focal point in the motivational process. Warren Bennis summarized the functions of the leader in his statements concerning an "agricultural" model of leadership. Bennis offered as the major function of the leader the development of the climate and conditions that favor individual involvement in group effort. Leadership is a process more than a structure; the leader creates the climate for change so that the organization will have the adaptability needed for its survival.[13]

Styles of Leadership

The manner in which a manager interacts with subordinates reflects a cluster of characteristics that constitute a style of leadership. While any manager uses several styles of leadership—choosing the style most appropriate for a given situation—one style generally emerges as that manager's predominant mode of interaction.

Autocratic Leadership

Also referred to as *authoritarian, boss-centered,* or *dictatorial leadership,* autocratic leadership is characterized by close supervision. The manager who employs this style gives direct, clear, and precise directions to employees, telling them what is to be done and how it will be done; there is no room for employee initiative. Employees do not participate in the decision-making process. There is a high degree of centralization and a narrow span of management.

The chain of command is clearly and fully understood by all. Autocratic managers use their authority as their principal, or only, method of getting work done because they feel that employees could not properly or efficiently carry out work assignments without detailed instruction.

Although this style of leadership apparently gets results, it can be fatal over the long run. Employees easily lose interest in their assignments and stop thinking for themselves, since there is no occasion for independent thought. Under certain conditions and with specific employees, however, a degree of close supervision may be necessary. Some employees prefer to receive clear and precise orders, because close supervision reassures them that they are doing a good job. Even so, it can generally be assumed that the autocratic, close leadership style is the least effective and least desirable method for motivating employees.

Bureaucratic Leadership

Like the autocratic leader, the bureaucratic leader tells employees what to do and how to do it. The basis for this leadership style is almost exclusively the institution's rules and regulations. For the bureaucrat, these rules are the laws. The bureaucratic manager is normally afraid to take chances and manages "by the book." Rules are strictly enforced, and no departures or exceptions are permitted. The bureaucrat, like the autocrat, allows employees little or no freedom.

Participative Leadership

In participative leadership, the contribution of the group to the organizational effort is emphasized. This style is the opposite of autocratic, close supervision. The manager who employs the participative method involves the employees in the decision-making process and in the maintenance of cohesive group interaction. The manager consults with employees concerning goals and objectives, work assignments, and the extent and content of a problem before making a final decision and issuing directives or orders. This approach is an attempt to make full use of the talents and abilities of the group members; the manager is the facilitator of this process. It is difficult for employees who have participated in the consultative process not to accept the resulting decision.

Some managers use a pseudoparticipative method of leadership to give employees the feeling that consultation has taken place. Employees quickly sense that the manager is manipulating people, however, and that their participation in the decision-making process is not real. The manager who employs the participative style of leadership must take it seriously and must be willing to listen to and evaluate employees' opinions and suggestions before making a final decision.

Participative management does not weaken a manager's formal authority, since the manager retains the right to make the final decision. The obvious advantage of the participative style of leadership revolves around the meaningful involvement of the employees, which greatly enhances the implementation of the decisions that have been made.

Laissez-faire Leadership

Laissez-faire or "free rein" leadership is based on the assumption that individuals are self-motivated. Employees receive little or no supervision. Employees, as individuals or as a group, determine their own goals and make their own decisions. The manager, whose contribution is minimal, acts primarily as a consultant and does so only when asked. The manager does not lead but allows the employees to lead themselves. Some managers consider this approach true democratic leadership, but the usual end result is disorganization and chaos. The lack of leadership permits different employees to proceed in different directions.

Paternalistic Leadership

The manager who is paternalistic treats employees like children. The manager tells employees what is to be done but does so in a nice way. It is the paternalistic manager's belief that employees do not really know what is good for them or how to make decisions for themselves. In this approach, everyone is watched over by the benevolent manager—the benign dictator—and the employees eventually become extremely dependent on their "paternalistic boss."

Continuum of Leadership Styles

Another way to view leadership behavior is on a continuum ranging from highly boss-centered to highly group-centered.[14] The relationship between the manager and the employee in the continuum ranges from completely autocratic, in which there is no employee participation in the decision-making process, to completely democratic, in which the employee participates in all phases of the decison-making process (Figure 10-1). The following is a brief description of the seven gradations along the continuum:

1. *Manager makes decision and announces it.* The manager identifies a problem, considers alternative solutions, selects a course of action, and tells employees what they are to do. Employees do not participate in the decision-making process.
2. *Manager "sells" decision.* The manager again makes the decision without consulting the employees. Instead of announcing the decision, however, the manager attempts to persuade the employees to accept it. The manager details how the decision fits both the goals of the department and the interests of group members.

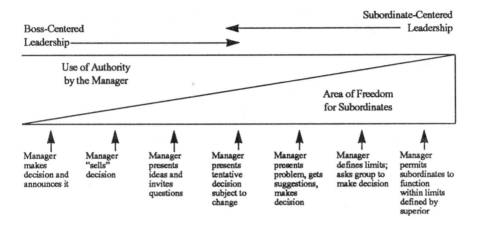

Boss-Centered
Leadership

Subordinate-Centered
Leadership

Use of Authority
by the Manager

Area of Freedom
for Subordinates

| Manager makes decision and announces it | Manager "sells" decision | Manager presents ideas and invites questions | Manager presents tentative decision subject to change | Manager presents problem, gets suggestions, makes decision | Manager defines limits; asks group to make decision | Manager permits subordinates to function within limits defined by superior |

Figure 10-1 Continuum of Leadership Behavior. *Source:* Reprinted with permission from "How to Choose a Leadership Pattern" by Robert Tannenbaum and Warren H. Schmidt, *Harvard Business Review* 36, no. 2 (1958): 96. Copyright © 1958 by the President and Fellows of Harvard College; all rights reserved.

3. *Manager presents ideas and invites questions.* The manager has made the decision but asks the employees to express their ideas. Thus, the manager allows for the possibility that the initial decision may be modified.
4. *Manager presents tentative decision subject to change.* The manager allows the employees the opportunity to exert some influence before the decision is finalized. The manager meets with the employees and presents the problem and a tentative decision. Before the decision is finalized, the manager obtains the reactions of employees who will be affected by it.
5. *Manager presents problem, gets suggestions, makes decision.* Up to this point on the continuum, the manager has always come before the employees with at least a tentative solution to the problem. At this point, however, the employees get the first opportunity to suggest solutions. Consultation with the employees increases the number of possible solutions to the problem. The manager then selects the solution that he or she regards as most appropriate in solving the problem.
6. *Manager defines limits; asks group to make decision.* For the first time, the employees make the decision. The manager now becomes a member of the group. Before doing this, however, the manager defines the problem and the limits and boundaries within which the decision must be made.
7. *Manager permits subordinates to function within limits defined by superior.* For the maximum degree of employee participation, the manager defines the problem and lists the guidelines and boundaries within which a

solution must be achieved. The limitation imposed on the employees comes directly from the manager, who participates as a group member in the decision-making process and is committed in advance to implementing whatever decision the employees make.

In summary, the manager's relationship with the employees influences morale, job satisfaction, and work output. Employee satisfaction is positively associated with the degree to which employees are permitted to participate in the decision-making process. On the other hand, poor supervision causes employee dissatisfaction, high turnover rates, and low morale.

Factors That Influence Leadership Style

No one style of leadership fits all situations. A successful manager selects a method appropriate for a given situation. Before selecting a style of leadership or deciding to blend several styles, the manager must consider a number of factors:

1 Work Assignment. If the work assignment is repetitious, the properly trained employee does not need constant or close supervision. If the assignment is new or complex, however, close supervision may be required.
2. Personality and Ability of the Employee. Employees who are not self-starters react best to close supervision. Others, by reason of their personality and work background, can take on new and important responsibilities on their own; these individuals react best to participative leadership. The occupational makeup of a department may also influence the leadership style used by the manager. For professional people (e.g., physical therapists, occupational therapists, medical records personnel) or other highly skilled employees, the employee-centered participative leadership style is often most effective. When employees are unskilled or unable to act independently, the boss-centered or autocratic style of leadership may produce better results.
3. Attitude of the Employee Toward the Manager. Managers cannot begin to lead or influence behavior unless they are accepted by the group. Employees give managers their authority only when they believe that the goals and objectives of the managers are consistent with their own personal and professional interests.
4. Personality and Ability of the Manager. The manager's personality has a very definite effect on the behavior and performance of employees. The manager must treat employees' opinions and suggestions with respect and must sincerely encourage employee participation.

When faced with different work group encounters and situational factors, the good manager shifts from one style of leadership to another, often without conscious recognition of a shift in style. Table 10-1 shows examples of the adjustments in leadership style that a manager makes in order to stimulate maximum effort from employees.

MENTORING*

Professional practitioners may find themselves in the special leadership role of mentoring. Mentoring is a process where an older or more experienced person guides and nurtures a younger, or less experienced one. The

Table 10-1 Variables in Leadership Style

Work Group	Key Activities	Leadership Style
Hospital transporters	Transport of patients Safety considerations Schedule considerations Mode of transport	Bureaucratic—policies and procedures must be followed
Staff physical therapist with experience	Patient evaluation "Need evaluation today" Neurological case Conference at 10:00 A.M.	Laissez-faire—manager does not need to tell physical therapist such typical evaluation elements as motor, sensory, and cognitive tests
Total physical therapy professional staff (5 physical therapists)	Vacation schedules Consideration of patients, students, and overall coverage. One staff resignation in July	Participative—manager consults with employees concerning vacation schedule and the need for proper coverage during the summer months
Staff physical therapist	Call from physician to staff therapist; wishes to see therapist at patient's bedside promptly at 9:15 or "Sorry to interrupt but just had a call from Dr. Jones and he requests you be at the patient's room #343 in 5 minutes" (*Note:* Even, nice, tone)	Autocratic, nonnegotiable

* The author would like to acknowledge the assistance of Michael S. Klein, OTR, Cape May Therapy Services, Inc., and Wendy White, OTR/L, Staff Therapist, A.I. duPont Institute for Children, for the development of this section.

person who serves as the guide is the mentor and the person who accepts the guidance serves as the protégé or mentee. Mentoring can be best described as a set of behaviors that operate in a relationship rather than as a set of "innate abilities possessed by the mentor."[15] There is a paternalistic aspect of mentoring that some authors refer to as "hierarchical." Mentoring is compared with the Erikson concept of "generativity," in which the older person guides the next generation through role modeling, counseling, guiding, supporting, critiquing, and believing in the mentee's skills. Like a "good" parent, the "good" mentor responds to the mentee's needs and promotes independence and self-knowledge.

Definitions

Some terms commonly used to discuss this professional relationship are defined below.

Mentor

A person who is willing to select an individual and shape his or her career by teaching, sponsoring, hosting, guiding, and serving as a role model and counselor. The mentor is usually an older person who believes in the mentee and is willing to nurture the mentee through the difficult aspects of charting a future in the field. The relationship is intense, and the mentor must be willing to devote time to the mentee. The mentor is motivated by a desire to influence the next generation and assumes responsibility for shaping the mentee's career and offers feedback to improve performance. This affirms the competence of the mentee and gives the mentor an opportunity to nurture someone.

Mentee

The mentee is a protégé who commits time and effort to becoming competent. Willing to listen and learn, the mentee trusts the mentor and acts on the ideas offered. Protégés or mentees are grateful for the attention and help they receive and they are able to demonstrate their appreciation. Williams claims that mentees make themselves receptive to this relationship by displaying a teachable attitude and a willingness to learn.[16] Mentees can take feedback and use the advice to further their own development.

Sponsor

A sponsor is someone who takes responsibility for someone else's learning. Some authors use *mentor* and *sponsor* interchangeably; others feel that there is less paternalism and commitment in the sponsor relationship.

Mentor Relationship

Kelly defines the mentor relationship as a formal or informal relationship between a prestigious, established, older person and a younger one wherein the older guides, counsels, and critiques the younger, teaching him or her how to survive and advance in a certain field or profession.[17] Levinson delineates the functions of various kinds of mentors as follows[18]:

1. A teacher develops knowledge and skills.
2. A sponsor facilitates entry and advancement in the workplace.
3. A host and guide welcomes a mentee into the appropriate groups to promote the mentee's career.
4. A role model provides an example of appropriate values, behavior, habits, and roles.
5. A counselor is willing to listen and guide the mentee using advice, feedback and support for ideas.

Rogers maintains that the essence of mentorship lies in a more experienced person accepting responsibility for developing a less experienced person.[19] Mentors teach what textbooks and teachers cannot—namely, how to be successful in the profession.

Network

A network is a group of individuals who communicate through formal and informal channels and willingly promote each other for mutual benefit. The network members trade services, ideas, recommendations, and "tips" to further their own development and success. The AOTA, the APTA, the AMRA, and state associations are examples of networks.[20]

Peer Pals

Peer pals boost each other's career by sharing information and strategies. They share each other's strengths and weaknesses since they are on the same developmental level.

Why Act as a Mentor?

The stress of current health delivery makes mentoring seem like a burden to both parties. Yet those who have been on either side of the relationship describe it as satisfying and useful. Mentoring transmits current values to another generation of professionals at the same time that young practitioners are warmly welcomed into the field. Professional development and continuity are results of the mentor relationship.

Pilette maintains that the deepest of human needs is to believe in oneself and the next most important need is to receive affirmation from another.[21] Thus, the two basic elements of the mentoring process are human-relatedness and direction. Human-relatedness is the relationship between the mentor and the mentee. Direction is the dual notion of inner direction or motivation and the external directedness of the mentor guiding the mentee. There are four stages in the process: invitational, questioning, informational, and transitional.

The *invitational stage* is when an invitation is proffered "to try out one's thinking and test out one's dreams within the boundaries of a nurturing relationship."[22] The mentor encourages the relationship by being open, authentic, and responsive to the mentee. The mentee invites the relationship by wanting to learn and by respecting the mentor. The mentee and mentor share a vision of the mentee's future, but the mentor might perceive the mentee as having more potential than the mentee is aware of.

In the *questioning stage*, the mentee begins to question the mentor. Vacillation, anxiety, and fear of being unable to meet expectations and goals are common. They provoke further thought about goals and interests. The mentor will direct the mentee and clarify future issues. The mentor serves as "a footbridge aiding the mentee to reach far beyond her initial, comfortable grasp."[23] "You can do it" is the theme of this stage.

During the *informational stage,* ideas are gathered, more data are collected, and ideas are tested. The mentor serves as a sounding board and initiates the neophyte into the professional network. The mentee must assimilate information and reconceptualize ideas. In particular, the mentee must learn how organizations function and how to recognize and use power.

The *transitional stage* occurs when the mentee becomes less dependent. In many instances, the mentor relationship is terminated or the influence of the mentor becomes more limited. Kram uses the term redefinition to refer to the adjustment that occurs when the mentor and mentee become peers and develop, in many cases, a friendship among equals.[24]

A good mentor is an effective teacher who guides the mentee. Using communication skills, the mentor offers a feedback in a fashion that promotes the mentee's feelings and self-worth and competence. Mentors enjoy power and can make things happen.

Johnsrud offers a conceptual framework for understanding mentoring as an interdependent rather than a hierarchical, one-way process of giving and receiving.[25] Johnsrud rejects the paternalistic model of mentoring according to which the dependent mentor develops by becoming independent of the mentor. Kegan argues that the evolution toward maturity is basically a series of resolutions of the tension between autonomy and connectedness.[26] Full maturity is the ability to be interdependent. As in any human relationship, the mentor and mentee struggle with feelings of wanting to be autonomous and connected at the same time. The tension between these contrasting emotions shapes the quality of the relationship.

Kegan, whose work is based on the work of Piaget and Perry, suggests that individuals construct reality or make meaning of their experiences based on their perceptions. Perceptions shift as a person differentiates the self from the environment and the self from others. Kegan describes six constructions of self that occur from birth to mature adulthood, each representing a balance between self and other. Maturity is the stage where the self can be differentiated from others but also can be integrated with others. These contradictions create a dialectic of yin and yang where contradictory feelings create a tension. Kegan describes three stages of adult development that are applicable to the mentoring relationship: interpersonal, institutional, and interindividual.

In the *interpersonal stage* we define ourselves by our relationships with others. "I" and "we" are fused. In this stage, a mentee determines his or her worth based on the perceptions of the mentor. The mentor must provide confirmation, feedback, and continuous support while the mentee establishes a unique self. Opportunities for independence must be offered so the mentee can develop.

As the mentor encourages more independence and the mentee establishes a unique identity, the mentee begins to self-monitor and collaborate with greater ease. The mentor should support this autonomous behavior and encourage the mentee to make independent decisions. This is the *institutional stage* of the relationship.

Finally, if the other stages have been completed, the mentor and mentee balance the need for connectedness and the need for independence. This occurs at the *interindividual stage*. During this stage the relationship becomes reciprocal, and each individual's differences and separate identities are recognized and honored. This is a difficult stage to attain, but reaching it benefits the individuals involved as well as their profession.

Johnsrud's application of Kegan's ideas follow the stages of ego development when the self is differentiated from the environment and then the mother. Her ideas focused on academic women but could be utilized in a male dominated culture.[27] Johnsrud speculates that female mentees have more hurdles to cross at the beginning of their relationship but that they also have the ability to attain interindividuation with greater ease.

Urbano and Jahns identify four developmental stages: initial adjustment, adaptation stage I, adaptation stage II, and termination.[28] During the initial adjustment stage, the mentee experiences anxiety and role dysfunction, clinging to concrete aspects of learning, such as mastering terms and procedures. Technique is important during this stage of development. In the second stage, a period of calm sets in, because the mentee begins to understand the demands of his or her role. Integration of knowledge and skills is evident as the mentee performs clinical skills with increased ease. Independent judgments are still not easily made. The mentee usually checks with the mentor. The mentor should be supportive during this phase, but constructive criticism and counseling can lead the mentee to greater independence. New demands, such as dealing with families or presenting a case at a conference, may be stressful. If the mentee feels vulnerable, he or she may regress to some of the behaviors seen during the initial adjustment period. Once the mentee learns to use professional support networks, real progress can continue.

During the next stage, adaptation stage II, the mentee moves toward more independent behaviors. Questions are asked and eager learning takes place as knowledge and skills are integrated. The mentor must help the mentee to choose appropriate outlets for newfound knowledge and skills. Some mentees may become rebellious and may need opportunities to test out their independence. This is a vulnerable time for the mentee, who needs to gain independence without turning everyone else off. The mentor should help the mentee to take on new responsibilities and should guide the mentee into new relationships so that the mentee can give and receive feedback. The mentee must learn to function independently and take responsibility for his or her actions.

In the termination stage, the mentee internalizes a new role and can function without the intervention of the mentor. The mentee should have a peer group, and new opportunities and challenges should be encouraged. The identification of stages is important for mentor and mentee.

Although individuals succeed without a mentor, research indicates that a mentor seems to smooth the way and make the future more satisfying.[29] Anyone who has supervised students knows that some individuals seem to seek advice while other students fight the learning process and appear brittle and resentful of any feedback. The best mentees demonstrate a willingness to learn, curiosity, a desire to do well, an interest in their mentors' ideas, an ability to take feedback and act on it, an ability to consider new ideas and test them out, and a desire to develop as a professional.

Mentoring is a rewarding relationship that can satisfy professional and personal needs. The time invested by both the mentor and mentee is often well spent, especially as other parties usually benefit from the relationship. At some point the mentee should outperform the mentor and either surpass the mentor's knowledge and abilities or develop new areas for growth and personal satisfaction. It can be helpful to keep in mind that altering the relationship and reshaping the mentee's role may prove stressful for both parties.[30]

Case Example

Ralph, a recent graduate, started in a new position at a rehabilitation center. Wanting to expand and reinforce his management skills, he attended lectures, medical rounds, and other organizational events and tried to meet individuals outside of his department. The third month of his employment, he was introduced to John, the director of rehabilitation engineering, who was friendly and open during their discussion. Ralph decided to make an appointment with John and ask for his ideas on a patient mobility problem that he wanted to solve.

Ralph found that John was eager to share his knowledge, and Ralph asked if he might consult with him again. After three more sessions, Ralph felt comfortable enough to ask John if he would serve as his mentor. John met with Ralph once every other week and listened to Ralph's ideas and offered suggestions and new ideas. Ralph used this help and acknowledged John's assistance. Within four months, John helped Ralph develop a new telephone dialing device for bilateral amputees. A model was constructed, and John taught Ralph how to pilot-test equipment. Ralph learned this step and mastered the other stages of equipment design, construction, and presentation to patients.

ORDERS AND DIRECTIVES

The manager's role is to direct the employees toward achieving the goals and objectives of the department and the institution. Regardless of the leadership style employed, the manager must issue orders and directives to indicate what must be done. The terms *orders* and *directives* may be used interchangeably, although *orders* has a more autocratic tone.

Giving orders is a major function of the manager's day-to-day operation of the program. Too often, it is taken for granted that every manager knows how to give orders. Unfortunately, this is not true. The manager must remember to convey to the employees *what* is to be done, *who* is to do it, and *when, where, how* and *why*. At times, some of the components are implied or omitted. For example, "Effective July 1, John Doe will be the Senior Physical Therapist of the Amputee Service." This statement answers the *what, who, when,* and *where* but omits the *how* and *why.*

Verbal Orders versus Written Orders

The form of an order depends on the situation. The verbal order is the most frequently used. Because it is given on a one-to-one basis with immediate feedback, the manager can observe the employee's reaction, ask questions, and appraise the degree of understanding. Disagreements can be handled immediately. Observation of the employee's body language provides additional feedback.

When permanence is important, written orders are more appropriate. This form is most effective when information is to be disseminated to employees as a group. Written orders are more carefully thought through, since there is less opportunity for explanation. The use of long sentences, excessive adjectives, and involved word patterns should be avoided. The written order also carries a degree of formality not present in the verbal order. It is difficult, however, to keep written material up to date and impossible to clear up obscure meanings.

Making Orders Acceptable and Effective

The issuing of effective orders requires attention to timing and language. Planning to issue the order involves content, format (oral or written), and the manner in which the order is actually issued. When there is rapport between the manager and employee, a simple request may be suitable; an implied order is sometimes given with the same informality. When certain action must be taken, precision is involved, or misunderstanding must be avoided, the written, direct order is the best method. The sense of command may be foreign to many managers, yet commands may be needed on some occasions, such as emergencies. Although policies, work rules, and procedures may not be considered orders, they do set required courses of action as determined by management.

Since a critical aspect of the manager's function is communicating, effort must be given to making orders acceptable and effective. Acceptability is enhanced by the general processes of leadership that the manager has developed over time. In effect, the manager prepares the employees in many ways so that, when orders are actually given, they are normally both acceptable and effective in terms of essential communication.

DISCIPLINE

The attitudes and emotions of each employee within an organization not only affect the degree to which goals and objectives are met but also influence the behavior of other employees. The manager of any unit or department must be concerned with the conduct or discipline of all employees within that unit or department. Control can best be maintained by establishing reasonable standards of conduct or work rules, informing employees of these standards, and enforcing them wisely.

Because the word *discipline* is immediately associated with the use of authority, it carries the disagreeable connotation of punishment. Discipline should be used to improve employee behavior, however, and to motivate employees so that they will be self-disciplined and effective in the performance of their jobs. Calling attention to correct behavior is more effective in promoting self-discipline and cooperation than calling attention to incorrect behavior.

Even in an organization where employees have a high degree of self-discipline, a manager must occasionally take some type of disciplinary action because rules have been broken. At this point, the manager is confronted with a situation in which the more restricted meaning of *discipline* is required. Disciplining becomes a response to unacceptable behavior, and the imposition of penalties is the only course open to the manager for correcting the employee's behavior and maintaining control of the department. Distasteful as it may be, it is the manager's responsibility to act promptly, firmly, and consistently. This means that disciplinary action should follow the misconduct as closely as possible. Since harsh words may be exchanged during the discussion, the manager must maintain self-control. The manager who feels that loss of control is a risk should avoid taking any action until a later date.

The manager must handle all disciplinary action as a private matter. If the manager can be overheard in disciplining, the other employees of the department will judge the manager's performance. Being observed or overheard by others may only confuse the situation and foster ill feelings among the manager, the employee, and the coworkers. This situation may further damage manager-employee relationships. Therefore, privacy during any disciplinary action is essential.

Progressive Disciplinary Action

When an institution has a union contract, the disciplinary process is usually outlined in the policy and procedure manual or in the work rules of the institution. Many institutions that do not have these documents have accepted the idea of progressive discipline, which has become fairly well standardized as a result of custom and practice. In order of increasing severity, the disciplinary steps are as follows:

1. general counseling
2. oral warning with a notation in the employee's employment record
3. official written warning noted in the employment record
4. disciplinary layoff without pay, varying in length from one day to two weeks
5. termination

Consistent with the concept of positive, corrective discipline, oral or written warnings are given for minor offenses. The oral warning is used when it is believed that the employee does not fully understand the significance of the actions or behavior. It is hoped that emphasizing the need for a change in behavior at this point will make further disciplinary action unnecessary. The employee who continues to violate established standards should be warned in writing. The warning should state how the employee's performance or conduct is unacceptable and what particular punishment is prescribed by institutional rules and regulations for continued infractions. A copy of the warning should be given to the employee, and a duplicate copy should be placed in the employee's personnel file so that it becomes a part of the employee's permanent record (Exhibit 10-1).

The disciplinary layoff may be used when all previous disciplinary steps have produced no change in the employee's behavior. The length of the disciplinary layoff depends on the seriousness of the offense and the number of times it has been repeated; it may vary from one day to several weeks. An employee who continues misconduct after oral warnings and an official written warning will find a disciplinary layoff without pay a rude awakening.

Termination is the most severe form of disciplinary action and should be used only for the most serious offenses, such as stealing, falsification of records, drinking of alcoholic beverages, or use of narcotics during work time, or for a record of repeated offenses. When termination is necessary, every effort should be made by management to maintain pleasant relationships with the employee who is about to be terminated.

In all disciplinary actions, the time element is important. How long should an infraction of the rules and regulations of the institution be held against an employee? Current practice is to wipe the slate clean and disregard offenses committed one or two years ago. There is no justification for continual reference to offenses of past years if the employee has maintained a good record for at least one year.

The disciplinary action used by the manager should match the severity of the offense, and the manager must remember that the purpose of the action is to correct the employee's behavior and to avoid similar offenses in the future. Whatever the disciplinary action, it should be done as impersonally as possible. It is the specific offense that requires discipline, not the personality of the employee. If the

Exhibit 10-1 Official Written Warning

May 18
To: S. Jennings
From: H. Morgan, Director of Physical Therapy
Subject: Lateness

On February 22, I counseled you regarding your frequent lateness and cautioned you about the continued violation of this specific work rule. I also reviewed that portion of the work rules, Section 5, Lateness, for the exact wording and the need to conform to established procedures. On two separate occasions after this, we again discussed your pattern of late arrival. Verbal warnings were issued on March 15 and April 3.

Since February 22, your pattern of late arrival has continued. Therefore, on this date, May 18, in my office, we again discussed your failure to be at work at the designated time of 8:30 A.M. This memorandum is to confirm our conversation and to issue an official written warning that continuation of frequent lateness could result in progressive disciplinary action as noted in the work rules of the institution.

A copy of this memorandum has been placed in your personnel file.

---

manager criticizes the offense, not the employee, the individual is likely to accept discipline more willingly.

Appeal Procedure

In every organization, there must be a grievance procedure whereby employees have the right to appeal a disciplinary action that they feel is unfair. If an employee belongs to a union, the right of appeal and the grievance procedure are specifically outlined in the union-management contract. (A typical grievance process under a union contract is included in Chapter 16.) The right of appeal should also be available to an employee of an institution where there is not a union. In either situation, the grievance procedure is an orderly way of resolving conflict. In most cases, the appeal process follows the chain of command. The privilege of appealing disciplinary action through a specified grievance procedure gives the employees confidence that they will be treated fairly.

TRAINING

A basic responsibility of every manager is to shape and modify the behavior of employees so that they have the necessary knowledge, skill, and attitude to perform their assignments according to the policies, rules, and regulations of the institution. Advances in technology necessitate continual retraining of experienced employees to perform new and changed tasks. Training and staff development are the fundamental means by which behavior can be changed in order to meet the immediate and long-range needs of the institution.

An organized formal training program to meet certain objectives is the most effective method of changing the behavior of employees. To establish such a program, the manager and those individuals involved in the organized training program must (1) identify the training needs, (2) establish training objectives, (3) select appropriate methods and techniques, (4) implement the program, and (5) evaluate the training outcomes. (See Appendix 10-A for excerpts from a training program designed for release of information specialists.)

Identification of Training Needs

The manager reviews various aspects of the work, including individual employee performance, to determine training needs. Such a detailed review might include the following:

1. Comparison of specified job requirements (as stated in the job descriptions) with current or new employee skills.
2. Analysis of performance ratings. Where are workers having difficulty meeting accuracy or productivity standards? Where are errors concentrated? Is there a pattern of difficulty in some technical aspect of the work?
3. Analysis of personnel records and reports. Is there a pattern of lateness, absenteeism, accidents, safety violations, client complaints, or equipment damage?
4. Analysis of short- and long-range plans. These often indicate the need for training in new procedures or in skills for dealing with new client groups.

A director of health record systems used an analysis of grievances over five months (Exhibit 10-2), a quarterly audit of the storage and retrieval function (Exhibit 10-3), and a four-year long-range plan excerpt (Exhibit 10-4) to determine training needs.

Training Objectives

Once training needs have been identified, the objectives for the program must be established. The objectives should be written in measurable terms and should

Exhibit 10-2 Analysis of Grievances (May to October)

Substance/Issue	Employee	Outcome for Mgt.
1. Harassment by supervisor: inconsistent application of late/absentee docking	File clerk	Lost
2. Arbitrary & excessive work standards in file area	File clerk	Lost
3. Excessive work standards in file area	File clerk	Sustained
4. Firing for unauthorized release of record	File clerk	Sustained
5. Arbitrary change in procedure for delivery of records to outpatient clinics	File clerk	Lost
6. Excessive work standard for transcription	Transcriber	Lost
7. Arbitrary employee evaluation	Transcriber	Lost
8. Inconsistent merit money allocation	Release of info. clerk	Sustained
9. Harassment: inconsistent application of work rules re: dress code	Release of info. clerk	Lost
10. Arbitrary selection of candidate for job promotion	File clerk	Lost
11. Firing for failure to meet work standards for chart retrieval	File clerk	Lost
12. Unequal rate of pay	Coder	Sustained
13. Harassment for failing to meet work standard	Transcriber	Sustained
14. Suspension for insubordination	File clerk	Sustained

Exhibit 10-3 Audit of Storage and Retrieval System (July to September)

Percentage of misfiles: active records; terminal digit, color-coded system	14%
Percentage of missing or incorrectly placed outguides	11%
Percentage of loose reports misfiled in records	8%
Percentage of "permanently lost" records	4%
Percentage of records unavailable *at time* of appointment (appointment request had clear patient ID)	33%

# of Accidents/Incidents:

Falls from ladder	3
Back strain: moving/accessing boxes of emergency room reports	1
Eye injury: hit in eye by falling outguide	1
Bruised hip due to file cabinet drawer jammed open	1

Other Problems Noted

20% turnover rate
All employees in unit = entry level
Poor "housekeeping" in inactive area; active storage = o.k.
Active storage area: terminal digit and color coded
Inactive storage area: middle digit and different color-coded record jackets

Exhibit 10-4 1991–1995 Long-Range Plans (excerpt)

Organizational Expansion:

Sports medicine outpatient clinic	July 1992
Participation in regional tumor registry program	July 1992
Affiliation with local university's college of allied health professions	September 1992
Home care program	July 1993
Hospice program	December 1993

Departmental Objectives (in addition to plans stemming from organizational expansion):

Conversion to automated appointment system	September 1993
In-house microfilming	September 1994

state the specific outcomes to be achieved at the conclusion of the training program. For example, if a training program for physical therapists is to introduce the SOAP (subjective, objective, assessment, plan) format for writing notes, the manager must establish an objective that states, "Record physical therapy progress notes using the SOAP format for all patients receiving treatment in the department." This objective is specific and stated in measurable terms, since the desired results can be factually determined through recordkeeping. Written objectives serve as the fundamental guide for organizing the program and evaluating the desired outcomes.

Training objectives are stated in stylized language. Usually each objective contains

- the statement of the main focus (what is to be demonstrated or stated)
- the level of mastery *or* an acceptable performance level (e.g., "error-free" or "with 100% accuracy"); when mastery-level performance is adopted, a realistic time limit to obtain mastery (e.g., after a certain number of practice sessions) may be stated
- any conditions, such as use of specific regulations or use of designated equipment
- a time frame/performance standard, which may be presented in stages, with an initial phase of untimed performance followed by progressively increased performance levels until the work standard is met

These training objective elements may be stated in whole or in part at the beginning of the training design for each unit and need not be repeated. For example, the various activities or processes that the trainee carries out must be in "accordance with the specified policies and procedures. Having stated this condition initially, the training specialist need not repeat it for each learning objective."[31]

Training Methods and Techniques

The manager has many training methods available to achieve the desired outcomes. The methods most often used are as follows:

Job Rotation

This is a popular approach to staff training and development. Under a rotational schedule, job assignments usually last anywhere from three to six months. This approach gives an employee the opportunity to acquire the broad perspective and diversified skills needed for professional and personal development. Job rotation can also be used to introduce new concepts and ideas into the various units within the department and to help individual employees to think in terms of the whole program rather than their immediate assignments.

Selma manages a department of occupational therapy in a large urban acute care hospital. After years of rapid staff turn-over, Selma decided to rotate staff every 6 months. There was overlap between new assignments so "old" staff trained the "new" staff. Staff enjoyed the change and felt that they were gaining invaluable experience and increased knowledge and skills. Selma noticed that staff turn-over was reduced.

Formal Lecture Presentations

The lecture method is one of the oldest techniques used in training and development programs. The fundamental purpose of the lecture is to inform. The lecture format saves time because the speaker can present more material in a given amount of time than can be presented by any other method. The lecture should be supplemented by visual aids, however, or the results are likely to fall short of the instructional goals. During the lecture, employees are passive. Outside disturbances or mental wanderings frequently distract individuals and render the lecture ineffective.

Alice had two years of therapy experience and wanted to change her area of practice. She had three interests: pediatrics, hand therapy, and sports medicine. She found that she could get a job in any one of these areas and wondered how she could begin to narrow her choices. As she glanced through her professional newspaper, she discovered an announcement for a lecture on hand therapy. She attended the one hour presentation and was excited by the description offered by the physician and therapists. Based on her new experience, Alice searched for a hand therapy position.

Seminars and Conferences

The major purpose of seminars and conferences is to allow for the exchange of ideas, the discussion of problems, and the finding of answers to questions or solutions to problems. The opportunity for employees to express their own views and to hear other opinions can be very stimulating. Employees who actively participate are more committed to decisions than they would be if the solution were merely presented to them. It must be remembered that learning takes place in direct ratio to the amount of individual involvement in the discussion process.

James owned a private practice group. To keep the staff informed and up-to-date, he mandated that each employee must attend at least three seminars and one conference each year. He urged the attendees to discuss ideas with other professionals at the conference and to bring the ideas back so they can be shared with other members of the practice group.

Role Playing

Acting out situations between two or more persons is a training method used successfully with all levels of employees. Interviewing, counseling, leadership, and human relations are a few of the content areas in which role playing has been used. By playing the role of others, employees gain valuable insight not only from their own action but from the comments of observers.

> Jan was surprised when she heard David, a recent graduate, talking to an elderly patient as if she were deaf when, in fact, she had Alzheimer's disease. Jan set up a role play situation at the next staff meeting and asked David to play the patient. Almost immediately, David realized that he was stereotyping the patient and assuming that she could not hear.

Committee Assignments

Through committee assignments, employees can explore a topic or problem to gain a wider or new perspective, experience situations involving the resolution of different ideas, learn to adjust to someone else's viewpoint, and practice reaching decisions. Committee assignments also offer opportunities for employees to assume positions of leadership that they would not otherwise have.

> The State Association needed help with justifying a renewal of the Sunset Clause of their licensure act. The task of proving the importance of licensure to a new group of legislators seemed overwhelming. One member spoke up and suggested dividing the work into tasks that could be assigned to several committees. Each committee was given a portion of the work and the State Association officers were amazed at the increased interest in the renewal process since members were helping rather than standing on the sidelines.

Case Studies

Based on the premise that solving problems under simulated conditions enables employees to solve similar problems in an actual work situation, the case study method requires employees to become actively involved in a problem-solving situation, either hypothetical or real. The case studies used in developing problem-solving skills should be carefully selected and pertinent to the job so that their use meets the training and development requirements of the employees.

> Glen had no idea how to treat a patient who was wearing an elaborate wrist splint. Then he remembered a case study which was presented

during one of the conferences he attended. The case study reminded him of the correct protocol to use during treatment. The human example stuck in his mind and promoted better application of the knowledge.

Program Implementation

Throughout the implementation phase, the physical and psychological environment must be constantly monitored. For example, the time schedule, the learning environment, and the pace need to be checked periodically.

The primary consideration in any training program is to establish a time schedule to provide the greatest educational impact possible without reducing work output or, in health care institutions, patient care. The training program and the methods to be used should be announced well in advance. This allows everyone involved sufficient lead time to arrange individual schedules so that work assignments can be adequately covered during the employee's absence.

The arrangement of the room in which the training is to occur can either promote or handicap the process of learning. It is important to ensure that each participant see and hear each member of the group. The traditional classroom setting in which the "teacher" sits in the front of the room and the participants are seated in neat rows should be avoided whenever possible because it creates a stiff and formal atmosphere. One of the best arrangements for a training session is to put the tables in an open-ended rectangle, with chairs placed only on the outside perimeter. In addition, the room should be well lighted and adequately ventilated.

The pace and timing of each session are also important during the implementation phase of a training program. The function of pace is to maintain interest; therefore, the pace should be quickened when interest begins to sag or it should be slowed if individuals are having difficulty absorbing content. A training session should not last longer than two hours. In fact, a one-hour session is believed to produce better results. If a two-hour session is necessary, a break should be allowed at the midpoint. Common sense and individual attention spans dictate how long adults accustomed to active work can be kept relatively immobile.

Evaluation of Outcomes

Probably the most difficult aspect of a training program is to evaluate the desired outcomes, because there are no concrete and precise measuring tools to determine changes in behavior and attitudes. Outcomes must be measured indirectly and conclusions based on inference. The evaluation is not just a single act or event but an entire process. If objectives have been clearly stated in measurable terms, however, evaluation is easier.

A before-after comparison may be a useful way of evaluating change. If the manager and those individuals involved in the training program assess the behavior factors they wish to change before training and examine the same factors after the training has been concluded, they can determine if a change occurred.

For material of a factual nature, where precise knowledge should be demonstrated, fact tests are used. More commonly, trainees are evaluated through performance tests. Each trainee has activities to carry out; these are drawn from the usual work of the job. The final evaluation may be carried out in stages: practice activity, followed by real work activity under immediate supervision, followed by real work activity with diminishing levels of immediate supervision.

The evaluation brings the training process full circle. Each trainee has been given specific training objectives to attain, appropriate didactic and practice materials have been explained, and practice activities with appropriate correction and feedback have been given. The evaluation, therefore, consists of determining the trainee's capacity to perform the work described in the job description and specified through the detailed policies and procedures of the department.[32]

NOTES

1. Chester Barnard, *The Functions of the Executive* (Cambridge, Mass.: Harvard University Press, 1968), 167–69.

2. Herbert Simon, *Administrative Behavior* (New York: Macmillan, 1965), 12.

3. Ibid., 129.

4. Robert Presthus, "Authority in Organizations," in *Concepts and Issues in Administrative Behavior,* edited by Sidney Mailick and Edward H. Van Ness (Englewood Cliffs, N.J.: Prentice-Hall, 1962), 122.

5. Edgar H. Schein, *Organizational Psychology* (Englewood Cliffs, N.J.: Prentice-Hall, 1965), 11.

6. H.H. Gerth and C. Wright Mills, *From Max Weber: Essays in Sociology* (New York: Oxford University Press, 1946), 196–204.7. Ibid.

7. Ibid.

8. H.C. Metcalf and L. Urwick, eds., *Dynamic Administration: The Collected Papers of Mary Parker Follett* (New York: Harper, 1942).

9. Ibid.

10. Ibid.

11. P.F. Drucker, "Leadership: More Doing than Task," *Wall Street Journal,* January 6, 1988.

12. Philip Selznick, *Leadership in Administration* (Evanston, Ill.: Row, Peterson, 1957).

13. Warren Bennis, "New Patterns of Leadership," in *Health Care Administration: A Managerial Perspective,* edited by Samuel Levy and N. Paul Loomba (Philadelphia: J.B. Lippincott, 1973), 163.

14. Robert Tannenbaum and Warren H. Schmidt, "How to Choose a Leadership Pattern," *Harvard Business Review* 36, no. 2 (1958): 96–101.

15. M. Bunjes and D.D. Canter, "Mentoring: Implications for Career Development," *Journal of the American Dietetic Association* 88 (1988): 705–7.

16. M. Williams, *The New Executive Woman* (Radnor, Pa.: Chilton Book Company, 1977).

17. L.Y. Kelly, "Power Guide: The Mentor Relationship," *Nursing Outlook* 26 (1978): 339.

18. D.J. Levinson, *The Seasons of a Man's Life* (New York: Knopf, 1978).

19. J.C. Rogers, "Mentoring for Career Achievement and Advancement," *American Journal of Occupational Therapy* 40 (1986): 79–82.

20. M.M. Kapustiak, S.M. Capello, and L.R. Hofmeister, "The Key to Your Professional Success Is You: Networking, Mentor-Mentee Relationships, and Negotiation," *Journal of the American Dietetic Association* 85 (1985): 846–48.

21. P.C. Pilette, "Mentoring: An Encounter of the Leadership Kind," *Nursing Leadership* 3 (1980): 22–26.

22. Ibid., 23.

23. Ibid., 24.

24. K.E. Kram, "Phases of the Mentor Relationship," *Academic Management Journal* 26 (1983): 608.

25. L.K. Johnsrud, "Mentoring between Academic Women: The Capacity for Interdependence" (Paper presented at the annual meeting of the American Educational Research Association, Boston, April 1990).

26. R. Kegan, *The Evolving Self: Problems of Process in Human Development* (Cambridge, Mass.: Harvard University Press, 1983).

27. Johnsrud, "Mentoring between Academic Women."

28. M.T. Urbano and I.R. Jahns, "A Developmental Approach to Doctoral Education," *Journal of Nursing Education* 25 (1986), 76–78.

29. G.R. Roche, "Much Ado about Mentors," *Harvard Business Review* 57 (1979): 14–16, 20, 24, 26–28.

30. L.K. Galbraith, A.E. Brueggemeyer, and D.L. Manweiler, "Failure to Flourish: Indications for Mentoring," *Pediatric Nursing* 14 (1988): 405–8.

31. Joan Gratto Liebler, *Medical Records: Policies and Guidelines* (Gaithersburg, Md.: Aspen Publishers, 1991).

32. Ibid..

Appendix 10-A

Training Design: Release of Information

1. Assumptions
2. Overall learning objective
3. General orientation and introduction
4. Privacy and confidentiality principles
5. General requirements for authorization
6. Special authorization requirements
7. Selection of medical record information for the response
8. Administrative and procedural steps
9. Telephone inquiries and requests
10. In-person inquiries and requests
11. Subpoenas and court orders
12. Final evaluation

ASSUMPTIONS*

The learning objectives presented in this training design are based on these four assumptions.

1. Performance condition: the activity is carried out according to the prescribed policy and procedure.
2. Acceptable level of performance:
   a. alternative one: 100 percent accuracy is attained.
   b. alternative two: mastery-level competence is attained (no stated accuracy level is given).

---

* *Source:* Reprinted from: *Medical Records: Policies and Guidelines, Supplement 1*, by J.G. Liebler, pp. 10:91–10:94, Aspen Publishers, Inc., © 1991.

3. Time frame/performance standard:
    a. during training: the activity is accomplished at [60 percent] of the established performance [time] standard.
    b. final, comprehensive evaluation: the trainee meets fully the stated performance [time] standard.
4. These learning objectives relate to the release of information; therefore, this phrase is not repeated in each objective or evaluation statement.

OVERALL LEARNING OBJECTIVE

At the conclusion of this training sequence, the trainee/employee will demonstrate the ability to process written and oral requests for the release of information

- according to the standard policies and procedures of this facility
- with 100 percent accuracy
- within the performance [time] standards established for this work

The training sequence that follows is intended to develop the trainee's capacity to meet this comprehensive objective.

GENERAL ORIENTATION AND INTRODUCTION

Purpose

To acquaint the trainee with the general content and scope of the release of information processes.

Content

- review of job description: release of information specialist
- overview of policy and procedure manual
- explanation of learning objectives:
  –performance conditions
  –accuracy level (or mastery level)
  –performance standards

Methods

- In-basket activity: The trainee is given a representative sample of the various types of requests in the usual form in which such requests are received. (*Note*: All examples used at this stage of orientation and training are fictitious.)
- Discussion: The trainee has a brief discussion with the trainer in order to answer immediate questions and concerns and to present the outline for the detailed training to follow.

Evaluation

None: at this stage of the orientation, the trainee will not carry out activities.

GENERAL REQUIREMENTS FOR AUTHORIZATION

Purpose

To acquaint the trainee with general principles relating to the need for patient authorization.

Learning Objectives

- Given [_____] written requests containing various types of written requests, the trainee will determine the need for authorization for each request.
- Given the same set of written requests and a mix of authorizations, the trainee will determine the adequacy/validity of each authorization for those requests needing authorization.

Content

- general underlying principles used to determine need for authorization
- the patient's capacity to authorize
- designated representatives of a patient who may authorize on behalf of the patient

- circumstances in which no authorization is needed
- requirements for valid authorization
- formats of authorizations:
  −insurance claim form
  −patient's own wording
  −facility's recommended form

Methods

Lecture is followed by practice activity. The trainee is given a representative sample of written requests, including a variety of authorization formats and a mix of both adequate and inadequate authorization statements.

Evaluation

A performance test consisting of fictitious written requests and a mix of authorizations is used.

- The trainee will determine which requests require authorization.
- The trainee will determine which authorizations are adequate/valid when compared to the listing of the required content for an authorization.

ADMINISTRATIVE AND PROCEDURAL STEPS

Purpose

To acquaint the trainee with the detailed administrative and procedural steps for the release of information from patient's medical records.

Learning Objective

- Given [_____] written requests, the trainee will process each request in eight-step sequence established in the procedure manual.
  1. performing preliminary sorting and processing
  2. making entries in the release of information log
  3. determining patient status
  4. requisitioning the patient's medical record

5. preparing the cover letter
6. determining and calculating the fees
7. photocopying and reassembling the medical record
8. processing outgoing mail

Content

- examples of types of written requests:
  –U.S. mail
  –interdepartmental mail
  –fax
- categories of requests:
  –direct patient care
  –third-party payers
  –government agencies
  –review agencies
  –attorneys
- initial processing:
  –sorting and date-stamping
  –handling confidential mail
  –routing mail for further processing
- priority matrix: purpose and use
- release of information log:
  –purpose and use
  –content
  –staged entries: initial logging through final entry
  –computer security safeguards
- determining patient status:
  –accessing the patient master index
  –interpreting information in the patient master index
  –recording information on the request/inquiry
- requisitioning the patient medical record:
  –preparing the requisition form
  –coordinating with the Storage and Retrieval unit
- preparing the cover letter:
  –purpose
  –sample formats
  –appropriate response statements and cover letters

- processing fees:
  - —fee schedule and guidelines
  - —determining applicable fees
  - —calculating the fee
  - —handling money received
  - —transmitting fees to Accounts Receivable
- photocopy process:
  - —equipment use
  - —safeguards to prevent misfiling during processing
- reassembling the chart:
  - —chart order
  - —problem and misfile identification: notification of Storage and Retrieval unit and correction of misfile or problem
  - —inclusion of original request, authorization, and record of material released
  - —return of record to Storage and Retrieval unit
- final preparation for mailing the completed reponse

Methods

- lecture and demonstration of each step
- immediate practice activity following the lecture and demonstration of each step

Evaluation

Stage 1: The trainee will be given one standard request to process the complete procedural cycle.

Stage 2: The trainee will be given one nonstandard request to process through the complete procedural cycle.

Stage 3: The trainee will be given [_____] written requests reflecting a mix of materials typically received. The trainee will process these requests through the complete procedural cycle.

Chapter 11

Communication

CHAPTER OBJECTIVES

1. Define the various levels of communication.
2. Develop methods to promote personal communication.
3. Identify behaviors and situations that block communication.
4. Analyze the communication tools used by organizations.
5. Develop a personal communication style that is effective in a variety of communication settings—interpersonal relationships, small and large groups, and organizations.

In a large organization, decisions are usually presented as orders, and members are asked to comply. Work roles are specialized, and communication is carried out by means of formal channels, such as memos, regulations, and lectures. The situation is quite different with a small organization (e.g., one that has less than 20 people). Work roles overlap and are less specialized. Communication is informal, and the opportunity for shared information is increased. Formal communication is minimal. Clearly, just one factor, size, can influence the quality and type of communication used in an organization.

There are many other factors to consider. Communication is a complex process that requires skills on both an individual and group level. As one person interacts with more and more people, the complexity of the interaction also increases.

DEFINITION

Communication is an exchange of ideas, thoughts, or emotions between two or more people. Humans can also communicate with animals, and animals can communicate with each other; however, only humans exchange symbolic information through complex patterns of thought that are transmitted by language, gesture, and movement. Communication has a verbal and nonverbal component, with both conscious and unconscious aspects in each.

PERSONAL AND SMALL GROUP COMMUNICATION

Verbal Communication

Verbal communication is important in health care, since understanding the ideas of others is essential to the delivery of quality patient care. The three parts of a verbal exchange are the voice, the content of the message and response, and the method used to transmit the information. The voice conveys emotions. The tone used for delivery, the use of silences, the choice of words, the accents and intonation, and the speed of delivery are all factors in a verbal exchange.[1] Some of these factors are genetic, such as voice quality, and some are cultural, such as speed of speech. Health practitioners must also understand that their professional education has trained them to express ideas in a selected fashion.

The unconscious aspects of verbal communication are frequently overlooked. Conscious information is volitional because the speaker is aware of the content, direction, and reasons for the exchange. In greetings, information sharing, confrontations, and discussions, for example, the speaker can identify the reasons for the communication. On the other hand, there may be unconscious motives for the verbal communication, such as thoughts, aspirations, desires, anxieties, fears, or emotions that influence behavior but are hidden from the person's conscious thoughts. A slip of the tongue is an example of an unconscious verbalization.[2]

Nonverbal Communication

Comprised of movements, gestures, expressions, and silences, nonverbal communication may or may not accompany verbal communication. People may not speak, and yet ideas are exchanged. For example, telephone conversations are dependent on the voice, but intonation and silences frequently convey information beyond the spoken words. Two people who share a "knowing" look while waiting for a third have shared an idea without uttering a word.

Nonverbal communication can have both conscious and unconscious aspects. As mentioned above, conscious information is available for analysis and scrutiny. Unconscious thoughts also influence behavior, but these thoughts, feelings, or emotions are not part of the person's awareness. Analysis of the content of thoughts is difficult because the forces are hidden.

Dress is another nonverbal component of communication. Many people silently judge others by their clothing, hair style, jewelry, and make-up. Much has been written about this issue, and managers need to match their dress to the dress style of other managers in the organization. Clothing and accessories should not call attention to the wearer. Up-to-the-minute styles, flashy items, revealing clothing, excessive perfume and aftershave, false nails in bright colors all might be better used in social rather than work environments.

In health care management, conservative attire is the norm. Most managers wear suits in pleasant but not gaudy colors. If the manager carries a patient load, a laboratory coat or jacket can be used to protect clothing and provide a professional look. In pediatric, psychiatric, or community settings, staff may dress in casual clothing that does not create a barrier between them and their clients. Relying on slacks and shirts, sneakers and sweaters, they often look just like their clients. It is important to analyze the social norms in the organization and make decisions regarding dress based on what is commonly seen. This is essential after just being hired for a position or receiving a promotion. Appearance should not be overlooked, since patients feel more comfortable when their practitioners are well groomed and professionally attired.

Health professionals frequently overlook the importance of unwritten dress codes when they receive a promotion. By continuing to wear the clothing appropriate for a staff therapist, a recently promoted manager might meet resistance to his or her new authority. Dressing the part is another way to communicate nonverbally.

Communication levels can be presented on a matrix. Table 11-1 is based on the Johari Window, which was developed by Joseph Luft and has appeared in many group dynamics texts and courses in the last 20 years.[3]

Body language is a series of conscious or unconscious postures that convey information to others. Many studies, both popular and scholarly, have been done to explore this topic. Popularized versions seem to indicate that gestures are universal. Few gestures are, however; most are culturally bound. A nod of the head may mean yes in one society, but it may mean no in another.

Table 11-1 Examples of Personal Communication

	Verbal	*Nonverbal*
Conscious	Speeches, greetings	Wave hello, nod head to affirm interest
Unconscious	Slip of the tongue, mistake in verbalizing	Cross legs away from speaker, smirk while hearing suggestion

Birdwhistel made detailed studies of human gestures and analyzed the complexity of body language.[4] Interpretation of human gestures, expressions, silences, and body movement must be cautious. It is best to check perceptions with the other person.

Communication Distance

Hall discussed four levels of distance that are used by humans during communication.[5] His research was based on observations and interviews with middle-class adults from the northeastern seaboard of the United States. These crude observations are merely a first attempt to develop approximate categories. The four distance zones are as follows:

1. Intimate Distance (from 1 to 18 inches). Individuals are involved in love-making, wrestling, or comforting or protecting each other. Verbalizations are involuntary or very quiet.[6]
2. Personal Distance (from 1½ to 4 feet). Individuals can hold or grasp each other. Visual images are still distorted, but they begin to normalize as the person moves to arm's length. Verbalizations are moderate.[7]
3. Social Distance (from 4 to 12 feet). Individuals are less intimate. Voice level is normal, and conversations can be overheard. Impersonal business is conducted at this distance, but the interaction becomes more formal as the persons involved move to the 12-foot distance.[8]
4. Public Distance (from 12 to beyond 25 feet). Voice volume is increased, and details about the person are not noticed. Verbalization is formal.[9]

Impression Management

Verbal, nonverbal, and distance management are used to create impressions on others. During the 1980s a lot of effort was expended on "managing impressions." Molloy even wrote a book suggesting how women can "dress for success."[10]

Although Molloy offers helpful hints, the concept of an executive uniform is no longer accepted. Nonetheless, there are still unwritten rules that govern professional dressing. Complicating the expression of rules is the 1990s quest for authenticity and simplicity in life style, modes of dress, and presentation of self. In a way, this makes the integration of self and image more personal. Someone can "play" the role of a stranger only so long before the image is tarnished by the incongruence between fantasy and reality.

It is important for health professionals to think about their roles and responsibilities before they choose clothing. They should also pay attention to the way that others in the organization present themselves. In some institutions, the attending physicians wear operating greens all day, but in other institutions slacks and shirts are worn under laboratory coats. Function is important since some providers have to help patients with eating, dressing care, and toileting. Clothing that can be easily laundered and that looks neat and does not hinder comfort and movement is commonplace. On the other hand, some health professionals are not in contact with patients, so clothing choices are determined by different demands and needs. For example, a medical records administrator does not lift or ambulate patients, so a supportive shoe does not have to be worn for safety. An occupational or physical therapist may have to bend, lift, and support patients, so the choice of shoe must reflect this need.

It is also necessary to refrain from wearing accessories that might harm patients. Jewelry with sharp edges can catch on the clothing of patients or scratch them; shirts with elaborate and textured material can catch in a piece of equipment and harm the patient and practitioner; false nails can compromise grip patterns; and loose hair can fall on patients, get caught in equipment, and hinder movement.

Impression management is important, especially during interviews and presentations, but practitioners' dress and actions must reflect their role in patient care and their feelings about the institution and their profession.

Components of Communication

Communication has four components: initiation, transmission, reception, and feedback. For communication to occur, there must be a sender, someone who begins the interaction. Initiation, which includes the preparation for the interaction, might begin on a nonverbal level and move to a verbal exchange. Transmission is the movement of the communication from one party to another; it depends on verbal and nonverbal sharing methods. Reception is the manner in which the message is received. The receiver's perception shapes the way in which a message is decoded and acted upon. In order to ensure that the sender and the receiver are truly sharing ideas, the receiver offers feedback, which is a verbal or nonverbal signal that acknowledges the message. Acknowledgments include modification, suppression, or nonacceptance of the information.

Personal communication depends on assumptions, perceptions, feelings, past experiences, and present surroundings. Although people frequently talk, communication may prove taxing and difficult. People must transcend personal and cultural barriers that obstruct their understanding of an exchange.

Methods to Improve Communication

Communication is improved by observing, attending, responding to requests, and checking information. Each of these strategies depends on an objective analysis of an exchange. Observation is the activity of perceiving events, objects, and people. Skilled observers are objective and can separate their own inner world from outside reality. Accurate observation is dependent on self-knowledge, because inner reality can make someone "see" an event that did not happen. An event can be "real" in the mind of the person who really wants to "see" it.

Attending helps people hear or see events as they are. During a conversation, instead of planning their next remark, those who are attending direct their energy toward listening or empathizing with the other person. Attending is also called active listening. Responding is the behavior an individual selects to address the needs or requests of the other person. The behavior may be verbal or nonverbal, and the quality of the response shapes the remainder of the communication. If a person asks for the time and receives a pleasant answer, that person may decide to continue the exchange. In contrast, unpleasant replies may inhibit further communication.

Active listening can also help an individual decode less obvious requests. Sometimes a sender makes an indirect request, which may be symbolic or may indicate unconscious desires. A perceptive listener should try to "hear" the request and bring the buried topic into the conversation. For example, Allie asked Mary for her pathology notes. Mary responded by saying that she would be glad to duplicate the notes, and she began to rummage in her purse. Allie handed Mary a tissue. Mary seemed grateful and quickly wiped her nose. Allie then handed Mary some money to cover the cost of duplicating the notes. A less perceptive listener may have mistaken Mary's action as a hint for payment or as a rejection of the request. In reality, Mary's nose was running, and she was distracted for a minute while she attended to it.

Communication is also improved by checking information. Listeners can check information by matching their perceptions of a situation with the sender's intention. In the example given earlier, Allie could have asked Mary if she needed a tissue. Listeners can examine the validity of their perceptions by paraphrasing the sender's message and asking for feedback.

People must be aware of symbols that may be archetypal, cultural, or idiosyncratic.[11] A symbol is any object that represents something else. Archetypal symbols are shared by humans and extend back in history; for example, a circle means unity throughout the world. Cultural symbols are specific to a subgroup (e.g., a thumb extended upward means a victory or a good job). Idiosyncratic symbols are specific to an individual or small group. Men who wear one pierced earring share an idiosyncratic symbol that they are "cool." Symbolic meanings contribute to the variety and breadth of communication by forcing listeners to move beyond their personal understanding of gestures, body movements, expressions, and silences.

Personal Tools to Foster Communication

There are six personal tools to promote communication:

1. authenticity: the ability to be true to one's own feelings
2. acceptance of feelings (based on authenticity): people who accept their own feelings can extend this acceptance to the feelings of others
3. disclosure: the ability to share feelings, both positive and negative, with others (honest people are able to share information openly)
4. empathy: the ability to project one's own personality onto another person (this promotes understanding)
5. caring: the desire to help others on an individual and collective level[12]
6. humor: the ability to identify situations as ludicrous, comic, or happy[13]

All six tools require the integration of personal needs with goals and actions.

Communication Barriers

Communication can be blocked by internal or external forces. Internal forces, including both conscious and unconscious thoughts, may preclude listening, sharing, and caring so that the meaning of the exchange is confused and misinterpreted. Conscious behaviors that limit communication include facial expressions that are perceived as negative or inappropriate (e.g., smiling when reprimanding a subordinate), body postures that are perceived as rejecting or critical of the person (e.g., folding one's arms over one's chest although expressing a desire to share ideas), verbalizations that interrupt the flow of the exchange (e.g., saying "fabulous!" every time a speaker pauses), and interruption or disruption of the speaker's thoughts (e.g., changing topics abruptly, such as interrupting a request for assistance with a comment about football scores).

External forces also impede communication. Distractions, such as noise, motion, and confusion, compromise the quality of an exchange. The context for a communication adds to or subtracts from the interaction. For example, a crowded room with flashing lights and loud music is designed for sensory stimulation, not verbal communication. In this environment, intimate conversations are taxed and labored; communication is limited to nonverbal cueing.

COMMUNICATION IN ORGANIZATIONS

Communication between two people may be difficult, and small group communication may be taxing; however, the task of communicating in a large group may be overwhelming. Bureaucracies emerged at the turn of the century when industrialization promoted the growth of large organizations. The need to develop complex communication patterns became more pressing as organizations added more and more new members. Communication had to keep pace with production. The resulting strategies to increase organizational communication can be divided into two categories: formal and informal.

Formal Communication

Verbal

An organization is a stratified social system with a hierarchy of roles. The roles are arranged according to the degree of power and status assigned to each, and the assignment is based on the goal-oriented needs of the organization. Formal communication is sanctioned by the organization and is shared along communication channels that are established by the hierarchy of roles. The arrangement of roles determines the direction of the communication.

Formal communication is directional. The four traditional channels of communication are upward, downward, diagonal, and lateral (Table 11-2).

Formal verbal communication in organizations takes place through orderly channels. The exchanges are directional and promote organizational goals, such as a verbal exchange of orders or instructions. Department meetings can also be formal. An aide who wants to register a complaint must pursue a series of formal channels; the aide cannot walk into the president's office and discuss the grievance.

Because the size of organizations precludes face-to-face interaction among the majority of group members, they must rely on nonverbal communication (i.e., written and transmitted communication). Common examples include goal

---

Table 11-2 Example of Directionality

Four Channels	Examples
1. Upward	Staff person communicating with supervisor
2. Downward	Staff therapist giving orders to an aide
3. Diagonal	Department head of social work conferring with patient registrar in Admissions
4. Lateral	Nurse sharing night orders with another nurse

statements, policy and procedure manuals, directives, direct mailings to employees, inserts in pay envelopes, organizational bulletins, newsletters, magazines, bulletin boards, posters, and handbooks.

Written communication in the organization includes patient care plans, documentation, written materials for use at staff meetings and rounds, and training session handouts. Patient care plans and notes must be concise but clear and free of jargon. Abbreviations should be shared by the entire group, not just fellow professionals. Some organizations require dictated notes so that practitioners have to gather their thoughts before presenting findings. In other organizations, notes are typed into a computer terminal, which requires different communication skills.

Communication to Groups

There are a number of ways to convey information to groups. These methods include presentations, meeting minutes or reports, in-service programs, and professional communication channels.

Presentations at staff meetings should be preplanned, concise, and offer meaningful information to other professionals. Use of standardized evaluations and periodic assessments affords objective information on patient progress. Concrete proof should be offered that the patient progressed from the baseline to another level of functional performance (e.g., "the patient was ambulating 6 feet with maximum assistance and now walks 15 feet with minimal assistance").

Among the written documents used in organizations are committee reports. These are minutes or summaries of the issues addressed by a committee. Ideas should be expressed in a clear style that is able to convey information to all members of the group as well as to outsiders who did not attend the meeting.

Another important communication method is the annual report, in which past events are summarized. The report is useful to members of the organization as well as outsiders. Each department is asked for information by means of a standard form. Included are questions about yearly objectives, productivity, use of space, presentations made, honors received by members, professional activities, students trained, staff changes, and other items. It is useful to collect items for the report throughout the year so no item is forgotten.

In-service education programs offer another way to keep communication open and ideas flowing among department members. A department member might be scheduled for a presentation on a new treatment method or a new way of carrying out responsibilities. The presentation should be well thought out and planned and audiovisual aids should be used if appropriate. Slides and videos require additional preparation but increase the educational value of a presentation. Sometimes an in-service program is so useful that the practitioners can present the information at a professional meeting. Information sharing is moved from the institution to the external world of other practitioners.

Most professional associations solicit papers and workshops for local, state, national, and international meetings. An association may meet every year or convene for a particular issue of concern. Department managers should encourage staff participation, because ideas are exchanged and refined during and after presentations. Another level of formality is added to presentations when the ideas are evaluated by a jury of peers. An abstract is prepared and submitted for evaluation, and a panel of subject specialists review the content and score the proposal. All presentations are ranked, and the most valued papers are scheduled for presentation. This is an excellent way to keep fellow professionals informed of recent developments.

There are other forums to share professional ideas, such as newsletter articles, posters, and handouts. If an idea is noteworthy, an article explaining it should be written and forwarded to a professional journal. This type of formal communication is time consuming but very valuable, because other practitioners are made aware of the idea. Most journal articles are revised upwards of five times, so practitioners need to value writing and rewriting for increased clarity.

The way that information is shared outside the organization conveys a message about the organization.

Nonverbal

The use of space is a form of nonverbal communication. The goals of the organization determine the location and quality of space assigned to group members (who may resist adjustments and reassignments). The way that furniture is arranged, the selection of ornaments, the care given to the space all reflect the values of the group. If an organization has an elaborate waiting room and sloppy offices, it can be inferred that the company is more interested in its public face.

The arrangement of furniture can stimulate or stifle communication. Managers rely on spatial relationships to strengthen their communication. For example, asking for a raise while the manager looks over a desk is more difficult than asking while both parties are seated next to each other.

Informal Communication

Because informal communication is not sanctioned by the social system, it may or may not promote the goals of the organization. Informal communication is not directional; it may circumvent formal channels. Informal communication may be anonymous, and sources cannot be double-checked.

Informal communication, such as small talk and gossip, may not be accurate. Even so, the use of informal communication should not be neglected. Managers and supervisors can use this type of communication to determine the success of formal communication patterns. Rumor and gossip, although inaccurate, may gauge the feelings of group members. Perceptions about events can also be examined. Informal communication is a barometer of the organization, because information can travel at a fast rate of speed. Future events may be foreshadowed by listening to information communicated informally.

Tools to Improve Communication

A number of formal and informal tools can be used to promote communication. Assessment instruments require an analysis of the conscious and unconscious goals of group members. Some can be used to assess individual interaction styles, members' perceptions of each other, perceptions of leadership, roles that members play with each other in the work group, and members' feelings about the organization. Group members complete questionnaires, and the results are compared and discussed. The goals of the members are compared with the goals of the leaders. The results are discussed in nonthreatening ways. Strategies for promoting change can be generated in the group.

Sometimes, group communication becomes so difficult that outside experts, called *facilitators*, are brought in to resolve the issues. Facilitators are trained in a number of disciplines, including business, psychology, education, and sociology.

Barriers to Communication in Organizations

A number of factors can block communication or distort the goals of organizational exchanges:

1. Language. There may be a lack of a common understanding of certain important terms. The use of slang, jargon, or technical language can create problems.
2. Unconscious Motives. Inner thoughts, ideas, and emotions that are not readily available for examination may cloud a group's ability to perceive or interpret events. A group may share a collective mentality that may not be based on real events. The collective thought has been shaped by emotions.
3. Psychological Factors. Past experience and ideas impinge on the communication process. Feelings such as mistrust, fear, anger, hostility, or indifference may shape group perceptions.
4. Status. Real or perceived differences in rank, socioeconomic status, or prestige may detract from the communication process. People develop preconceived notions about others and act on their preconceptions instead of reality.

5. Organizational Size. The larger the social system, the greater the number of communication layers. Each layer provides an opportunity for additional distortion.
6. Logistical Factors. Groups may lack the time, place, or space to communicate clearly. Feedback may be neglected because it is difficult to collect.
7. Overstimulation. Members may be bombarded with so many events that they are unable to process any more information. People who are stressed must be managed carefully so that they are not burdened additionally.
8. Cultural Clashes. One group may misinterpret another's ideas because of a difference in cultural factors, such as age, socioeconomic status, the region of birth, and education level.
9. Organizational Structure. Communication may be blocked by the structure of the communication channels. One person's role may serve as a bottleneck for open communication. In another instance, roles may overlap, and some groups may not receive the information that they need.
10. Phase in Life Cycle of Organization. Communication may be taxed during the organization's developmental stage. In later stages, the old channels may not have been adapted to new situations. Sometimes, organizations rely on one type of communication and ignore other methods.

NOTES

1. Evelyn W. Mayerson, *Putting the Ill at Ease* (Hagerstown, Md.: Harper & Row, 1976), 1–36.
2. Sigmund Freud, *A General Introduction to Psychoanalysis,* trans. Joan Riviere (New York: Washington Square Press, 1964), 40.
3. Joseph Luft, *Group Process* (Palo Alto, Calif.: National Press Books, 1963).
4. R.L. Birdwhistel, *Kinesics and Context* (New York: Ballantine Books, 1970).
5. E.T. Hall, *The Hidden Dimension* (Garden City, N.Y.: Anchor Books, 1966), 113.
6. Ibid., 116–119.
7. Ibid., 119–120.
8. Ibid., 121–123.
9. Ibid., 123–125.
10. J.T. Molloy, *The Women's Dress for Success Book* (New York: Warner, 1979).
11. A.C. Mosey, *Three Frames of References for Mental Health* (Thorofare, N.J.: Charles B. Slack, 1970), 52. Taken from J. Mazer, G. Fidler, L. Kovalenko, and K. Overly, *Exploring How a Think Feels* (New York: American Occupational Therapy Association, 1969).
12. Naomi I. Brill, *Working with People* (Philadelphia: J.B. Lippincott, 1973), 31–46.
13. V.M. Robinson, *Humor & the Health Professions* (Thorofare, N.J.: Charles B. Slack, 1977).

Chapter 12

Controlling

CHAPTER OBJECTIVES

1. Define the management function of controlling.
2. Relate controlling to planning.
3. Identify the basic control process.
4. Develop specific tools of control: the Gantt chart, the PERT network, the flow chart, the flow process chart, and the work distribution chart.

Controlling is the management function in which performance is measured and corrective action is taken to ensure the accomplishment of organizational goals. It is the policing operation in management, although the manager seeks to create a positive climate so that the process of control is accepted as part of routine activity. Controlling is also a forward-looking process in that the manager seeks to anticipate deviation and prevent it.

The manager initiates the control function during the planning phase, when possible deviation is anticipated and policies are developed to help ensure uniformity of practice. During the organizing phase, a manager may consciously introduce the "deadly parallel" arrangement as a control factor (see "Basic Departmentation" in Chapter 6). Close supervision and a tight leadership style reflect an aspect of control. Through rewards and positive sanctions, the manager seeks to motivate workers to conform, thus limiting the amount of control that must be imposed. Finally, the manager develops specific control tools, such as inspections, visible control charts, work counts, special reports, and audits.

THE BASIC CONTROL PROCESS

The control process involves three phases that are cyclic: establishing stand-ards, measuring performance, and correcting deviation. In the first step, the specific units of measure that delineate acceptable work are determined. Basic standards may be stated as staff hours allowed per activity, speed and time limits, quantity that must be produced, and number of errors or rejects permitted. The second step in the control process, measuring performance, involves comparing the work (i.e., the goods produced or the service provided) against the standard. Employee evaluation is one aspect of this measurement. In manufacturing, inspection of goods is a routine part of this process; studies of client satisfaction are key elements when services are involved. Finally, if necessary, remedial action is taken, including retraining employees, repairing equipment, or changing the quality of the raw materials used in a manufacturing process.

CHARACTERISTICS OF ADEQUATE CONTROLS

Several features are necessary to ensure the adequacy of control processes and tools:

- Timeliness. The control device should reflect deviations from the standard promptly, at an early stage, so there is only a small time lag between detection and the beginning of corrective action.
- Economy. If possible, control devices should involve routine, normal processes rather than special inspection routines at additional expense. The control devices must be worth their cost.
- Comprehensiveness. The controls should be directed at the basic phases of the work rather than later levels or steps in the process; for example, a defective part is best inspected and eliminated before it has been assembled with other parts.
- Specificity and Appropriateness. The control process should reflect the nature of the activity. Proper laboratory inspection methods, for example, differ from the financial audit and machine inspection processes.
- Objectivity. The processes should be grounded in fact, and standards should be known and verifiable.
- Responsibility. Controls should reflect the authority-responsibility pattern. As far as possible, the worker and the immediate supervisor should be involved in the monitoring and correction process.
- Understandability. Control devices, charts, graphs, and reports that are complicated or cumbersome will not be used readily.

Types of Standards

Standards may be of a physical nature, both in terms of quantity and quality (e.g., pounds of laundry that are clean and without stains or the number of charts processed according to the required regulations). Such standards make it easier to develop inspection processes, because such information can be recorded relatively simply on visible control charts, work logs, and similar tools. Standards may also be set in terms of cost; a monetary value is attached to an operation or to the delivery of a service (e.g., the cost per square foot per employee, the cost per patient per visit, or the cost per object in a factory). Occasionally, the standard is expressed somewhat intangibly, such as the success of a volunteer drive, competence or loyalty in an employee, or ability in a trainee. Whenever possible, however, a quantifiable factor should be introduced. For example, behavioral objectives could be developed for each level of trainee functioning.

The Intangible Nature of Service

Health care organizations face a special difficulty in that their primary activities are services, which do not always lend themselves to quantifiable measurement. Furthermore, it is difficult to monitor the delivery of a service because of its dynamic nature. Patient privacy is a major consideration. Another dilemma stems from attempts to delineate services in terms of cost; many services must remain available even if they are not used every day. A highly specialized burn unit must be ready to receive patients even if the patient census has dropped during a given period. An emergency room must have adequate coverage no matter how many patients come for service at a particular time.

TOOLS OF CONTROL

Certain tools of control may be combined with the planning process. Management by objectives, the budget, the Gantt chart, and the PERT network are examples of tools used both for planning and controlling. The flow chart, the flow process chart, the work distribution chart, and work sampling all may be used in planning workflow or assessing a proposed change in plan or procedure. They also may be adapted for specific control use, such as when the flow chart is employed to audit the way in which work is done, as compared with the original plan. Some control tools are directed at employee performance, such as the principle of requalification, discussed later in this chapter. Specific, quantifiable output measures may be recorded and monitored through a variety of visible control charts. In addition to these specific tools, the manager exercises control through the assessment and limitation of conflict, through the communication process, and through active monitoring of employees. These concepts were discussed in earlier chapters. Specific tools of planning and control are dealt with here.

GANTT CHART

A visual control device, the Gantt chart was developed by Henry L. Gantt (1861–1919), one of the pioneers in scientific management. Sometimes referred to as a *scheduling and progress chart*, it emphasizes the work-time relationships necessary to meet some defined goal. The time needed for each activity is estimated, and a time value is assigned. This information is plotted on the chart. As the work progresses, entries are made to reflect the work completed. The chart focuses on the interrelationships among the phases of work within a given task. The Gantt chart may be used to reflect different aspects of the work:

- machine or equipment scheduling (in this application it is also called a *load chart*)
- overall production control
- individual worker production

Basic Components of Gantt Charts

Each Gantt chart contains the same basic components regardless of the application. The estimated time allotted for the work is plotted against a time scale that shows the appropriate time frame in days, weeks, or months, as well as calendar dates (Figure 12-1). The calendar legend may be placed at the top or bottom of the chart. As work progresses, items completed are entered and compared to those planned. In using the chart as a visual control tool, the manager uses shading or color coding to enter lines proportional in length to the percentage of work accomplished.

Standard Symbols

Standard symbols are used for plotting the Gantt chart:

1. The "opening angle" is entered under the date an operation is planned to start. $\ulcorner$

2. The "closing angle" is entered under the date the operation is planned to be completed.

3. A straight line joining the opening and closing angle shows the time span within which the operation is to be done.

4. A heavy line shows work completed. This progress line usually is proportional to the amount of work completed.

5. A check mark is placed at the date when the progress was posted and is entered on the time scale.

An additional entry may show cumulative work done as time progresses. Codes may be entered to show the reason for being off schedule, such as

- W: worker unavailable due to illness or personal day
- M: lack of materials
- E: equipment breakdown

In constructing and reading any charts, codes should be used and interpreted consistently. (Figure 12-2).

THE PERT NETWORK

The program evaluation review technique (PERT) is a planning and coordinating tool for use with large, complex undertakings that are nonrepetitive in nature and require integrated management of several projects. If a hospital plans to build an entirely new facility, for example, each department head must plan and coordinate the layout, equipment selection, workflow determinations, and staffing pat-

Employee	Month: June			Days				
	12	13	14	15	16	17	18	19
M. Higgins		sorting						
S. Morton	sorting							
K. Ollis				filing				
S. Watkins				filing				

Figure 12-1 Gantt Progress Chart for Planning and Controlling Filing Backlog: Laboratory Reports

Therapist		Week 1						Week 2					
		M	T	W	Th	F	S-S	M	T	W	Th	F	S-S
A. Clay	AM												
	PM		acute-2nd								Emerg. Acute W W		
D. Francis	AM							Acute admiss.					
	PM												
S. Scott	AM	W W											
	PM							Emerg. Acute-2nd					
L. Matt	AM		Progress										
	PM		Update staff										
O. Rank	AM												
	PM												

Figure 12-2 Gantt Chart for Evaluating New Admissions

terns for the operations of his or her department. These, in turn, must be coordinated with the work of other departments. Other managers in the health care setting may face similar projects of a complex nature. An occupational therapist may be assigned to develop and implement a home care program within six months, a medical technologist may be assigned to oversee the conversion of several manual laboratory techniques to a computerized system, a medical record administrator may face the task of converting 100,000 medical records from a serial filing system to a terminal digit system with unit record while maintaining the availability of records on a day-to-day basis, or a project manager may have to oversee the development of a fully operational quality assurance or risk management program by a specific date.

PERT's major components are the final goal, the events to be accomplished, the activities to be carried out, and the critical time calculations to be monitored.

Historical Background

During the 1950s PERT networks were used extensively by the Department of the Navy. The Polaris missile system project needed a master planning and scheduling process to reflect the work of the many aspects of the project.

Planning and controlling charts were in use in industry, but each had limitations. The Gantt chart, for example, was widely used in industry, but had an inherent limitation; while it shows relationships within tasks, it does not necessarily show relationships among all tasks. Although the Gantt chart shows progress along the projected time span for each activity, it cannot readily be determined if the task listed can be

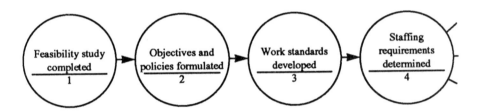

Figure 12-3 PERT Network: Conversion to In-House Transcription Service

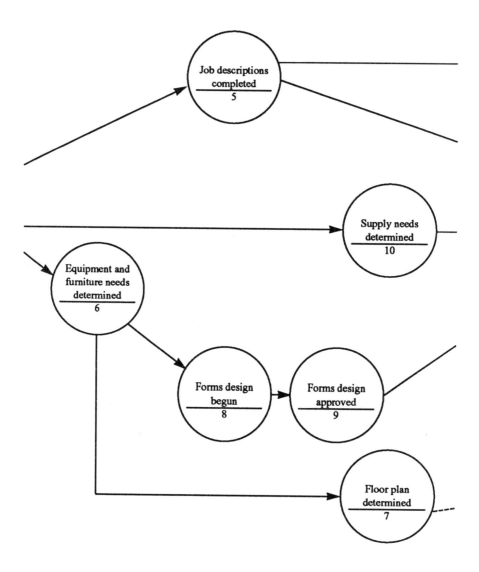

Figure 12-3 continued

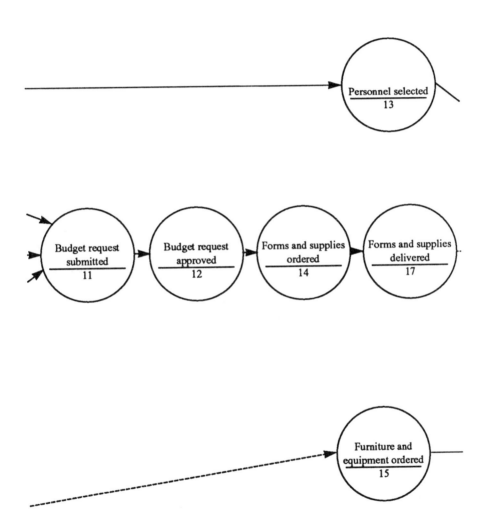

Figure 12-3 continued

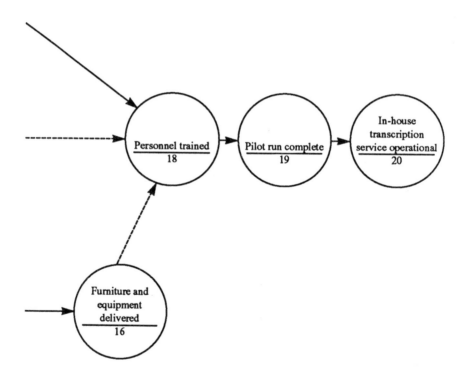

Figure 12-3 continued

started before the successful completion of the previous task. For the Polaris project, a planning and controlling technique that reflected the dependent relationships of various aspects of the work was needed. The PERT network (Figure 12-3) was developed to show such relationships.

Advantages of Network Analysis

Seasoned experts at PERT network application caution users not to spend more time on constructing the network than on carrying out the project. If the project is characterized by complex, nonrepetitive, interrelated activities, however, time probably is well spent on network construction; such detailed planning both permits and forces the manager to examine each major program and project in its entirety and in detail. The manager must identify and anticipate possible delays, which helps resolve difficulties. Network analysis enables the manager to identify deadlines that can be met ahead of schedule through the constant built-in monitoring aspect; consequently, the manager can save money, staff, and resources.

Fundamental Concepts

There are three phases in the PERT network: planning, scheduling, and controlling. These activities involve a specific goal that must be defined in detail. All events within the network and all activities performed flow from and are aimed toward accomplishment of this goal.

The Goal

The most basic component in the PERT network is the goal. The network essentially is a diagrammatic representation of the plan for achieving this goal. The following are examples of goal statements for network construction:

- Home care program fully operational.
- Medical audit program fully operational in medical, surgical, and obstetrics units.
- Pilot test of computerized system completed.
- Conversion to automated laboratory system completed.
- Medical record storage system under terminal digit system fully operational.
- Nurse's aide trained to established level of performance.

Events

The work is divided into events so that the manager can check accomplishments against the plan. These events are the recognizable control points. They are discrete points in time and do not consume per se resources or time; they reflect either the starting or ending point for an activity or a group of activities. The following are examples of the statement of events:

- Job description completed.
- Training of home health aides begun.
- Computer selected.
- Renovation of storage area begun.
- Telephone system installed.

Although events are most frequently stated as work completed, the start of some events is a significant milestone. A network, therefore, contains both events stated as completed and events stated as begun. Events are depicted in the network by circles, rectangles, or ovals that contain the descriptive wording of the elements. Usually, events are numbered for ease of reference, but letters may be used if there are only a few events. The events depicted in Figure 12-3 are numbered.

Certain events actually are subgoals in that no further activities and no additional events (except the final goal) flow from them. Such events are called "hanging events," because no other activities are needed to complete them. No successor event follows them, so they flow directly to the final goal.

Activities

An activity is defined as a recognizable part of a project that requires time and resources for its completion. Activities are the work operations necessary to progress from one event to another (i.e., from one point in time to another in the project schedule) and, ultimately, to the goal. These operations require time, money, resources, and staff. Activities connect events. The network is a diagrammatic representation of activities to be performed and events to be completed in terms of the goal to be reached. Normally, activities are depicted by solid lines between the events to which they are related. Activities are characterized by a specific initiating event, the *predecessor* event, and a specific terminal event, the *successor* event.

No descriptive wording is placed on the activity line. The activities are delineated in detail on an accompanying activity specification form, which includes the predecessor events, the successor events, and the responsible individuals (Exhibit 12-1). This facilitates, even forces, thorough planning. The wording of activities reflects their nature as work being done:

Exhibit 12-1 Activity Specification Sheet

Activity:	Completing job descriptions
Predecessor Event:	Staffing requirements determined
Successor Event(s):	1. Budget request submitted
	2. Personnel selection, Phase one

Task Specifications	Responsibility	Optimistic Time	Most Likely Time	Pessimistic Time
Carry out task analysis	Department manager	One week	Two weeks	Three weeks
Review supervisory relationships	Department manager and Associate director	Half day	One day	Two days
Write preliminary job descriptions	Associate director	Two days	Three days	Five days
Complete job rating process	Department manager	Half day	One day	Two days
Review for union contract compliance	Labor relations	Half day	One day	Two days
Finalize job descriptions	Associate director	Two days	Three days	Five days
Finalize job rating	Department manager	Half day	One day	Two days

- developing job descriptions
- training home health aides
- selecting the computer
- renovating the storage area
- installing the telephone system

An activity of a PERT network is indicated using the beginning and ending events as the reference points. Thus, the name of the activity as determined from the network refers to those specific elements involved in moving the plan from the beginning event to the desired state in the ending event. Table 12-1 shows the proper way of indicating the activities of the following network:

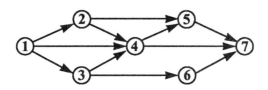

Table 12-1 How To Indicate Activities on a PERT Network

Activity	Beginning Event	Ending Event
1–2	1	2
1–3	1	3
3–4	3	4
2–4	2	4
1–4	1	4
4–5	4	5

Interrelationships of Activities and Events

All activities and events in a program are related to each other in various ways. These relationships are called *dependencies* or *constraints*. Activities can be related to one another because they employ common resources; for example, those that must use the same facilities, equipment, or personnel and cannot do so concurrently are dependent on each other. Most dependency relationships result simply from the fact that a particular activity cannot begin until the product of the preceding action is available. In other words, certain events cannot occur until previous ones have been completed. For example, a computer obviously cannot be installed until after it has been selected. A merge event is one that is constrained immediately by two or more activities; a burst event is one constraining two or more activities. Large networks often contain many merge and burst events.

The following examples illustrate the interrelationship of activities and events as well as the sequence of events.

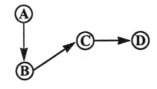

Event A = walls of building completed
Event B = walls of building painted
Event C = special interior design completed
Event D = roof completed

Activity AB must obviously be completed before activity BC can be started and completed.

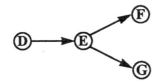

Event D = roof completed
Event E = siding completed
Event F = TV antenna installed
Event G = rainpipes installed

Activity DE must be completed before either activity EF or activity EG can be started. It is not necessary to start activities EF and EG at the same time; the diagram simply emphasizes the relationship of event E to event F and that of event E to event G. If events F and G stood in some special relationship to one another, this would be shown through the use of the dummy or zero-time activity line.

In some cases, more than one event must be satisfied before a subsequent event can be started:

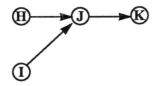

Both activities HJ and IJ must be completed before activity JK can be started. For example, an excavation must be completed and the building material received before construction can be started.

Dummy or Zero-Time Activities

The relationship between events in some instances is simply a matter of constraint: no real activity occurs, no time is spent, no resource is consumed. This type of dependency is represented by a dummy or zero-time activity, which is usually depicted as a dotted or broken line rather than the solid line of a real activity. A network may contain a cluster of dummy activities as various subgoals are reached. Although no further activity occurs, it is necessary to show that the final goal is constrained by the preceding events. Dummy activities may also occur within the body of the network. The activity lines between events 16 and 18 and between events 17 and 18 in Figure 12-3 illustrate dummy activities.

Figure 12-4 demonstrates the difference between real and dummy or zero-time activities. These examples are not from the same PERT network, nor are they related to each other; they are provided for emphasis. In the first example,

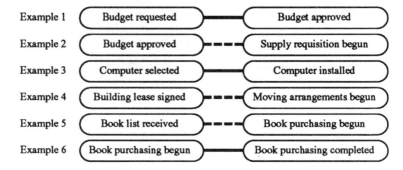

Figure 12-4 Real versus Zero-Time Activities

budget requested and budget approved, many activities are involved. The activity specification sheet for this activity line might include such detailed elements as obtaining cost estimates for equipment, calculating salary increases for personnel, adjusting the budget after preliminary review, and merging unit budgets into a master budget. The time needed to complete these activities and the individuals responsible are stated on the activity specification sheet. The length of an activity line on the diagrammatic network is not necessarily proportional to the number of detailed activities nor to the amount of time needed to perform them. It is simply a result of the mechanics of drawing the network and has no significance in itself.

Level of Indenture

The network is specific to the given program or project. The level of detail and degree of specificity should be custom-made for the project and should be consistent within the network. Highly detailed statements for some events and much more generalized statements for others create an imbalance. Because the network is first of all a planning tool, both the event statements and the activity specifications should be relatively specific. The planner may start with a gross network and refine it for greater specificity. Subnetworks may also be used for events that require a greater level of detail than that accorded most events in the network. Interface points are used on the master network to show the relationship points of the subnetworks. In order to maintain control as the project is implemented, the manager needs to monitor specific and critical points; again, there is need for a consistent level of detail.

Use of Time Estimates

Because PERT involves control of projects after the planning stage is complete, it is necessary to estimate how long the project as a whole will take so that the manager can determine how much ahead of time or behind time it is at any given phase. Ordinarily, time in a PERT network is never estimated in units of less than a week, since most activities are of such magnitude that they take considerable time to accomplish. The Activity Specification Sheet (Exhibit 12-1) reveals the importance of time in that it includes the following terms related to time:

1. optimistic time
2. most likely time
3. pessimistic time

Usually, the individual with overall responsibility for an activity is involved in determining these times. Three estimates are obtained for each activity:

1. the worst (if everything goes wrong)—pessimistic, t_p
2. the best (no breakdown in equipment, no personnel turnover, no delay in obtaining materials)—optimistic, t_o
3. the probable (realistic considerations)—most likely, t_m

Estimates for an activity assume not only full-time utilization of given resources but also successful completion of the predecessor events. At this point, the cumulative effect of a failure to complete predecessor events according to assigned deadlines can be seen. The manager actively monitors these deadlines, usually requiring periodic reporting of progress.

Constructing the PERT Network

The following steps are suggested in the construction of a PERT network:

1. State the final goal in detail. Then either work forward from beginning to end, stating all the events that must be completed to achieve the final goal, work backward from the goal to the beginning point, or use a combined approach.
2. List all possible events. It may be useful to write one event per card and work out the sequence later, which is sometimes best accomplished in a brainstorming session.
3. List activities. Although this is optional, it may help the manager differentiate activities from events or recall events to be specified.
4. Analyze events and place them in proper sequence. Look for critical relationships, logical flow, and dependencies.
5. Review the activities carefully to distinguish between real and dummy activities.

6. Remember that there may be a number of merge and burst events.
7. Diagram events and activities; number or letter the events.
8. Remember that the flow of activities and events is always forward; there are no backward loops in a PERT network.

The Critical Path

The expense of the overall project is the primary concern of the critical path method. Managers seek to reduce the cost by reducing the length of time required to accomplish the most time-consuming set of activities in the network. Managers assess the cost of a "crash" program and compare the increase in expense with the dollars saved if the goal is met earlier. If there is a saving, it is worthwhile to allot greater resources to critical activities. This approach is used commonly in construction projects. A similar technique is used in the field of manufacturing. The possibility of capturing the market ahead of a competitor sometimes makes it feasible to expend more money in reducing the critical path. This all ties in with probability, forecasting, and related techniques. At times a particular outcome is vital, and use of the critical path method may be warranted even though specific dollars will not be saved.

THE FLOW CHART

The manager may use a flow chart to depict the chronological flow of work. A flow chart is a graphic representation of an ordered sequence of events, steps, or procedures that take place in a system. The following are various types of flow charts:

- Procedure flow chart: a graphic depiction of the distribution and subsequent steps in processing work.
- Program block diagram: a detailed description of the steps that take place in computer routines. Specific operations and decisions, as well as their sequence in the program, are indicated.
- Logic diagram: a graphic representation of the data-processing logic.
- Two-dimensional flow chart: a depiction of complex workflow. This type of flow chart allows the procedures analyst to show a number of flows at the same time, such as a procedure that begins with a single action and branches out into several workflows (Figure 12-5).
- Systems flow chart: a display of the information flow throughout all parts of the system. These flow charts may be task-oriented (i.e., emphasize

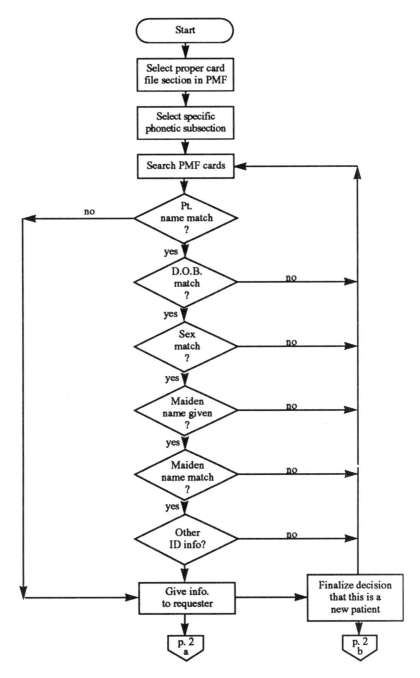

Figure 12-5 Two-Dimensional Flow Chart

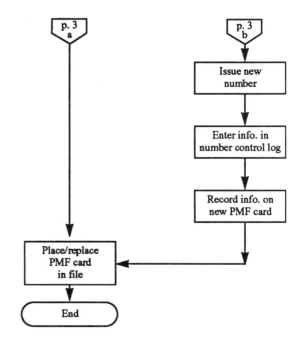

Figure 12-5 continued

work performed) or forms-oriented (i.e., depict the flow of documents through the functional structure).

Flow charting is associated with computerized data processing because of its emphasis on logical flow, but it is not restricted to program documentation. The flow chart may be used to advantage by any manager who must analyze, plan, and control workflow.

Uses of the Flow Chart

The flow chart may be used for both planning and controlling activities. As a planning tool, it may be used for the following purposes:

1. To develop a procedure. It forces the manager to think logically, since it reveals how one aspect of the task is linked to others, which areas of workflow must be made consistent, and where coordination mechanisms are needed.

2. To illustrate and emphasize key points in the written procedure. The flow chart may be used as companion documentation to the written procedure, as it provides an overall picture of the workflow in concise form. Key points in the workflow may be emphasized by color-coding critical decisions or actions.
3. To compare present and proposed procedures. A comparison of a flow chart for a proposed procedure with a flow chart for the existing procedure may show that there are as many, or more, delays in the proposed procedure.

It is less costly to assess the probable outcome of a procedure before it is implemented than to find that the procedure is not workable after it has been implemented. As a control device, the flow chart may be used for these purposes:

1. To compare the actual workflow with that originally planned. In order to remain effective guides to actions, procedures must be updated and the workflow must be monitored for changes that occur imperceptibly. By developing a flow chart of a procedure as it is currently performed and comparing it with the original plan, the manager can see changes that have occurred in the workflow and may then decide whether to change the procedure so that it reflects existing practice or to enforce compliance with the original plan.
2. To audit the workflow. Every loop in a flow chart is a potential delay; the manager can pinpoint areas of delay, investigate the legitimacy of the delays, and determine how to shorten or eliminate them.

Flow Chart Symbols

On a flow chart, each distinctive symbol stands for a certain kind of function, such as decision making, processing, or input-output. Symbols provide a shorthand method of describing the processes involved in the work. These symbols, which have become standardized in data processing, are used for flow charts in connection with both computer programs and with noncomputerized systems analysis. Commonly accepted flow chart symbols are shown in Figure 12-6.

Support Documentation

Sometimes the flow chart is a companion document to a fully written procedure. When the flow chart depicts the overall systems flow or when the procedure has not yet been developed, support documentation is needed to complement the infor-

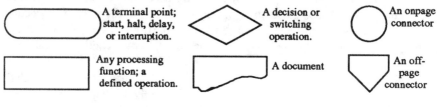

Figure 12-6 Flow Chart Symbols

---

mation on the chart. This documentation may be in the form of notes in the body of the flow chart or in the form of a narrative statement. Notes are brief, clarifying statements that supply information in conjunction with a process. They are keyed to their proper place in the chart by a number or a letter. Notes are placed in side or bottom margins where they will not interfere with the flow chart proper. A narrative statement covers assumptions, questions, and areas that need additional follow-up. A brief summary of the overall setting of the workflow may be included. Any special terms or abbreviations used are defined in this document.

THE FLOW PROCESS CHART

Sometimes referred to simply as a *process chart*, the flow process chart is a graphic representation of events that depicts the chronological flow of work or a product through an entire workflow cycle or through some part of it. Each detail of the workflow is clearly recorded with the appropriate symbols; each step can be questioned and analyzed to identify areas for possible improvement.

The flow process chart may be developed to present the process in terms of the material flow or in terms of the activity of the workers. The specific focus, materials or workers, must be decided at the beginning of the study; information about both materials and workers cannot be recorded on the same chart. Should information about both be needed, two separate charts must be developed.

Flow Process Chart versus Flow Chart

Although both charts are graphic representations of the workflow, the flow process chart differs from the flow chart. The symbols used to record the information are different for the two charts, and the information recorded and made available for analysis differs in its emphasis. The flow process chart contains specific entries for time units, distances, and qualities; it also contains specific questions for step-by-step analysis (Exhibit 12-2). On the flow chart, in con-

Exhibit 12-2 Flow Process Chart

Process		
☐ Man or ☐ Material		
Chart Begins	Chart Ends	
Charted By	Date	

Actions
- ○ Operations
- ◇ Transportations
- ☐ Inspections
- D Delays
- ▽ Storages
- Distance Travelled (Feet)

Summary

	Present		Proposed		Difference	
	No.	Time	No.	Time	No.	Time

Analysis
- Eliminate
- Combine
- Sequence
- Change: Place, Person
- Improve

Details of	Method ☐ Present ☐ Proposed	Operation	Transportation	Inspection	Delay	Storage	Distance in feet	Quantity	Time	Analysis — What? Where? When? Who? How?	Notes
1		○	◇	☐	D	▽					
2		○	◇	☐	D	▽					
3		○	◇	☐	D	▽					
4		○	◇	☐	D	▽					
5		○	◇	☐	D	▽					
6		○	◇	☐	D	▽					
7		○	◇	☐	D	▽					
8		○	◇	☐	D	▽					
9		○	◇	☐	D	▽					
10		○	◇	☐	D	▽					
11		○	◇	☐	D	▽					
12		○	◇	☐	D	▽					

trast, this information is shown in supplementary notes; furthermore, it is not gathered as precisely as it is in the flow process chart. In addition, the flow process chart does not have the branching capability of the flow chart; simultaneous flow of work must be shown on separate flow process charts and cross-referenced by special notes.

The flow process chart permits the recording of information in great detail, which is both an advantage and a limitation. The mass of details may be so great that it becomes excessively time consuming to analyze the results properly. Also, information on the flow process chart may be distorted, especially when the focus is on materials. Reasons for apparent delays must be carefully analyzed. For example, a laboratory requisition slip may be placed in a temporary file while the results are being obtained; this appears as a delay, although important activity is occurring.

Uses of the Flow Process Chart

The flow process chart is used to break down and analyze individual operations in detail in order to

1. develop and verify procedures
2. compare present and proposed procedures
3. obtain specific information about time factors and delays in operations as well as about distance factors in transportation and work movement
4. analyze workflow to improve procedures by eliminating overlap and minimizing delays
5. assess physical layout with emphasis on (a) transportation distance between equipment and workstation and (b) relationship of one workstation to another
6. gather information to use with other data to set work standards, especially when delay and transportation are factors
7. establish a basis for further study, such as detailed analyses of bottlenecks in the workflow, excessive delays, and backtracking

Standard Symbols

The standard flow process chart symbols are those endorsed by the Administrative Management Society and the American Society of Mechanical Engineers (Table 12-2).

Table 12-2 Approved Flow Process Chart Symbols

Symbol	Element
○	Operation
◊	Transportation
▽	Storage
□	Inspection
D	Delay

Operation

An operation occurs when an object is changed in any of its physical characteristics, when information is given or received, when planning or calculation takes place, or when a worker carries out an activity. Operations are the main steps in a process. The end result is usually something produced or accomplished; something is being done to or by the subject or is being created, changed, or added to. The symbol for an operation is a large circle ○. Unshaded, this symbol is used for nonproductive activities, such as make-ready or put-away operations (e.g., sort appointment cards, arrange orders in account number sequence, or pick up medications). Shaded, the operation symbol shows a "do" or productive operation (e.g., clean a needle, type a letter, or fill in monthly rates).

Transportation

Except when the movement is a part of the operation or is caused by the operator at the workstation during an operation or inspection, movement of an object from one place to another is considered a transportation process. The symbol for transportation is an arrow ◊. Examples of transportation processes include carrying appointment slips to work area, carrying medication cards to medication cabinet, returning empty trays to cart, and carrying supplies to table. Placing a letter in the outbasket is an operation, while carrying a letter to the mailroom (from one workstation to another) is a transportation process. The distance travelled is usually included on the chart as supplementary information.

Storage

When an object is kept, protected against unauthorized removal, and made available for future use, it is in its authorized storage place. The object either is disposed of permanently or remains in one place for a period of time awaiting further action. The symbol for storage is an inverted triangle ▽. Examples of storage include medical records placed in permanent files, medications stored in a cabinet at the nurses' station, reagents placed in a bottle, and medication cards put in the medication card file until the next medication is given.

Inspection

During an inspection, an object is examined for identification or verified for quality or quantity in any of its characteristics. Objects are checked, verified, reviewed, or examined, but no change is made. The symbol for inspection is a ☐. Examples of inspection include scanning appointment slips for patient identification, proofreading letters, and comparing medications with the master medication sheet entries.

Delay

When conditions do not permit or require immediate performance of the next planned action, a person or object is interrupted or delayed in flow. An action such as placing an object in temporary storage (e.g., in a desktop file), where it awaits the next action is included in the concept of delay. A delay is shorter in duration than storage. The symbol for delay is a stylized D. Examples of delay include a wait by a nurse while medications are taken by the patient, a letter in an outbox waiting for pickup, a patient's wait for a visit to a clinic, a worker's wait for an elevator, equipment awaiting transportation, and appointment slips placed in a chronological file. A standard unit of time (e.g., minutes) is usually used to indicate the amount of delay.

Factors Outside the Study

Certain outside influences that temporarily disrupt the workflow may be outside the scope of a designated study. If the analyst considers some process impractical to evaluate, it is noted as an outside interference, usually of a temporary nature. An elevator may be broken, an area may be under renovation, or equipment may not be functioning properly. If the same influencing factor is noted repeatedly, the manager should take some corrective action; if it is beyond the control of the manager, it should be taken into account in the assessment of overall constraints on the workflow. To determine which of the elements in the process is involved in such a constraint, it is useful to review them in terms of the intent of these definitions of standards symbols:

Element/Process	*Intent*
Operation	Produces or accomplishes
Transportation	Moves
Inspection	Verifies
Delay	Interferes
Storage	Keeps

Flow Process Chart Format

The format typically used for a flow process chart contains standard elements of information, although these elements may be arranged in different ways. After the header information has been completed, the body of the flow process chart is developed:

1. Step numbers are listed chronologically, and numbers are assigned to each step for easy reference in the note section or in the related narrative documentation.
2. Events are described as briefly as possible, but clearly. It is helpful to use the active voice when describing a worker's movement (e.g., fill out medication card) and the passive voice when describing the flow of material (e.g., medication card filled out).
3. The appropriate symbol for each step in the process is determined and entered in a column reserved for that entry.
4. Supplemental information, such as distance in feet, quantity, or time, is entered. This is tallied and summarized after all the data have been gathered for the entire workflow under study.
5. Analysis questions are raised as part of the review of the workflow. These may be simply checked off and analyzed in detail as a separate step. The questions are straightforward: Who? What? When? How? Where?
6. Space is provided to make special notes, such as cross-references to a previous step, additional factors to be examined, or factors in the physical layout.
7. Action questions concerning possible changes are included: Eliminate the step? Combine? Improve sequence, place, or a person? These action questions are combined with the analytical questions.

Space is provided for a summary section, which contains a tabulation of the various operational steps or elements. Space is also provided to enter the totals for time spent and distance travelled. Data for the present and proposed methods may be included, as well as a calculation of the differences in the two methods.

Steps in Developing Flow Process Chart

The usual steps in developing a flow process chart are summarized here for review and reference:

1. Choose the job to be studied. Be specific.
2. Refine the focus of the study by selecting:

    a. the subject to be studied (person or material present or proposed method)

    b. the starting and stopping point of the study

3. Complete identification section of the chart.
4. List each step in sequence and enter any explanatory notes in the appropriate column.
5. Apply the correct symbol for each activity. Be consistent in the use of accepted symbols. Shade the productive operations to highlight them.
6. Enter time, distance, and quantity where appropriate. Use consistent units to enter these data (e.g., inches or feet, seconds or minutes).
7. Draw a line to connect each symbol to emphasize the idea of the flow of the work.
8. Summarize the findings and enter the figures in the appropriate spaces.

THE WORK DISTRIBUTION CHART

Although its overall goals may remain constant, every organization is in a state of continual change. Therefore, continual monitoring of the organizational structure is needed. If the actual distribution of work shifts from the original workflow plan, the manager must determine whether the present distribution of work among the organizational units is an improvement. If so, the structure should be adjusted; if not, appropriate measures should be taken to restore the original workflow plan and the original organizational structure.

One managerial tool for gathering factual data about the present organizational system is the work distribution chart, which focuses on work assignments and job content within any single unit or work group. This chart is designed to show (1) major activities of the unit, (2) total hours (per standard time period) spent on each activity, and (3) total hours (per standard time period) spent by each worker on each task. If the chart has been properly prepared, it shows

1. the amount of time spent on each activity
2. the degree of specialization
3. any overlap in work distribution
4. any fragmentation in work
5. any uneven distribution of work

This information must be analyzed to determine whether the degree of specialization is adequate or excessive; whether the amount of time is appropriate, excessive, or disproportionate to the significance of the activity; whether the fragmentation is unavoidable or is the result of overspecialization; and whether some employees are overloaded while others lack work.

The purpose of the work distribution chart is to gather information in a consistent manner and to display this information in a way that facilitates critical review (Exhibit 12-3). It is customary to list workers in descending order by job rank. Name and job title are placed along the horizontal plane left to right. Major activities and time tallies are listed in vertical columns.

The work distribution chart is prepared by the unit supervisor or manager from the information contained in the daily task lists (Exhibit 12-4) kept by each worker. The daily task list is a record of the time each worker spends each working day on each activity. The manager develops the basic form and gives the appropriate instructions to the staff, emphasizing that work distribution studies are not used for employee evaluation and that the focus is on the distribution of the work, not personal productivity.

The manager provides a list of definitions for each activity so that the usage of terms is consistent. Instructions are also given as to the time units to be used, usually segments of 15 minutes. It is not necessary, however, to account for every minute. The idle times, rest periods, and delays could be grouped under the miscellaneous category. If that category's total seems unusually high (above the customary 10 to 15 percent allowed for personal, fatigue, and delay factors in work standards and time studies), a separate investigation should be done.

The supervisor or manager collects the daily task lists and compiles the summary task list for each worker in the unit. These summary task lists are assembled at the end of some predetermined period, e.g., at the end of a work week (Exhibit 12-5). In constructing the work distribution chart, the manager follows the customary rules for conducting a work study, such as consistency in gathering facts, selection of a representative work period, and inclusion of the entire work cycle.

BIBLIOGRAPHY

Archibold, Russell D. *Network-Based Management Systems* (PERT/CPM). New York: John Wiley & Sons, 1967.

Bettersby, Albert. *Network Analysis for Planning and Scheduling*. New York: St. Martin's Press, 1964.

Levin, Richard, and Kirkpatrick, Charles. *Planning and Control with PERT/CPM.*

Lott, Richard. *Basic Systems Analysis*. San Francisco: Canfield Press, 1971.

Exhibit 12-3 Work Distribution Chart: Medical Records Division

Department: Medical Records
Unit: Correspondence
Week of May 14 to May 18

ACTIVITY	Total Hours (all employees)	Augusta Bernard Supervisor	Hours	Laura Case	Hours Clerk II	Martha Cossian Clerk I	Hours
Telephone Requests	8		1		3		4
In-Person Requests	14		11		3		
Subpoena/ Depositions	12	• Prepare charts • Attend court sessions	12				
Obtaining Patient ID for Requests	6					• Checking patient master file	6
Chart Retrieval	11			• Complete chargeout cards • Retrieve charts	1		10
Abstracting Reply	42		10		26		6
Photocopying	7					• Daily Photocopying	7
Miscellaneous	20	• Supervisor's Meeting • Session with trainees 2	4	• Emergency Coverage in files 5/15	7	• File area coverage 5/16	7
TOTAL	120		40		40		40

Exhibit 12-4 Daily Task List

Time Period	Task Performed
Employee:	Date:_____
Job Title:	

Exhibit 12-5 Weekly Task List

Tasks Performed	Hours
Employee:	Week of:_____
Job Title:	

Chapter 13

Work Sampling

CHAPTER OBJECTIVES

1. Define work sampling.
2. Relate work sampling to the control process.
3. Cite uses of work sampling.
4. Relate the concept of random sampling to work sampling.
5. Understand how to apply alignment charts, random number tables, and observation tables to departmental work sampling.

Work may be measured by means of several approaches, such as stopwatch studies, micromotion studies, and work sampling. The technique of work sampling (i.e., making a series of observations at random intervals) is based on the statistical principle that observations made at random provide information as complete as that provided by a continuous method of study. Work sampling is sometimes called *ratio delay*, as it was developed in the British textile industry, where the ratio of delays to productive work was determined through a process of random observations.

The technique consists of periodic, but frequent, spot checks of workers, equipment, or activities; the observations are recorded and then analyzed. Specific uses of work sampling include

- determining downtime on a machine
- identifying patterns of delay or interference in the workflow
- verifying job content (comparing job duties assigned or originally described with actual job content)
- determining discrepancies in workflow between what was planned and what is occurring
- determining what percentage of the workday is spent on each job or activity

- determining what percentage of an overall job is done by each worker
- establishing delay factors in setting work standards

The work sampling technique allows the manager or observer to carry out a study while concurrently doing other work, since it is not a continuous time study (as is a stopwatch study). Work sampling is relatively inexpensive to do and may be carried out by a nonstatistical practitioner. Because the content is closely related to other managerial data, the major items for study are readily identifiable. For example, the job description lists the major duties of a worker, task assignment records contain the major worker assignments, and systems and workflow statements contain details of the planned work.

The work sampling technique is best suited for the study of jobs with a few major tasks. Limits of the technique include the possibility of worker tendency to perform when under observation and the possibility of observer bias in developing the study and carrying out the observations. These problems can be overcome by adherence to the underlying principles of sampling, however. The observations should be made at random rather than casually or haphazardly. The worker should be informed that the study is a series of observations to evaluate the work process, not employee performance. The study should be carried out over a period of time long enough so that the worker becomes accustomed to being observed and becomes relatively unaware of the process. The sample size should be representative, and the degree of precision or confidence level of the study should be sufficiently high to give validity to the study. The observation period should reflect a suitable work cycle that includes both peak and nonpeak loads.

KEY CONCEPTS

Work sampling is based on the statistical principle of probability or "the law of averages." The following are key terms:

- *Population* or *Universe*. All the things of the kind one is interested in; the subject of the study, such as all the beans in a jar, all the patients in an outpatient clinic, all the students in a class, all the employees of a department, or all the residents in long-term care facilities for the mentally retarded.
- *Sample*. A small part of the population or universe intended to reflect or represent the quality or nature of the whole, such as a handful of beans from the jar, a few patients from the outpatient clinic, or some of the students in the class.
- *Random*. The condition that exists when every element of the population has the same probability of being selected as an item in the sample.

The basic law of statistical probability is based on the premise that a small sample selected at random from a given population tends to reflect the same pattern and to have the same distribution as the whole.

Random sampling is commonly illustrated by visualizing a container of black and white marbles. Given a container of 50 black and 50 white marbles that have been well mixed, there is a 50-50 chance of pulling either a black or a white marble from the container. Each time a marble is pulled, its color is noted. After it has been returned to the container and the marbles mixed, additional marbles are pulled to complete the sample. Returning the marble to the container after noting its color is termed "sampling with replacement," a technique that allows the researcher to approximate an infinite population. Failure to replace the pulled marble alters the mix of colors and changes the odds as to which color will be drawn next.

The larger the sample size (the more times a marble is drawn from the container), the more closely the sample results approach the true percentage in the population or universe of the study. After only 3 draws, for example, all the marbles drawn might easily be of the same color. As more draws are made, the sample will more closely reflect the equal mix of the entire population.

SELECTION OF SAMPLE SIZE

The size of the sample selected is a function of statistical calculation and common sense. The sample must be large enough to reflect the universe to be studied but not so large that it will be unwieldy, time-consuming, and expensive to analyze. It is costly to analyze a large sample, and it may be unnecessary, depending on the purpose of the study. The analyst must choose a sample that is large enough to be valid and small enough to be economical. Sample size is also dependent on the desired degree of accuracy. The analyst must determine the level of confidence that is desirable for the study. Usually, a 95 percent confidence interval is used. The width of such an interval is defined by placing 1.96 standard deviation units around the arithmetic mean or average. In effect, the analyst is accepting a 5 percent error on either side of the results. "Give or take 5 times out of a hundred, the following results are accurate" summarizes the implications of a 95 percent confidence interval. Given a group of random observations, the results will be correct 95 percent of the time; stated another way, the results will be incorrect only 5 percent of the time.

Statistical formulas are available to calculate sample size. As a shortcut for the nonstatistical practitioner, alignment charts can be used to calculate the number of observations required to achieve a specific level of precision at a given confidence level. Figure 13-1 is an alignment chart that can be used for all 95 percent confidence levels. To use the alignment chart, several steps must be

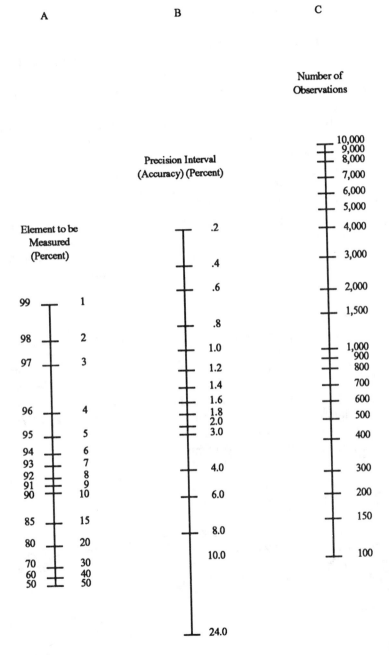

Figure 13-1 Alignment Chart

followed. The analyst must estimate the time spent on the job element; this information would be obtained from past records, common sense observations, and rough sampling of observations.

Column A of the alignment chart shows the element to be measured by listing the percentage of the work constituted by the element. In this example, the major tasks were roughly assessed through 64 observations. Of these, 51 showed that the major duties constituted the bulk of the work, as had been planned in the original division of the work. Dividing 51 by 64 gives 80 percent as the percentage for the element to be measured. This percentage is plotted on the chart by aligning a straight edge at 80.

The next step involves choosing the desired precision. For example, if the maximum deviation allowed is to be 4 percentage points of 80 percent (80% ± 4%), 4 percent is plotted on the precision interval scale of column B. A straight edge is aligned so that it crosses through the 80 percent in column A and through the 4 percent in column B.

Extension of the line connecting columns A and B over to column C indicates the number of observations required for 95 percent accuracy on a major job constituting 80 percent of the activities or elements to be measured. The number of observations needed in this example is 400.

By way of further illustration in the use of the alignment chart, determine the number of observations needed for 95 percent accuracy in the following example:

Given a major activity that constitutes 80 percent of the job and a desire to be within 1.6 percentage points of 80 percent (80% ± 1.6%), align the straight edge at 80 in column A, locate and plot 1.6 percent in column B, and construct a line to column C. A total of about 2,500 observations would be needed. Clearly, the smaller the error tolerance, the larger the sample size must be.

INTERVAL SAMPLING

Certain aspects of work may be assessed by means of interval sampling, a technique in which the specific elements to be studied in the total population are determined through the use of an interval fraction. Interval sampling would be suitable for use in answering the following sorts of questions:

- Given 10,000 medical records per week to be refiled accurately, how many records were returned to their proper location?
- Given an average of 16,000 outpatient visits per month, how many patients' records have appropriate progress note entries?

- Given 630 laboratory studies per week, how many were left incomplete because of an inaccurate specimen draw?

The first example is described in detail to illustrate the use of interval sampling. A sample of 500 records is to be drawn from the population of 10,000 refiled records:

1. Calculate the average number of charts to be refiled per week; in this example, 10,000 is the total population of the study.
2. Calculate the sample size (see earlier discussion of sample size): in this case, 500 charts will be checked for proper location.
3. Calculate the interval by dividing the total population (10,000 records per week) by the sample size (500):

$$\frac{10,000}{500} = 20$$

The result is an interval of 20, which means that every 20th element is to be selected from the total population in the study.

4. Select the starting point by choosing a random number between 1 and 20. Use a random number table or a calculator to obtain this number. In this example, the random number table in Exhibit 13-1 was consulted. Random entry into the chart was at the second batch of numbers on the right hand side, precisely at the second line of numbers: 52 53 37 97 15. The number 15 was the first usable one accessed. Therefore, beginning with the 15th record returned, every 20th record returned in the study week is checked to determine if it has reached its proper location in the file. Numbers studied are 15, 35, 55, 75, 95, etc.

To carry out this particular study, the chargeout/tracer forms must be saved for the week so that it can be determined which medical records were returned that week. The analyst in the study must anticipate such a need and take the necessary steps.

SELECTION OF OBSERVATION TIMES

In selecting observation times, the manager must take into account the work cycle and the working days and hours within a weekly or monthly work cycle. If a total of 800 observations must be made over one month of working days (weekends omitted), 40 observations per day must be made (800 observations divided by 20 working days). This cycle of a full month of working days allows the manager to sample the work without subjecting the worker to intense observation on any one workday and without missing important variables in the workday as it is influenced by the flow of work throughout a month's cycle of activity.

Specific times in the workday must be chosen for making the observations, and these times should be selected randomly. One way is to write each time on a slip, mix all the slips, place them in a box, and choose the times for each day's observations from all the times in the box. This process can be cumbersome and time consuming, however.

Random Number Tables

In random number tables, sequences of numbers are displayed in such a way that it is just as likely for any given digit, 0 through 9, to follow any other given digit. This is true whether the path for number selection is horizontal, vertical, or diagonal. Random number tables are used to draw a truly random sample (Exhibit 13-1). Such tables may be found in standard form in compilations of statistical tables. Some calculators have a random number function, which is another source of random number generation.

The table is consulted in a random manner. The user simply opens to some page in the random number table and accepts the first digit or set of digits displayed. The number is recorded on a work sheet, and additional numbers are taken from the random number table and recorded until sufficient usable numbers have been selected. If

Exhibit 13-1 Random Number Table

91	76	21	64	60		94	21	78	55	09		55	34	57	92	69
00	97	79	08	06		34	41	92	45	71		69	66	92	19	09
36	40	18	34	94		53	14	30	59	25		86	96	98	29	06
88	98	99	60	50		88	59	53	11	52		90	92	10	70	80
04	37	69	87	21		65	28	04	67	53		74	16	32	23	02
63	02	06	34	41		73	43	07	34	48		16	95	86	70	75
78	47	23	53	90		48	62	11	90	60		52	53	37	97	15
87	68	62	19	43		28	97	85	58	99		56	61	87	33	12
47	60	92	10	77		02	63	45	52	38		21	94	47	90	12
56	88	87	59	41		76	96	59	38	72		23	32	65	41	18
02	57	45	86	67		79	88	01	51	48		26	29	13	56	41
31	54	14	13	17		08	25	58	94	43		77	80	20	75	82
28	50	10	43	36		84	99	87	40	75		46	40	66	44	52
63	29	62	66	50		36	37	34	92	09		61	65	81	98	60
45	65	58	26	51		01	16	96	65	27		93	69	64	43	07

the table in Exhibit 13-1 is entered randomly, for example, the second block of numbers on the extreme left of the table might be chosen. Accepting the numbers as given (and neglecting the spacing), the user would find the following three-digit numbers by reading from left to right across the chart: 630, 206, 344, 173, 430, 734.

The randomness of the table must not be destroyed by starting on the same page and in the same place each time. The odds are against this, unless the book is so well-worn that it opens often to the same page. Another potential distortion in the use of the random number table results from the tendency to read only from left to right. Numbers may also be selected by reading up and down, right to left, diagonally, and so forth.

One way of developing observation times with the use of a random number table is given by Ralph Barnes.[1] The first digit of a number taken from the table might indicate the hour of the day; the second and third digits, the minutes. Thus, if the number taken from the table is 950622, 950 would indicate 9.50, which is 9:30 (0.50 equals one-half of 60 minutes, or half past the hour). The second number 622 might indicate 6.22, or approximately 6:13 (0.22 of 60 minutes, or 13 minutes past the hour). If the company hours are 8:00 A.M. to 5:00 P.M., the number 6.22 would be discarded, and the next random number listed on the table would be selected and translated into a time of day. The manager continues this process until enough observation times for the day have been obtained.

Observation Table

In an observation table, each minute in a workday is listed and a number assigned to that minute. For example, in Exhibit 13-2, the tenth minute of this workday is 8:39 (010). An observation table may be used in conjunction with a random number table to select observation times.

The following is a detailed example of the use of the random number table (Exhibit 13-1) in conjunction with the observation table (Exhibit 13-2):

1. Select numbers from the random number table, starting at the same point as used earlier (the numbers are listed in columns to be read top to bottom):

630	867	605
206	075	253
344	784	379
173	723	715
430	539	876
734	048	862
481	621	194
695	190	etc.

Exhibit 13-2 Observation Table: 8:30 A.M. to 4:30 P.M. Workday

001	8:30	016	8:45	031	9:00	046	9:15
002	8:31	017	8:46	032	9:01	047	9:16
003	8:32	018	8:47	033	9:02	048	9:17
004	8:33	019	8:48	034	9:03	049	9:18
005	8:34	020	8:49	035	9:04	050	9:19
006	8:35	021	8:50	036	9:05		
007	8:36	022	8:51	037	9:06	Such an obser-	
008	8:37	023	8:52	038	9:07	vation table would	
009	8:38	024	8:53	039	9:08	continue in this	
010	8:39	025	8:54	040	9:09	manner through	
011	8:40	026	8:55	041	9:10	480, that is,	
012	8:41	027	8:56	042	9:11	4:30 P.M.	
013	8:42	028	8:57	043	9:12		
014	8:43	029	8:58	044	9:13		

2. Because this observation table spans the numbers 001 to 480, only these and any other numbers that fall between them may be used. Numbers above 480 are discarded for this study. Should the manager wish to carry the work study into workhours beyond 4:30, the observation table would be adjusted accordingly (e.g., 481 would indicate 4:31 P.M.).

3. Arrange the remaining numbers in numerical order:

048

075

173

etc.

4. Correlate the numbers with the times of day given in the observation chart:

048 = 9:17

075 = 9:44

173 = 11:22

etc.

5. Enter the numbers in the column for "Observation Time" on the work sampling record form (Exhibit 13-2).

THE WORK SAMPLING OBSERVATION RECORD

In order to gather the work sampling observations in a systematic and consistent manner, a work sampling observation record is developed (Exhibit 13-3).

Exhibit 13-3 Work Sampling Observation Record

DEPARTMENT: Medical Records

JOB TITLE: Chart Assembly

INCUMBENT: A.L. Spark

DATE:

OBSERVER: M.S. Brown

PAGE 1 OF 1

OBSERVATION TIME	Set up	Clean up	Personal	Telephone	Away from work station	Assembling charts	Checking disc. list	Pulling new folders	Obtaining pt. ID for misc. reports	Making out control cards	Working with review clerk	Observation time missed	Comments
9:02													
9:57													
10:18													
11:22													
12:08													
12:31													
1:16													
2:31													
3:02													
3:58													

The observation form includes a section of identifying information, for example, department, job title, incumbent, analyst, date of study, and number of pages. Observation times, which vary for each day, are listed.

Time is allotted for worker preparation of the workstation and for clean up. Personal time refers to coffee breaks, lunch breaks, and similar permissible time away from the workstation. Even when an employee is not designated as a person to answer the telephone, this activity is included as a possible category. The worker under observation occasionally is not at the workstation when the manager/analyst makes the sampling observation; this is so noted. Should excessive entries occur in this category, the manager pursues this information in detail at another time. The remaining header entries are custom-made to suit the job activities.

Occasionally, the analyst fails to make the observation at the time indicated. Since the number of observations missed affects the study and its reliability, it is important to include spaces where missed observations can be noted. Finally, there is room for comment, spaces to make additional notes or entries that explain and augment the observations made during the sample study. The manager develops a specific observation record for the study; prepares sufficient copies of the form; chooses the observation times, either on a daily basis or in one concentrated effort; and proceeds with the study over the designated days and weeks.

TABULATION OF RESULTS

The results obtained from the sampling study are compiled in a summary tabulation. The manager gives additional attention to areas where the results are not consistent with the expected range. Such selected areas are studied separately and in further detail, with corrective action taken as indicated. Table 13-1 shows the results of observations made of a discharge analysis clerk in the medical records division of a hospital.

CONCLUDING EXAMPLE

A final example is presented here, drawing from the direct patient care interaction. The background problem for this work sample stems from delay in patient transport from a hospital inpatient unit to the physical therapy department. The manager assesses the situation by means of the sampling technique.

Step 1. Calculate sample size using Exhibit 13-1. Patient population per month = 1,000. Precision level of this study equals 4% (3.9% on the chart). This gives you a population size of 400 patients to be studied. Summary: 400 patients needing transportation will be studied.

Table 13-1 Example of Work Sampling Summary

Task or Function	Percentage of Time Spent
1. Checking charts for deficiencies	36
2. Making out deficiency slips	11
3. Making out Rolodex cards	7
4. Hunting for missing charts	8
5. Assembling charts (Mondays only)	6
6. Taking charts to doctor's boxes	3
7. Away from office to pick up missing reports	2
8. Time to set up in the morning	2
9. Time to clean up desk in the evening	3
10. Filing loose reports	1
11. Personal time	20
12. Other miscellaneous duties	1
	100

Step 2. Develop a fact gathering form:

Time patient left inpatient unit =
Scheduled arrival time =
Actual arrival time =
Summary:

Step 3. Study the results. Calculate average delay time (e.g., which inpatient unit exhibits highest frequency of delay).

Step 4. Initiate corrective action based on the study.

NOTE

1. Ralph Barnes, *Work Sampling* (Dubuque: Wm. C. Brown, 1956), 43.

Part II

Organizational Environment and Dynamics: The Context of Management Practice

Chapter 14

The Organization as a Total System

CHAPTER OBJECTIVES

1. Understand the uniqueness of an organization by assessing the organizational environment.
2. Differentiate between an informal organization and a formal organization.
3. Classify organizations according to primary characteristics.
4. Classify health care organizations according to various organizational types.
5. Identify the characteristics of classic bureaucracy.
6. Identify the consequences to the manager of the organizational environment.

Social evidence abounds with support for the basic observation that humans form groups: families, clans, neighborhoods, churches, political parties, businesses, fraternities, work groups, professional associations. The study of these groups as social organizations is the proper domain of the social scientist; their study as formal organizations is the proper focus of administrative analysis.

The successful manager recognizes the impact of the organizational environment on clients, members of the organization, and the public at large as well as on the manager's specific role. An organization does not exist in a static world; rather, it is in a continual state of transaction with its environment. As an open system, the organization receives inputs from its environment, acts on them and is acted on by them, and produces outputs, such as goods and services (and even organizational survival, which can be considered an essential output). Consequently, the organizational environment consists of both internal and external components. The specific functions of the manager are modified by the organizational environment (i.e., the specific attributes of the given work setting). Classic organizational theory provides the manager with concepts to assess the organizational environment.

The organizational environment may be assessed by an examination of its characteristics and components through a typology of organizations, a review of the organizational life cycle, and an analysis of the purpose and functions of organizations. The use of clientele network and systems models yields further information about the internal and external components of the organizational environment. Managers may anticipate organizational conflict when stated purposes or goals and actual practices become disparate; such an occurrence should alert managers to changes in the organizational environment so that they can develop an anticipatory response rather than a reactive response.

FORMAL VERSUS INFORMAL ORGANIZATIONS

An organization is a basic social unit that has been established for the purpose of achieving a goal. A formal organization is characterized by several distinct features:

1. a common goal; an accepted pattern of purpose
2. a set of shared values or common beliefs that give individuals a sense of identification and belonging
3. continuity of goal-oriented interaction
4. a division of labor deliberately planned to achieve the goal
5. a system of authority or a chain of command to achieve conscious integration of the group and conscious coordination of efforts to reach the goal

An informal organization may be characterized by some of the features of formal organizations, but it lacks one or more of these features. Individuals who share a common value may meet regularly to foster some goal, and this group may become a recognizable formal organization. Some informal groups never develop the consistent characteristics of a formal organization, however, and simply remain informal.

Formal organizations almost inevitably give rise to informal organizations. Such informal groups may be viewed as spontaneous organizations that emerge because individuals are brought together in a common workplace to pursue a common goal, which makes social interaction inescapable. Informal organ-izations arise as a means of easing the restrictions of formal structures, as in the cooperative communication and coordination that may occur outside of the officially mandated channels of authority. Through an informal organization's communication network, an individual may gain valuable information that supplements or clarifies the formal communications. Also, informal groups help to integrate individuals into the organization and socialize them to accept their specific organizational roles. A manager must remain aware of the existence and composition of the informal groups in the organization so that their functioning affects the formal structure in positive rather than negative ways.

CLASSIFICATION OF ORGANIZATIONS

When an organization's managers understand and accept its nature, organizational conflict can be reduced and organizational viability increased, because the managers function in a manner consistent with the type of organization shaping the interactions. Personal conflict can be reduced. Should an individual be unwilling or unable to accept certain aspects of a particular organizational type, that individual may decide to move to a different organizational climate. For example, if an individual practitioner prefers not to function in a highly structured, bureaucratic setting, it is better to recognize this before accepting employment in a government-sponsored health care institution. An individual who believes that health care should not be "for profit" would do well to seek employment in health care settings that are not predicated on the business model. An individual may gain an insight into the climate of a particular organization through the use of organizational classifications based on prime beneficiary, authority structure, and genotypic characteristics.

Prime Beneficiary

Peter Blau and W.R. Scott presented a classification of organizations based on the prime beneficiary.[1] Their suggested model for the analysis of organizations focuses on this question: Who benefits from the existence of the organization? Four types of organizations result from the application of this criterion[2]:

1. mutual benefit associations, where the members are the prime beneficiaries; examples include a professional association, a credit union, and a collective bargaining unit
2. business concerns, where the owners are the prime beneficiaries
3. service organizations, where the clients are the prime beneficiaries
4. commonweal organizations, where the public at large is the prime beneficiary; police and fire departments are examples of commonweal organizations

Managers may formulate goals, establish priorities, and monitor activities to determine the effectiveness of the organization in meeting the needs of the prime beneficiary. Actions that do not foster such goals are eliminated and proper priorities formulated. Because the clients are the prime beneficiaries of a service organization, decisions about hours of service, the scope of services offered, and similar matters are made with the needs of clients in mind. In health care, the growing development of home care, flexible hours in outpatient care clinics, and alternatives to full hospitalization are attempts at meeting the needs of the prime beneficiaries, the patients and their families. At the same time, health care worker units involved in collective bargaining can be considered mutual benefit associations. Managers in health care settings must balance the demands made by both types of organizational forms within one organization.

Authority Structure

The organizational environment can also be classified according to the modes of authority that are operative in the institution. Managers must adopt leadership styles, develop procedures and methods for worker interaction, and determine client interactions in a manner that is consistent with the predominant authority structure. Health care organizations tend to embody more than one pattern of authority structure; for example, there are few limits on the activities of professional staff and greater limits on the activities of semiskilled and unskilled workers. The work of Amatai Etzioni provides a typology of organizations based on the authority structure predominant in the institution.[3] The classification that results from this approach may be summarized as follows:

1. predominantly coercive authority; prisons, concentration camps, custodial mental institutions, or coercive unions
2. predominantly utilitarian, rational-legal authority; use of economic rewards; businesses, industry, unions, and the military in peacetime
3. predominantly normative authority; use of membership, status, intrinsic values; religious organizations, universities, professional associations, mutual benefit associations, fraternal and philanthropic associations
4. mixed structures: normative-coercive (e.g., combat units); utilitarian-normative (e.g., most labor unions); utilitarian-coercive (e.g., some early industries, some farms, company towns, ships)

Genotypic Characteristics

Like the prime beneficiary concept, the classification of organizations by genotype is based on an analysis of their fundamental roots and purposes. Daniel Katz and Robert Kahn viewed organizations as subsystems of the larger society that carry out basic functions of that larger society. These basic functions are the focal point in this system of classification. The typology of organizations developed by Katz and Kahn is based on genotypes, or first-order characteristics: What is the most basic function that the organization carries out in terms of society?[4] These first-order, basic functions are as follows:

1. productive or economic functions: the creation of wealth or goods as occurs in businesses
2. maintenance of society: the socialization and general care of people as occurs in education, training, indoctrination, and health care
3. adaptive functions: the creation of knowledge as occurs in universities and as a result of research and artistic endeavors
4. managerial/political functions: adjudication and coordination functions and control of resources and people as occur in court systems, police departments, political parties, interest groups, and government agencies

The charter, articles of incorporation, and statement of purpose are official documents of the organization that can be used to classify the organization according to this typology.

Goal statements are derived and priorities set in terms of primary function. Managers can monitor organizational change when the actual function performed differs from the stated function. When a social service agency spends a great deal of effort determining eligibility of patients for service under a variety of government programs, it is assuming some of the characteristics of a managerial/political organization. Sometimes this adjudication interferes with the delivery of the health care service; managers must make decisions in the light of this conflict. If priority is given to research and education over direct patient care, the health care practitioner must again come to terms with the true nature of the organization.

CLASSIFICATION OF HEALTH CARE ORGANIZATIONS

When a health care organization is classified according to these typologies, the complexity of the setting becomes apparent. Classification by prime beneficiary offers several possibilities. In terms of direct patient care, for example, the health care organization can be classified as a typical service organization. On the other hand, if it is a for-profit institution, classification as a business organization is more appropriate. If the health care organization has a mixed goal, as does a teaching hospital associated with a medical school, it can be defined as a service organization with respect to its clients—both the physicians to be educated and the patients to be treated. The potentially conflicting priorities of teaching and direct patient care underlie the selection of patients for treatment, however; preference may be given to those patients who are "interesting" cases for teaching purposes. Even when a health care institution is not directly associated with a medical school, a variety of clinical affiliation arrangements may be developed to meet the needs of such practitioners as occupational and physical therapists, medical technologists, social workers, health record administrators, dietitians, and other groups that require clinical practice as part of their educational sequence. In developing goal statements for a department, the chief of service must keep this secondary goal in mind.

A health care organization also is a commonweal organization insofar as it protects the public interest in matters of general community health, such as the benefits of the facility's research efforts for the public at large. Health care institutions also offer a variety of free health-monitoring programs as a means of fostering health maintenance in the community.

Etzioni included the hospital as an example of normative authority structure. This point could be argued, however, depending on the focus of organizational analysis. Professional staff members tend to function in the normative mode; their codes of ethics, their professional training, and the general level of behavior expected of them modify individual participation in the organization as much as, if not more than, the formal bylaws and contractual arrangements. In this sense, the normative authority structure predominates. When the health care organization is viewed from another perspective, it seems to function more as a mixed normative-utilitarian structure. With business orientation and the increasing unionization of workers in the health care field, the utilitarian model seems to be a more appropriate category.

A coercive element is sometimes introduced into the health care setting, as when individuals are assigned to health care jobs in wartime as an alternative to military service or when hospital volunteer work is given as part of a court sentence. In such cases, a mix of normative-utilitarian-coercive authority is required and the manager must adopt a variety of leadership and motivational styles in working with the different groups in the organization. Worker or member motivation and the source of the manager's authority differ for these different groups.

In the Katz and Kahn genotypic classification, the health care organization fits two categories, again indicating the mixed mandates of such entities. As an organization concerned with restoration, the health care establishment functions to maintain society. It also performs adaptive functions when higher education and research are major goals.

CLASSIC BUREAUCRACY

Bureaucracy is such a common aspect of organizational life that it is often treated as synonymous with formal organization. The study of bureaucracy in its pure form was the work of the structuralists in management history: Max Weber, Peter Blau and W. Richard Scott, and Robert K. Merton. Weber's work is pivotal, since it presented the chief characteristics of bureaucracy in its pure form. Weber regarded the bureaucratic form as an ideal type and described the theoretically perfect organization.[5] In effect, he codified the major characteristics of formal organizations in which rational decision making and administrative efficiency are maximized. He did not include the dysfunctional aspects or the aberrations that occur when any characteristics are exaggerated, as in the popular equation of bureaucracy with "red tape." From the works of Weber and others, a composite set of characteristics or descriptive statements may be derived concerning the formal organization or bureaucracy[6]:

1. size
    a. large scale of operations, large number of clients, high volume of work, and wide geographical dispersion
    b. communication beyond face-to-face, personal interaction
2. division of labor
    a. systematic division of labor
    b. clear limits and boundaries of work units
3. specialization
    a. a result of division of labor
    b. each unit's pursuit of its goal without conflict because of clear boundaries
    c. areas of specialization and division of labor that correspond with official jurisdictional areas
    d. specific sphere of competence for each incumbent
    e. promotion of staff expertise
    f. technical qualifications for officeholders
4. official jurisdictional areas
    a. fixed by rules, laws, or administrative regulation
    b. specific official duties for each office
5. rational-legal authority
    a. formal authority attached to the official position or office
    b. authority delegated in a stable way
    c. clear rules delineating the use of authority
    d. depersonalization of office; emphasis on the position, not the person
6. principle of hierarchy
    a. firmly ordered system of supervision and subordination
    b. each lower office or position under the control and supervision of a higher one
    c. systematic checking and reinforcing of compliance
7. rules
    a. providing continuity of operations
    b. promoting stability, regardless of changing personnel
    c. routinizing the work
    d. generating "red tape"

8. impersonality
    a. impersonal orientation by officials
    b. emphasis on the rules and regulations
    c. disregard of personal considerations in clients and employees
    d. rational judgments free of personal feeling
    e. social distance among successive levels of the hierarchy
    f. social distance from clients
9. the bureaucrat
    a. career with system of promotion to reward loyalty and service
    b. special training required because of specialization, division of labor, or technical rules
    c. separation of manager from owner
    d. compensation by salaries, not dependent on direct payment by clients
10. the bureau (or office or administrative unit)
    a. formulation and recording of all administrative acts, decisions, and rules
    b. enhancement of systematic interpretation of norms and enforcement of rules
    c. written documents, equipment, and support staff employed to maintain records
    d. office management based on expert, specialized training
    e. physical property, equipment, and supplies clearly separate from personal belongings and domicile of the officeholder

These characteristics are interwoven, each flowing from the others; for example, the growing size necessitates a division of labor, which, in turn, fosters specialization.

One of the dreams of many direct patient care practitioners is a health care delivery system that does not become bogged down in formalities. The private practice model seems to offer the solution; if the private practice or small group practice flourishes, however, the characteristics of formal organizations inevitably begin to emerge, for example, specialization and division of labor, procedures for uniformity, some form of authority structure, and a variety of rules. The wisest approach seems to involve taking the best features of formal bureaucracy and making particular efforts to avoid the negative elements, such as impersonality. Family-centered approaches to health care or the team approach are models that tend to offset the impersonalization associated with large health care organizations.

CONSEQUENCES OF ORGANIZATIONAL FORM

Managers work in specific organizational environments, and their specific functions are shaped and modified by the organizational form, structure, and authority climate. Some specific consequences concern the following organizational characteristics:

- Size. The more layers in the hierarchy, the greater (potentially) the limits on managers' freedom in decision making. Their decisions may be subject to review at several levels, and more decisions may be imposed from these higher levels.
- Organizational Climate. The degree to which clients, workers, and other managers participate in planning and decision-making processes is determined in part by the authority climate. Managers may have to modify their management or leadership style if it is inconsistent with the organization's authority structure. The basis of motivation may vary. In the highly normative setting, for example, members willingly participate; in the coercive organization, the basis of motivation tends to rest on the avoidance of punishment.
- Degree of Bureaucracy. A highly bureaucratic organization may be associated with great predictability in routine practices but less innovation and more resistance to change. Efforts to offset distortion caused by layering in communication may constitute a large portion of the activities of a manager in a highly bureaucratic organization.
- Phase in the Life Cycle. The openness to innovation and the vigorous, aggressive undertakings through goal expansion and multiplication that characterize some stages of the life cycle may permit the manager to undertake a variety of activities that are precluded by concerns for organizational survival in other phases of the life cycle.

For these reasons, managers must assess the organizational setting and their own roles. The major concepts of the clientele network, organizational life cycle, and analysis of organizational goals are tools for such assessments. Their active use fosters in the manager an awareness of the overall organizational dynamics that shape managerial practice, worker interaction, and client service.

NOTES

1. Peter Blau and W.R. Scott, *Formal Organizations* (San Francisco: Chandler Publishing Company, 1962), 42.
2. Ibid., 43.
3. Amatai Etzioni, *A Comparative Analysis of Complex Organizations* (Glencoe, Ill.: The Free Press, 1961).
4. Daniel Katz and Robert L. Kahn, *The Social Psychology of Organizations* (New York: Wiley, 1967), 11.
5. Max Weber, *The Theory of Social and Economic Organization*, A.M. Henderson and Talcott Parsons, trans., and Talcott Parsons, ed. (Glencoe, Ill.: The Free Press, 1947), 324–86.
6. Ibid.

Chapter 15

The Clientele Network

CHAPTER OBJECTIVES

1. Define the concept of clientele network.
2. Identify the impact on management activities of each group in the clientele network.
3. Understand the significance of support, competition, and rivalry among groups within an organization.
4. Apply the concept of the clientele network to the health care setting.

A major charge given implicitly to any manager is the building of external relationships. In order to do this, the manager must identify critical relationships, develop satisfactory working relationships with the several key individuals and groups involved, and, finally, work at maintaining these relationships. With the conservation of organizational resources, time, money, and personnel as a mandate, the manager seeks to capitalize on available external sources of power, influence, advice, and support as well as to identify those areas of potential difficulty, such as competition and rivalry, erosion of client good will, and shifting client demand and loyalty. In an era of increasing regulation of health care, the contemporary manager in the health care setting must identify and comply with multiple sets of changing regulations and guidelines issued by federal and state government agencies as well as by the various accrediting agencies, such as the Joint Commission or the American Osteopathic Association.

Like a living organism, an organization exists in a dynamic environment to which it must continually adapt. The manager identifies these units and constructs a network of the pattern of interrelationships. Bertram Gross developed the concept of the clientele network (Figure 15-1), noting that any organization is usually surrounded by a complex array of people, units, and other organizations that interrelate with it on the basis of various roles. He called these people, units, and organizations the "publics with opinions."[1]

376

PUBLICS WITH OPINIONS

Figure 15-1 The Clientele Network. *Source:* Reprinted with permission of Macmillan from *Organizations and Their Managing.* Copyright © 1968 by the Free Press, a division of Macmillan Publishing Company.

Wherever the concept of organization is used, a department manager could well substitute individual service or department. Although such a department or service is obviously a part of the organization, the development of the clientele network for a unit within the organization yields information about the critical relationships, clients, adversaries, and supporters of that department. Department-level managers must be aware of the unique environment of their department or service as well as the overall environment of their organization.

CLIENTS

The most obvious and immediate individuals and groups who make significant demands on the organization are the clients. Gross used the term in a broad sense, that is, to refer to those for whom goods and services are provided by the organization.[2] Immediate, visible clients in health care, both for the organization and for any department directly involved in patient care services, are the patients.

The providers of direct health care services are immediate, visible clients for certain units within the organizations. The business office, the legal staff, and the medical record department offer support services to assist physicians, nurses, and social workers in the provision of patient care. Given the traditional and historical development of the modern hospital, it could be said that the physicians are a special class of clients in that the organization of the hospital or clinic gives them the necessary support personnel and services for patient care. Physicians in different specialties are clients of each other, since they depend on each other for consultative services and referrals.

Certain services may be placed into the client category vis-a-vis each other. Some service units, such as physical therapy, are income producing; because the resources obtained are used on behalf of the whole organization, other units may be considered clients of the income-producing units. The business office relies on the medical record service to supply certain documentation to satisfy financial claims, and the safety committee relies on the several patient care and administrative departments to supply the information necessary to perform its function.

The use of the broadest possible definition of client alerts the manager to the subtle facets of organizational relationships. The manager who recognizes the number of distinct client groups can more effectively monitor their several and sometimes conflicting demands for services.

Although one step removed from the immediate services or goods offered by the organization, less visible clients are nonetheless legitimate users of the services or goods. By identifying these secondary clients, the manager has a key to the primary and secondary goals of the organization or unit. In the many educational programs offered within health care organizations, for example, the sponsoring institutions (e.g., a college or university), the health professionals, and the technical students are secondary, less visible clients. Hospitals traditionally have direct patient care as a primary goal, with teaching and research as secondary goals. The ordering of priorities should stem from recognition of the multilevel client demands.

The same physicians who are immediate clients in terms of their need for support services for their direct patient care activities are less visible clients in terms of their need for opportunities for education and research. The employees of the organizations are, in a sense, less visible clients, since one of the organizational outputs is the provision of jobs. Occasionally in health care the provision of jobs is an explicit goal; the neighborhood health centers sponsored by the federal government were intended not only to provide health care services but also to afford job opportunities to area residents.

The clients twice removed from the immediate goal of the organization may be termed the remote clients. Many of these individuals and groups do not even know they are being served. In addition to patient care, teaching, and research, a third goal of health care organizations is generally given as the protection of the public at large, that is, remote clients.

The manager, in assessing the stated and implied goals, may readily identify them by analyzing the needs of primary, visible clients as well as those of the less visible and remote clients. If the client demand is relatively stable, the planning, organizing, and staffing functions of the manager may be done on the basis of some predictability; that which can be predicted can be reasonably controlled. Workflow, organizational pattern, and staffing needs may be assessed in a stable manner. The net effect is efficiency in the allocation of resources of money, space, and personnel.

There is within the client group a potential capacity to control the organization. When a business has only one major purchaser of its goods or an agency has only one group to serve, the clients could easily take charge of the organization, limiting its independence. On the other hand, the organization with multiple clients must set priorities, balance conflicting demands, and maneuver so as to satisfy several groups.

SUPPLIERS

Three categories of suppliers are given by Gross: (1) resource suppliers, (2) associates, and (3) supporters.[3]

Resource Suppliers

Since no organization is totally self-sufficient, it must take into itself the necessary resources, raw material, money, and good will that it needs to survive and function. In this sense, the organization is the client of other organizations.

Within the given organization, one department or service is the supplier of another. In assessing workflow patterns, this concept is useful in identifying which aspects of the work are within the unit's immediate control and which originate in one or several other departments. The medical record department is the client of several other units in this sense. The proper gathering of patient identification information is the work of the several admissions and intake units; a medical record department is dependent on these units for that part of the workflow. Resource suppliers, such as the ward clerk or secretary, control the medical record at the time of a patient's discharge; consequently, its timely receipt in the medical record department after discharge is somewhat dependent on that unit's workflow. A centralized, computerized data processing system is dependent in the same way. The laboratory, radiology department, physical therapy department, and occupational therapy department all depend on the nursing service literally to bring, send, or prepare the patient so that they can proceed with their own work in a predictable manner. Essential information for the formulation of job descriptions concerning interdepartmental relationships or for the development of cross-training programs within the organization is obtained from an awareness of those organizational components that act as resource suppliers to each other.

In the same sense, the chief executive officer can be seen as a resource supplier, making the final adjudication in the allocation of space, money, and personnel to the units. The manager of the department or service should know the needs of other departments and should develop strategic alliances in the competition for scarce resources.

Associates

Individuals or groups outside the organization who work cooperatively with the organization in a joint effort are associates of the organization.[4] Associates have a common interest and common work that unites them with the organization. The manager who recognizes the efforts of associates will actively obtain their cooperation. Through informal sharing of ideas among themselves, the various health care practitioners frequently act as associates to each other. The medical record practitioners from several area hospitals may collaborate informally on a release of information policy so that there is areawide consistency in dealing with requests for data from patient records. The medical technologists of a region may cooperate in a joint venture for blood-banking processes.

Supporters

Various politically, socially, and economically powerful individuals and groups in the society may be supporters of the organization. They mobilize "friendly power" for the organization, giving it encouragement and developing a climate of good will toward the organization. Such supporters can coordinate major activities, such as fund raising, public relations, and intermediate services for the organization. This type of support helps the organization to conserve its own resources for direct application to immediate goals, such as providing direct patient care. Individual organizations may quite simply lack the power to mobilize certain political or economic resources on their own behalf and may depend on a "friend in the castle" to help in these matters. The traditional pattern of appointing the political, social, and economic elite to the board of trustees in health care organizations is often an effort to mobilize such power on behalf of these organizations.

Occasionally, a nationally prominent figure demonstrates a particular interest in health care because of some personal experience with a particular health problem. In a sense, poliomyelitis, heart disease, and breast cancer received more attention because they affected a president or a member of his family. A leading political figure may work toward the passage of legislation on behalf of some specific health care need. A number of well-known entertainers and sports figures have supported fund-raising activities for one or another health care issues (e.g., the Jerry Lewis Telethon for Muscular Dystrophy). Such individuals command resources unavailable to a single institution.

The Lions Club programs to support eye care, the Easter Seal program in fund raising and coordination of volunteers to work with handicapped persons, and the Shriners' traditional support of health care for crippled children illustrate the typical activity of supporters. The traditional hospital auxiliary is yet another example of a support group. Supporters may help to coordinate activities to the mutual benefit of all participants, offsetting the destructive aspect of competition and facilitating compliance with standards set by controllers by making resources available for use by the organization.

Although an organization may not actively declare itself a supporter, the net effect of its activities may provide support. The concern of the American Civil Liberties Union for privacy in general, for example, has helped raise the social consciousness of the public toward all issues concerning privacy, thus helping health care institutions to develop guidelines for the restrictive release of information. In such situations, collaboration in the development of and lobbying for pertinent state legislation becomes possible.

ADVISERS

Although they are like supporters in some ways, advisers have more specific activities that tend to set trends for the industry. Advisers provide a particular form of resource or support through their advice. Gross stressed an important difference between supporters and advisers: The assistance and support of advisers helps the organization use its resources and the support it receives from other sources.[5] Advisers stand apart from the organization and often have a more impersonal relationship with the organization than do supporters.

The advice may be in the form of overall guidelines, position papers, data analysis, sample procedures and methods, or model legislation. Examples of documents that are advisory in nature include the American Hospital Association's *Guidelines on Patient Rights,* the American Medical Association's *Model Legislation Concerning Disabled Physicians,* and the American Health Information Management Association's *Position Paper on the Confidentiality of Patient Records.*

CONTROLLERS

Those individuals or groups who have power over the organization are controllers. Health care organizations must comply with the regulations of several federal and state government agencies, for example, as well as with the mandates of the various accrediting agencies. Table 15-1 gives a listing of organizations and agencies that have such control power. The level of detail varies greatly from the optimal standards stated by the Joint Commission to the highly detailed regulations (e.g., required room size) in a state law.

Certain controllers are internal to the organization and yet constitute a kind of separate organization. Workers as individuals are a part of the organization, but the unions that represent them stand outside the organization, exerting specific pressure on it. The governing board is an integral part of the hierarchical structure, but in some ways the board of trustees is separate from the line managers,

Table 15-1 Key Controllers

Controller	Requirement
Federal government	Conditions of participation for Medicare and Medicaid, special standards resulting from specific program funding and grants
State government	Institutional licensure regulations, individual professional licensure regulations
Local government	Zoning codes, fire and safety requirements
Accreditation bodies	Accreditation standards
Professional associations	Codes of conduct, professional educational requirements
Collective bargaining agreements	Detailed contract provisions
Organizational policy	Detailed provisions for each organizational unit
Various regulatory agencies	Personnel laws and regulations, such as Civil Rights Act, Workers' Compensation, Fair Labor Standards Act, Occupational Safety and Health Act
Third-party payers	Detailed contractual provisions concerning patient eligibility, mode of treatment covered, and similar provisions

who are controlled by the decisions made by the top-level management group. The assessment of the net effect of such controllers' input gives the manager a sense of clear boundaries for planning and decision making. However innovative an idea might be, for example, the manager must still keep management practices in line with these constraints.

Controllers may also impose conflicting regulations on the institution, such as the mandate of the federal government to maintain almost absolute confidentiality of alcohol and drug abuse records and the mandate of third-party payers to provide satisfactory evidence of treatment for reimbursement. Managers may be forced to change their managerial style as a result of certain constraints imposed by a controller (e.g., the details of a union contract may limit severely the use of a laissez-faire style of management). By means of survey questionnaires and site visits, the manager may assess the net effect of these multiple regulations on workflow, services offered, staffing patterns mandated, and job descriptions restricted and refined.

ADVERSARIES

Health care traditionally carries overtones of great compassion and deep charitable roots. Like any other organization, however, health care organizations have opponents and enemies as well as competitors and rivals. The rising cost of health care tends to make health care professionals and the organizations in which they work a source of conflict and even a target for opposition at the present time. Indeed, clients themselves at times take an adversarial stance.

Outright opponents or enemies are those individuals or groups who seek actively and aggressively to limit the organization in its activity. These opponents or enemies may have the power to bring an activity to a halt or to prohibit an activity from being started. For example, clients do not wish to have certain facilities, such as drug treatment centers or group homes for the mentally retarded, too close to their homes. Furthermore, they may want ample parking and easy access to their hospital, but they do not want to disturb the local housing units or the business areas. Zoning codes may be enforced in order to prevent the development of alternative treatment facilities or the expansion of existing facilities. Clients may withdraw financial support as evidence of displeasure.

The concept of competition is well understood and accepted in the economic arena. Within reasonable boundaries, competition is favorable for clients because it forces providers to make products or services better or more accessible. The sharp edge of competition is also evident in health care delivery, possibly because certain factors in contemporary culture are producing shifts in client loyalty. These factors include (1) erosion of strong ethnic and religious ties to one hospital or health center; (2) the passage of the Civil Rights Act, which removed certain barriers to access; (3) urban and suburban migration patterns; (4) the lowered birth rate; and (5) the passage of the National Health Care Planning and Resource Development Act, which mandated the certificate-of-need process and created the health systems agencies (HSAs).

Given a dropping inpatient census, a hospital may compete actively with a free-standing medical clinic by offering its own outpatient clinic services. In order to attract patients, one obstetrics unit may offer the latest in fetal monitoring, while another may stress family-centered childbirth. An urban medical school or medical center may offer the benefits of highly specialized techniques to offset a census drop due to the fact that certain clients seek to avoid the city. A hospital seeking HSA approval for an expanded facility or for some special activity may engage in active outreach to increase its patient population.

Rivals, according to Gross, are those who produce different products, but compete for resources, assistance, and support.[6] In the health care setting, specialty hospitals could be considered the rivals of general hospitals (e.g., a children's hospital versus a pediatrics ward in a general hospital, a lying-in hospital versus an obstetrics unit). When the emphasis in definition is placed on competition for the same resources, there is evidence of rivalry among health care institutions for scarce personnel (e.g., registered nurses for the 3 P.M. to 11 P.M. shift, trained medical transcriptionists, physicians for the emergency room).

Within an organization, one department may be cast as rival to another for needed space, additional personnel, and special funds. Managers may find that the same departments that are clients may also be supporters and rivals.

Additional discussion of competition and rivalry may be found in the examination of bureaucratic imperialism (Chapter 16) and conflict and cooperation (Chapter 8).

CASE STUDY A

Many individuals and groups affect the management of a single unit. The elements of the clientele network are identified in this review of the Registry of Melrose Occupational Therapists, a private practice group that includes five full-time and two part-time therapists. The organization was developed by Mary S., who is now the president of the corporation. The group members hold contracts with three home health agencies and two nursing homes. Mary S. supervises the members, who treat patients daily. The group members are paid for their work on a fee-for-service basis, meaning that they are paid for direct service only. Fringe benefits are not available, because the therapists are not employed by the agency in the traditional manner.

The immediate clients of the group are clearly its patients, who either reside in their own homes or in a nursing home. When Mary S. receives a referral, she forwards the request to the appropriate therapist, who then visits the patient, performs an evaluation, and designs a treatment regime. Physical, emotional, social, and cognitive aspects of the patient's illness must be considered during the treatment process. Frequently, the families of these patients must be included in the therapist's treatment.

Less visible clients are the agencies that hold contracts with the group. The agencies determine the services that are required and the rate of reimbursement. They supervise the quality of the services and will take action if the services are not meeting the needs of the patients. The agencies need the therapists to provide these selective services, thus creating a mutuality of interaction.

The Melrose group members use their professional knowledge and skills to promote independent living for their patients. At the same time, the members must satisfy the needs of their other clients, the home health agencies and the nursing homes that hold contracts for their services. The existence of several client groups influences the decision making and priority setting in which the manager of this group engages.

Resource suppliers offer (1) material goods, such as splinting equipment; (2) emotional support, such as a newspaper article that describes a new type of service; and (3) financial support, such as items donated to raise money for special needs. Each agency is a resource supplier because it supplies necessary administrative items, such as the charting forms for documenting patient progress and the payment for each patient treatment. Furthermore, some agencies provide the therapist with splinting supplies, adaptive equipment, and exercise modalities. Each of these items may seem somewhat inconsequential individually, but the cumulative effect of resource provision may spell economic success or failure for a private contractual group such as this small agency. Attention to such detail also reduces interorganizational misunderstanding and conflict, freeing energies to be directed at patient care.

The Melrose group also acts as a resource supplier. In one nursing home, group members order eating equipment and toileting supplies for the nursing staff, thus freeing nursing personnel for direct patient care. The therapist also constructs simple aids to improve wheelchair and bed positioning.

Susan S., a Melrose group member, and Barry Z., a member of the Austin Practice, are developing a check-off progress note. Barry and Susan are designing this progress note to facilitate documentation of patient progress. Therapists can check off patient services that are routine and use the space at the bottom of the progress note form to focus on new areas. The form will benefit members of both private practices. Barry Z. is an associate of the Melrose group; Susan S. serves in the same capacity for the Austin group.

The Melrose group is fortunate to have a supporter in the college of health professions at the local university. Alice D. teaches in the college's occupational therapy department. When prospective clients call to ask for community services, Alice refers the calls to this private practice group.

Advisers can be compared to supporters, but their activities are more special-ized and their relationship is further removed from the organization. John G., a lawyer who drafted the state licensure bill, is an adviser to the Melrose group. This lawyer's research for the licensure bill helped to delineate clearly the roles of the physical and the occupational therapists, and the Melrose group used his services when they developed guidelines for their own practice. The activities related to the drafting of the licensure bill provided this lawyer with a sensitivity to the problems that arise in daily practice within these specialties.

Controllers are evident in the variety of contractual relationships into which the Melrose group must enter. The group holds contracts with the Bureau of Health Insurance, the Worker Compensation Bureau, Sun Insurance Company, Blue Cross and Blue Shield, Consolidated Medical Service/Health Maintenance Organization, and the Anderson Nursing Home Association. Each of these or-ganizations has established its own guidelines and regulations concerning reim-bursement. The individuals who work for the Melrose group define their list of reimbursable services to fit the criteria of the controller; the nature of these decisions shapes the scope of the practice.

Other controllers include the State Licensing Board and the American Occupational Therapy Association, the only national organization for occupa-tional therapists. The association provides guidelines for private practice, ethics, and standards. The American Physical Therapy Association and other profes-sional groups provide guidelines for delivering patient services.

The Melrose group seems to have no outright opponents and enemies, but there is the natural competition with other private practice groups. The members once concentrated on pediatric evaluation, but the interests of the group mem-bers now extend to nursing homes. Northwood Health Services, which has been in the nursing home contract service business for several years, is a competitor of the Melrose group. Adversaries need not be enemies. In health care it is advisable to work cooperatively. Members of the groups mentioned here wel-come the competition, because they feel that it improves their practice and pro-vides a stimulus to excellence.

CASE STUDY B

A tabulation method can be used to analyze a departmental clientele net-work. The development of such a reference tool for the internal environment of the organization provides the manager with much information concerning rela-tionships to be developed, aspects of the workflow to be considered, and regu-lations and guidelines that must be satisfied. The following is the clientele net-work of a spinal cord treatment service in a physical therapy department:

I. Clients
  A. Immediate clients
    1. Patients on the spinal cord injury service
    2. Hospital personnel assigned to the spinal cord injury service
  B. Secondary clients
    1. Family members
    2. Hospital medical staff for in-service education and clarification of policies and procedures
    3. Physical therapy students on clinical affiliation
    4. Local hospitals requesting information on special programs dealing with treatment of the spinal cord–injured patient
  C. Remote clients
    1. Local hospitals
    2. Home health agencies
II. Suppliers
  A. Resources
    1. Physicians within the hospital who refer patients to the spinal cord injury unit
    2. Medical supply companies that supply equipment for both the patients and the department
    3. Bureau of Vocational Rehabilitation, which covers the cost of treatment and equipment
    4. Hospital transport system
  B. Associates
    1. National spinal cord treatment centers
    2. Other direct patient services (e.g., nursing, occupational therapy, speech, psychology, social services)
    3. Home health agencies
    4. Professional journals
  C. Supporters
    1. Hospital physicians and residents
    2. Community service organizations
    3. Auxiliary organizations serving the spinal cord service
    4. Medical supply companies
    5. County Wheelchair Sports Association
    6. Public relations department of the hospital
III. Advisers
  A. Hospital administrators
  B. Other direct patient care services within the hospital
  C. Insurance companies

IV. Controllers
    A. Accreditation agencies
        1. Joint Commission on Accreditation of Healthcare Organizations
        2. Commission on Accreditation of Rehabilitation Facilities (CARF)
        3. Accrediting Council for Graduate Medical Education for Residency Program (CGME)
    B. Federal government
        1. Medicare reimbursement regulations
        2. Equal employment opportunity
        3. Working conditions
    C. State government
        1. Licensing regulations for physical therapists
        2. Medicaid reimbursement regulations
    D. County Hospital Association
    E. Professional association codes of ethics
    F. Unions
    G. Hospital policies
V. Adversaries
    A. Opponents and enemies
        1. Consumer groups
        2. Hospital personnel resistant to change
    B. Rivals and competitors
        1. Other local rehabilitation centers sharing the same clientele network

---

NOTES

1. Bertram Gross, *Organizations and Their Managing* (New York: The Free Press, 1968), 114.
2. Ibid.
3. Ibid., 119–21.
4. Ibid., 121.
5. Ibid., 122.
6. Ibid., 130.

Chapter 16

Organizational Survival Strategies

CHAPTER OBJECTIVES

1. Identify the need for organizational survival as a fundamental goal of organizational effort.
2. Identify selected management strategies that are used to foster organizational survival: bureaucratic imperialism; cooptation; hibernation and adaptation; and goal succession, expansion, and multiplication.
3. Identify the phases in the organizational life cycle that reflect major changes.
4. Relate the phases of the organizational life cycle to the functions of the manager.
5. Identify the organizational change process.
6. Relate the actions of the manager as change agent to the change process.
7. Identify specific strategies for initiating change in organizations.

Organizational survival and growth are implicit organizational goals, requiring the investment of energy and resources. Normally, only higher levels of management need give attention to organizational survival; it may be taken for granted by most members of the institution, who may even take actions that threaten survival (e.g., a prolonged strike). There may be an unwillingness to admit the legitimacy of survival as a goal because of its seeming self-serving aspect. Managers disregard the concept of organizational (including departmental and unit) survival only at their peril, however.

So fundamental is the goal of organizational survival that it underpins all other goals. Fostering this goal contributes to the satisfaction of the more explicit goals of the group or organization. Bertram Gross described this implicit goal as "the iron law of survival." The unwritten law of every organization, he said, is that its survival is an absolute prerequisite for its serving any interest whatsoever.[1]

Survival is articulated as a goal in certain phases of organizational development. The clientele network includes competitors, rivals, enemies, and opponents that must be faced. Certain threats to organizational survival may be identified:

- lack of strong, formal leadership after the early charismatic leadership of the founders
- too rapid change either within or outside the organization
- shifting client demand, with either the loss of clients or with the increased exercise of control by clients
- competition from stronger organizations
- high turnover rate in the rank and file or the leadership
- failure to recognize and accept organizational survival as a legitimate, although not the sole, organizational purpose

These factors drain from the organization the energy that should be goal directed.

An organization ensures its survival through certain strategies and processes, such as bureaucratic imperialism, cooptation, patterns of adaptation, goal multiplication and expansion, use of organizational roles, conflict limitation, and integration of the individual into the organization. Astute managers recognize such patterns of organizational behavior and assess them realistically. A weak organization or unit cannot pull together the money, resources, and power to serve clients effectively.

BUREAUCRATIC IMPERIALISM

Organizations develop to foster a particular goal, serve a specific client group, or promote the good of a certain group. In effect, an organization stakes out its territory. Thus, a professional association seeks to represent the interests of members who have something in common, such as specific academic training and professional practice. A hospital or home health agency seeks to serve a particular area. A union focuses on the needs of one or several categories of worker. A political party attempts to bring in members who hold a particular political philosophy. A government agency seeks to serve a specific constituency.

The classic definition of bureaucratic imperialism reflects the idea that a bureaucratic organization exerts a kind of pressure to develop a particular client group and then to expand it. It becomes imperialistic in the underlying power struggle and competition that ensues when any other group seeks to deal with the same clients, members, or area of jurisdiction. Matthew Holden, Jr., coined the term *bureaucratic imperialism* and defined it in the context of federal government agencies that must consider such factors as clients to be served, political aspects to be assessed, and benefits to be shared among administrative officials and key political clients. According to Holden's definition of the concept, bureaucratic imperialism is "a matter of interagency conflict in which two or more agencies try to assert permanent control over the same jurisdiction, or in which one agency actually seeks to take over another agency as well as the jurisdiction of that agency."² The idea of agency can be expanded to include any organization, the various components of the clientele network can be substituted for the constituency, and the role of manager can replace that of the administrative politician in those organizations that are not in the formal political setting.

Managers in many organizations can recognize the elements of this competitive mode of interaction among organizations. There may even be such competition among departments and units within an organization. In the health care field, competition may be seen in the areas of professional licensure and practice, accrediting processes for the organizations as a whole, the delineation of clients to be served, and similar areas.

Professional licensure has the effect of annexing specific "territory" as the proper domain of a given professional group, but other groups may seek to carry out the same, or at least similar, activities. For example, there is the question of the role of chiropractic in traditional health care settings. Is the use of radiological techniques the exclusive jurisdiction of physicians and trained radiological technicians or should the law be changed to permit chiropractors greater use of these techniques? Psychiatrists question the expanding role of others who have entered the field of mental health. As each health care profession develops, the question of jurisdiction emerges.

The accrediting process in health care reflects similar struggles for jurisdiction. Which shall be the definitive accreditation process for mental health facilities—that approved by the American Psychiatric Association or that approved by the Joint Commission? Should all these processes be set aside, leaving state governments only to exercise such control through the licensure of institutions?

Other examples may be drawn from the health care setting. There is the jurisdictional dispute over blood banking between the American Red Cross and the American Association of Blood Banks, as well as the competition of health maintenance organizations (HMOs) with the more traditional Blue Cross and Blue Shield plans and commercial medical insurance companies. The area of health care planning also reflects this territorial question; several agencies, including both government and private agencies, require hospitals and other health care institutions to submit to several sets of planning mandates.

Although the charitable nature of health care has been emphasized traditionally, the elements of competition and underlying conflict must be recognized. With shifts in patient populations and changes in each health care profession, health care managers must assess the effects of bureaucratic imperialism in a realistic manner. The competition engendered by bureaucratic imperialism and the resultant total or partial "colonization" of an organizational unit or client group may be functional. Holden noted that conflict not only forces organizational regrouping by clarifying client loyalty and wishes but also sharpens support for the agency or unit that "wins." Furthermore, it disrupts the bureaucratic form from time to time, causing a healthy review of client need, organizational purpose, and structural pattern.

COOPTATION

Another method that organizations use to help ensure their survival is cooptation, an organizational strategy for adapting and responding to change. Philip Selznick described and labeled this strategy, which is viewed as both cooperative and adaptive. He defined cooptation as "an adaptive response on the part of the organization in response to the social forces in its environment; by this means, the organization averts threats to its stability by absorbing new elements into the leadership of the organization."[3] The organization, in effect, shares organizational power by absorbing these new elements. Selznick called it a realistic adjustment to the centers of institutional strength.[4]

Formal versus Informal Cooptation

In formal cooptation, the symbols of authority and administrative burdens are shared but no substantial power is transferred. The organization does not permit the coopted group to interfere with organizational unity of command. Normal bureaucratic processes tend to provide sufficient checks and balances on any coopted group, just as they tend to restrict the actions of managers. Through formal cooptation, however, the organization seeks to demonstrate its accessibility to its various publics.

In health care, the cooptation process is suggested by the practice of appointing "ordinary" citizens to the board of trustees. Community mental health centers and some neighborhood health centers tend to emphasize consumer or community representation. Health planning agencies include both providers and consumers in planning for health care on a regional or statewide basis. The formalization of nursing home ombudsmen or patient care councils is still another example of this process.

Professional associations in those disciplines that have technical-level practitioners have sought to open their governing processes in response to the growing strength of the technical-level group. Increases in numbers, greater degree of training, further specialization, and a general emphasis on the democratic process and provision of rights for all members have fostered changes in these associations. Without cooperative adaptation to such internal changes, there is a risk that additional associations will be formed, possibly weakening the parent organization.

When an organization seeks to deal less overtly with shifting centers of power and to maintain the legitimacy of its own power, cooptation may be informal in nature. For example, managers may meet unofficially with informally delegated representatives of clients, employees, or outside groups. Organizational leaders may deal regularly with some groups, but there are no visible changes in the official leadership structures. No new positions are created; committee membership remains intact. The emphasis is on the substance of power, not its symbolic forms, such as title, official appointment, or power to vote. Informal cooptation may be more important than formal cooptation because of its emphasis on true power, although each form serves its unique purpose. An organization can blend formal and informal cooptation processes, since they are not mutually exclusive.

Control of Coopted Groups

Although the coopted group could gain strength and attempt to consolidate power, this does not happen frequently for several reasons. First, the organization has the means of controlling participation. For example, only limited support may be given to the group; there may be no physical space, money, or staff available to give to the coopted group, or management could simply withhold support. Another possible course is to assign so much activity to the coopted group that it cannot succeed easily. Key leaders of the coopted group generally retain their regular work assignments but now have in addition projects and tasks relating to their special causes. Coopted leaders also become the buffer individuals in the organization, since the group has placed its trust in them and looks for results faster than they can be produced. Such leaders may find their base of action eroded and their activity turning into a thankless task.

In a more Machiavellian approach, organizational authorities could schedule meetings at inconvenient hours or control their agenda in such a way that issues of significance to the coopted group are too far down on the list of discussion items to be dealt with under the time constraints. Absolute insistence on parliamentary procedure may also be used as a weapon of control; a novice in the use of Robert's *Rules of Order* is at a distinct disadvantage when compared with a seasoned expert.

The subtle psychological process that occurs in the coopted individual who is taken into the formal organization as a distinct outsider acts as another controlling measure. The person suddenly becomes, for this moment, one of the power holders and derives new status. Certain perquisites also are granted. Consumer representatives, for example, may find their way paid, quite legitimately, for special conferences or fact-finding trips to study a problem. The individual, in becoming privy to more data and sometimes to confidential data, may start to "see things" from the organization's point of view.

Certain subtle social barriers may make the coopted individual uncomfortable, even though they may not be raised intentionally and may be part of the normal course of action for the group. For example, a female nonvoting representative of a constituency who has been invited to attend a portion of a board meeting at an exclusive downtown club where women are permitted only in special areas may well be overwhelmed when ushered into the suite where the power elite sit at a long table, portfolios closed, business seemingly concluded except for this final agenda item—her cause. Even an informal setting, such as a swimming party or golfing match, may be intimidating if the coopted person feels out of place.

Individuals representing pressure groups find that their own time and energies are limited, even if they desire power. Other activities continue to demand their energies. In addition, certain issues lose popularity, and pressure groups may find their power base has eroded. Finally, the agenda items that were causes of conflict may become the recurring business of the organization. The conflict may become routinized, and the structure to deal with it may become a part of the formal organization. In the collective bargaining process, for example, the union is a part of the organization, and its leaders have built-in protection from factors that erode effective participation. Labor union officials commonly have certain reductions in workload so that they may attend to union business, space may be provided for their offices or meetings, and they may seek meetings with management as often as executives seek sessions with them. Cooptation has occurred but without a loss of identity of the coopted group. In health care organizations, consumer participation has become part of the organizations' continuing activity through the development of a more stable process for consumer input, such as the HSA and the community governing board models.

HIBERNATION AND ADAPTATION

To maintain its equilibrium, an organization must adapt to changing inputs. This adjustment may take a passive form of hibernation in which the institution enters a phase of retrenchment. Cutting losses may be the sensible option. If efforts to maintain an acceptable census in certain hospital units, such as obstetrics or pediatrics, are unsuccessful, there may be an administrative decision to close those units and concentrate on providing quality patient care in the remaining services. An organization may adjust or adapt to changing inputs more actively by anticipating them. Staff specialists may be brought in, equipment and physical facilities updated, and goals restated. Finally, the overall corporate form may be restructured as a permanent reorganization that formalizes the cumulative effects of changes. A hospital may move from private sponsorship to a state-related, affiliated status, or a health care center may become the base service unit for mental health or mental retardation programs in the area.

The relationships among the concepts of hibernation, adaptation, and permanent change can be seen in the following case history of a state mental hospital. After the state legislature cut the budget of all state mental hospitals, the institution director began to set priorities for services so that the institution could survive. The least productive departments were asked to decrease their staff. The rehabilitation department lost two aide positions. The institution director had to force the organization into a state of hibernation in order to accomplish some essential conservation of resources.

The director of rehabilitation services revised the department goals to improve the chances of departmental survival. After closing ancillary services, the director concentrated staff on visible areas of the hospital and asked them to make their work particularly praiseworthy. At the same time, the director emphasized the need to document services so that patients' progress in therapy programs could be demonstrated. The director adapted to the change in the organization.

The program changes proved successful. The director of the rehabilitation department consolidated the changes and modified the department's goals. Instead of offering periodic programs to adolescent, neurological, geriatric, and acute care patients, the staff would concentrate on acutely ill geriatric patients. The staff applied for funds that were available to treat this population. At the same time, the staff determined that the adolescent unit could benefit from their services. Although funds were shrinking, the staff serviced this unit because needs in that area were unmet. The director and the staff decided to apply for private funds to service neurological and acute care cases so that these programs could also continue. By adopting a combined strategy of hibernation and adaptation, with alternate plans for expansion, the department director was able to foster not only departmental survival, but, ultimately, departmental growth.

GOAL SUCCESSION, MULTIPLICATION, AND EXPANSION

Because an organization that effectively serves multiple client groups can attract money, materials, and personnel more readily than an organization with a more limited constituency, leaders may seek actively to expand the original goals of the organization. In addition to the pressures in the organizational environment that may force the organization to modify its goals as an adaptive response, success in reaching organizational goals may enable managers to focus on expanded or even new goals. The terms *goal succession, goal expansion,* and *goal multiplication* are used to describe the process in which goals are modified, usually in a positive manner.

Amatai Etzioni described this tendency of organizations to find new goals when old ones have been realized or cannot be attained. In goal succession, one goal is reached and is succeeded by a new one.[5] Etzioni cited David Sill's analysis of the goal evolution of the Foundation for Infantile Paralysis (March of Dimes). Having achieved its goals of arousing public interest in infantile paralysis and raising money for research and assistance to its victims, the organization could have ceased operations. Instead, it continued to function through its network of volunteers, national leaders, and central staff to achieve a new goal: prevention of birth defects.[6]

Sometimes an organization takes on additional goals because the original goals are relatively unattainable. A church may add a variety of social services to attract members when the worship forms and doctrinal substance per se do not increase the church's membership. A missionary group may offer a variety of health care or educational services when its direct evangelical methods cannot be used. The original goal is not abandoned, but it is sought indirectly; more tangible goals of service and outreach succeed this primary goal.

Goal expansion is the process in which the original goal is retained and enlarged with variations. Colleges and universities expand their traditional educational goals to include continuing education. The Joint Commission continues to focus primarily on inpatient acute care hospital accreditation but has expanded its standards and accreditation process to include home care, outpatient, and emergency care units. A collective bargaining unit negotiates specific benefits for its workers and takes on the administrative processing of certain elements, such as the pension fund; the basic goal of improving the circumstances of the workers is retained and expanded beyond immediate economic benefits. Another example of goal expansion may be seen in the work of the Red Cross. Organized to deal with disaster relief in World War I, it subsequently expanded its work to assist in coordinating relief from all disasters, regardless of cause. In all these examples, the basic goal is retained and the new ones derived from it; the new goals are closely related and are essentially extensions of the original goal.

Goal multiplication is also a process in which an original goal is retained and new ones added. In this case, however, the new goals reflect the organization's effort to diversify. Goal multiplication is often the natural outgrowth of success. A hospital may offer patient care as its traditional, primary goal. To this it may add the goal of education of physicians, nurses, and other health care professionals. Because excellence in education is frequently related to the adequacy of the institution's research programs, research subsequently may become a goal. The hospital may take on a goal of participating in social reform, seeking to undertake affirmative action hiring plans and to foster employment within its neighborhood. It may offer special training programs for those who are unemployed in its area or for those who are physically or mentally impaired. It may coordinate extensive social services in order to assist patients and their families with both immediate health care problems and the larger social and economic problems they face.

Similar examples can be found in the business sector. A large hotel-motel corporation, with its resources for dealing with temporary living quarters, may go into the nursing home industry or the drug and alcohol treatment facility business by offering food, laundry, and housekeeping services; it may even operate a chain of convalescent or of alcohol and drug rehabilitation centers itself. Several real estate firms might consolidate their efforts in direct sale of homes and then offer mortgage services as an additional program. Organizations take on a variety of goals as a means of diversification; resources are directed toward satisfaction of all the goals. Such multiplication of goals is seen as a positive state of organizational growth.

ORGANIZATIONAL LIFE CYCLE

Organizational change can be monitored through the analysis of an organization's life cycle. This concept is drawn from the pattern seen in living organisms. In management and administrative literature, the development of this model stems from the work of Marver Bernstein, who analyzed the stages of evolution and growth of independent federal regulatory commissions.[7] This model of the life cycle can be applied to advantage by any manager who wishes to analyze a particular management setting.

The organization is assessed, not in chronological years, but in phases of growth and development. No absolute number of years can be assigned to each phase, and any attempt to do so in order to predict characteristics would force and possibly distort the model. The value of organizational analysis by means of the life cycle lies in its emphasis on characteristics of the stages rather than the years. For example, the neighborhood health centers established in the 1960s under Office of Economic Opportunity sponsorship had a relatively short life span in comparison with the life span of some large urban hospitals that are approaching a century or more of service. Both types of organizations have experienced the phases of the life cycle, with the former having completed the entire phase through decline and—in its original form—extinction.

The phases of the organizational life cycle usually meld into one another, just as they do in the biological model. Human beings do not suddenly become adolescents, adults, or senior citizens; so, too, organizations normally move from one phase to another at an imperceptible rate with some blurring of boundaries. Finally, not every organization reflects in detail every characteristic of each phase. The emphasis is on the cluster of characteristics that are predominant at a specific time.

Gestation

In this early formative stage, there is a gradual recognition and articulation of need or shared purpose. This stage often predates the formal organization;

indeed, a major characteristic of this period is the movement from informal to formal organization. The impetus for organizing is strong, since it is necessary to bring together in an organized way the prime movers of the fledgling organization, its members (workers), and its clients.

Leadership tends to be strong and committed, and members are willing to work hard. Members' identification with organizational goals is strong, because the members are in the unique situation of actualizing their internalized goals; in contrast, those who become part of the institution later must subsequently internalize the institution's objectives. Members of the management team find innovation the order of the day. Creative ideas meet with ready acceptance, since there is no precedent to act as a barrier to innovation. If there is a precedent in a parent organization, it may be cast off easily as part of the rejection of the old organization. A self-selection process also occurs, with individuals leaving if they do not agree with the form the organizational entity is taking. This is largely a flexible process, free of the formal resignation and separation procedures that come later.

Youth

The early enthusiasm of the gestational phase carries over into the development of a formal organization. Idealism and high hopes continue to dominate the psychological atmosphere. The creativity of the gestational period is channeled toward developing an organization that will be free of the problems of similar institutions. There is a strong camaraderie among the original group of leaders and members. Organizational patterns have a certain inevitability, however. If a creative new organization is successful, it is likely to experience an increase in clients that will force it to formalize policies and procedures rapidly in order to handle the greater demand for service.

Some crisis may occur that precipitates expansion earlier than planned. A health center may have a plan for gradual neighborhood outreach, for example, but a sudden epidemic of flu may bring an influx of clients before it is staffed adequately. Management must make rapid adjustments in clinic hours and staffing patterns to meet the demand for specific services and, at the same time, to continue its plan for comprehensive health screening. A center for the mentally retarded may schedule one opening date, but a court order to vacate a large, decaying facility may require the new center to accept the immediate transfer of many patients. Routine, recurring situations are met by increasingly complex procedures and rules. Additional staff is needed, recruited, and brought into the organization, perhaps even in a crash program rather than through the gradual integration of new members.

At this point, a new generation of worker enters the organization. These workers are one phase removed from the era of idealism and deeply shared commitment to the organization's goals. The organizational structure (e.g., workflow, job descriptions, line and staff relationships, and roles and authority) is tested. For the newcomer brought in at the management level, formal position or hierarchical office is the primary base of authority. Other members of the management team, as the pioneers, know each other's strengths and weaknesses intimately, but these managers may need to test the newcomer's personal attributes and technical competence. Sometimes, because the new organization attempts to deal with some problem in an innovative manner, an individual health care practitioner is hired in a nontraditional role; not only the professional and technical competence but also the managerial competence of that individual is tested.

Communication networks are essential in any organization. During an organization's youth, it is necessary to rely on formal communication, because the informal patterns are not yet well developed, except within the core group. This lack of an easy, anonymous, informal communication network forces individuals to communicate mainly along formal lines of authority. The core group may become more and more closed, more and more "in," relying on well-developed, secure relationships that stem from a shared history in the developing organization, while the newcomers form a distinct "out" group.

The jockeying for power and position may be intense. If managers hold an innovative office, those who oppose such creative organizational patterns may exert significant pressure to acquire jurisdiction or to force a return to traditional ways. Since there may be much innovation in the overall organizational pattern, managers have little or no precedent against which they can measure their actions.

Certain problems center on the implementation of the original plans. The planners may start to experience frustration with managers who enter the organization during this period of formalization. Perhaps the original plans need modification; perhaps the innovative, ideal approach of the original group is not working, largely because of the change in the size of the organization. The line managers find themselves in the difficult situation of seeming to fail at the task on the one hand and being unable to make the original planners change their view on the other. The promise of innovation becomes empty, however, if the original planners guard innovation as their prerogative and refuse to accept other ideas.

In the youth phase of an organization, more time must be devoted to orientation and similar formal processes of integrating new individuals into the organization. Certain difficulties may be encountered in recruiting additional supervisors and professional practitioners; for example, there may be no secure retirement funds, no group medical and life insurance, and no similar benefits that are predicated on long-term investments and large membership. Salary ranges may be modest in comparison with those of more established organizations simply because insufficient time has passed for the development of adequate resources. The strong normative sense of idealism may have a negative effect on potential workers as well as a positive one; a certain dedication to the organization's cause may be expected, and it may also be assumed that personnel should be willing to work hard without being rewarded monetarily.

Bernstein stressed the increased concern for organizational survival in this youthful stage. The organization may become less innovative, because it is not sure of its strength. It may choose to fight only those battles in which victory is certain. In the case of regulatory bodies, which were Bernstein's major focus, the businesses subject to regulation may be perceived as stronger than the agency itself. In a health care organization, the new unit may be treated as a stepchild of related health care institutions. A new community mental health center or a home care organization, for example, may have to choose between competing with older, traditional units within the parent organization and being completely independent, still competing for resources but with less legitimacy of claim. A struggle not unlike the classic parent-adolescent conflict may emerge. Thus, organizational energy may go into an internal struggle for survival rather than into serving clients and expanding goals.

If the client groups are well defined and no other group or institution is offering the same service, a youthful organization may flourish. A burn unit in a hospital may have an excellent chance of survival as an organization because of the specificity of its clients as compared, for example, with the chance of a general medical clinic's survival. A similar positive climate may foster the development of units for treatment of spinal cord injury or for rehabilitation of the hand as specialized services. In effect, a highly specialized client group may afford a unit or an organization a virtual monopoly, which will tend to place the unit or organization in a position of strength.

Middle Age

The multiple constraints on the organization at middle age are compounded by several factors. In addition to the external influences that shape the work of the organization, there are internal factors that must be dealt with, such as the organizational pattern, the growing bureaucratic form, the weight of decision by precedent, and an increasing number of traditions.

On the other hand, the organization also reaps many benefits from middle age. Many activities are routine and predictable; roles are clear; and communication, both formal and informal, is relatively reliable. These years are potentially stable and productive. There is a reasonable receptivity to new ideas, but middle age is not usually a time of massive or rapid change and disruption, even the positive disruption resulting from major innovation. The manager in an organization in its middle age performs the basic traditional management processes in a relatively predictable manner.

Periods of rejuvenation are precipitated by a variety of events. A new leader may act as a catalytic agent, bringing new vision to the organization; for example, the president of a corporation may push for goal expansion by introducing a new line of products, or an aggressive hospital administrator may push for the development of an alternate health care service model. Mergers and affiliations with new and developing types of health care institutions, such as HMOs, community mental health centers, and home care programs, may be the catalyst. Although primarily negative events, the fiscal chaos associated with bankruptcy or the loss of accreditation as a hospital may cause the organization to reassess its goals and restructure its form, thus giving itself a new lease on life.

Some external crisis or change of articulated values in the larger society may make the organization vital once again. The recent emergence of alternate modes of communal living reflects individuals' search for a mode of living that combats the alienation of urban society; organizations that provide alternative modes of living can be revitalized because of this renewed interest in shared living arrangements. The effect of war on the vitality of the military is an obvious example of crisis as a catalytic agent that causes a spurt of new growth for an organization. The growth of consumer and environmental agencies is another organizational response to change or crisis in the larger society.

In health care, family practice is developing as a specialty in response to patients' wishes for a more comprehensive, more personal type of medical care. The hospice concept for the terminally ill is gradually becoming an alternative to the highly specialized setting of the acute care hospital.

An organization may experience a significant surge of vitality because of some internal activity, such as unionization of workers. During the covert as well as the overt stage of unionization, management may take steps to "get the house in order," including greater emphasis on worker-management cooperation in reaching the fundamental goals of the organization. Service of strong client groups may become more active, both to focus attention on the institution's primary purpose and to mobilize client good will in the face of the potential adversary (i.e., the union). Such internal regrouping activities foster rejuvenation in the organization as an offshoot of their primary purpose, avoiding unionization or reducing its impact.

Legislation of massive scope, particularly at the federal level, may have a rejuvenating effect. The infusion of money into the health care system via Medicare and Medicaid is partly responsible for the growth of the long-term care industry, although population trends and sociological patterns for care of the aged outside of the family setting are contributing factors. The passage of the National Health Care Planning and Resource Development Act rejuvenated some of the existing health planning agencies; its gradual phasing out, of course, has had the opposite effect in some instances by forcing a decline in certain planning groups. Changes in state professional licensure laws may bring certain professional groups into a season of new vigor.

The bureaucratic hierarchy protects managers who derive authority from a position that traditionally is well defined by the organization's middle age. Planning and decision making are shared responsibilities, subject to several hierarchical levels of review. The same events that may spur rejuvenation also may hurl the organization into a state of decline, the major characteristic of the final stage: old age.

Old Age

Staid routines, resistance to change, a long history of "how we do things," little or no innovation, and concern with survival are the obvious characteristics of an organization in decline. There may be feeble attempts to maintain the status quo or to serve clients in a minimal fashion, but the greater organizational energy is directed toward efforts to survive. If the end is inevitable, resources are guarded so that the institution can fulfill its obligations to its contractual suppliers and to its past and present employees (e.g., through vested pension funds, severance pay, and related termination benefits). There may even be a well-organized, overt process of seeking job placement for certain members of the hierarchy; time and resources may be made available to such individuals. Sometimes key individuals from the dying organization attempt to develop a new organization.

Because of its dwindling resources, the organization no longer may serve clients well, and all but the most loyal clients will look for other organizations. The organization in decline cannot attract new clients; the cycle is broken. Without clients, the organization cannot mobilize financial and political resources to maintain its physical facilities, expand services, respond to technological change, or remain in compliance with new licensure or regulatory mandates. The end, which may come swiftly, may be brought about by a decision to close and a specific plan to do so in an orderly way. For example, a department store might announce a liquidation sale that ends with the closing date. Only the internal details of closing need attention. As far as clients are concerned, the organization has died.

A final closing date may be imposed on an organization; in a bankruptcy, for example, the date may be determined in the course of legal proceedings. Legislation that initially establishes certain programs may include a termination date, although the date is more commonly set when legislation to continue funding the program fails. The changes in medical care evaluation under professional standards review organizations (PSROs) and the Office of Economic Opportunity neighborhood health centers are examples in the health care field of programs that moved into a state of decline or closure when funding was no longer available through federal legislation.

The closing decision may be a more passive one; there may be a gradual diminution of services and selective plant shutdowns and layoffs, as may occur in manufacturing corporations that rely primarily on military or space contracts. Bankruptcy is costly in economic and political terms in some cases, so the decision is implemented slowly. Indeed, it sometimes seems that no one actually makes a decision in some institutions that decline. Because of its unpopularity, the decision to close certain services, such as health care services, may be made in a somewhat passive way; however, the seemingly gradual slipping away of clients and the deterioration or outright closing of urban hospitals may be accompanied by the emergence of competitive forms of health care, such as home care units, neighborhood health centers, mobile clinics, and community mental health centers.

Although some organizations cease to exist entirely, others may change form or come under new sponsorship. For example, some of the neighborhood health centers under Office of Economic Opportunity sponsorship were absorbed into other federal government systems of health clinics. Several major railroad divisions were reorganized under Amtrak or Conrail. Some hospitals that had been owned and controlled by religious orders became community-based, nonprofit institutions. Some organizations seem only to change title and official sponsorship. The various types of agencies for health care planning over a decade or so have included regional medical programs, regional comprehensive health planning programs, HSAs, and statewide health planning agencies; the organizational structure, not the total mandate, of these agencies has changed.

The managers in the declining organization may find themselves in a caretaker role that involves such difficult activities as allaying the anxiety of workers, monitoring contradictory formal and informal information about closing, and developing a plan for closing while continuing to give a modicum of service to the remaining clients. Managers must continue to motivate the workers without a traditional reward system, even in its most limited form. Staff may be reduced, and workers may seek to use up all benefits that they may lose if the organization closes (e.g., sick days and vacation days). Line managers may be forced to deal with the hostility of the workers facing job loss. Finally, a personal decision must be made: stay to the end or leave and cut theoretical losses.

Paradoxically, this may be a time of great opportunity for managers. Middle managers may have an opportunity to participate in activities outside their normal scope as the executive team grows thin. This may be the ideal time for middle managers to try their hand at related jobs, because failure may be ascribed to the situation rather than to their inexperience or even incompetence. Valuable experience may be gained, because this may also be a time of great creativity as the gestational phase begins for a new organization with its unique opportunities, challenges, and frustrations. The organizational phoenix rises—sometimes.

We now move from general survival of the total organization to the specifics of individual change strategies.

ORGANIZATIONAL CHANGE

Recognition of and response to organizational change is yet another survival strategy. The astute manager anticipates change and is, sometimes, an active change agent.

The Change Process

Organizational change is a process by which a person or group of persons develops a strategy for effecting change in a social system. The changes are deliberate and, if successful, fulfill predetermined long- and short-term goals. Organizational change is carried out by an individual change agent who spearheads the change process. The change agent may work alone initially but eventually will require the support of a small group. Efforts to change a group with more power and prestige than the change agent group require the support of a higher echelon group or sponsor to make the change successful.

There is no single correct method to initiate organizational change; however, observation, description, reflection, and focus are all necessary components of the strategy-building process.[8] The change agent must monitor results and be aware of any new events or participants in the change process. Organizational change requires observational and analytical skills as well as a working knowledge of formal and informal power roles.

The change process is spiral. It begins on a small scale and assumes bigger proportions as more events can be linked to the desired goals (Figure 16-1). It includes the following steps:

1. Assessment. This includes evaluation of the formal and informal power systems, examination of individual and unit roles, and isolation of a problem.
2. Focus. The boundaries of the problem must be determined. At the same time, long- and short-term goals must be established. It is important to identify possible allies and resources that might promote the change process. Obstacles must also be studied.
3. Strategy Building. The change agent must develop an approach or a strategy. The change agent or the support group initiates events that promote goal attainment. Strategies are analogous to a plan for action.
4. Working Through. The first three steps are repeated as many times as deemed necessary.

5. Resolution. The end of the change process is the appropriate time to eval-
    uate the effect of the changes.

Because of its circular nature, the change process requires direction; therefore,
success also depends on the methods selected to introduce the change process.
John Kotter and Leonard Schlesinger presented six strategies to make change
less threatening[9]:

1. *Education and communication*[10] are two easy ways to overcome resistance
    to change, since the logic of a change is understood before the process
    begins. Individual and group discussions, memos, and reports are used to
    open a communication network. This process is time consuming and requires
    a good relationship between the initiators and the group affected by the
    change.
2. *Participation and involvement*[11] engages potential resisters in some aspect
    of the design and implementation of the change on the assumption that
    involved participants become committed to the change. This strategy takes a
    great deal of time; furthermore, if not managed well, the strategy can produce
    poor results.

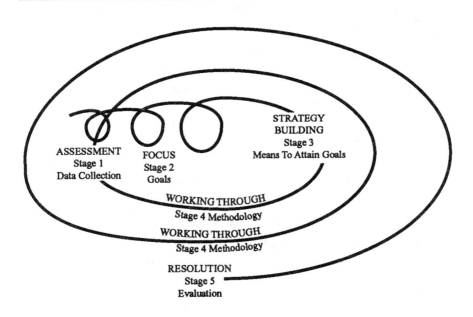

Figure 16-1 Organizational Change Process

3. *Facilitation and support*[12] can foster new changes by dissipating fear and anger. This approach may be time consuming and expensive. Even so, after energy has been expended in offering support, the change process may well fail.
4. *Negotiation and agreement*[13] can be used to offer incentives to active or potential resisters. The burden of adjustment is eased by trade-offs and negotiations. This strategy makes it possible to avoid major conflicts, but initiators might have to compromise.
5. *Manipulation of cooptation*[14] involves covert attempts to influence others by the selective use of information and the intentional structuring of events. Coopted individuals may become angry if they discover their endorsement is valued above their ideas. If handled poorly, manipulation can also foster distrust and increase resistance to change.
6. *Explicit and implicit concern*[15] can force change on subordinates if the change agent has sufficient power. This method is quick, but dissatisfied individuals may work to undermine the changes.

Change is resisted for four reasons: (1) lack of trust, (2) a different assessment of a situation, (3) a desire to protect the status quo, and (4) protection of self-interest.[16] Successful change strategies depend on careful assessment of the people who will be affected by the changes. The extent of the resistance should be determined by observation and the change process should then be initiated again. The best strategy can be selected once the nature of the resistance is known.

Change is a part of life, but unregulated change in organizations can prove taxing and difficult for group relations. Organizational change is a planned process in which the social structure of the group is altered by formal or informal interaction. Social change can improve patient services and increase the status of allied health care professionals.

CASE STUDY: SEDENTARY PATIENTS IN A GERIATRIC FACILITY

Background

Shore Acres is a 125-bed health care facility owned by a corporation and managed by a health care administrator who is responsible for all the hospital functions (Figure 16-2). The director of nursing, a nurse-practitioner, oversees all direct patient services. Routine functions are carried out by nursing aides. The speech therapist, physical therapist, dentist, and activity director all report to the director of nursing. The director of nursing uses her power to control the other services. Because the medical director is a part-time employee, she is also influenced by the director of nursing.

Assessment

The speech therapist and physical therapist note that patients are frequently undressed and lying in bed. Both feel that this is detrimental to the patients' health, since elderly individuals lose functional skills if they do not keep moving.

Focus

The speech therapist and physical therapist would like to strengthen the rehabilitation program of the facility. They would like to introduce an occupational therapist into the hospital social system. Do you agree with the focus selected by the physical therapist and social worker? Can you generate another focus that would address the problem? The director of nursing would probably claim that she needed more staff to improve patient care. She might maintain that patients must remain in bed because she has so little help. Does this solution address the original problem?

Goals must be established for the change process, for example, "to keep patients engaged in activities." This goal would require the cooperation of the director of activities. Another goal might be "to increase functional independence of patients." This goal clearly identifies the self-care skills needed by patients. Select a goal and refine it. Break the goal into short-term pieces.

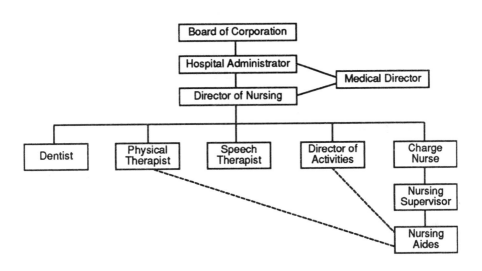

Figure 16-2 Organizational Chart

Strategy Building

What strategies would you use to accomplish the goal? Select a strategy from the six listed earlier and discuss whether each would work and why or why not. Who would need to help institute the change process? Which people might support the change and which people might oppose the change?

The physical therapist decided to use the strategy of education and communication. The therapist met with the physician and discussed the problem. The physician was concerned and asked for the physical therapist's solution. The social worker used the same strategy to enlist the help of the director of activities. Once the physician and the director of activities were engaged in the change process, the group decided to include the director of nursing, using the participation and involvement strategy.

Working Through

The director of nursing used this opportunity to expand her staff. The change group encouraged her to hire two "rehabilitation aides." These two nursing aides would be supervised by the therapists. The director of nursing agreed to support the idea of hiring an occupational therapy consultant. This stage was advanced by the strategy of negotiation and agreement.

There are several more stages to working through the problem. The aides must be trained and the consultant hired. The group must again address the best strategy to keep the patients moving.

Resolution

This case study will be ended when the patient problem is solved. The group must use the new positions and resources to address the original problem.

Clearly, the change process can be initiated by an individual or a small group. The change may be planned by people who have no power, but the ultimate success of the change requires the support of a person or group who enjoys some power in the social system. Strategies are evaluated and adjusted during the working-through stage, which is why feedback is so important. Change can improve social organizations if it is well conceived and executed.

NOTES

1. Bertram Gross, *Organizations and Their Managing* (New York: The Free Press, 1968), 454.

2. Matthew Holden, Jr., "Imperialism in Bureaucracy," *American Political Science Review* (December 1966): 943.

3. Philip Selznick, *TVA and the Grass Roots* (New York: Harper Torchbooks, 1966), 13.

4. Ibid., 13, 260–61.

5. Amatai Etzioni, *Modern Organizations* (Englewood Cliffs, N.J.: Prentice-Hall, 1964), 13–14.

6. David L. Sills, *The Volunteers* (Glencoe, Ill.: The Free Press, 1957), 64, cited in Etzioni, *Modern Organizations*, 13.

7. Marver Bernstein, *Regulating Business by Independent Commission* (Princeton, N.J.: Princeton University Press, 1955).

8. Virginia Schein, "Individual Power and Political Behaviors in Organizations: An Inadequately Explored Reality," *The Academy of Management Reviews* 2 (1977): 64–72.

9. John P. Kotter and Leonard A. Schlesinger, "Choosing Strategies for Change," *Harvard Business Review* (1979): 106–14.

10. Ibid., 109.

11. Ibid.

12. Ibid., 110.

13. Ibid.

14. Ibid.

15. Ibid.

16. Ibid., 111.

Conclusion

This work began with a discussion of the traditional functions of the manager. What qualifies an individual to assume the role of manager? As with the grant of organizational authority, the first pillar is the manager's technical and professional ability. In the health care setting, department heads and chiefs of service are specialists, usually trained in a specific health care discipline, such as nursing, physical therapy, occupational therapy, medical technology, or health record administration. Education for specific health disciplines usually includes some training in management techniques, but this is not the primary focus.

What, then, is the suggested plan of action for the health care practitioner who assumes a greater, more specific management role? What program of study and activity will equip the manager to deal with conflict, change, shifting balances of power, and authority? How does the manager avoid the extremes of "bureausis" and "bureaupathology"? Education is the answer. Managers must seek to increase their skills in the management area through formal study. This program of study should go beyond specific technical and professional skills (e.g., cost accounting in budget preparation) to embrace a wide range of social science areas. Psychology and sociology can provide insights into interpersonal relationships; history and political science can help in identifying and understanding changes in the social and political culture.

Managers must develop the capacity for balance and inner harmony that characterizes the whole person. They turn to music, art, philosophy, and related disciplines to enrich their own spirits, mindful of the Greek aphorism: "One becomes similar to what one contemplates." The work of health care, with its long history of compassionate involvement with the ill and infirm, demands much from the health care practitioner, who must balance the science of management with the art of human relations.

Index

411

About the Authors

JOAN GRATTO LIEBLER, RRA, MPA, is Professor in the Department of Health Records Administration, College of Allied Health Professions, Temple University. In addition to working in a variety of health care settings, Professor Liebler has taught a variety of workshops in the areas of applied management practice, with particular emphasis on long-term care practices. She has been a member of the editorial boards of *Topics in Medical Record Administration* and *Health Care Supervisor*, quarterly publications of Aspen Publishers. She is also the author of *Medical Records: Policies and Guidelines*.

RUTH ELLEN LEVINE, Ed.D, OTR, FAOTA, is Professor and Chairperson of the Department of Occupational Therapy, College of Allied Health Sciences, Thomas Jefferson University. She is a graduate faculty member, grant reviewer, editorial board member of four journals, and Co-Principal Investigator on a national research study. She has also published several articles on the effects of culture and environment on health care delivery. She received her education at the University of Pennsylvania and Temple University. In 1989–1990 she was a Research Fellow at St. Loye's School of Occupational Therapy, Exeter University, England. As the former President of the Pennsylvania Occupational Therapy Association, she was able to test many of her ideas on planning, communication, management and supervision.

JEFFREY ROTHMAN, PT, Ed.D, is Director of Health Sciences at The College of Staten Island of the City University of New York. He received his education at New York University and Rutgers University. He is an experienced administrator in a variety of clinical and academic settings. He was formerly Administrator of the Department of Physical Medicine and Rehabilitation at a major medical teaching hospital and Chairman of the Department of Physical Therapy at the College of Allied Health Sciences of Thomas Jefferson University. He is co-editor of *Applying Prevention Strategies in Physical Therapy and Occupational Therapy Practices* and has written numerous articles for professional journals. Dr. Rothman has lectured nationally and internationally with particular emphasis on the "Evolving Role of Physical Therapy in the Health Care System". He is a member of the American Physical Therapy Association and has held office at both the state and national level.